AF385817

Gladiators in the
Greek World

Gladiators in the Greek World

How A Roman Blood Sport Took Ancient Greece By Storm

Alexandra Sills

PEN & SWORD HISTORY

AN IMPRINT OF PEN & SWORD BOOKS LTD.
YORKSHIRE – PHILADELPHIA

First published in Great Britain in 2026 by
Pen & Sword History
An imprint of
Pen & Sword Books Ltd
Yorkshire – Philadelphia

ISBN 978 1 03613 048 0

A CIP catalogue record for this book is available from the British Library.

Typeset by Simon and Sons ITES Services Private Limited
Printed and bound in the UK by CPI Group (UK) Ltd, Croydon, CR0 4YY.

The Publisher's authorised representative in the EU for product
safety is Authorised Rep Compliance Ltd., Ground Floor,
71 Lower Baggot Street, Dublin D02 P593, Ireland.
www.arccompliance.com

For a complete list of Pen & Sword titles please contact:

PEN & SWORD BOOKS LIMITED
47 Church Street, Barnsley, South Yorkshire, S70 2AS, England
E-mail: enquiries@pen-and-sword.co.uk
Website: www.pen-and-sword.co.uk
or
PEN AND SWORD BOOKS
1950 Lawrence Road, Havertown, PA 19083, USA
E-mail: uspen-and-sword@casematepublishers.com
Website: www.penandswordbooks.com

Contents

Foreword

Ben Gray, Dan Stewart and Jane Masséglia have my eternal gratitude for encouraging and nurturing this research, and it is through their mentorship that it reaches publication. Any errors within are mine and mine alone. Thanks also to Jen Baird, Paola Ceccarelli, Graham Shipley and Simon James for their invaluable teaching. I also owe a debt to Owen Rees, George Connor, Miri Teixeira, Samuel Azzopardi and Liv Albert for giving my early research a home, and for sharing it with the world. My deep thanks must also go to Philip Sidnell, my commissioning editor, for allowing this dream to become the reality you now hold in your hands, as well as Ian Hughes and Matt Jones at Pen & Sword.

The life of an independent researcher working from home has the potential to be an isolated, lonely existence. Thank goodness, then, for the online community of classicists, ancient historians, archaeologists and enthusiasts to whom I can turn for companionship, discussion and top tier memes. This entire process would have been interminable were it not for the following people in particular, who provided their research, advice, proofreading, cheerleading and camaraderie with generosity, grace and patience. I am sure for some of those listed their help and support seemed so small as to be insignificant, but for me, every piece of encouragement meant the world. My deepest appreciation goes to Livia Adams, Leah Bernardo-Ciddio, Manda Binns, Margrethe Birkler, Chance Bonar, Glynn Davis, Bret Devereaux, Dan Diffendale, Liz Gloyn, Georgina Homer, Christina Hotalen, Roel Konijnendijk, Derek McCann, Peter Miller, Carlos Noreña, Jeremy Swist, Rebecca Todd and the many more friends who have made this process a pleasant one.

I have utmost respect for the epigraphers, archaeologists, philologists and historians who have paved the way in the various aspects of this niche subtopic; even when I draw differing conclusions, it has been an honour and a privilege to build upon their existing scholarship.

Several individuals and institutions have donated their photographs to this book, improving it no end. Their generosity is only matched by my gratitude.

I have enormous appreciation for Edwin Vaughan-O'Hagan, who convinced me that becoming a mature student and obtaining a degree or two would change my life for the better. You were right, as usual. Thank you, my dear friend. To Franki Webb, Danielle Sandwell, the bottle of limoncello and (less directly) Russell Crowe: who gently persuaded me to invest in myself and fulfil my potential, I will be forever grateful for your encouragement. Also to Christy Constantakopoulou, for teaching me that the real history is found between the lines, and for never once making me feel absurd to dream of one day writing a book. If it were not for her confidence in me and the example she set for me, this book would still be an idle daydream. My perpetual thanks are also owed to the Fairy Godmother of this book, which without her expert guidance would still be a pumpkin. Thank you.

My final and deepest thanks go to my parents, Janet and Patrick, for their unconditional love and support, and to my beloved husband Edward, who never once doubted that one day I would be thanking him at the beginning of a book. He was right, I was wrong. It happens once a decade. My family believed in me even when I did not myself, and this book would not exist without their support. I will never be able to adequately express how much I love my family, and how grateful I am that they tolerate me.

This book is dedicated to Imogen Amelie, my Sistine Chapel. You're my favourite!

Author's Note

This book is about the blend of Greek and Roman, and as such I have elected to use neither (anglicised) Greek names nor Latin names exclusively. Greek gladiators preferred to use Greek names wherever possible, so I have tried to follow suit out of respect, though it would be distracting (and frankly pretentious) to refer to Athens as Athenai, or even to refer to Corinth as Korinthos. Achilleus is too well-known as Achilles for me to refer to him otherwise throughout, and I fear Aias is unrecognisable unless I call him Ajax, though I hope the reader will indulge me if I use Eteokles and Polyneikes instead of Eteocles and Polynices. Consistency either way would be unsatisfactory, and so I have aimed for a happy medium.

In lesser-known cities in the eastern Mediterranean I have chosen to use the non-latinised version of names; for instance, Laodikeia on the Lykos in place of Laodicea on the Lycus or Pergamon in place of Pergamum. This is only partly because of aesthetics, as many tourist guidebooks, maps and road signs also elect to use non-latinised names for all but the most famous of sites. Internet search engines will return results regardless of the spelling used, for those who want to read further.

A word on the title: *Gladiators in the Greek World*. It is imperative to note that while the Romans certainly viewed the Greeks as eastern, Greeks definitely did not. It is always tricky for a historian to discuss geography without falling into age-old and frankly imperialist traps that centre Rome because Rome and subsequent historians of Rome have chosen to centre Rome. After all, while Rome marked the centre of their world with the Milliarium Aureum monument in the Roman Forum, the Greeks had their own, more ancient centre of the world in Delphi. To try and achieve some balance, I alternate between 'Greek East' (in reference to the culturally Greek portion of the Roman empire), 'Eastern Mediterranean' and, on occasion, 'Western Asia' when discussing the areas relevant to this book, which incorporates a vast and disparate area of regions with close ties to Greek culture.

Glossary

Achaea	A small region of the Peloponnese. In the *Iliad*, even Greeks from outside this region are referred to as 'Achaeans'. When the south of the Balkan peninsula was made a Roman province, it was known as Achaea.
Agon	A Greek word meaning competition or contest
Amphitheatre	'Theatre on both sides' – a building that resembles two theatres placed back-to-back to create a continuous oval
Arena	from '*harena*', the Latin word for sand
Arete	A Greek philosophical concept of individual excellence in any aspect of life
Attalids	A Greek royal dynasty who ruled Pergamon
Bestiarius	A beast hunter
Bouleuterion	Greek council house
Cavea	'Hollow' – the curved area of seating in a Roman theatre
Circus	'Ring' – a Roman building designed for chariot racing
Comitia Centuriata	Legislative and electoral assembly in the Roman Republic, responsible for electing praetors, consuls and censors, and for declaring war
Cuneus	pl. *cunei*. Wedge-shaped section of seating in a Roman theatre
Diadochi	The successors of Alexander the Great who fought over control of his empire
Diazoma	'Girdle' – a horizontal, curved walkway separating the upper and lower bands of seating in a Greek theatre
Dromos	Greek – 'racecourse' – the track of a stadium
Editor	The organiser and financier of a gladiatorial games
Epigraphy	The study of texts inscribed onto durable materials such as stone
Epitaph	Commemorative inscription on a tombstone
Eques	A gladiator who fought on horseback

Essedarius   A gladiator who fought from a moving chariot

Gladiator   A competitive combatant in Roman bloodsports, who typically wielded a *gladius* style sword – literally 'swordsman'

Gladius   A Roman short sword used by gladiators and legionaries alike

Hippodrome   'Horse track' – a Greek building designed for equestrian racing

Hoplomachus   A gladiator whose equipment mimicked a Greek hoplite warrior

Kerkis   pl. *kerkides*. Wedge shaped section of seating in a Greek theatre

Kleos   A Greek word meaning eternal fame, glory and renown, earned through great deeds and achievements

Koilon   'Hollow' – the curved area of seating in a Greek theatre

Lanista   Owner of a gladiatorial troupe

Logeion   'Speaking place' – the high stage in a Greek theatre

Monomachos   A duellist, literally 'one-on-one fighter'

Munera   Latin. 'duty' or 'obligation' – the provision of a monument or entertainment given by an individual to the public as an obligation of an official post

Munerarius   The organiser and financier of a gladiatorial games

Murmillo   pl. *murmillones*. From the Greek word *'mormuros'*, meaning 'sea bream' – a gladiator whose crested helmet resembled the fin of a fish

Orchestra   'Dancing place', the circular or semi-circular area of a Greek theatre where the chorus of a play performed

Orthostate   Upright squared stone block, higher than they were thick, typically built into the lower portion of a wall

Palaestra   Wrestling school

Pankration   Extremely violent ancient Greek contact sport, similar to modern MMA fighting

Parapet   Protective barrier wall

Parma   A small shield used both by gladiators and in the Roman army – typically around 3 feet in diameter, and often square, oval or circular

Parmularius   A gladiator who fought with the smaller shield known as the *parma*

Philotimia   Greek. 'Love of honour' – an act of *euergetism* which earns the individual praise and prestige in return

Podium	A raised base of a building – in this case, raising the level of seating by creating a wall
Pomerium	The religious boundary of the city of Rome
Praetor	An elected magistrate in the Roman political system
Proskenion	'In front of the skene' – an umbrella term for the structures between the *skene* and the *orchestra*, including the stage itself
Provocator	'Challenger' – a heavily armed gladiator
Prytaneion	Greek seat of government
Ptolemies	A Greek–Macedonian dynasty who ruled territories including parts of modern Iraq, Syria, Iran, Afghanistan and Türkiye
Pulpitum	The stage of a Roman (or Romanised) theatre – lower in height than a *logeion*
Retiarius	'Net-man' – a lightly armoured gladiator who resembled a fisherman, wielding a large net and trident
Scutarius	A gladiator who fought with the larger shield known as the *scutum*
Scutum	A large shield used by both gladiators and in the Roman army – rectangular and curved into a semi-cylindrical shape
Secutor	'Pursuer' or 'Chaser' – a gladiatorial type armed to chase his opponent (typically a *retiarius*)
Seleukids	A Greek–Macedonian dynasty who ruled territories including parts of modern Iraq, Syria, Iran, Afghanistan and Türkiye
Skene	The 'backdrop' built behind the stage of a Greek theatre. Literally 'tent' or 'hut', reflecting the early origins of this structure
Sphendone	pl. *sphendonai*. Semicircular area at the end of a racetrack
Stadium	A Greek venue for foot races, so named for its track length of 600 feet
Thraex	Pl. *thraeces*. A type of gladiator styled like a Thracian warrior
Venatio	pl. *venationes*. Beast hunts
Venator	A beast hunter
Virtus	Roman concept of individual excellence and virtue

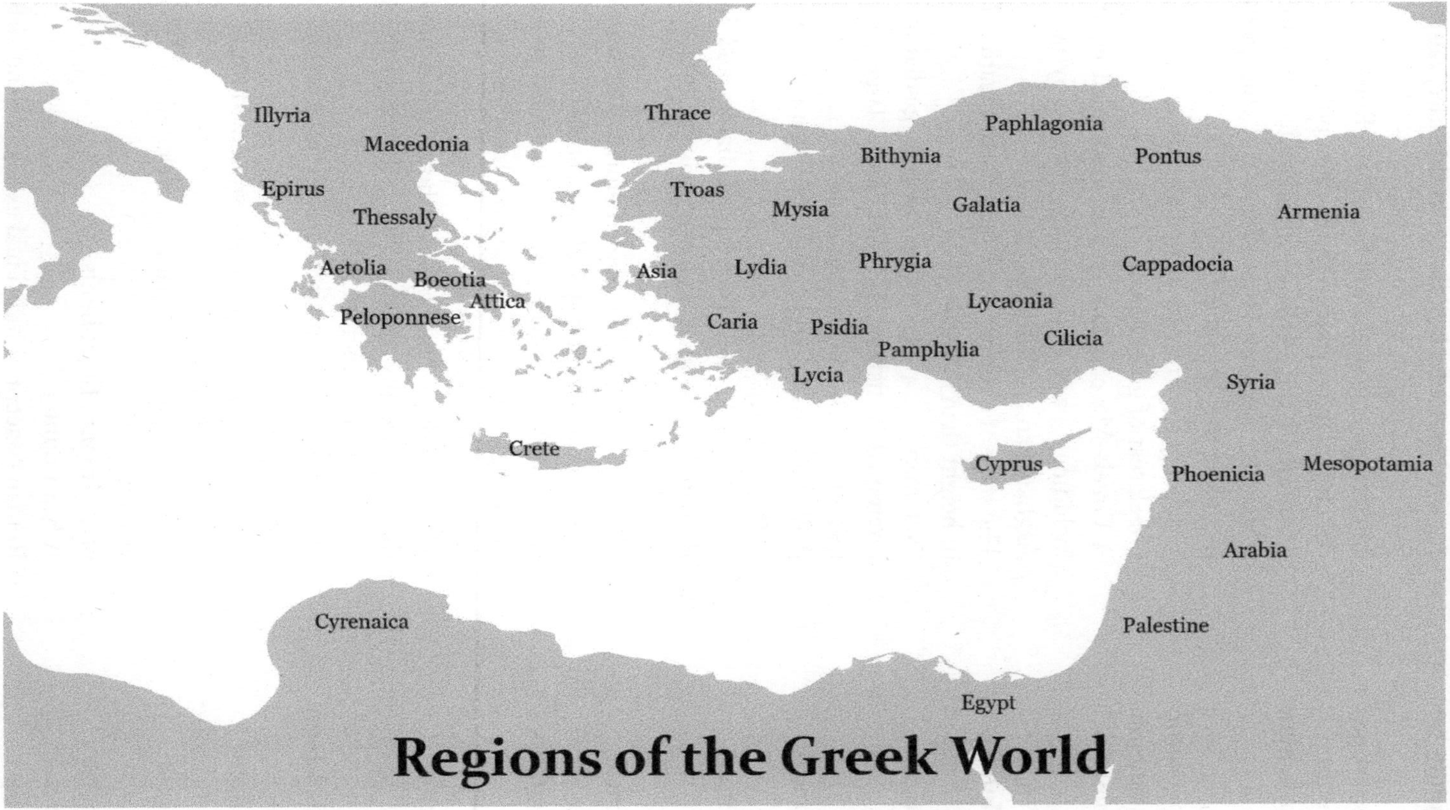
Regions of the Greek World
Illyria
Macedonia
Epirus
Thessaly
Aetolia
Boeotia
Attica
Peloponnese
Crete
Thrace
Troas
Asia
Mysia
Lydia
Caria
Lycia
Psidia
Bithynia
Phrygia
Pamphylia
Paphlagonia
Galatia
Lycaonia
Cilicia
Pontus
Cappadocia
Armenia
Syria
Cyprus
Phoenicia
Mesopotamia
Arabia
Palestine
Egypt
Cyrenaica

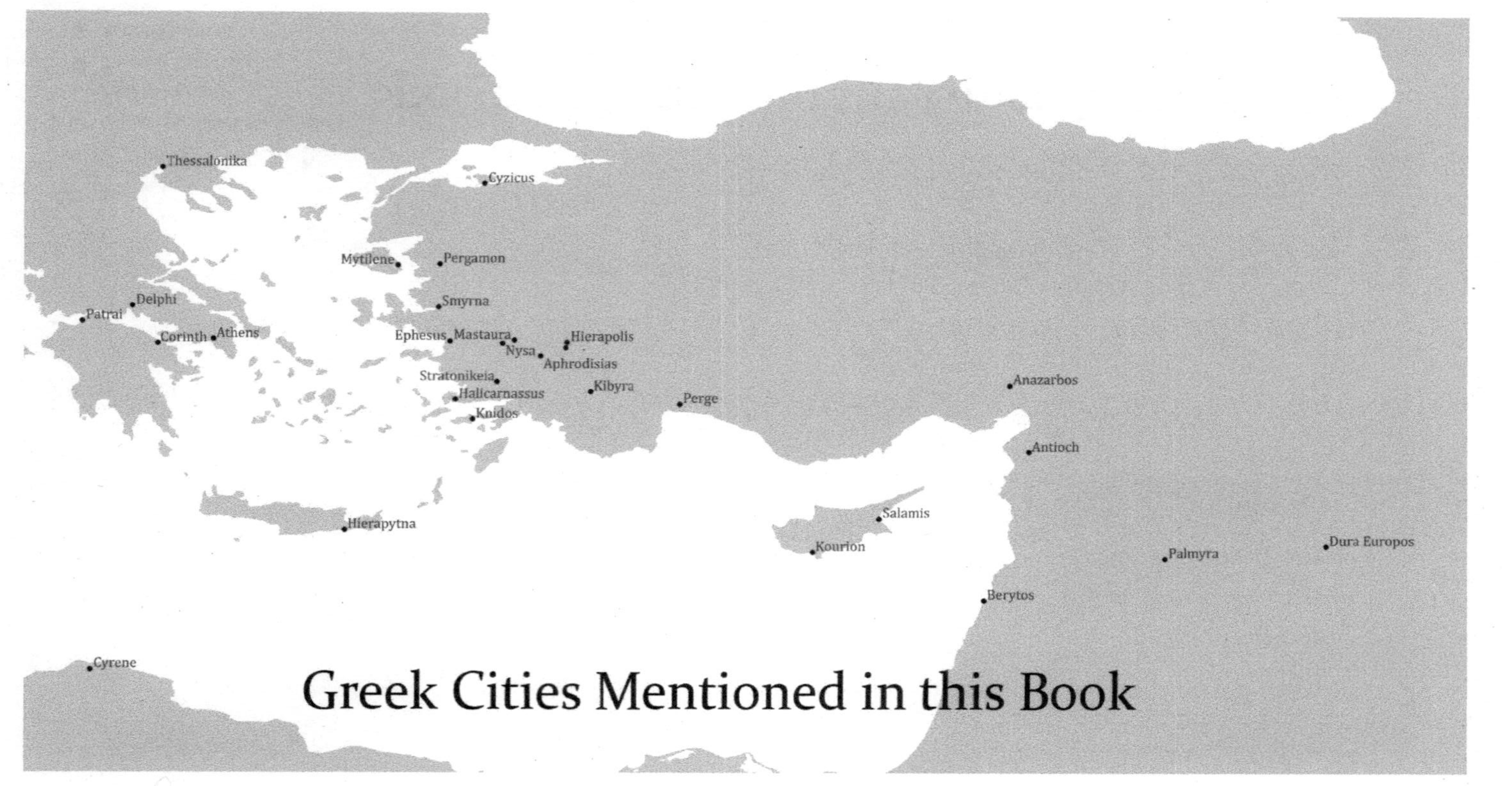

Greek Cities Mentioned in this Book

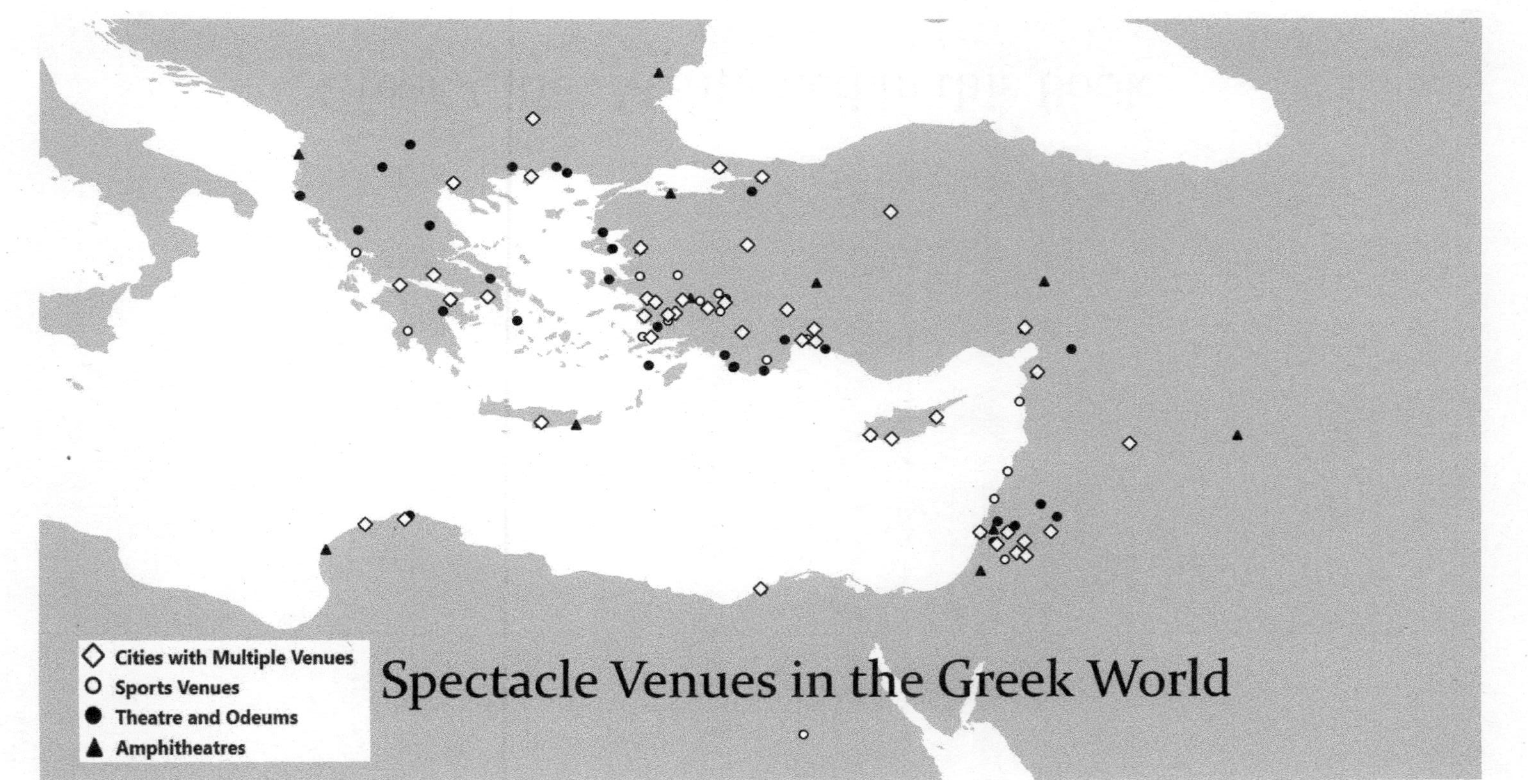

Spectacle Venues in the Greek World
Cities with Multiple Venues
Sports Venues
Theatre and Odeums
Amphitheatres

Images

Front Cover: Relief showing a gladiatorial fight in chronological stages. Found in Kibyra. Image courtesy of Carole Raddato.

Back Cover: Gravestone of Satornilos, a *thraex* from Smyrna. Image courtesy of Rijksmuseum van Oudheden, Leiden.

1. Relief showing a gladiator fight in chronological stages. Provenance uncertain, possibly from Ephesus. The inscription names the fighters as Parthenopaios and Nympheros, both of the First Rank and hailing from Cappadocia. Image courtesy of Yale University Art Gallery.

2. Relief showing a gladiator fight in chronological stages. Found in Hierapolis. The fighters are named Pinnas and Odysseus. Image courtesy of Carole Raddato.

3. Relief showing a gladiatorial fight in chronological stages. Found in Kibyra. Image courtesy of Carole Raddato.

4. Terracotta lamp depicting a gladiator fight. Made in Anatolia. Image courtesy of Getty's Open Content Program.

5. Funerary stele of Satornilos, a *thraex* from Ephesus who was buried in Smyrna. His tombstone was erected for him by his colleagues. Image courtesy of Rijksmuseum voor Oudheden, Leiden.

6. Fragments of a glass beaker painted with gladiatorial images. Found in Egypt. Image courtesy of The Metropolitan Museum of Art, New York.

7. Architectural remains of Cyzicus Amphitheatre. Image courtesy of Carole Raddato.

8. Pergamon Amphitheatre, viewed from the acropolis. Image courtesy of Carole Raddato.

9. A mosaic featuring two fighters being separated by the referee. Found in the House of the Gladiators, Kourion, Cyprus. Image courtesy of Carole Raddato.

10. A mosaic featuring two gladiator fights. Found in the House of Silenos, Kos. Image courtesy of Robert Caudill, www.roamintheempire.com.

11. An unusual gladiator monument in the shape of a *scutum* and helmet. Found in the necropolis of Claudiopolis, now in the Bolu Museum. Erected by a priest named Secundus, the inscription names the gladiators of his *familia:* Campanus – *scutarius* with sixty-five victories; Myron – *essedarius* with forty-three victories; Apleros – *provocator* with fifty-two victories; Chrysampelos – thirty-five victories; Margareites – *essedarius* with seventy-five victories; Victor – fifty-eight victories; Poseidonius – twenty – four victories; Skirtos – *retiarius* with eighteen victories; Spekles – *eques* with thirty-five victories; Achilleus – forty victories; Euchorous – fifty victories; Panter – *retiarius* with fifteen victories.

12. Perge stadium, viewed from the *sphendone.* Note the addition of a wall bisecting the track, creating an arena.

13. Aphrodisias stadium, viewed from the *sphendone.* Note that the stadium has not been as extensively restored as Perge, yet the same additional arena wall is discernible.

14. Kibyra stadium excavations. The trench shows that the track level of stadiums is typically lower than the current surface, and the restoration work demonstrates how the high *podium* wall was constructed.

15. Xanthos theatre, with a high *podium* wall separating spectators from combatants.

16. The Theatre of Dionysus in Athens, with parapet wall in situ.

17. The rough-hewn parapet wall of Patara theatre

18. The rough-hewn wall of Alabanda theatre, showing the blocked row of seating in the front.

19. Halicarnassus theatre, the likely location of Amazon and Achillea's bout. Post holes are discernible around the arena edge.

20. The theatre at Myra, with a *podium* wall topped with a parapet wall of *orthostates,* of which only a few stand upright.

21. Gravestone of a *murmillo* from Tralleis. Now in Aydin Archaeological Museum.

22. Gravestone of the *murmillo* Penelais, probably from Sparta. Now in the National Archaeological Museum in Athens. Note the four victory wreaths and palm frond.

23. Stele of a *thraex* named Stephanos. Ephesus Museum.

24. Stele of Anicetus, a *secutor* from Aphrodisias.

Prologue: Anything Rome Can Do, Greeks Can Do Better

Antiochus IV Epiphanes shifted in his saddle, impatient to begin. He needed today to go well, and had invested much money in ensuring it. The annual festival of Apollo was always of utmost importance, of course. One must always make sure that religious rites were performed in the appropriate manner. Gods and citizens alike were eased when the ceremonies were observed correctly. But it was not just Apollo that needed to be impressed today. This year, the festivities would not be as normal. This year, Antiochus had made sure, would be unlike anything seen here before. He would put on a spectacle that his people would remember with awe for decades to come – but his ambitions were far greater. This festival would outshine all that had gone on at the sanctuary of Daphne before, even those of the sanctuary's founder and his illustrious ancestor, Seleucus I Nicator.

His own father, Antiochus III, called 'the Great', had never dreamt of a spectacle such as this. As he always did, Antiochus cringed almost imperceptibly when remembering his father. Seleucus, the founder of their dynasty, had been the great friend of Alexander the Great, and in the wake of Alexander's death had fought tooth and nail to seize control over as many of Alexander's conquests as possible. At his death, Seleucus had secured an empire that stretched from the Hellespont to the Bactrian and Sogdian plains. The great cities of Ecbatana, Susa, Babylon, Damascus and more fell under his control, and Seleucus and his descendants founded dozens of others. That should have been Antiochus IV Epiphanes' inheritance: the greatest empire in West Asia, a collection of varied lands and varied people all united under the Hellenism of the Seleukid dynasty. It was not to be, as the empire's borders had been eroded and chipped away over the generations. Asia Minor was gone, Parthia had broken away, Bactria had won their independence. His father had promised that the Seleukid Empire would be restored. A myriad of cities had once paid them homage and tribute; soon they would again. Antiochus III had meant to reclaim it all and conquer more besides.

Antiochus III had consolidated Seleukid power in the east, regaining much glory and prestige to the Seleukid dynasty. How could he help but be flattered when an envoy of Aetolians begged him to take control of Greece? Antiochus III had styled himself the defender of the Hellenistic world's freedom from Roman interference. For a while, it had seemed as if Antiochus III would succeed, capturing cities the Seleukids had once held, annexing territories that Seleucus I had failed to take, and claiming Euboea. It had all been for naught: Antiochus had drawn the ire of Rome, who preferred the bickering in the region to be on a smaller scale. The Battle of Magnesia had been an utterly embarrassing defeat, and the consequences even more so. The Seleukid dynasty had been stripped of their recent conquests in Thrace and Asia Minor, forced to pay reparations and their western territories demilitarised. They had been humiliated, emasculated and diminished by Rome. He himself had been dragged to Rome as a political hostage for over a decade to keep his father in check. His father had died a pathetic death soon afterwards, attempting to pillage a temple.

Well, Antiochus IV Epiphanes would succeed where his father had faltered. He had spent over a decade in Rome and the early years of his reign acting with great deference to Rome. Rome, in his opinion, was a squalid little city, ugly and ramshackle. It had been arduous to languish there for so long, pining for the elegant cities of home. He had been kept under close surveillance, disguised as hospitality; the Romans clearly hoping to learn of his intentions when he was finally allowed to return. No doubt they thought their cordiality would earn them unquestioned loyalty. Well, he had watched and listened and learned too. He knew how Romans operated, and he knew they were increasingly cocky – all pride and swagger, having defeated first the Carthaginians and now the Antigonids. Well, cockiness tended to evaporate once the run of good luck ran out, which it would. Just ask the Carthaginians and the Antigonids. All in good time.

It may come as a surprise to learn that the Romans were not the first to bring Roman gladiatorial combat to the Greek world they eventually conquered and ruled. After all, gladiators are considered quintessentially Roman and not really associated with the Greek world at all. Instead, it was one of Rome's chief antagonists, a Seleukid king with a chip on his shoulder. More surprising is that Antiochus disregarded gladiators as a (then) component of funerary practice, something that the Romans had yet to do; *his* gladiators were to fight in a programme including footraces, banquets and dramatic plays — quite the innovation. The opening procession of the festival was a parade of wealth, power and cultural cachet. The festival at Daphne in 166/65 BCE was on a scale that would dazzle a Greek world already accustomed to grand shows.[1]

For a Hellenistic king, parading wealth and power in such a manner was par for the course and entirely expected of him, but Antiochus IV had a deeper motive for making his festival so bombastic. After his father was defeated by Rome at Magnesia, the Treaty of Apamea stipulated that the Seleukids must cede all territory north and west of the Taurus mountains, which Rome had handed over to the Attalids (rulers of Pergamon) and to the city state of Rhodes, both loyal Roman allies. The Seleukids were ordered to restrict their fleet to a mere twelve ships and were limited on where they could sail. Antiochus III was banned from hiring mercenaries from the territories ceded to Pergamon and Rhodes, was forced to surrender all prisoners of war and had to pay a substantial indemnity to Rome. Any enemies of Rome harboured by the Seleukids were to be handed over.[2] Antiochus III was forced to send twenty prominent Seleukids to Rome as hostages; Antiochus IV had been one of them.

After the Treaty of Apamea, the Seleukids still held a vast amount of territory, but the loss of Antiochus III's conquests stung deeply. Asia Minor, now held by Roman allies as a buffer zone between Rome and the Seleukids, was still much coveted by both Antiochus III and IV. It had been part of their empire at its founding by Seleucus I Nicator after the successors of Alexander, known as the Diadochi, had fought to carve up his many conquests, but, like its far eastern territories, was now lost. The empire, while larger than Antiochus III had inherited upon his succession, was still smaller than it had once been. How could any Seleukid king be content with anything less than what they were entitled to? The treaty was an insult, albeit one that it had been necessary to swallow at the time.

Antiochus IV had watched his father try to restore their dynasty's legacy with pride. Antiochus III had made enough conquests to earn himself the epithet 'Megas', meaning the Great. He'd even invaded areas that Seleucus I had not managed to secure; however, while successful in Thrace, his invasion of mainland Greece had failed. It should have been easy; Rome's repeated defeats of the Antigonids in Macedon had left so many power vacuums across the Aegean that Antiochus should have filled them with ease. The cities of Asia Minor would have easily fallen into Seleukid hands, had they not pathetically called for Rome to defend them.[3] Even the Ptolemies had taken to begging Rome for assistance, like cowards. Antiochus III was a king; he shouldn't have had to deal with being scolded by Rome like he was a naughty child. Western upstarts should not have had the audacity to dictate to a king which territories and cities he could and could not conquer. Every time Antiochus marched north, west or south, pitiful pleas had been sent to Rome and every time, Rome had responded by meddling in affairs that had nothing to do with them.[4] Antiochus had complained to them as much, once enquiring why Rome insisted on wading into Greek affairs when no Greek had ever stuck their noses into Roman business.[5] How dare Rome treat Seleukid kings like clients that they could order around at will?

Despite seeing his father fail in his own quest, Antiochus IV was not to be deterred. Like gaudy parades, conquests were expected of a Hellenistic king. It was simply the done thing. Epiphanes would succeed where Megas had not. Antiochus IV had been sure to cause no trouble during his years in Rome and had ascended the Seleukid throne while making a great show of deference to Rome and her ally, Pergamon. His meekness had disguised his steeliness. A few years before the festival, in 170 BCE, Egypt had tried to wrest back Coele Syria (which Antiochus III had annexed from them), and Antiochus IV had moved to defend it with significant strength. He would show the whole Mediterranean that the Seleukids had not been enfeebled by the Treaty of Apamea. Aware of Egyptian intentions, Antiochus IV had managed to pre-empt any invasion. As the Egyptian forces marched from Pelusium, they were ambushed in the Sinai desert by Antiochus' army. The Egyptians were caught off guard and fell easily, with Antiochus IV chasing the survivors back to Pelusium, which surrendered to him immediately.

Politics in Egypt were already fractious, with two brothers sharing the throne – both of them children. The news of the defeat had a swift and devastating effect. The city of Naukratis fell to Antiochus soon after; buoyed by his success, he'd pressed on further into Egypt – the first to successfully invade Egypt since Alexander himself. There he'd hoped to play one sibling against the other, manipulating one child into becoming his client king. Dismayed at the idea of foreign rule, Alexandrians quickly threw their weight behind the other brother.

Alexandria, then, would not be as easy an acquisition as the rest of Lower Egypt for Antiochus IV. Oh, but how it would be worth the effort; a jewel of a city, housing the entire Ptolemaic treasury – wealth that made his own wealth look like a few old coins. Antiochus IV considered Egypt to be both weak at this time and worth the effort to annex. If he could seize Alexandria, then he would have the whole of Egypt and a massive war chest at his fingertips. He could still install a brother as a client king, or – and why not? – become Pharaoh himself. The Romans at that very moment were destroying the Antigonids and draining Macedon of its populace. One Hellenistic rival was out of the way, ripe for Antiochus IV to grab and surpass his father.[6] If he could oust the

Ptolemies from Egypt first, he would be the last of the successors of Alexander left standing. The possibilities would then be endless.

The great city of Alexandria was a tough nut to crack, however, and so Antiochus had returned the following year and laid a second siege. The Egyptians, for once putting aside their internal squabbles in face of external threat, had a dilemma: to accept Antiochus' terms would mean that they became Seleukid vassals; the alternative was to send pleas of help to Rome and pray that the price would not be too high. They had seen time and time again that once Rome had pacified upstart kingdoms of the eastern Mediterranean they were content to go home afterwards with minimal fuss. And owing Rome a favour, when they had seemed so disinterested in maintaining an eastern presence, would surely be a lesser evil than submitting to Antiochus who would clearly not leave them to their own devices. The decision was made and envoys sent.

Meanwhile, by 168 BCE, Antiochus had seized Cyprus and his armies were plundering it for as much loot as they could carry. He had secured most of the Nile Delta, including Memphis. He was camped outside the walls of Alexandria. The city was difficult to besiege and had ample provisions, but it was a necessary endeavour. If he needed to dig his heels in, he would. These Egyptians needed to be taught that Seleukid territory was off limits and their incursion must be punished. The Alexandrians waited anxiously for a Roman intervention and a response had indeed been sent. Rome was in no rush, caught up in yet another war with Macedonia. After crushing Perseus utterly at the Battle of Pydna in the summer, the business at Alexandria was the only mess left to tidy up. The former Roman consul, Gaius Popilius Laenas, had been docked at Delos, waiting to see if Antiochus would finally admit that Alexandria was impregnable. When he realised that Antiochus was being stubborn, he sailed out to Alexandria to finally put an end to the matter. He had found Antiochus in a suburb named Eleusis, camped out and plotting. Antiochus had held out his hand in a gentlemanly gesture of friendship, but Popilius Laenas was in no mood for pleasantries. He shoved a document into Antiochus' open hand and scowled at him as Antiochus scanned the lines. It was a *senatus consultum*, orders from the Roman Senate. It instructed Antiochus that he should evacuate Egypt and Cyprus immediately, or consider himself at odds with Rome. They meant it this time, and wouldn't hesitate to march an army against him if he refused to leave.

Antiochus IV now had a dilemma. When his father had provoked the Romans, the result had been a couple of battlefield defeats and some harsh terms in a treaty. Then Antiochus III had been left alone. Previously, when the Antigonids had repeatedly gone to war with Rome, they'd faced the same consequences. But the shock of the Battle of Pydna a few months before had reverberated around the Mediterranean. The Romans had raised the stakes. They weren't content to knock a few Hellenistic heads together and then go home – this time, they'd annihilated the Antigonid army once and for all (an army that even Antiochus had to admit was the best of any Hellenistic kingdom) and enslaved 150,000 civilians, looting everything they could from seventy cities and destroying the rest.[7]

Rome had grown weary of the constant Hellenistic bickering, and now they were putting their foot down. They'd defeated every Hellenistic army they'd encountered for three decades with unsettling ease. While he was a hostage, Antiochus IV had taken a keen interest in watching how Rome prepared for war. He had been impressed by their tactics, their discipline, their efficiency and perhaps most of all, the cutting edge arms and armour that were far superior to anything Hellenistic armies possessed.[8] He also knew that Rome had an almost inexhaustible supply of troops from their *socii* – allied troops who, unlike his own units of mercenaries, didn't have the habit of disappearing from the battlefield at the first sign of a little hard fighting. If Rome brought their army now, Antiochus knew he couldn't beat them with what he had at that moment and the consequences of a loss would be different – the Romans weren't playing games anymore. There would be no second treaty of Apamea; the Seleukids would be wiped from the face of the earth, just as the Antigonids had been. Egypt was a glittering prize, but it wasn't worth the risk to claim it. Yet.

Sobered, Antiochus had asked for time to deliberate the terms with his advisors, as was common practice. Popilius Laenas, never one for small talk, lost any semblance of patience he had had. He grabbed a stick and drew a circle in the dust around Antiochus' feet. 'You had better give me your answer before you cross that line!', he reportedly said. Antiochus' assembled compatriots baulked. Not only was this no proper way to address a king, but it went against all etiquette of proper negotiation – this upstart barbarian was yelling at a king as if he were a common soldier.

As far as Rome was concerned, the terms were fair. The Ptolemies weren't blameless, and had brought this siege upon themselves. They were banned from ever attempting to invade Seleukid territory again. Coele Syria was therefore safe, at least. Rome also knew that continuing the siege would be a lengthy, costly and probably futile venture. As far as they were concerned, Antiochus could return to Syria with his dignity intact; undefeated, with his territory protected and a load of plunder to smooth any dents in his ego. The region would be calm once more and their own headache soothed. For his part, Antiochus was furious. He had been backed into a corner and embarrassed. More than that, he didn't want to abandon his dreams of an annexed Egypt. He'd been so close! But the threat of facing a Roman army was far, far worse than the paltry troops of the Ptolemies. Being publicly scolded by a *Roman* was an insult that cut deeply, but being annihilated would hurt far worse. Through gritted teeth, Antiochus had had no choice but to acquiesce to the Senate's demands.

On his journey home, stinging from the humiliation, Antiochus had vented his full fury on his vassals in Judaea, where a former High Priest of Jerusalem with an axe to grind was stirring up trouble. This was Antiochus' thanks for letting the Jewish population retain their customs? He sacked Jerusalem, massacring tens of thousands of Jews and enslaving tens of thousands more. He was at least able to show that he was no pushover in Judaea. Most of his rage was assuaged by the time he returned to Antioch, although he could not forget his embarrassment at the hands of the Romans. He decided that to restore his prestige, he needed to demonstrate strength – and not just against some ungrateful Jews. He would head east at the head of a massive army, consolidating Seleukid power and tackling Parthia and Armenia. With the eastern territories of his traditional empire secured once more, he would have more options for expansion. Egypt, perhaps, or possibly Macedonia. The Attalids in Pergamon would be easily dealt with. If he wanted, he could even take mainland Greece, as his father had once attempted. Rome would find him a formidable foe.

After his victory at the Battle of Pydna, the Roman general Lucius Aemilius Paullus had held a victory festival at Amphipolis, before returning to Rome for his triumph. For all intents and purposes, the festival was that of a Hellenistic king. Delegations from across the Greek world had been invited to watch this Roman general parade around as if he were one of them, while simultaneously crowing of his victory over one of their own. Not content to meddle in Hellenistic affairs, the Romans had started play-acting as Hellenistic kings. For any Greeks squirming at the attempts to imitate their customs, it caused apprehension as well as consternation. The Antigonids were gone, the Ptolemies were under the thumb. Without Carthage to distract them, these Romans seemed poised to interfere much more often.

Antiochus' festival at Daphne the following year was a message to the entire Mediterranean that he was only just getting started; Rome wasn't the only player in town. His parade of troops were fresh from their campaigns in Egypt, Cyprus and Judaea and could claim that they were undefeated in battle. He was about to embark on an *anabasis* that would outshine that of his father.[9] Once he had truly made his mark, no Roman would rebuke him – and none would match him. His parade was him flexing his military and cultural muscles, to intimidate as much as to dazzle. Anything a Roman could do, a Hellenistic king could do better. And if Aemilius Paullus wanted to have a go at hosting a Greek festival? Well, Antiochus would show the whole Greek world that a Seleukid could put on a Roman spectacle on a scale Rome had never managed to achieve. This festival would outshine those of generations of great Hellenistic kings, let alone the imitations of an interloping Roman general. The opening parade was designed to showcase Seleukid capabilities, but it was also a sign of intent.

The usual military units were all present: nearly 10,000 cavalry in various units, a phalanx of 20,000 men kitted out in the Macedonian style, plus 5,000 infantry bearing glittering bronze shields and many more with silver.[10] Among the infantry were 16,000 mercenaries, recruited from Mysia, Cilicia, Thrace and Galatia. This recruitment was in direct contravention of the Treaty of Apamea, which forbade Antiochus from hiring troops beyond the Taurus mountains, i.e. the Roman sphere of influence. At his parade, Antiochus was brazenly rejecting those terms. Why shouldn't he? That was a treaty signed by his father, it should have died when he did. These troops combined were on a par with the great armies his father had fielded at Raphia and Magnesia, as well as his *anabasis*. The demilitarisation imposed in the treaty was finished.

One of the most cruel stipulations in that treaty was that his father had been forced to euthanise his prized herd of war elephants, a unit so iconic they'd graced Seleukid coins. In another contravention, Antiochus paraded a chariot pulled by two elephants and then another pulled by four. Following them were thirty-six elephants in full military regalia. The rest of the parade included 140 chariots drawn by horses, 800 beautiful youths each carrying ivory tusks, 780 beautiful women in elegant gowns and wagon after wagon of treasure looted from Egypt and Judaea. All of this was normal in style (if excessive in scale) for such a Hellenistic royal parade. More unusual were 480 gladiators, placed not with the entertainers, but between the infantry and cavalry components. Even more striking, at the very head of the parade, was a unit of 5,000 men clad in Roman mail armour, bearing the *gladius hispaniensis* so prized by Roman legions. Any participant of the parade who had faced a Roman legion in battle knew how effective Roman kit was, alien though it looked. The number of men was significant too; 5,000 was the exact number of a Roman legion in times of crisis. Antiochus IV had raised his own Roman-style legion.

Antiochus IV had personally witnessed the exact reasons that Rome was becoming such a loud, bossy voice in the Mediterranean world; their military was infinitely superior to anything any Hellenistic king had mustered so far. But Antiochus wasn't too proud to take notes. His replica of a Roman legion was a very good one, and his campaign to the east would give him the chance to test it out away from Roman eyes. He could then raise more, trained and kitted out in the Roman style that Antiochus would copy down to the letter. If Rome was only unbeatable because their legions were superior to Hellenistic armies, what would happen if a Hellenistic king came back from the middle east with Roman-style legions of his own, but bigger and better? Well, then Antiochus IV could fulfil every Hellenistic king's greatest dream of reuniting Alexander's conquered lands under one leader once more, and maybe even venture to the west, scooping up the battered remains of Carthage and succeeding where his father's great pal Hannibal had failed on the Italian peninsula. In order to achieve any of this, he had to prepare to face Rome eventually; and to face Rome, he had to think and act like a Roman. As well as cribbing from their military, Antiochus was the first to admit that even barbarian Romans had a few customs worth replicating, and he was quick to copy his favourite at home.

Over the month of the festival, there were 240 pairs of gladiators scheduled to perform. His people, as well as emissaries from the entire Greek world, watched them fight and die among the elegant gentility of the leafy sanctuary. His subjects no doubt saw it as a bizarre inclusion to an otherwise familiar cultural programme; this bloody Roman entertainment was alien and a little peculiar, but he had been fascinated by it during his time at Rome. Besides, Antiochus did love to defy expectations.

Tiberius Gracchus was incredibly cosy, having arrived in Antioch after arduous travelling. He'd been sent to gauge if Antiochus IV was hostile, and he was uncomfortable recalling how his colleague had humiliated the king in Eleusis. He'd considered it incredibly reckless behaviour, albeit effective, and was intending to be the very picture of respect in comparison when dealing with Antiochus himself, assuaging any latent grievances with deference and faultless etiquette.

Tiberius needn't have anticipated a frosty welcome, to his relief. He'd expected to be given the usual show of intimidation, the king dressed in that excessive finery that Hellenistic royals were so fond of, surrounded by haughty courtiers with their beady eyes fixed on the scruffy Roman. He couldn't have been more wrong; Antiochus was the epitome of xenia, and had greeted Tiberius as if he was an old friend. Tiberius had been quick to embrace him on equal terms. He and his companions were invited to dine with Antiochus in the Roman manner and even to sleep in his own hall. Antiochus had left his gaudiest apparel firmly in his chests, and was almost indistinguishable from anyone else at court. They'd laughed and joked over a fine dinner and swapped anecdotes. Antiochus asked after some acquaintances of his from his days in Rome, and Tiberius filled him in on some gossip from home. Why had he worried? Antiochus was a delightful interlocutor and a very thoughtful host. This work trip had taken an exceedingly pleasant turn. He'd have to ask for copies of recipes for the rich recipes for his cook to try and master.

Chatter among the Antiochene milieu was abuzz with talk about Antiochus' grand festival, which Tiberius was rather upset to have missed by a matter of days. The faux Roman legion sounded very ... cute, though he'd made sure not to make any condescending remarks. He sipped a very nice wine as he listened to excited descriptions of musical recitals, acrobats and dancing girls with beautiful dresses. He would dearly have loved to have seen elephants pull a chariot. His aide was too uptight and didn't understand the flamboyancy of these Greek kings like he did. They simply loved any opportunity to put on a show.

That said, Tiberius was most surprised to hear that Antiochus had presented gladiators. He knew Antiochus had spent an awfully long time in Rome, but he'd never assumed he'd have acquired that particular taste. Greeks were too spoiled and soft for that kind of thing, he'd supposed. Certainly, Antiochus' courtiers were slightly bemused by the whole thing and didn't seem to quite appreciate the finer aspects of technique and style. Squeamish, these Greeks. From what Antiochus was saying, the gladiators were among the finest money could buy, imported from Rome. And Antiochus had bought 480 of them! Wait until the lads at home heard about that – they'd never known such a large show back in Rome. It would have bankrupted a fair few senators. These Greeks might be a bit squeamish, but they could sure put on a show. He would have dearly loved to see them himself, for he was very partial to a bit of combat and nobody important had died for a while. He diplomatically refrained from correcting Antiochus and telling him that gladiators were to be saved for grand funerals, not religious festivals. It would be awfully rude of him, and Antiochus was so infectiously genial. Why ruin the mood with a dull lecture on Roman customs?

Beside him, his aide muttered under his breath that this was all a little too chummy, wasn't it? Some nonsense about a false sense of security. Tiberius hushed him and reached for some more spiced meat strewn with herbs. Antiochus was a charming fellow and he fully intended to report exactly that back to the Senate. No need to see conspiracies where there clearly were none. Besides, Antiochus had confided in Tiberius his plans to consolidate power to the east. In a few months he'd be hundreds of miles in the other direction, tied up in regional squabbles for a couple of years. Something or other about Armenia. The Aegean would be as calm as a pond. No, his report would tell of a budding friendship and those 480 gladiators! Tiberius would be able to dine out on that for weeks.

Chapter 1

Arena

Did the Greeks love Roman gladiators? I wouldn't blame you if your immediate instincts lead you to reply with an emphatic 'no'. The commonly accepted picture we have of Rome is of an empire earned at the point of a sword; ruthlessly efficient legions of soldiers conquering their neighbours. The Greeks, meanwhile, are known for their beautiful art and architecture and for their famous poets and philosophers. If this is an accurate picture, the two had little in common. This dichotomy is itself over 2,000 years old; take the Latin quote above, for which an English translation is: 'Greece, conquered [by Rome,] conquered her savage victor and brought the arts to rural Latium.'[12] It's a line from a poem in the form of a letter. In this case, the poet Horace is writing to the emperor Augustus about the state of Roman literature in comparison to the poems and plays of Classical Greece and this line is essentially saying that Rome may have defeated the Greeks on various battlefields in order to conquer them, but the subsequent influx of Greek art and literature to the Italian peninsula conquered Rome culturally. Rome conquered Greece, but Greece then *civilised* Rome.

Horace has a point. Roman plays began as copies of Greek plays. Roman poets tried to write like Greek poets. Roman houses, and now museums, were filled with statues labelled 'Roman copy of a Greek original.' Romans adopted Greek architecture. Romans invented their own alternatives to the Olympic Games. Roman intellectuals styled themselves as Greek philosophers. However, as Horace complains elsewhere in this poem (to the emperor, no less!) the general consensus seemed to be (and often still is) that all of this copying largely resulted in inferior facsimiles.

Greeks had not managed to best Rome on a battlefield, but as far as art, literature and philosophical thought went, Rome simply could not compete. They may have excelled at law making, logistics and warfare, but Roman culture was always going to be seen as inferior to Greek. For many, Rome's most iconic cultural phenomenon, the gladiatorial arena, is proof positive that Rome was incapable of reaching the heady heights of Greek writers, athletes and thinkers. The Greeks were elegant sophistication personified, and in comparison the brutish Romans gathered to watch two brutes stab each other for fun.

We tend to view Greece civilising Rome as a one-way system of culture travelling westwards, and that's because writers now, as Horace did then, tend to present Greek culture as 'superior' and influencing the Roman 'inferior' culture. They present Greek culture as improving Roman culture, even if, in their opinion, Rome never quite got the hang of it. When we are trained to think this way, it can be difficult to break from the habit long enough to consider what culture travelled in the opposite direction. What did the Romans give the Greeks? Even Monty Python never suggested Roman *culture* was their primary export. After all, why would a 'superior' culture accept any form of entertainment for an inferior one? It makes little sense.

This is why some historians and archaeologists were a little perplexed to find evidence of gladiators in their excavations; they weren't digging in Italy; they were digging in Greece and Anatolia. This evidence was in the wrong place, surely? There was muttering; these gladiators didn't belong here, and it must surely be those brutish Romans imposing their coarse entertainments on unwilling, elegant Greeks. Is this fact, or conjecture?

Being an historian is much like being a detective on a case. We're handed a pile of evidence from an event we haven't witnessed and we need to piece all of it together to try to work out an accurate picture of how events played out. Sometimes evidence is lost, or partial, and some of our witnesses may turn out to be less than reliable, with inconsistent statements and personal bias that distorts their testimony. Detectives and historians, juries and readers, all have their biases too, which influence their perspective. It is for this reason that so many historians can draw such different conclusions from their peers and why none of us will ever agree on everything entirely. The best that we can do is to assemble our evidence, comb through it as carefully as we can, and produce a 'case' that stands up to scrutiny. My own rubric is to ask if a theory passes the Three Ps: is it Possible? Is it Plausible? Is it Probable?

This book, then, is my forensic investigation, presented to you, the reader, to judge for yourself. Can we prove, beyond reasonable doubt, that gladiatorial combat was adopted and absorbed into the Greek cultural landscape? How enthusiastic were the Greeks about this process? Did Greeks view gladiation from the same perspective as their western counterparts? Were the gladiators in the eastern territories of the empire more Roman, or Greek? And why does all of this matter?

I will be presenting the case that the majority of Greeks not only really took to Roman spectacle, but that they came to view it as quintessentially Greek. This is my defence case against the much older opposition argument: that Greeks were too culturally sophisticated to ever take Roman violent bloodsports to their hearts, and that they resisted gladiators being shoved down their throats as much as they could. By the end of this book, I hope to have convinced you that the traditional viewpoint needs a drastic revision. I'll guide you through the necessary historical and cultural context and present focused groups of different types of evidence to you as case studies, so you can judge for yourselves.

Throughout this investigation, it will be important to look at as many types of evidence as possible. To do anything else would result in a partial and skewed picture of what was going on, and, because so much evidence has already been lost to us by the passage of time, we must ensure we use as much evidence as we have left to the best of our abilities. The questions about the popularity of gladiators in the Greek part of the Roman empire are a perfect example of both the problem of patchy evidence from the ancient world and how much we can still learn if we collect all the evidence and examine it carefully.

The question about where gladiators fought in the Greek world is, for instance, a little trickier than we might expect. As we will see in Chapter 11, amphitheatres were quite rare in the Greek part of the Roman empire. Greece and Asia Minor have fewer amphitheatres between them than the tiny province of Britannia, which is the opposite of what we might expect: the Romans had had to introduce the Britons to the concept of cities, let alone large civic monuments, whereas Greeks were living in sophisticated cities with elaborate architecture when Rome was still a backwater. Some have taken this as evidence that Greeks never bought into the whole gladiatorial phenomenon because they were perfectly capable of constructing the building designed to host Roman spectacle yet largely chose not to, but, when we look at the small changes made to existing Greek entertainment buildings like theatres and stadiums, sometimes almost imperceptible, we realise that Asia Minor in particular can now be seen as the region with the third highest distribution of buildings capable of hosting gladiators after the Italian peninsula and the area of the African coast that is now Tunisia.[13]

A few writers from the ancient world mention gladiators, usually in passing, and some of it still survives. We can take their offhand comments and read between some lines to mine literature for nuggets of information. We're also lucky that some extraordinary works of gladiatorial art survive to us from this half of the empire – from crude graffiti made by fans to souvenirs bought from merchandise stalls and expensive mosaics in the houses of the rich. Thanks to the Greek love of inscriptions, we also have a lot of written information about gladiatorial fights and the gladiators themselves.

That evidence requires context to properly understand it, however. For example, if we only looked at gravestones of gladiators, we might think that gladiators weren't really popular until the second and third centuries CE, when we find a huge spike in the numbers of gravestones being made. However, these were centuries when inscriptions in general soar in number in the eastern provinces – so we can't say that gladiators were only popular then, only that they were more likely to want an inscribed epitaph then, in keeping with local patterns.

Not all of our evidence is readily accessible: the vast majority of portable finds are stored away in museum back rooms, and not on display; each individual museum makes curatorial choices about what objects they put on view and what they keep in boxes. Our evidence fills many, many boxes. Not every archaeological site is entirely open to the public, because some monuments are deemed unsafe, particularly if they are in areas that are difficult to reach, or in a perilous state of disrepair. In such cases, our evidence must be gleaned from the testimony of the archaeologists who found the objects and buildings by reading their scholarship that is stored in academic libraries.

To get as accurate a picture as possible, we then need to combine all of our different kinds of evidence, otherwise the evidence can become misleading. The first thing to do is look at the Greek world as what it was – a patchwork of small regions that had lots in common with their neighbours but also their own distinct heritage and traditions. A survey of the evidence reminds us of this.

It is possible to place different types of evidence onto a map; we can put a dot on every entertainment venue where gladiators fought, and on every place we find their tombstones. More dots can be added for every place we find an object or artwork relating to gladiators. For a gladiation historian, it would be really nice if all of these dots matched up into a neat pattern, where the cities with the biggest venues also had the biggest concentrations of inscriptions, tombstones and artworks. The problem is, there is no neat pattern. The concentrations of gladiatorial epigraphic material (where text has been inscribed onto stone) don't always match up with how many venues are in those small regions: some, like Caria, Ionia and Macedonia, just had a much stronger epigraphic tradition than other regions.[14] In other words, they were keener to write information down in stone at that point in time. Other regions don't have huge amounts of gravestones, but had just as many (if not more) venues for gladiators to fight in. One might assume that a traditionally Roman amphitheatre in a city such as Pergamon might result in a particularly large number of inscriptions made about or for the people who performed there, but it actually has very little epigraphic material relating to gladiators from this city. In fact, forty-five cities that boasted a venue for gladiatorial combat haven't yielded a single tombstone, while Beroia has an astonishing twenty-seven tombstones (second only to Smyrna's twenty-nine) but no venue has yet been firmly identified.

These anomalies indicate just how incomplete our evidence is. There are many potential entertainment venues across the eastern Mediterranean that have been built over, torn down, or remain unexcavated. We can make educated guesses as to whether those cities were likely to want gladiatorial shows, but we may never be able to prove that they hosted them. Inscriptions, graffiti and small objects decorated with gladiatorial imagery are even more likely to fade, be destroyed or lay undiscovered. Archaeological excavations (when done properly) are expensive, time consuming and invasive. Financing, scheduling and modern buildings being inconveniently built right where we want to dig most are just some of the reasons why artefacts may have to remain under the earth. For now, we can say that coastal areas around the Aegean Sea (which generally had a longer cultural relationship to mainland Greece) had a stronger epigraphic tendency, while venues are pretty evenly distributed across most of the region. There are exceptions, which we will explore as we go.

As well as acknowledging the gaps in our evidence, we need to compare it to the evidence we find in the western territories of the empire. Are the amphitheatres in the same style as those we find in Italy, the heartland of the Roman gladiator phenomenon? Do the tombstones of Greek gladiators give us different information from ones elsewhere? Are the gladiators presented differently in artworks such as mosaics and lamps? And can the sheer amount of evidence tell us anything about why Greeks grew to love gladiators? For this, we'll not only need to compare evidence to that in the west, but to other evidence of other professions in the Greek world.

We'll explore the cultural, political and social history of the Greek world and encounter some of the most famous architecture, art and literature in history through the fascinating perspective this investigation provides. After all, we can't understand the popularity of gladiators in the Greek world in isolation. As we weigh the evidence together, an interesting picture emerges – and perhaps a surprising one to many readers. But, as with all good investigations, we should start at the very beginning.

Chapter 2

Edutainment in the Caput Mundi

Most people have a vague sense that the ancient Roman and Greek worlds, while overlapping in many ways, had distinctive cultural differences. The focus of this book is one of those perceived key cultural differences: gladiatorial combat and the particular ways in which the Greek world in the eastern Mediterranean engaged with this major cultural export from the Roman west for their own purposes, in ways we haven't appreciated before. However, we can't get to grips with this topic without having a little context about Roman cultural life more broadly, and specifically without understanding what gladiators meant to cultural life for Romans themselves.

So our first question to investigate is: what was cultural life like in the Roman empire and how widespread were the main cultural elements?

Roman bathing customs, for instance, spread across the entire empire. The ritual of bathing, with hot and cold plunge pools and steam rooms were a marker of Roman civilisation, and to go to the bath house (*thermae*) was to demonstrate one's participation in Roman culture. Yet the Romans were not averse to 'alien' ideas. As a result, they added 'Greek' palaestrae to the bath houses, combining Greek and Roman concepts in a single complex.

The archaeological remains of *thermae* (bathing houses) of all sizes can be found from Hadrian's Wall to Lebanon to the tiny islands of Malta. While Greeks had developed their own, less complex bathing rituals, Roman baths were soon constructed in many Greek cities, and even great religious sanctuaries like Delphi and Olympia. Hours at a time were whiled away at bath houses, where politics was debated, business deals struck, and bodies oiled, plucked and massaged. Cleanliness and good health were the signs of a sophisticated society, and it quickly became a social expectation that baths were to be used regularly by all able to do so. *Thermae* were far more significant than merely a place to wash away the grime of the street; they were hubs of the community and markers of identity. When we consider the export of gladiation, we should keep the deeper significance of bath house construction in mind; neither are as superficial as we might suppose.

To those who know of the fervent love of chariot racing in Rome itself, it may come as a surprise that the sport was not a popular export of Roman culture – certainly far less than gladiatorial combat was. There were far, far more amphitheatres than circuses in the empire, but, in the city of Rome, the Circus Maximus was king. Festival days that included races were frequent, reaching up to 135 days a year by the early Imperial period. Each race day consisted of ten to twenty-four races, and each race consisted of twelve chariots hurtling around the track for seven nail-biting laps. Four *factiones*, or teams, competed in the races. Fans and emperors alike were loyal to the different teams called Greens, Blues, Reds and Whites, who were operated by consortiums of wealthy investors. Rivalries between teams and supporters were fierce, regularly descending into scuffles. The factions were big businesses, each employing over a thousand drivers, grooms, carpenters, wheelwrights, et cetera. Charioteers were the de facto celebrities of the city, and their massive prizes often catapulted them into the richest strata of society. After all, in a career that all too often ended both quickly and painfully, the incentives needed to be considerable. In comparison, gladiatorial shows were less frequent, hosted in smaller venues and featured more modest prizes. In Rome itself, gladiatorial combat was the lesser sport. As the Roman empire expanded, it absorbed cultures with chariot racing traditions more ancient and embedded than their own. In the capital city, rulers produced racing festivals on a scale never before seen. Yet it was gladiatorial combat that saturated the Roman world. Why?

There is a concept known by ancient historians as 'Romanisation'. It's a theory that suggests that Roman rulers consciously began a process of 'civilising the barbarians' they had conquered, by making them culturally Roman. Essentially, Rome required newly conquered people to start acting Roman: speak Latin; worship Roman gods; dress in togas; and fill their time off as a citizen in Rome would – with Roman entertainments. That, presumably, included attending gladiatorial shows, which would then explain why gladiator games seem like the premier Roman entertainment export. To explore this theory, detective notebooks in hand, we need to first understand why Rome wanted to export gladiators instead of, say, chariot racing. Why did gladiators matter to Rome? What was their purpose? Hollywood depictions of gladiators too often reduce combat into a bloody frenzy to satisfy the violent cravings of crazed spectators, but this is a simplification that misunderstands why the Romans developed gladiatorial combat in the first place. Secondly, we must investigate the evidence that would prove whether or not Romans were forcing gladiators upon foreign, conquered cultures. This chapter will tackle that first task: establishing the purpose and popularity of gladiator games in Roman society. It is only then that we can consider the second task of why and how the popularity of gladiators spread.

Firstly, can we say that Romans believed gladiators were quintessentially Roman, and chariot racing was not? We know that many other ancient cultures had chariots and that some used them for racing. Races feature in the *Iliad* during the funeral games of Patroklos, and chariot racing was introduced as an Olympic event in 680 BCE. The Etruscans, who appreciated the culture of the ancient Greeks and likely encountered chariot racing through their contacts with the Greek city states in Sicily and southern Italy, enthusiastically put on their own races and made beautiful artworks depicting their charioteers.[15] The Etruscans were a sophisticated culture that originated in the Etruria region of Italy, though they grew to control a far greater percentage of the peninsula at their height. If the Romans are often accused of stealing much of their religion and customs from the Greek world, it was largely filtered through to them via the Etruscans, or from the Greek colonies of Sicily and southern Italy. While the Etruscans didn't produce the literary evidence of their Greek and Roman counterparts, they left behind remnants of a rich material culture that hints at a highly sophisticated society, highly respected by their peers. It's likely the Romans first encountered chariot racing-as-sport from them. If chariot racing wasn't a novelty for the people Rome started to conquer, was a traditionally 'Roman' entertainment chosen instead?

It turns out that gladiatorial combat isn't any more 'Roman' in this sense than chariot-racing as a cultural pursuit. Because evidence is in such short supply, historians aren't exactly sure who invented gladiatorial combat, but even Roman historians knew it hadn't been them. Unfortunately, neither ancient writers nor modern scholars can find enough proof to definitively give credit where it is due. There are two main schools of thought: the first suggests that, like chariot racing, Rome copied gladiatorial combat from the Etruscans. Tomb paintings and imported vases from Corinth and Greece indicate that Etruscans were familiar with Greek myths and epic poems, as well as athletic competitions and the aforementioned chariot races. Some of these tomb paintings depict warriors, but there is nothing to suggest that these are early gladiators instead of local warriors or even characters from the *Iliad*, of which the Etruscans were fond. None of the warriors are depicted mid-combat, crucially.

The other potential inspiration for Roman gladiators comes from Campania. This region, to the south of Rome, consisted of both local tribes and Greek colonies such as Cumae, Neapolis (Naples) and Poseidonia (Paestum), and at one point had been within the Etruscan sphere of influence. As such a melting pot, it too had a rich culture. Evidence for gladiators in this region is a little stronger. Several tombs from the late-fourth century BCE feature paintings of warriors fighting duels. Significantly, these images also feature specific references to the Underworld, such as pomegranates, which were associated with Persephone, goddess of the Underworld, and funeral biers. At least one of the tombs is for a woman, and so the picture of male warriors can't be a scene from her own life; it's more likely to be a permanent image of her funeral. This is where the archaeological evidence stops, but historians pick up the narrative. According to several Roman writers, captured enemies were forced to fight to the death as part of the entertainment for Campanian victory feasts.[16] Apparently, these writers find this practice distasteful – not because of the cruelty, but because fights were not seen as an appropriate dinner show.

Rome may not have invented gladiatorial combat, then, but it certainly perfected it. The first recorded gladiatorial combat in Rome took place in 264 BCE. The date is significant, as Rome was hurled headlong into their first war with the superpower of the day: Carthage. Livy is the first to record it, deliberately noting this innovative addition to the funeral of a former consul of Rome to emphasise 264 BCE as a year of change.[17] As an historian, he knew well the twists and turns of the Punic Wars, and understood that they had irrevocably changed Rome to its very core. As we shall see, this won't be the first time Livy connects gladiators with this particular enemy.

The fights themselves were part of the funeral ceremony of one Decimus Junius Brutus Pera.[18] A member of an august family, the funeral was to be a grandiose affair. Livy wrote about the funeral in the sixteenth book of his vast *History of Rome*, which sadly has not survived. We only have a summary of that section that was written centuries later, in which the description of the funeral is condensed into a single sentence. As you can imagine, this is extremely frustrating. For more detail, we have to find other writers who used Livy as a source. Valerius Maximus gives us the location: the Forum Boarium.[19] That forum was already home to the *Ara Maxima*, the great altar of Hercules, and the Temple of Portunus. It was also home to the cattle market. Ausonius comments that the fight consisted of three pairs of gladiators.[20]

It is Servius the Grammarian who gives us the most detail, in his commentary of Vergil's *Aeneid*. He's trying to give further context to that poem, but handily for us manages to give us more context on the funeral itself. He tells us that guests had brought prisoners of war for the grieving family, who then paired them off and made them fight.[21] Servius is discussing an epic poem that was a conscious Latin continuation of the Greek epic cycle of poems that recounted the Trojan War, because the Romans were convinced that their city had been founded by Trojan refugees. As such, Vergil writes with a similar structure to the Epic Cycle and follows many of the same tropes and themes. In the *Iliad*, Trojan prisoners of war are sacrificed at the funeral of Patroklos. In the *Aeneid*, the hero Aeneas similarly sacrifices four young men at the funeral of Pallas, their blood sprinkled on the pyre as 'an offering to shades of the dead'.

Just as the poem is a continuation of Greek literary tradition, Vergil is continuing Greek concepts of death and the afterlife. The halls of Hades were not a place where the souls of warriors went to feast for eternity, like the Norse Valhalla, or a tranquil paradise like the Christian concept of Heaven. The Greek (and later Roman) concept of the afterlife was an Underworld – dark, silent and cold. For all but a few initiates of certain cults, the afterlife was distinctly uncomfortable and dull. When Odysseus needs to speak to the spirits (known as 'shades') of the dead in the *Odyssey*, he is told that in order for them to be capable of recalling their memories and being able to communicate with him, they need to be partially rejuvenated. He has to travel to the edges of the Underworld, dig a trench in the ground and fill it with milk, honey, wine and the dark blood of freshly sacrificed sheep. This causes hundreds of shades to swarm around the trench, as they are utterly parched. Only when they drink from this will they be strong enough to speak. This episode in the *Odyssey* tallies up with what we know about libations; drinks could be poured out as an offering to the gods, but also onto the ground for the dead. As the liquid dripped down into the earth, the shades could have a taste and momentarily enjoy a little nourishment, as a treat. It was common for Romans to picnic at the tombs of deceased relatives so that they could continue sharing meals; some tombs even had little drains specifically for pouring wine or honey into the grave. But, as suggested in the *Odyssey*, the shades also feel a longing for blood, having none themselves. Animal sacrifices were considered slightly more generous offerings to the dead than normal drinks, and across the ancient world the blood of animal sacrifices was poured onto the tombs of heroes. The slaughter of captives by Achilles at Patroklos' funeral is an extreme version of such sacrifice, one that Plato thought was abominable.

By mentioning the first gladiator fight in Rome as part of a funeral in his commentary on this part of the *Aeneid*, Servius definitely appears to be making a deliberate connection for us. Killing captives hadn't been confined to literature, and hadn't always been carried out as a sacrificial process, but Servius is pointing us in that direction. Whether or not he himself truly understood the motives behind this innovation is unclear. Should we take this comment to mean that gladiators were considered to be human sacrifices? Some scholars do say so, but I disagree. Firstly, the ritual of animal sacrifice required the victim to accept death without protest, which does not describe combat, and also does not explain why gladiators were frequently allowed to live, even if defeated, or for fights to end in a draw.[22] The idea of sacrifice instead seems to stem from early Christian writers like Tertullian, who abhorred 'pagan' practices like this and wished to paint them in as bad a light as possible to prevent converts hanging on to old cultural habits. Tertullian predates Servius, who may even have been influenced by Tertullian's rhetoric.

We need to go back to Livy, who doesn't mention gladiators at a funeral again until 216 BCE – nearly fifty years later. The gap is for two reasons: firstly, his books covering 292–220 BCE are missing, as we have seen. The summaries that survive are brief, and so we cannot know if we're missing another display of gladiators during this period. Secondly, we should not assume that gladiators were not used during this half a century, but consider *why* Livy mentions them when he does. It is reasonable to assume that others quickly followed suit after the first show of gladiators in 264 BCE, but that they were funerals for less notable men or modest in scale. Livy is not writing a history of gladiation, but a history of Rome. He mentions them when he needs to make a point. If the first gladiators in Rome coincided with the eruption of the first war with Carthage, the second funeral Livy describes coincides with the catastrophe inflicted by Carthage in 216 BCE.

This is the second war Rome would enter with the Carthaginians, after Hannibal had crossed the Alps two years previously. By 216 BCE, Rome had already suffered humiliating defeats at Ticinus, Trebia and Lake Trasimene. It is crucial for us to remember that Rome was not yet the highly organised, professionalised military machine that it would one day become; its forces were formed of male citizens of all types of profession, who were called upon in times of war and responsible for providing their own kit. Those citizens were joined by units from Rome's Italic allies, known as *socii*, who – in return for Rome's 'protection' – were obliged to provide Rome with troops in all military campaigns. Hannibal had brought fewer troops than the Romans could themselves field, but his mercenaries were professional, and he was also recruiting additional thousands of warriors from tribes in Gaul who were themselves tired of resisting Rome's attempts to expand north. Rome did have the benefit of fighting on home turf with a larger force, but they were being defeated again and again by Hannibal's superior army. Frustrated, the voters elected two new consuls to take the Roman offensive up a notch. Lucius Aemilius Paullus and Gaius Varro decided to field the largest army Rome had ever sent into battle, to meet Hannibal at the small town of Cannae in Apulia. By now, Hannibal had amassed a diverse army of allies, numbering around 50,000. The consuls decided to go all in, and the Roman forces consisted of around 85,000.[23] Unfortunately for the consuls, their combined plan of attack was no match for Hannibal's military genius.

The battle was such a disaster that the previous three defeats combined looked mild in comparison. By the end of the day, Livy estimates that 48,200 Romans and their allies lay dead.[24] Thousands more were captured, and fewer than two in every ten men managed to flee for their lives, only to find themselves exiled to Sicily for their cowardice. Vivid, terrifying rumours swirled about the extent of the carnage. We should imagine that there was hardly a street in Rome that hadn't lost a resident on the battlefield, and Livy tells us that because the Cerealia festival rites could not be performed by mourners, it had to be cancelled altogether.[25] Adrian Goldsworthy compares the slaughter and the subsequent shock it caused to the British casualties on the first day of the Somme in the First World War.[26] But Cannae was perhaps even worse; Lucius Aemilius Paullus was killed, along with a proconsul, twenty-nine of the forty-eight military tribunes, two quaestors and eighty senators, many of them who had also been consul. Many more magistrates were captured. Hannibal didn't just wipe out the Roman army at Cannae; he wiped out a significant portion of the government.

The losses on the battlefield sent panic throughout the Italian peninsula. Rome was teetering on the brink of annihilation, and in the aftermath of Rome's defeat many *socii* switched allegiance to Hannibal and Macedonia seized the opportunity to ally with Carthage, declaring war on Rome. In Rome, stress levels were running high, and the populace wailed that the gods must be angry with them. Scapegoats were found. Two Vestal Virgins were blamed for the calamity, as surely they must have broken their vows of celibacy to bring down such divine disfavour. The traditional punishment for disgraced Vestals was to be buried alive in a subterranean cell with food and water, so that Rome could still claim the women weren't technically harmed, as their blood could not be spilled. One of the Vestals committed suicide, but the other was executed as intended.[27] One of their accused lovers was beaten to death. Also, four enslaved foreigners were also buried alive beneath the Forum Boarium: a man and a woman from Greece, and a man and a woman from Gaul. To modern sensibilities, this is horrifying – and, while it's important to remember how differently Romans saw the world from us, this was still an extreme solution, which even Livy notes was thoroughly out of character.[28]

Hannibal had captured between 8,000 and 12,000 prisoners from the battlefield, and sent an envoy to Rome demanding a ransom. (What was left of) the Senate refused to pay, and they forbade private citizens to raise funds either. The prisoners would be left to their fate; Rome washed her hands of them. Some were slaughtered straight away, but many were sold into slavery. Rather than spend money on men tainted by their perceived cowardice (and simultaneously fill Hannibal's coffers), the Senate appointed Marcus Junius Pera dictator, who immediately bought 8,000 men from slave markets and armed everyone who volunteered to fight, though it is unclear whether the men were allowed to say no. They were more expensive than paying Hannibal's ransom demands, but the enslaved, so low in Roman estimations, were still considered better than disgraced citizens. The message was clear: a slave who fights is better than a citizen who surrenders, and dying with honour is preferable to surviving in dishonour.

Donald Kyle writes that the disaster 'crystallized the ideology of military virtue', and it did cause a monumental shift in how Rome approached warfare afterwards. Livy clearly thought along similar lines, and it is in the months after the battle that he mentions the next gladiatorial fight occurring in Rome. It was very different from the first. Rome was in turmoil, and they were struggling to reckon with their losses and find psychological coping mechanisms. The former consul Marcus Aemilius Lepidus had recently died, and his funeral was now furnished with forty-four gladiators. The fights lasted three days. In a city reeling from military disaster, we can detect a shift in their mindset. Dead Vestals, buried foreigners, and more gladiators than Rome had ever seen; Rome was a city reeling from a military catastrophe, fighting for survival, and frantically looking for solutions. Depleted, demoralised and desperate, Rome sought to redeem themselves from so much death by dealing out even more death.

In the years that followed, funerary gladiator shows continued to grow. Marcus Valerius Laevinus was a former consul who had been sent to keep the Macedonian forces at bay, as the Macedonians had used the Roman defeats at the hands of Hannibal as an opportunity to expand westwards. Later, he commanded the Roman fleet in Sicily. When he died in 201 BCE his funeral boasted fifty gladiators.[29] Publius Licinius Crassus died in 183 BCE. He too had been consul and also Pontifex Maximus. As Pontifex, he was not permitted to leave the Italian peninsula, however as consul he was one of the heads of the army, and led the war against Hannibal in Calabria towards the end of the Second Punic War, by which point Rome had the upper hand. His funeral was even more spectacular, with feasting following fights from sixty pairs of gladiators.[30] This was only fitting for a man so rich he gained the nickname '*dives*', the ancient version of 'Mr Moneybags'.[31] Livy describes 174 BCE as a year of many 'unimportant' gladiatorial games, but the one he deems noteworthy is also significant in our story. Titus Quinctius Flamininus, the victor of the Second Macedonian War who had declared Greece to be liberated at the Isthmian Games in 196 BCE, lay dead. His funeral was not as lavish as Crassus', having only seventy-four gladiators, though Livy does stress that this number at the time was still considered large.[32] What all these men have in common is prestige, wealth and consulships, which by extension involved leading the Roman military forces. This is why Livy mentions these funerals and not the dozens of others that must have occurred.

Polybius adds one more funeral to the pile, and it is that of another man we have met before: Lucius Aemilius Paullus 'Macedonicus', the victor of Pydna and the Third Macedonian War.[33] He died in 160 BCE, and Diodorus mentions that his funeral attracted huge crowds, not just of Rome's residents but scores of people from neighbouring towns who travelled to Rome to witness it.[34] Polybius recounts that his sons struggled to afford the minimum thirty talents that hiring gladiators would cost for a suitably 'generous' show.[35] Within a century, gladiators at elite funerals had become a necessity worth the eye-watering expense. The men were significant to Livy and Polybius; not just the presence of gladiators at their funerals, but the emphasis on the military subtext is heavily implied. Roman generals who had waged war against barbarians were honoured by having those same barbarians, the prisoners of Rome's wars, fight to the death in a celebration of their life.

This new custom fits in with elite funerals as a whole, for which Polybius gives us a description: the deceased was carried on a bier into the Forum Romanum, where he was placed upon the Rostra. This was the platform for orators, decorated with the rams of captured enemy ships. Also on the Rostra were men wearing the death masks and official magisterial togas of the deceased's ancestors, so that he was surrounded by his illustrious forebears. A male relative, usually the eldest adult son, would deliver a eulogy that recounted the great deeds of the deceased, and the assembled people were reminded of his exemplary service and deeds. Polybius stresses that the crowds were not just friends and acquaintances: the city gathered en masse to bear witness. This show of respect was rewarded with public feasts and entertainments, of which the gladiators formed their part. Rome had long ceased to have a royal family, and the top positions in government were tussled over by the men of great families, who were in constant competition to gain and maintain their prestige. Spectacular funerals honoured the deceased, reminded the city of the family's pedigree, and provided the deceased's heir with a public platform on which to promote his own suitability for office in one fell swoop.

It is impossible to reconstruct the exact influences and reasons for early gladiatorial combats in Rome, no matter how much scholars would like a concrete answer, and much excellent scholarship on later gladiation is not applicable to this period. But what *is* clear is that, from the start, gladiation was linked to militarism. It would remain so for centuries. Between 160 BCE and the later Republic, we find gladiators mentioned less often, as their presence became less extraordinary. We can still see glimpses of them, scattered through literature: Terence, a comic playwright working in the 160s BCE, complained that he lost half his audience for the debut of his play *Hecyra* once they learned that a gladiatorial show was occurring elsewhere;[36] Pliny recounts the first person to show gladiatorial art; Gaius Terentius Lucanus started a custom of hanging portraits of popular fighters in the sanctuary of Diana on the Aventine hill, having himself provided thirty pairs of gladiators for his grandfather's funeral.[37] In 122 BCE, the hero politician of the everyman, Gaius Gracchus, caused a stir by tearing down some temporary seats that had been installed in the Forum for a gladiator show.[38] We learn from this anecdote that various magistrates had each built blocks of bleacher-style temporary stands, and were selling tickets for profit. Gracchus found this distasteful, believing funeral games were supposed to be accessible by anyone in the city, and as a solemn occasion were not something to be monetised. By having the stands torn down, Gracchus ensured that everyone could view without paying any money. The idea of optimising views stuck, however, and Chapter 11 will discuss how temporary structures developed to address concerns over getting a good enough view of the action.

It seems likely that these elite funeral displays with their pomp, shows and public feasts were a welcome event for the residents of the city – entertainment, of a type. Arranging such events became an obligation of the role of *aedile*, a junior magistracy. The post of *curule aedile* was an important step on the *cursus honorem*, the ladder of magisterial posts that formed the career path for ambitious men. Technically, it was a rung that could be skipped while still being allowed to proceed, for the *aediles* were required to spend a lot of their private money on public projects; a year in post was a drain on resources that few could afford.

That said, the popularity that came from splashing the cash as *aedile* came in very handy later, and those who had served as *curule aedile* ascended to the consulship more often than those who hadn't. A young Julius Caesar is a useful example. He started his career on the back foot. His family had been close to Gaius Marius and Lucius Cornelius Cinna, the powerful and influential statesmen whose rivalry with Lucius Cornelius Sulla dragged Rome into civil war. Caesar was Marius' nephew by marriage; Caesar's closeness with his paternal aunt Julia was instrumental in bringing him to the attention of the Marian faction, though Marius himself died before he could personally aid Caesar's ascension. As a teenager, Caesar was married off to Cinna's daughter Cornelia, and his new father-in-law nominated him for the prestigious (if distinctly odd) post of *flamen Dialis,* the high priest of Jupiter. Before Caesar could take up the post, Cinna was murdered by his troops in 84 BCE. All of Cinna's appointments were voided when Sulla triumphantly marched into Rome the following year.[39] For the ambitious Caesar, losing the role of Jupiter's high priest was perhaps a relief, as the restrictions that came with the position would have prevented him from ever leaving the city or even looking at an army. He would never have been able to ascend the *cursus honorum.* As well as forbidding Caesar from taking up the priesthood, Sulla also demanded he divorce Cornelia. Caesar refused. At the time Sulla was drawing up proscription lists of Marians to have murdered and their properties confiscated.[40] Caesar's defiance was extraordinarily bold, particularly as he was still only around eighteen years old. Whether or not he was officially placed on a proscription list for this audacity is debated by scholars, but we know that he felt forced to flee the city, where he lived rough, moved often to escape assassins, and contracted malaria. He was only allowed to return when Vestal Virgins and two relatives on his mother's side in Sulla's faction petitioned Sulla on his behalf.[41] In short, Caesar was very, very lucky to be alive. Even after Sulla died in 78 BCE, his faction dominated Roman politics. Caesar could have chosen to live a quiet life, but he chose to stick with the boldness that had nearly gotten him killed.

It was in 69–68 BCE when he was serving as quaestor that Caesar first used funerals to his political advantage. His beloved aunt Julia, wife of Marius, died. As her closest living male relative, it fell to Caesar to give an *encomium* to her in the Forum, as was customary at the funeral of elite Roman matrons. She had been allowed to survive the Sullan proscriptions, and had spent widowhood mourning a husband who was officially remembered as a public enemy. In open defiance of the Sullan faction, Caesar included images of Marius in Julia's funeral procession. Few had dared speak of Marius in the intervening years, particularly since a group of Marians under Quintus Sertorius had waged a bloody yet futile civil war across the Iberian Peninsula from 80–72 BCE in which yet more Romans died. Sulla had banned any honours for Marius, and a few in the crowd protested at seeing his image. However, many more who still admired Marius drowned out the booing. It was a public reminder that, though the protégés of Sulla held Rome, the memory of Marius was still a positive one for many Romans. After all, Marius had achieved much, amidst the slaughter of the era. Caesar, in emphasising his personal connection to Marius, boosted his own popularity, while his speech lauding his aunt's impeccable pedigree (descended from deities, no less) showcased his own illustrious ancestry. Within months, he was speaking at another funeral – that of his beloved wife Cornelia. For a much younger woman like Cornelia, such a large public funeral was unheard of. The city took this break from standard protocol as the touching grief of a loving husband and he received much sympathy. No gladiatorial shows are mentioned for either funeral, but then no gladiatorial shows had been recorded for other funerals of women, and were likely to have been an inappropriate innovation too far for Caesar in 69 BCE. We shouldn't doubt whether the sorrow for his aunt and young wife was genuine, but the timing of their deaths at this point in his career was undeniably ideal for such funerary displays that so appealed to the public. He left the quaestorship more popular than he entered it – a reflection of the political opportunities of public funerals.

In 65 BCE, Caesar became *curule aedile* alongside Marcus Bibulus. Their shared responsibility was to subsidise public festivals, and though each contributed money towards the normal festivals, Caesar made sure to fund extra beast-shows and plays by himself, in order to take sole credit for the entire year's programme.[42] He was particularly extravagant, borrowing obscene sums to fund his largesse. He would remain in debt for years afterwards, but it was a price well-worth paying. Now was the ideal time for a gladiatorial show that would cement him as the politician most beloved by the people, though Caesar had one problem: none of his prominent male relatives were dying. Gladiators were an increasingly essential feature of elite funerals, but rather more essential was a distinguished corpse to bury.

Once again, Caesar employed some funerary lateral thinking. His father had died in 85 BCE, when Caesar had been only fifteen or sixteen. He had died suddenly, while putting on his shoes. Nothing is recorded of the subsequent funeral. Twenty years later, Julius Caesar elected to present the gladiatorial games separately, ostensibly to honour his father in the appropriate manner now that he was finally in a position to do so. His plans were ambitious, and the show featured an unprecedented 640 gladiators, all clad in silver armour. Suetonius remarks that he would have loved to have presented an even bigger display with even more fighters, but that his preparations had made his political rivals so jumpy that an emergency law had been passed to cap the number of gladiators allowed in a single event.[43] After all, as Plutarch notes, this show eclipsed the efforts of every politician who had gone before him, and few could ever hope to match Caesar's show without bankrupting themselves; in such a competitive environment, Caesar had set the new bar far too high for the comfort of his opponents.[44] Moreover, where once it may have been tacitly acknowledged that a funerary gladiatorial show was increasingly now used to boost the prospects of the surviving male relative, and less to honour the deceased, Caesar's decision to commemorate his father during his aedileship was a naked attempt to curry favour with the electorate as he prepared to stand for the praetorship. Within two years, Cicero made sure to pass a law that prevented all politicians from presenting gladiatorial games if they were eligible for a magistracy in the next two years, whether they planned to stand or not.[45]

Such blatant politicising of funerary gladiatorial shows was difficult to carry off for men less charismatic and audacious than Caesar, or those who lacked his deftness of political touch. As Caesar increasingly participated in the thuggish tactics of the time (usually one step removed from disorder itself), his bending of the rules of gladiatorial *munera* gave his lackeys licence to do the same, albeit with less delicacy. By 56/5 BCE, Caesar was part of the First Triumvirate, an unofficial and powerful political alliance with Sullan protégés Crassus and Pompey. That year the three had moved to push for the second dual consulship for the latter two, and sought to pack the magistracies with men loyal to them. One Vatinius, a man long in Caesar's service, was their choice for praetor as they fervently wished to block Cato the Younger, their vocal opponent, from the role. During his candidacy, Vatinius put on a lavish *munera* that was clearly intended to sway the electorate; he was prosecuted for electoral bribery for this and other misdemeanours as soon as his praetorship ended in 54 BCE. It is a testament to how deeply Cicero was inserted into the triumviral pockets that he successfully defended Vatinius for breaking a law Cicero himself had written.

In 59 BCE, we hear of plots to publicly assassinate Pompey at the gladiatorial show given by Gabinius, that Caesar may or may not have concocted.[46] By 57

BCE the infamous Clodius was borrowing gladiators that were supposedly intended for family *munera* to use as armed heavies, intimidating the crowds to vote against recalling Cicero from exile.[47] Many civilians were wounded or killed. Clodius himself was murdered by an ex-gladiator-turned-hired-thug on Milo's instructions, following a brawl on the Appian Way in 52 BCE.

In short, by making such a break from funerary traditions and using gladiators opportunistically, Caesar had opened a can of violent worms.[48] Gladiators became an essential weapon in the gang warfare that dominated Roman politics in the dying Republic, and every politician of means had a reasonable excuse to keep a stable of them for future family *munera*. By 49 BCE, Caesar himself owned no less than 5,000.[49] In 46 BCE Caesar made his final gladiatorial innovation: in contrast to the funerals of his aunt and wife, the funeral games of his beloved daughter Julia (his only legitimate child, daughter of Cornelia) featured gladiatorial combats, the first funeral for a woman to do so. She had died in childbirth in 54 BCE, to the devastation of both her father and her husband, Pompey Magnus. The people had requested she be buried on the Campus Martius, only the second to be granted that honour after Sulla.[50] However, 46 BCE was the perfect year for these *munera*. Her widower Pompey was dead, assassinated in Egypt two years before. Caesar had defeated nearly every rival; the Senate meekly voted to grant him dictatorial powers for an unprecedented decade. The commemoration of his daughter was part of a victorious return to Rome that also involved four triumphs. The funeral games themselves featured a feast that required 20,000 dining tables. There were athletic competitions of races and combat sports. Actors performed plays, and dancers and musicians entertained the crowds. There were beast hunts boasting 400 lions and forty elephants, as well as a special basin being excavated by the river so that a mock naval battle (known as a *naumachia*) could be played out with crews of prisoners of war. Romans were treated to an exhibition of the first giraffe to grace the city. So many people travelled to the city to see the spectacles that several got crushed in the crowds.

Everything was coming up Caesar – until it wasn't. He was rising too high and accruing too much power as an individual. In the early months of 44 BCE, the Senate decreed that Caesar be given unprecedented honours and privileges; among them, one day of every calendar year should be devoted to gladiator shows in Caesar's name, across the whole of Italy.[51] He was also given a golden curule chair, kingly raiment (to the horror of many dyed-in-the-wool anti-monarchist Romans), and dictatorial powers in perpetuity. Accepting these sycophantic honours did nothing to quell the fear that Caesar was after monarchical power, and within weeks he lay stabbed twenty-three times on the Senate floor, murdered by his peers. Had Caesar lived long enough for the *munera* for him to be held, they would have marked both the first gladiatorial show in Rome to honour a living person, and the first organised by the state rather than an individual. Within two years of his death, state sponsored gladiatorial shows were presented for the first time, but as part of the ancient and annual *Cerealis* festival, where the fighters replaced the traditional chariot racing.

It would be Augustus who, like Caesar, saw the benefit of utilising gladiatorial *munera*. By 27 BCE, he had emerged as *de facto* ruler of Rome, enjoying the power his uncle had dreamt of. The crucial difference was Augustus' insistence that he was merely the *princeps*, the first man in Rome. However, the Senate's power was reduced, and magistracies slowly became more or less an honorific title. The competitive demonstrations of largesse by ambitious individuals were now pointless, as Augustus was in control. In 22 BCE, Augustus passed a law that ensured that beast hunts and gladiatorial shows were now the responsibility of the praetors, and not private individuals anymore. Their costs were to be borne by the treasury, although if praetors wished to subsidise shows they could, as long as all praetors contributed an equal amount to their colleagues. Gladiatorial shows were restricted to two events per year, with no more than sixty pairs of fighters.[52] In the city of Rome, gladiators were now a state-controlled commodity, and nobody could threaten Augustus by outshining him with spectacle.

Chapter 3

It's All Greek to Us

So, Rome was getting more and more entangled and enmeshed with the Greek world – but what do we mean by 'the Greek world'? The modern nation state of Greece (or, to give it its official title, the Hellenic Republic) didn't exist until 1830 CE, and no such comparable country existed in the ancient world. When I use the term 'Greek world', I run the risk of painting a large region of the eastern Mediterranean with a very broad brush, and creating a simplified picture that none of its inhabitants would have ever recognised. This also applies to time – the various peoples of 'the Greek world' would not have recognised the eras that modern historians have imposed upon their history, e.g. Archaic, Classical, Hellenistic. Historians argue over when those eras begin and end, as well as squabble over the constantly shifting borders of what we consider the Greek world to have been over time. And, if historians find these questions to be such bones of contention, it pales in comparison over the arguments various ancient Greeks had with each other over who was, and very much wasn't, considered truly Greek.

What did it mean to be Greek? Who were the Greeks? The answer was never truly set in stone, and usually changed depending on who exactly was asking (and answering) the question. Because it was already an old question by the time Rome arrived on the scene, it might be best to travel back a little further in time to look at ancient ideas of identity.

The Greek Map

The first issue to address is one of geography: *where* was the Greek world? The answer that likely springs to mind is the southern part of the Balkan peninsula, home to the great cities of Attica and the Peloponnese, like Athens, Corinth and Sparta. This was indeed the region with the oldest Greek cities, but the Greek world was far, far larger than a single peninsula. Some of the notable Greeks who we are still familiar with today aren't from the region that is now modern Greece. Herodotus, known as the 'father of history',[53] was born in Halicarnassus (now Bodrum, Türkiye). Long before Socrates and Plato were philosophising in Athens, philosophers like Thales, Anaximander and Anaximenes were attempting to answer the big questions about life and the universe in Miletus (near modern Balat, Türkiye). The notorious Cynic philosopher Diogenes was not Athenian by birth, but had emigrated from Sinope on the north coast of the Black Sea. One of the most beloved Olympic athletes, a wrestler named Milo, was from Croton (now Crotone, southern Italy). The mathematician Eratosthenes, who calculated the circumference of the Earth,[54] was from Cyrene in what is now Libya, and the famous scientist and inventor Archimedes was a native of Syracuse, Sicily. All these people considered themselves to be very much Greek.

This geographical spread was the result of extensive Greek expansion, as various cities from what is now the mainland sent out colonies of settlers to found new cities across the Mediterranean. When the urban population grew too large, colonists set out to found new towns and took their traditions, language and culture with them. Particularly in the eighth–sixth centuries BCE, in what is known to us as the Archaic period of Greek history, there was a boom in colonisation of this type. The land around the Aegean and beyond became a patchwork quilt of over a thousand independent city states, known as *poleis*. The multiple meanings of *polis* betray how complicated the concept is; the word can be translated into 'city', 'state', 'city-state', 'community', or even sometimes 'country' interchangeably. Generally, a *polis* consisted of an urban city, known as the *asty*, (such as Argos or Thebes) that was surrounded by a band of countryside that it controlled, known as the *chora*. The *chora* was home to the majority of the population, and could consist of small towns and villages as well as farmland. Cities situated away from the coast often had port towns, for example Athens and Piraeus. Rivers, mountain ranges, thick forests and the Aegean Sea provided convenient natural borders or buffer zones between *poleis*, who were usually engaged in various rivalries that frequently erupted into war. Most inhabitants of the Aegean didn't refer to themselves as Greeks (a word actually deriving from the Roman term for people from that region: *Graeci*) or Hellenes (after the mythical progenitor of the Greek tribes, Hellen), but would identify themself as a member of their *polis*.

What Greeks Shared

Greekness was largely determined by what these *poleis* did or did not have in common. Politics was a huge priority across the board, though a common form of government was most certainly not. Between them, the cities trialled every form of government they could imagine. Monarchies (the staple mode of government during the earlier Mycenaean period) were not in vogue in the Archaic and Classical ages, though for a period Sparta had two kings at a time. Others were ruled by oligarchs, a few elite families that dominated the majority. Athens broke away from the pack to develop radical democracy in the fifth century BCE, which many of us now consider to be quintessentially Greek but was viewed by their various neighbours at the time with a mixture of curiosity and disgust.

What allowed people to be considered 'Greek', even in the colonies founded in Spain, France, Italy, North Africa and Türkiye, was not how the *poleis* functioned, but what they shared with each other. The first was language. For many, if you grew up speaking Greek as your first language, you were considered Greek. There were different regional dialects, but generally it was very easy to communicate with citizens of other *poleis*. Anyone who couldn't speak Greek was a barbarian, because their foreign languages made it sound like they were saying 'bar bar bar-bar bara'. That said, some Greeks were happy to be bilingual; for instance, the city of Side in Pamphylia (a region in southern Türkiye) was founded, according to sources, by a city named Cyme in Aeolis (a region in western Türkiye,) around the seventh century BCE. We know less about which city had founded Cyme, but we know they spoke Greek. When colonists founded Side, they interacted with local groups who had their own language. Rather than stamp out the indigenous language, the Greek colonists not only learned it, but preserved it, using it on coins and inscriptions for several centuries alongside Greek translations.

Religious cult practices were another part of culture shared amongst the Greeks and influenced every aspect of daily life. The Greeks had a pantheon of gods in common, though various *poleis* favoured some deities more than others, or characterised various gods slightly differently to their neighbours. Religious festivals had basic rites in common, even if they each had their own regional flair; Greeks were able to take part in festivals in other cities without sticking out like sore thumbs, and were frequently encouraged to do so. Wandering Greeks could therefore expect to find a temple, sanctuary, or festival dedicated to the core gods of the pantheon in any city, and were able to participate in rites as they would at home. Some sanctuaries and festivals became so important that they thrived on becoming meeting points for pilgrim Greeks from across the Aegean and beyond, such as the sacred island of Delos, the festivals of the Panhellenic Games, and oracles such as Delphi and Dodona.

Race, as we understand it today, was not a unifying factor. Dividing people into groups based on the colour of their skin is a phenomenon that developed more recently than the period we are discussing, and while the Greeks certainly noted that humans have an array of skin tones, the colour of one's skin was never a factor in determining Greekness, nor was it used as a measure of one's worth. Greeks did group themselves into *ethne*, but this has nothing to do with modern concepts of ethnicity. The various groups (Ionians, Dorians, Achaeans, Aeolians) had distinct dialects of Greek, some distinct religious rites, and had various collective origin myths and preferred heroes in common. These *ethnos* distinctions were pretty superficial most of the time, though, unless it was politically expedient to mark your city as superior to another belonging to a different *ethnos*, such as in times of war. For the vast majority of the time, belonging to the Ionians or Dorians was just another layer of an individual's identity; it might generate some minor local pride, or result in some stereotyping from Greeks from other groups. These distinctions grew less and less relevant, and by the Hellenistic period even the distinct dialects had fallen out of favour, and been replaced with universal *koine* Greek.

The rhythms of daily life were largely similar across Greek cities, with a set of preferred activities (and associated buildings) in common. Pausanias, a second century CE travel writer, sniffily claims that a city can hardly call itself a Greek *polis* if it doesn't boast government offices, a *gymnasium*, a theatre, a large communal drinking fountain and an *agora*, the marketplace-cum-town square that was also used for any large gatherings.[55] Pausanias was also partial to a lovely set of defensive city walls. While not every city had the entire list checked off (indeed, Pausanias uses his list to insult a little town called Panopeus), most had at least half of the buildings he deemed so essential. The list itself is illuminating, because it reveals what Pausanias (and likely many Greeks like him) considered important about daily life. Far from being homebodies, Greeks lived to be part of a community. Regardless of their form of government, nearly all cities had a council house for their officials, which was called a *Bouleuterion*. These council houses were in use even in cities under foreign rule (by Persia, the Athenian empire, or, later, Hellenistic dynasties) because Greeks were fiercely protective of autonomy, and were (usually) content to provide their overlords with the mandatory tributes and troops if they were left alone to manage city-level affairs 'in house'.[56] That Greek cities were generally allowed such autonomy is testament to their flair and fanaticism for city management, whether officials were elected or not. The *gymnasium* wasn't a place to exercise in silence whilst avoiding eye contact with neighbours, it was a social hub where men got together to train, talk and relax. Theatre-going was a similarly communal activity, and theatres were used for entertainments like music, dances and poetry recitals, as well as plays. Some cities also had an *odeon* for smaller performances, which (unlike the theatre) was roofed. The agora was a perpetually bustling centre of town, where locals met to trade, chat, take part in rituals, and have celebrations and processions. Even the public fountains weren't just functional; they became a place of congregation where people socialised. Being Greek was not for the introverted.

Having much in common should also not lead us to believe that the Greek world was a peaceful and cooperative one. Cities had fierce rivalries and disagreements, and the most common solution to minor disputes was a quick war. The Greeks were obsessed with fighting, and they fought each other far, far more often than they fought 'barbarian' foreigners. Armed squabbles were so common that sacred truces needed to be implemented for major festivals, such as the Olympic and Pythian Games, to allow pilgrim spectators and participants from across the Greek world safe travel to and from the sanctuaries. For centuries, the closest Greek *poleis* got to any form of cohesive cooperation was the formation of various leagues of cities or towns. *Poleis* would group together for military, economic or occasionally religious purposes, whilst theoretically retaining autonomy at city level.[57] Individual *poleis* would therefore find themselves as part of a faction, and tailor their foreign policies accordingly.

Over the centuries, the importance of individual *poleis* waxed and waned. Athens was such a minor entity in the Bronze Age that it was barely included in the epic poems of the *Iliad* and *Odyssey*. However, self-respecting cities always wanted a long and illustrious history, which is why playwrights in fifth century BCE Athens made sure to give their city a starring role in their tales of the Trojan War. Take Euripides' *Trojan Women*, which takes place in the aftermath of the fall of Troy. The surviving women of the Trojan royal family await their fates on the beach, as they prepare to be shipped off as the war trophies-cum-slaves of various Greek heroes. In most traditions, Cassandra was bound for Mycenae, Andromache for Epirus, and so on. Euripides makes sure they all state that if they had to be sent anywhere, they wished it could be Athens! In the fifth century BCE, Athens had ballooned into the largest city in the Greek world, with an estimated 30–50,000 male voting citizens. Even the cities whose heroes feature prominently in the epic poems, like Sparta and Argos, usually had around 1,500 citizens, and most of the less notable *poleis* had less than 1,000. But it wasn't enough for Athens to be dominant in the present, it wanted to have been dominant in the idealised past, and so its writers tweaked the tales.[58]

Cities wanted a connection to the glorious past of epic poetry because connection boosted their cultural cachet; for instance, Sparta had built a shrine to commemorate Menelaus and his beautiful wife Helen as early as the seventh century BCE. Tombs were built for heroes who the Greeks believed to be entirely historical. Such a tomb would be called a *heroön*, and most cities wanted to have one to show off that they were linked to the fabulous exploits of their stories. Such tombs needed bones; Plutarch recounts that the Athenian statesman Cimon, on the advice of an oracle, travelled to the island of Skyros to retrieve the remains of Athens' beloved hero Theseus.[59] He did indeed return with bones, but who they belonged to we will never know. Herodotus recounts a similar tale, wherein an oracle advised Sparta that the only way they could defeat the city of Tegea was to steal the bones of Orestes from them.[60] The Spartans dutifully retrieved some exceedingly large (and definitely not human) bones from the countryside around Tegea, and buried them in the Spartan agora. The possession of the bones of 'Orestes' was a smart piece of propaganda; Sparta wanted to be the heirs of the House of Atreus, and by building a *heroön* for the son of Agamemnon, they staked an ideological claim to be the dominant Peloponnesian *polis*. Even before the Classical period (which is what most of us consider to be the heyday of the ancient Greek world), Greeks craved a cultural connection to the past.

A Sliding Scale

The Greek world, then, was one of thousands of independent towns and cities with enough differences to ensure that they were constantly in-fighting, but with enough similarities that they acknowledged their kinship. Siblings and cousins may squabble, but family is family. Families are complicated entities, with extended relatives, in-laws and exiles. We all probably consider the members of our nuclear families very differently from the distant cousins we see twice a year, and each person in a family network sees certain members as more significant than others. In a similar way, were all Greek *poleis* equally Greek?

What follows is a necessarily brief account of several centuries of history, which loses a lot of nuance to its concision. However, if we are to understand the sliding scale of Greekness in the ancient world, it is necessary to summarise events in the eastern Mediterranean. As we've seen, from even before 700

BCE various *poleis* had sent out colonists to found new cities in search of fertile land, materials and trade. These colonies usually had little to do with their 'mother-city' afterwards, save for cultural touchstones. Most of the time, the colonies were independent and left to fend for themselves. Many of these cities eventually found themselves absorbed into foreign empires. For instance, the coast of Asia Minor has a dense string of Greek colonies along its shores, with the Aeolian cities of Assos, Adramyttion, Pitane and Larissa along the northwestern coast, the Dorian cities of Halicarnassus and Knidos on the southwestern coast, and Ionian cities including Smyrna, Ephesus, Priene and Iasos along the central western coast. The western half of the Anatolian peninsula had not been empty when they arrived, and while they aimed to remain independent alongside the kingdoms they neighboured, it was not to be. If we look at the twelve cities of Ionia, for instance, they first fell, one by one, to the Kingdom of Lydia between 700 BCE and the middle of the sixth century, when the Kingdom of Lydia was in turn conquered and absorbed into the Achaemenid Empire (more commonly known as the Persian Empire).

In 499 BCE, the Ionian cities revolted. Herodotus is our sole account for this, and his account is absolutely ridden with holes so we cannot be sure exactly why or how the revolt started. Herodotus suggests that the revolt erupted because of the ambitions of two men, but doesn't go into detail as to why many cities would agree to such a risky rebellion on their account; we simply don't know what prompted the Ionian Greeks to stand up against Persia. What we do know is that various cities along the Anatolian coast joined in over the next few years and were aided by an Athenian fleet (while most cities on the Greek peninsula opted to stay firmly out of it). By the time the revolt was quelled in 493 BCE, the Ionian cities were thoroughly beaten down and were not allowed to have the same amount of autonomy as they had previously enjoyed under the Persians. The Ionian Revolt is important because of its consequences, not in Ionia but in Greece itself. The Achaemenid emperor at the time was Darius I, and he'd already added Thrace, Paeonia and Macedonia to his collection of territories. He was now on the doorstep of Greece 'proper', and had the perfect justification for its invasion; retribution for the violence of the revolt, which had included the razing of Sardis. Darius was no doubt confident; from his perspective, Greece was a ragtag collection of squabbling towns, and Persia was the mightiest force on the planet. However, after a few minor victories, the Persians were roundly defeated by the Athenians and their allies at the Battle of Marathon in 490 BCE, effectively cutting the invasion of Greece short.

Ten years later in 480 BCE, Darius' successor Xerxes made a second attempt, keen to prove that Marathon had been a fluke. Several northern Greek cities, like Thebes, surrendered immediately when they saw the Persian invasion force. For other Greek cities, this was one of the few instances where we see them willing to work together in a semi-organised united front. The famous Spartan last stand at the Battle of Thermopylae delayed the Persian advance long enough to evacuate cities including Athens (which was indeed looted and razed by the advancing Achaemenid forces) and to organise combined Greek forces for the subsequent battles of Salamis, Plataea and Mycale, which were all significant Greek victories.[61] Knowing when to quit, Xerxes returned to Persia, with the Athenians snapping at his heels.

The Delian League was set up in 478 BCE, assembling a group of Greek *poleis* who collectively vowed to collaborate together to stand against a potential third Persian invasion (which never came) and to wreak revenge on Persia wherever possible. Having been such an active participant in the Ionian Revolt and both Persian invasions, Athens was, perhaps justifiably, worried about further retaliation, and knew that they had essentially painted a big target on their city. Fuelled by this anxiety, Athens soon took over the management of the League, suggesting (and then demanding) that member cities donate either ships and troops or cold hard cash to fund the military force that would be used to protect them, conveniently administered entirely by Athenians. The League swiftly morphed into what was to all intents and purposes an Athenian empire, and Athens quickly grew accustomed to imperialism, including cracking down hard on anything it saw as dissent. As most cities opted to pay their annual tribute in the form of cash, Athens ploughed enormous amounts of money into constructing the greatest fleet the Greek world had ever seen. This fleet, created to keep the Achaemenids at arm's length, was soon used to keep Athenian 'allies' in line.

In other words, the Greek cities of Anatolia swapped the Persian protection racket for an Athenian one, but, for some of the Aegean islands, this was their first experience of being under the yoke of an imperial power – and a Greek one at that. The documentary evidence tells us that, most of the time, Athens was content to leave her 'allies' alone as long as the tribute amounts (which Athens alone calculated) were paid in full and on time, and weren't interested in pushing Athenian ideology on the cities unless it was expedient.[62] For the majority of allied cities, life under Athens was certainly no worse than under any other empire, and, if Athens could be swift and cruel in punishing any dissent, their methodology was also in line with other imperial powers.

Whilst the Athenian empire grew in size and strength, the cities outside of the Delian League looked on with growing concern. They were part of their own consortium of cities, which we call the Peloponnesian League, and they resented Athens throwing its weight around. Resentments festered, particularly when Athenian imperialism directly affected their own interests. Where smaller cities could run to Athens for protection against Peloponnesian cities like Sparta and Corinth (in return for becoming paying allies, of course), the Peloponnesian League busied themselves with offering aid and protection to the allies who sought to break from Athens. Each League thus kept chipping away at the possessions of the other. A fifteen-year series of such conflicts (sometimes known as the First Peloponnesian War) erupted in 460 BCE, resulting in an uneasy peace treaty that did nothing to slow down Athenian ambition. When a second war eventually (and arguably inevitably) broke out in 431 BCE, it was to last intermittently for nearly three decades, and changed the face of the Greek world forever. As far as Greeks were concerned, the Peloponnesian war was a world war; it not only drew in participants from their own world, but neighbouring Persia, Macedonia and Sicily.

By the time the Peloponnesian War drew to a close in 404 BCE Athens was soundly defeated, losing most of her empire and her democracy. Sparta emerged victorious, but had only managed to win by turning to Persia for assistance. Sparta was now in control of many Greek cities, but they were unpopular and faced many difficulties trying to maintain order. The western cities of the Greek world had suffered enormous damage and depletion of their populations. Meanwhile, the Greek cities of the Anatolian coast, whose revolt against Persia nearly a century previously had set up all of the following events like a game of dominoes, were firmly back under Achaemenid control. Persia had not needed to invade Greece for a third time to eliminate them as a threat, all it had needed to do was let Greeks fight amongst themselves until they were weaker than they ever had been.

Here we come to a crucial moment in Greek history. No major city was as strong as it had been before the Peloponnesian War, and the whole network of *poleis* was now dangerously vulnerable. It would take decades before the Greek peninsula would be strong enough (and co-operative enough) to defend itself from foreign threats again. If an ambitious external power wanted to swallow up the whole of the Greek peninsula, the fourth century BCE was the time to do it. In the end, it was a northern backwater whom the *poleis* barely considered Greek at all that would step up to the challenge.

Philip II became king of Macedon in 359 BCE, and was responsible for turning Macedon from a rough, quasi-barbarian kingdom (as far as Greeks on the peninsula were concerned, at least) into a major player on the Greek stage. Using a combination of genius military reform and tactics, astute political manoeuvring, personal charm and outright bribery (as lucrative mines gave Macedon immense wealth), Philip was not only able to strengthen Macedon itself, but to rapidly expand its sphere of influence. Philip set out about defeating Macedon's neighbouring rivals, either via political marriages (he had four wives), or his crack military force. This expansionism didn't go unnoticed; the Athenian orator Demosthenes opposed Philip for decades, giving a number of impassioned speeches that first urged Athenians to resist negotiating with Philip, and later compelling them to take up arms against him to eliminate him entirely, on the basis that Philip was not only dangerous, he was entirely barbarian.[63] Isocrates, another of the Athenian orators, took the opposite view; he urged Philip to unite the Greek cities and lead an army against Persia, because, as a Greek king, Isocrates felt that Philip should be focussing his aggression outside of the Greek world, not within it.

So was Philip a barbarian or a Greek? Demosthenes and Isocrates clearly did not agree. This debate exists simply because Greekness was such a nebulous idea. Certainly, if we look at Philip with our checklist in mind, as a Macedonian he did speak Greek. Macedonians spoke in a dialect considered rather coarse by the Greeks of the peninsula, but, as an aristocrat, Philip probably spoke in the well-regarded Attic dialect anyway. He was highly educated, having spent his formative years as a political hostage in Thebes, where he spent much time learning from Epaminondas, one of the greatest Greek statesmen of the fourth century who briefly made Thebes the premier city in Greece. Philip could be charmingly eloquent when he wanted to, and was an excellent rhetorician. He participated in the Olympic Games, where he entered chariot teams (a standard mode of participation for nobles), and was a great patron of authors and actors. He followed all of the expected Greek religious rites, and was a courageous warrior. If we view Greekness as a verb, rather than an adjective, then Philip does indeed fit the bill. Of course, because Greekness was about the things that you did, rather than where you were born, Philip could dial up his Greekness whenever it was politically expedient. Conversely, he certainly behaved in ways that Greeks in the south were vocally opposed to, giving them the justification for calling him an outsider; he drank to excess, was sexually promiscuous and had expensive tastes. Most of all, he could be incredibly brutal towards Greeks who opposed his will; for instance, he completely destroyed the city of Olynthos and sold every single occupant (including an Athenian garrison) into slavery. To be clear, Greek cities (including Athens) had done startlingly similar, if not identical, things when they had been dominant: in order to criticise another for matching misdeeds, memories must have been either foggy or short. As for Philip, he was a multi-faceted character who chose to behave in a variety of ways depending on what he deemed appropriate for each occasion; when he wanted to be, he was Greek.

We know that some Athenians like Demosthenes were horrified by his imperialist ambitions – which is a little rich – but we also have evidence for Athenians like Aeschines and Isocrates who could perhaps see the writing on the wall. Philip was a force to be reckoned with, and he was methodically involving himself in the peninsula via both battlefield and *bouleuterion*. As it became increasingly clear that the threat from Macedon was growing more serious with every passing year, Athens and her allies (including Thebes and Corinth) finally followed Demosthenes' advice and put up a stand against Philip at the Battle of Chaeronea in 338 BCE. It was a disaster. The Greek cities had been fighting for their freedom, but simply could not resist Philip's military skill. Philip could have chosen to conquer the Greek peninsula at this point, but instead he strong-armed the cities into joining a confederacy (known as the Hellenic/Corinthian League) who would be his allies, not his subjects. He made all the cities (excluding Sparta, who stubbornly refused to have anything to do with the entire affair) swear an oath to remain peaceful towards Macedon and each other, and not depose him or his heirs, nor break from the League. Philip was to be the *hegemon*, or leader of the League, and in return he promised the cities a high degree of autonomy in civil matters. The terms may not have been ideal for the Greek cities (who were not permitted to choose exactly how autonomous they were to be, and were definitely unaccustomed to not squabbling with each other), but it was the best result they could hope for after Chaeronea.

Philip's first order of business was for the Macedonians and the League to launch a grand invasion of Persia to finally free the Greek cities of Anatolia once and for all. Whereas a few of the Greek cities of the Balkan peninsula had made their own failed, independent attempts, they had been unable to co-operate with each other to pose any serious threat to the imposingly huge Achaemenid empire. It took Philip marshalling the aggression that the cities too often pointed at each other to aim a united Greek force eastward. Unfortunately, Philip was assassinated at Aigai in 336 BCE before he could depart for the campaign.[64]

A Greek Conqueror Rises

The Macedonian expedition against Persia did go ahead, but under the command of Philip's twenty-year-old son, Alexander the Great, who succeeded him as King of Macedon and leader of the Hellenic League. In every way, Philip walked so that Alexander could run; without the father, the son would have been 'Alexander the Footnote'. In 334 BCE, Alexander marched his combined armies into Asia and did what no Greek had ever come close to achieving; he roundly defeated the Achaemenid armies in a succession of glittering military victories, and deposed their king, Darius III, in the space of four years. The entire Persian empire, not just the Greek cities, was now Alexander's.[65] The elimination of the Achaemenids fulfilled a long-held Greek dream, but Alexander wasn't content to stop there. By the age of thirty-three, his conquests stretched all the way to the Indus Valley, swallowing up Egypt, Syria, Mesopotamia and the regions now known as Iran and Afghanistan. The Greek colonisation of the eastern Mediterranean had taken a couple of centuries, but the expansion further east was like the Big Bang.

So did Alexander spread Greekness? Or did he spread Macedonian culture instead? The question over whether he should be considered Greek or Macedonian is a debate that has raged for over two millennia, and is still a hot button issue in modern Greece and Macedonia. Again, we must remind ourselves that ancient Greekness was a sliding scale and try to place Alexander on it.

Certainly, just like his father, he was a Greek speaker who ticks every cultural requirement on our list. Philip gave him the ultimate Greek education by assigning the Greek polymath Aristotle as Alexander's personal tutor, and Alexander was intimately familiar with the Greek canon of literature, even taking a personal, annotated copy of the *Iliad* with him on campaign. On the other hand, though he founded many new cities during his conquests, he never stayed in one place long enough to ensure that the cities had the necessary Greek institutions and civic buildings, which he delegated to others. Moreover, while he was happy to embody the epitome of Greekness when he made an emotional pilgrimage to the site of Troy, he also happily acted like an Egyptian in Egypt, taking part in Egyptian religious rites and allowing himself to be proclaimed the son of their god Ra (which Greeks accepted as him being son of Zeus). Equally, though he razed the great metropolis of Persepolis (an expedient act that nevertheless should be considered cultural vandalism), Alexander was attracted to the wealth of eastern royal courts and soon incorporated lavish foreign dress, feasting and court etiquette into his routine. While this may have eased the transition for locals from Persian rule to Alexander's rule, it nevertheless rankled amongst his Greek and Macedonian inner circle, one of whom he murdered in a rage when they voiced objection. Alexander was likely trying to find ways to ensure that Greeks, Egyptians, and Persians could live alongside each other in a merging of cultures, rather than suppressing Persian customs outright, particularly since the conquering Macedonians were very much outnumbered. But Greek xenophobia for the perceived effeminacy, subservience and self-indulgence of those they called 'easterners' had run deep since the First Persian Invasion. If Greeks were snobby about Macedonians, it paled in comparison to their derision for barbarians.

Alexander died in Babylon in 323 BCE, aged just thirty-three, before he could consolidate and organise his conquests into a proper empire, before he could produce and prepare an heir, and before he could convince his closest advisors that multiculturalism was the most logical and mutually beneficial step forward. They would have to work this out on their own, but not before they spent over three decades and four major conflicts fighting to carve up the defeated territories and grab what they could for themselves. These conflicts are known as the 'Wars of the Diadochi', meaning 'Wars of the Successors'. The dynasties they founded ushered the Greek world into what we call the Hellenistic Period, which lasted until the last of the successor's descendants, Cleopatra VII of Egypt, died in 31 BCE.

There were four main blocks of Greek power:

- Lysimachos was a Thessalian general in Alexander's army, and initially took control of Thrace, Asia Minor and Macedon. This empire was short-lived, and the main remnants in Asia Minor were usurped by one of his lieutenants, Philetairos. Philetairos founded the Attalid dynasty centred in Pergamon, which, despite its small size in comparison to other Hellenistic Kingdoms, was powerful and influential.
- Seleucus I Nicator was a Macedonian general, and founded the eponymous Seleukid Empire in Syria, Mesopotamia and the Iranian plateau. This was by far the largest of the Hellenistic Kingdoms.
- Ptolemy I Soter claimed Egypt, founding a dynasty of Macedonian Greek pharaohs. It was Ptolemy who turned Alexander's city of Alexandria from a port in a less-than-ideal location into one of the great Hellenic cities; Ptolemy is credited with both the famous Library of Alexandria and the Pharos (Lighthouse) that would become one of the seven wonders of the ancient world.

- Cassander ensured his own success by murdering Alexander's only surviving son, Alexander IV, when the boy was just fourteen years old, claiming Macedon for himself. He failed to leave behind heirs who weren't intent on murdering each other, and, shortly after Cassander's death, Demetrius I Poliorcetes took over Macedon. His heirs would eventually become the Antigonid dynasty.
- During this time, the independent cities of the Greek peninsula formed new Leagues (mainly the Achaean and Aetolian Leagues) to ensure that they, too, did not end up subjects of a successor.

And so, the conquests of Alexander were divided up, and these dynasties flourished until, one by one, each fell to Rome. In the interim, we should by no means assume that the Kingdoms weren't constantly tussling with both each other and neighbouring states, and their borders changed as frequently as the courses of great rivers. Just as individual Greek cities had been doing for centuries, the Hellenistic Kings made a habit of going to war with each other and their neighbours, but now with the massive armies that came with having an empire.

For many of the mature eastern Greek cities like Miletus, Smyrna and Halicarnassus, living under Roman hegemony was much like living under the rule of Persia, Athens, or Alexander and his successors. In cities such as these, Greeks had already been living in multicultural societies alongside other groups for centuries, and had adopted local customs and practices while enjoying Greek culture and institutions. These cities knew exactly what it meant to live under an imperial power, but were proud and needed delicate handling lest they revolt; the cities demanded as much autonomy as they could get away with. It was a question of dignity, which the Hellenistic dynasts largely respected if the cities maintained their imperial obligations of troops and tribute. The cities themselves continued to oversee their own internal affairs, and most kept a militia of local soldiers and maintained fortifications – just in case; this was no mere token gesture either, as the kings could be savagely brutal in their retribution against cities who they felt had provoked them to anger.

For cities that were theoretically more docile and loyal (and easier to extort), the Hellenistic kings followed Alexander's lead and added a long list of their own, new cities to the network of *poleis* in Thrace, Asia and Syria. These new cities were given everything they needed to be Greek: gymnasia, theatres for plays, temples, stadiums, agoras, etc., but on a new, massive scale. The older cities in Asia also chose to supersize and beautify their monuments, and rival cities vowed to outdo each other in how elegant and awe-inspiring their civic buildings were. Some of the Hellenistic civic buildings along the eastern shores of the Mediterranean dwarfed the Classical era buildings of the Greek mainland; the Temple of Artemis at Ephesus, was, for instance, about double the size of the Parthenon in Athens. The new cities were meticulously laid out on efficient orthogonal grid-systems with elegant straight roads that cut the layout of the urban quarters into uniform city blocks. Some of the new cities themselves grew much, much larger than their august counterparts on the 'mainland'; Alexandria and Antioch in particular became true metropolises, partly because of the huge numbers of mainland Greeks who chose to emigrate to these new centres of Greek life. Cities weren't isolated and insular, but were nodes in a vibrant network of communication and exchange. People travelled, traded, made pilgrimages, did business abroad. And every time a Greek moved about, they could find the familiar building blocks of Greek life in every new city they visited, however far away.

If the Greek colonisation of the eastern Mediterranean coast had been a slow drip, drip, drip over a couple of centuries, the Hellenistic spread of Greek culture, art and architecture was a tsunami that spread all the way to the Indus valley in Alexander's wake. Greekness abroad was no longer limited to enclaves clinging to the Aegean coast, but spread over a huge swathe of land. The Greekness of these cities matched the Greekness of the Hellenistic kings; bigger, bolder and brasher than the understated elegance of the Greek mainland, merging and melding into local cultures that had existed before the flood of Grecification. Subtlety was not part of the Hellenistic royal lexicon, and, if their pomp and pageantry was a turn off to mainland Greeks – as is often claimed – it had been part and parcel of Greek life under previous eastern empires; spreading Greek culture needn't mean a lack of continuity for local communities.

Hellenistic Greekness meant fusion. In many ways, this was a continuation of the old plurality of Greek identity; if we were to ask any Greek from the Archaic to Hellenistic periods who they were, few if any would answer 'Greek'. They were citizens of their city first and foremost. Some might add extra layers of detail, such as their tribe, or *ethne*, or a specific religious cult, but overall Greekness was a kind of umbrella for a mishmash of peoples who, for all of their incessant squabbling, did have quite a lot in common. Greekness wasn't the type of overarching identity that one needed to think about much – until that Greekness was threatened, or if being Greek ensured privilege. In cities across the Hellenistic kingdoms, Greeks got preferential treatment over local populations. Greeks got the key political roles, Greeks got the choice religious priesthoods, Greeks got prestige and deference. Because their kings identified as Greek, Greeks were the ruling class with all the privileges that came with it. This meant that, for the first time in the farthest eastern regions, Greekness was something that locals wanted to buy into. Positioning oneself as Hellenistic, or at the very least a Hellenophile, became a savvy move.

The Hellenistic kingdoms waxed and waned; for instance, as we've seen, the Seleukid empire gradually shrank as chunks of territory seceded. Greekness, however, seems to have endured more than we might expect. The Parthian empire grew from a nucleus that had once been Seleukid territory, and kept on growing until it was one of the greatest powers of the ancient world. Their initial territory was in what is now Iran, far from Greece, but even after the Seleukids were ousted from the area, Greek customs continued even as additional Iranian customs (which the Seleukids had also drawn on) were revived alongside them. Greek continued to be one of the many languages spoken in the empire, and they used Greek-style coins known as *drachmae*. We have no sources from the Parthians themselves, but a famous anecdote about one of their kings in the Late Republican Roman period mentions that he enjoyed watching the classic plays of Athenian tragedians.[66]

So, we can see that Greekness was fluid and fuzzy, a medley of customs, actions and beliefs, and an identity on a sliding scale that could co-exist with and within foreign cultures. We also understand that throughout their history Greeks had been consumed with destructive rivalries amongst themselves, were continuously at war with each other and entirely unable to co-operate for any significant length of time. Being bellicose, then, might be considered a feature of Greekness, had it not also been shared by a growing foreign neighbour: Rome.

Chapter 4

Rome Creeps Eastwards

Rome's first entanglement with the Greek world was not in the eastern Mediterranean, but in the southern end of the Italian peninsula, where the Greeks had planted a string of coastal colonies in the 700s BCE. This area, together with the Greek cities of Sicily, formed Magna Graecia— 'Greater Greece'. Rome, just as belligerent as any Greek city, wanted to control the entire Italian peninsula, and the Greek cities there stood in its way. Under the guise of offering the Greek cities of southern Italy protection, Rome planned to install their own garrisons in each one. The Greeks weren't under any illusions about who they actually needed protection from; Rome was determined to exert control and that meant their prized autonomy was at risk. The city of Tarentum (modern Taranto) did what any city under threat would at the time: find a bigger aggressor to scare off whoever was bothering them. The Tarentines chose King Pyrrhus of Epirus, who (like Alexander and his successors) seems to have had grand imperial ambitions of his own; the Tarentines were rejecting the rock and pinning their hopes on the hard place because at least the hard place was Greek. Pyrrhus was an excellent commander and strategist, who quickly set about giving Rome an absolute thrashing on a succession of battlefields.

The problem Pyrrhus faced was the key difference between Roman and Hellenistic imperialism; Greek kings (like the Persians before them) demanded that subjugated cities pay them tribute with towering piles of cash, and also the right to levy troops when needed. The Romans, on the other hand, just wanted troops. The price of Roman 'protection' was the male youth of the cities the Romans called *amicitiae* – 'friends', or more formally, *socii* – 'allies'. Whether this feeling of friendship was mutual is debatable. By the time Pyrrhus crossed over to the Italian peninsula in 280 BCE, Rome had enough *socii* that they had a steady and plentiful supply of troops. Pyrrhus, militarily gifted though he was, simply couldn't compete with Rome in terms of manpower. While he won battles, he didn't have a readily available reserve of fresh troops like Rome had. Even so, the Romans were genuinely threatened by Pyrrhus. We know that Pyrrhus eventually lost, and we still use the term 'Pyrrhic victory' to describe victories that come at too great a cost. But for Rome, their victory didn't seem inevitable at all; Pyrrhus was truly intimidating, and had brought terrifying cavalry and war elephants across to Italy in addition to his foot soldiers and slingers.

In 278 BCE, Pyrrhus turned his attention to Sicily, whose Greek cities seized the opportunity to ask for his help, just as Tarentum had done, but this time against the other great power in the west: Carthage. The Carthaginians held parts of the island and wanted more, and were currently besieging Syracuse. Pyrrhus broke that siege and was declared King of Sicily for his efforts, not that he proved to be a beloved or benevolent ruler. For the Sicilian Greeks, the hard place was far more uncomfortable than the rock, and many defected back to Carthage. In the meantime, Pyrrhus was still fighting his war on the Italian front, and his Sicilian expedition had given Rome plenty of time to eke out every young man of military age from the *socii*. At the Battle of Beneventum in 275 BCE, the Romans met Pyrrhus on a battlefield once again. The outcome wasn't particularly decisive, but it did convince Pyrrhus that perhaps Magna Graecia (with the ungrateful Sicilians in particular) was not worth the effort. The Pyrrhic war ended with the Epirote army returning home almost as empty handed as when they'd arrived, and the Italian and Sicilian Greek cities under a much stronger influence from Rome and Carthage, respectively.

This war had taught Rome two things: firstly, that having the Italian peninsula invaded was terrifying and must be avoided at all costs; the edge of the Greek world was geographically overlapping with the south of their territory, and Greeks had proven to be formidable opponents. Worse, Pyrrhus and Epirus were a minor threat compared to the other Hellenistic kingdoms emerging from the Wars of the Diadochi; there was a good reason Pyrrhus had attempted to build his empire to the west rather than to the east. A buffer zone would need to be carefully curated. Secondly, that they had in fact been able to stave off an invader, and had won control of the entire peninsula as a result. Imperialism presumably felt good; Rome wanted more. Sicily was a tantalising prize, and Carthage's own imperialism meant that they would, eventually, need to face each other. The western Mediterranean was getting too small to hold both of their ambitions.

Carthage

The first Punic[67] War did start a mere eleven years after the Battle of Beneventum, and successive wars with Carthage would keep Rome occupied on and off for nearly a century. The next time Rome faced a culturally Greek force would be in the Illyrian Wars of 229 and 219 BCE, which marked the first time Rome set hob-nailed sandals in the Greek world. The first war was ostensibly fought to curtail Illyrian piracy, and ended with the southern Illyrians becoming reluctant 'friends' of Rome. The second war a decade later was slightly different. The new king of Macedon was a teenaged Philip V, who wasted no time in marching south against the cities of Aetolia. In Rome, tensions in Spain meant that a fast-approaching second Punic War was becoming inevitable. In Illyria, Demetrius of Pharos had grown irritated with Rome's 'friendship' and was actively working to oust Roman influence from the region, including resuming piratical attacks on trading vessels. The Romans had learned from Pyrrhus that a war on two fronts was difficult to win, and they knew that Demetrius was amicable with Macedon, who were clearly on the ascendant. Rome couldn't afford for Macedon to become too strong before Carthage was decisively dealt with, and an alliance between Illyria and Macedon would do exactly that. It was crucial that Rome retained its Illyrian buffer, and quickly. The second Illyrian war was, in actuality, two short sieges, and ended with Rome reinforcing their 'friendship' with the defeated Illyrians.

Rome, satisfied, returned to dealing with Carthage in the west, but kept a close eye on the continual fighting between the Hellenistic kingdoms. In turn, Macedon watched Rome with interest, piqued at their willingness to interfere, in however minor a fashion, in the workings of the Greek world. Philip V was an ambitious young man, desperate to live up to the royal Hellenistic ideal of the warrior king, and, while he knew that his Greek rivals in Asia, Syria and Egypt were formidable, he also knew that Pyrrhus had come much closer to defeating the Romans than Rome cared to admit. Italy was laden with potential for conquest, particularly if Carthage brought them down a peg or two first.

Macedon

First, Philip made a show of allying with Hannibal following the utter carnage wrought upon the Roman army at Cannae in 216 BCE. Secondly, like Demetrius, he moved to prise Illyria away from Roman influence. After all, if Hannibal continued to raze the Italian peninsula, Rome would hardly be in a position to intervene, and Illyria would make an ideal springboard for a Macedonian invasion of Italy, should that become necessary. Nobody in Rome wanted another Greek king invading the peninsula, so the First Macedonian War (214–205 BCE) was started by the Romans to prevent the new allies of Carthage and Macedon teaming up. That the war ended in stalemate was moot; keeping each other at an uneasy arm's length was all Rome really wanted or needed. Rome also made sure to ally themselves with the Aetolian cities, who had their own reasons to ensure Philip remained hemmed in. It was a raw deal for the Aetolians, who found that Rome allowed Philip to keep his acquisitions in the region as part of Rome's peace treaty with Macedon when the war concluded.

Everyone was aware that matters were far from settled. Rome set about buddying up to the Greek cities who were most openly wary of Macedon. In the meantime, strife in Egypt left the Ptolemies vulnerable. Philip and Antiochus III of the Seleukid dynasty made a deal; each would take advantage of Egypt's turmoil to snap up some of what they saw as prime real estate, making sure not to tread on each other's toes. Antiochus wanted Coele Syria, Philip concentrated on coastal Caria and the Aegean islands, and Egypt was completely unable to intervene. Rome did not need Macedon cosying up to the Seleukids, particularly when both had such naked imperialistic ambitions, ones that would eventually clash with Rome's own naked imperialistic ambitions. Publius Sulpicius Galba, consul in 200 BCE, convinced the Senate that Philip should be dealt with in Greece before he had a chance to enter Italy. War was dutifully declared. Rome set about marketing themselves as the protector of free Greek cities, and rustling up hatred for Philip. This wasn't difficult, as Philip had a tendency for dealing with unco-operative Greeks with severity. Then again, Rome too had earned herself a reputation for massacring Greeks during the First Macedonian War. Who would prove to be the lesser of two evils?

An envoy from Rome sent Philip an ultimatum, which was never a sensible method of approaching a Hellenistic king. Conquer no more cities in Asia, mainland Greece, or Egypt's possessions in the Aegean – or be at war with Rome. Philip chose the latter, and so began the Second Macedonian War (200–197 BCE). The tide of this war was arguably turned by an ambitious young Roman general named Flamininus. He was consul in 198 CE at the staggeringly young age of twenty-nine, when most of his predecessors had reached this rank in their late thirties at the very earliest. As the war progressed, Flamininus repeated the Roman ultimatum, but now added a stipulation which they must have known Philip would be too proud to accept: surrender all previously conquered cities across the Aegean and be content to limit Macedonian hegemony to Macedon. Philip refused to budge, and the war continued – but not in Philip's favour. In 197 BCE, after a disastrous defeat at the Battle of Cynoscephalae, Philip was forced to sign an armistice, and on the terms originally stipulated by Flamininus. If Flamininus wanted to portray Rome as the lesser evil compared with Macedon, Cynoscephalae seriously threatened to ruin the facade; the Macedonians were forbidden to remove or bury their 8,000 dead from the battlefield. This treatment of enemy combatants was considered incredibly cruel, particularly since a proper burial was deemed essential for the souls of the deceased to be able to enter the Underworld.

Flamininus gathered his Greek allies at the sanctuary of Poseidon at Isthmia in 196 BCE and solemnly declared them to be liberated, though everyone present was aware that this freedom was illusory. They were free from Macedonian aggression (for the time being), but the price the Romans charged was high: 'friendship'. For the time being, this mode of friendship did indeed allow them more autonomy than Macedonian hegemony had; Rome seemed to have no interest in actively administering the region themselves at that point in time. In the immediate aftermath of the Second Macedonian War, the relief of the Greeks was palpable. Only the Aetolians were sceptical about Roman intentions at the time. Flamininus told the Greeks that now the job was done, the Roman army would leave and return to Italy. It was not to be a lasting absence.

The Seleukids

Antiochus III had been taking advantage of Philip's plummeting fortunes by hoovering up the cities of Asia Minor that had once been part of the Seleukid empire, which, as far as he was concerned, was restoring his inheritance. Rome's insistence that they were leaving Greece, having completed the task they had set themselves there, left a gaping power vacuum behind them. The Aetolians sought to exploit this by inviting Antiochus III to invade mainland Greece, which the Romans had already warned him against doing: they had declared the Greek cities to be free, after all, so why would Antiochus need to leave Seleukid territory? Antiochus, meanwhile, was already acting in a provocative manner (at least, from a Roman perspective) by expanding into Thrace, which could theoretically be used as a starting point for a march into Macedon and down into the mainland. When questioned about such intentions, Antiochus asked a question of his own: why were Romans so interested in Greek affairs? After all, did Antiochus ever meddle in Italian business? A further possible provocation was that Antiochus had welcomed the Carthaginian general-extraordinaire Hannibal into his inner circle. Hannibal certainly *had* meddled in Italian business, and no Roman wanted a repeat of Hannibal's campaigns on their peninsula. Was Antiochus so friendly with Hannibal because they were in cahoots, planning to destroy Rome together? It was just plausible enough to ensure that Rome couldn't – or wouldn't – stand idly by doing nothing.

Antiochus did bring a small, token force over to the mainland in the autumn of 192 BCE, expecting to bring a larger force over in the following spring for the usual campaign season. The Romans had evacuated, and the Aetolians had assured him of a warm welcome from fellow Greeks. However, he did not receive any welcome or support from Philip V of Macedon, who was licking his wounds and averse to annoying the Romans more than he already had. The Achaean League also chose to remain loyal to Rome; now that Philip's threat was eliminated, the League was salivating over the idea of expanding further into the Peloponnese. This itself was frustrating for Rome; the entire point of their policy in Greece was to prevent any of the power blocs there growing large enough to dominate the others, while keeping all of them dependent on or in awe of Rome. Macedon had been cut back down to an acceptable size, but if the Achaean League were to conquer Sparta their influence would then be dangerously large. Antiochus found his reception to be chillier than anticipated. He set about a winter of diplomatic persuasion, hampered only by one of his generals massacring a garrison of Romans at Delion, which gave the Romans the excuse they'd been waiting for to react with force, and so began the Roman–Seleukid War (192–188 BCE).

In the spring of 191 BCE, Roman troops arrived in Greece before Antiochus' reinforcements could arrive and met Antiochus' smaller army at Thermopylae; the very same place that the Spartans had slowed the Persian advance nearly three centuries previously. Antiochus was soundly defeated, and had no choice but to return to Asia Minor. The Aetolians attempted to continue the war with Rome alone, feeling abandoned, but it did not go well for them. Antiochus concentrated his attention on attacking Pergamon, whose king, Eumenes, was a staunch ally of Rome. This drew the Roman army and navy eastwards, and they defeated Antiochus again at the Battles of Myonessus and Magnesia. At Magnesia, the Roman force was no longer led by the philhellene Flamininus, whose Greek policy had been to 'do the job' of quelling unrest, placating the Greeks and then leaving them to it. Now, Scipio Africanus, hero of the Second Punic War, was in charge, and his policy was centred far less on diplomacy. As we've seen, the consequences of Antiochus' loss at Magnesia were significant, and the subsequent Treaty of Apamea was a humiliating document that severely shrunk the empire he had worked so hard to expand.

In two decades, Rome had fought major wars against Carthage, Macedon and the Seleukids, and come out on top. They were becoming as arrogant as any Hellenistic king, treating their allies with growing disdain. Eumenes of Pergamon, for instance, had long adopted a sycophantic position to Rome, and had benefitted greatly from Antiochus' fall from grace. Pergamon's territory was larger than it ever had been. Eumenes' enthusiastic bootlicking enriched him, beyond a doubt, but it didn't earn him their respect. Neither was Philip V thanked for refusing to join up with Antiochus; he was entirely snubbed. The illusion of 'friendship' was fading. If the Achaean League had clung on to the promise that their relationship with Rome was one of equals, they quickly realised the truth after they did, in fact, conquer Sparta in 188 BCE. Rome was not best pleased, and strongly urged the League to back off. Instead, the League called on Rome for military aid in its campaign against the Peloponnesian city of Messene, and were shocked when Rome rebuffed them. It turned out the obligations of Roman friendship were a one-way system.

For centuries, the Greek world had been divided between kings and leagues who were in constant competition, each seeking to expand its territories at the expense of the others. Now, they each found that Rome was not going to allow them to continue in this manner – not if it meant that one power bloc might actually end up successfully expanding. Competition and conflict were central to the Greek way of life, and now that was being curtailed, micro-managed by Romans. How far did Roman interference go? Philip V was certainly anxious. His younger son, Demetrius, had been taken as a hostage of Rome after Cynoscephalae and had fought for Rome *against* Antiochus. Demetrius was returned to Philip, but could Philip be sure that Demetrius, who was very popular with the Romans, wasn't some sort of double agent? Was Rome grooming Demetrius to be a compliant puppet king over Philip's elder son, Perseus? Philip wasn't taking any chances, and ordered the murder of Demetrius in 180 BCE. Although brutal, this was hardly out of character for Macedonian kings. Philip died within a year, and his son Perseus became king of Macedon.

Macedon 2.0

In 173 BCE, Eumenes, ever the willing minion, began whispering to Rome that Perseus was just as ambitious as his father had been, and that Macedon's new leader was a threat to them all. The Romans assured Eumenes that his worries were duly noted, but they had no intentions of intervening at the present moment. However, the seed was planted in the fertile soil of the Roman imagination, and Rome started to list grievances, imagined or exaggerated. Perseus was a gifted diplomat, and was amicable with his fellow Greeks.[68] This, in itself, was enough to rankle. Rome relied on Greeks viewing each other with mutual distrust, so that they believed that Rome was the only power they could rely on. Perseus becoming popular was too dangerous for this delicate balancing act. There was also the worry that Philip had charged Perseus with avenging his military defeats, according to the historian Polybius.[69]

Initially, Rome launched a smear campaign to try and prevent Perseus making any alliances. They sent emissaries to reaffirm their 'friendship', and, in an unprecedented move, sent troops to accompany them. The point was clear; war was coming, and it was the time to decide who would be on whose side. Rome gave the Greeks an offer they couldn't refuse: side with Rome or suffer the consequences. Perseus seemed reluctant to bring about a war with Rome, but, in the end, he had little choice in the matter. It wasn't his actions that had led him to this point, but the dual anxieties in Rome caused by his father's historical belligerence and his own potential for dominance; whether or not Perseus really did have a master plan of Macedonian vengeance (and if he did, his actual actions hid his intentions well) had become irrelevant. Rome was acting pre-emptively, and the old claim that they were the saviours of Greek freedom was becoming even more threadbare now that they were threatening a war with little clear justification. War was eventually declared against Macedon once more, which would be known as the Third Macedonian War (171–168 BCE).

The first battle, at Callinicus in Thessaly, came at the end of the summer campaign season and ended in a minor Macedonian victory. The Roman commander blamed their Aetolian allies for the loss, rather unfairly. Despite winning, Perseus still offered to sign a peace treaty, even going as far as to offer to pay Rome's war costs. Rome declined. Perseus spent the winter in Macedon, the Romans ('the protectors of Greek freedom', remember) spent it massacring three Boeotian cities for the crime of siding with Perseus. As optics went, it was not a move that endeared Greeks to the Roman cause. Many Greeks began to root for Perseus, but secretly. They knew what happened to Greeks who cheered for him out loud.

For the first portion of the war, Perseus was doing very well. Rome struggled, both with enemies and allies. When they docked at Abdera, a Pergamene ally, they demanded so much in supplies that the locals were forced to appeal to Rome. The Roman commander punished them for complaining by killing the lead protestors and selling many of the citizens into slavery. Seeing how Romans treated their 'friends', other Greek ports refused to let the fleet dock at all. The Senate eventually moved to mitigate the damage, sending over a fresh commander in 168 BCE. He would turn the tide of the war, which was not going as easily thus far as the Romans had expected or hoped. Lucius Aemilius Paullus was a seasoned commander who was far less likely to massacre allies, and could be trusted to wage war without tarnishing Rome's reputation quite as badly. Just a few months after his arrival, Aemilius met Perseus at Pydna; the subsequent battle was a bloodbath that left around 20,000 Macedonians dead and another

10,000 sold into slavery. Perseus attempted to flee, but was apprehended and taken to Rome as a prisoner. The Antigonid dynasty was over, and Macedon carved up into four puppet Republics who were to live under tight restrictions.

Retribution

If Aemilius Paullus was supposed to be less brutal than his predecessors, we should shudder to think what the aftermath of Pydna might have been had they still been present. Many cities were looted, which also involved violence towards civilians. Prominent citizens suspected of favouring Perseus over Rome were executed in large numbers, and pro-Roman Greeks took advantage of this brutality by eliminating their own rivals. Neighbours were encouraged to snitch on neighbours. Thousands of Greek elites on the mainland with even tenuous connections to Macedon were rounded up and taken to Rome as hostages, including a young man named Polybius, who would write a history of the Roman conquest of his homeland. Most never returned home. Anyone who had shown even the slightest amount of favour towards Perseus was dealt with harshly, and this included the power bloc of Rhodes, who had sent a mere five ships to help the Roman war effort, rather than the forty ships demanded of them. Rome sternly threatened Rhodes with war, and transformed Delos into a free port to deliberately harm Rhodian trade. By 164 BCE, Rhodes was reduced to the status of 'ally', ending any true independence.

The Molossians in Epirus, the only Greek group who had backed Perseus and not adopted a policy of wait-and-see-if-he-starts-winning, were punished severely. Their towns were looted and razed, their women sexually assaulted and 150,000 citizens sold into slavery. The region took over a century to recover, though some towns and villages remained entirely uninhabited because there were simply no more people left to live there. As for 'friends', even Eumenes of Pergamon, the toady of Rome, was treated with some cruelty, and seemingly for no other reason than his kingdom would now be larger than that of Rhodian territory, and Rome disliked imbalance. Rome was officially finished with pretending that any of their friendships were equal relationships. They had brought down a dynasty, and they could always bring down more.

The invasion of (mainland) Greece, then, was really a series of wars against Macedon that absorbed the rest of the Greek mainland into Roman power under the guise of alliances, but alliances were now not enough to prevent the spilling of blood. Rome was revelling in her power, buoyed up by destroying a mighty kingdom, and behaving badly because nobody was bold enough to protest anymore. With the defeat and capture of Perseus, the first domino had been dropkicked across the room.

The Seleukids 2.0

Antiochus IV had taken advantage of Rome's preoccupation with Macedon to harass the Ptolemies in Egypt, as we saw in the prologue, and it is at this point, in 168 BCE, that Gaius Popillius Laenas so baldly instructed Antiochus to end his siege of Alexandria and evacuate all Seleukid troops from Egypt. After Pydna, a single threat was now enough to stop a Hellenistic king in his tracks. Antiochus' festival at Daphne, replete with Roman-style gladiators, came a mere two years after Aemilius Paullus had his own victory festival with Greek art, music, literature and athletics. Rome was absorbing Greek culture, at least everything it could carry and cart back to Rome, even as it destroyed what it could not. Antiochus was simultaneously absorbing Roman military know-how, and re-arming his kingdom despite the terms of the Treaty of Apamea. After all, he must have known that, as with Perseus, the Romans didn't need direct provocation to start a war now.

Unfortunately for Antiochus, he died while testing out his new military formations in the east, and his nine-year-old son became King Antiochus V. Following the Daphne parade, a Roman ambassador named Gnaeus Octavius, a commander in the Third Macedonian War, arrived in Syria to demand and supervise the burning of the Syrian fleet and the hamstringing of its war elephants. In retribution, he was assassinated by a man named Leptines of Laodikeia, who stabbed Octavius as he was applying oil to his naked body in the gymnasium.[70] At this point, the fate of the boy-king Antiochus was sealed. Rome didn't send an army, they sent Antiochus V's older cousin Demetrius, whom they had been keeping as a hostage. Demetrius was trained by Rome, deferent to Rome, and the assassination plot gave Rome the ideal opportunity to fake his 'escape' to Syria, where Demetrius promptly murdered his young royal cousin and claimed the throne for himself.

At this point, Rome had created puppet rulers but no provinces for them to rule. This changed with events in Macedon, which was impoverished, suffering, and ripe for revolt. A young man named Andriscus claimed to be the son of Perseus. If he wanted the support of Demetrius, he didn't receive it; Demetrius sent him to Rome in chains. Andriscus was fortunate enough to escape back to the east, where he became a popular figure among the Macedonian diaspora. Royal relatives in Thrace lent him troops, and he soon captured the Macedonian royal city of Pella and began a campaign in Thessaly in 149 BCE. Because most of their army was tied up in the Third Punic War (149–146 BCE), the Romans sent a single legion out of curiosity more than panic, but were surprised to find that Andriscus annihilated the entire unit with ease. Macedon finally had a chance to regain independence. The Fourth Macedonian War thus began (149–148 BCE). Andriscus' early victory made him a popular figurehead for the anti-Roman factions still in Greece, and Carthage once again considered the enemy of their enemy to be their friend.

Of course, Rome wanted retribution for Andriscus' success, and they sent a far larger army to obtain it. It was bolstered by Pergamon, now ruled by their ally, Attalus II. The end of the war came swiftly, ending ironically at Pydna, where the Macedonian army was once again destroyed. The debacle had proven, however, that Macedonians longed for the good old days of Antigonid monarchy, and two more 'sons of Perseus' popped up in the next few years to attempt their own campaigns of independence. As far as Rome was concerned, Macedon could no longer be trusted to rule themselves, even under close supervision. In 146 BCE, it was formally transformed into an official Roman province. For the first time, a Greek region was under direct Roman rule, a mere seven decades after its first war with Rome. The rest of the Greek world would follow suit, bit by bit, over the following century.

The Achaean League

The Greek mainland was next, and swift on Macedonian heels. Half a century before the second Battle of Pydna, the Achaean League had chosen (not without internal debate) to throw in their lot with Rome over Macedon. Subsequent events would suggest that they had been correct in doing so, so why was there so much discontent with five decades of 'friendship'? One factor was the resentment felt about having to send so many hostages to Rome after the first Battle of Pydna twenty years previously. A second factor was increasing frustration that 'Greek freedom' was preventing their expansion into the Peloponnese. A third factor was the tumultuous, on-again off-again alliance between the Achaean League and temperamental Sparta, who, despite no longer being as powerful as they had once been, still preferred to do things in their own way – usually alone. The Achaean League had become tired of strong-arming Sparta into membership, and in 148 BCE launched a military campaign against Sparta to force them to return. They did this without consulting Rome, as the Greek member cities were labouring under the illusion that they still had some agency in conducting their internal affairs.

Rome, on the other hand, was under the impression that the Achaean League required their permission. Moreover, Rome was not comfortable with the idea of any league of Greek cities at all, let alone the possibility of the Achaean League getting any larger; it ran against their declaration that the Greek cities were 'free'. If Rome was their protector, why did they need a defensive League at all? In other words, the Romans tolerated the League's existence as long as they weren't causing any trouble. Crushing Sparta and executing its leading citizens was, in their opinion, causing trouble.

In 147 BCE the Romans sent an embassy to the League, declaring that the recently conquered Sparta was to be removed from the League. Not just that, though: Corinth, Orchomenus, Argos and Heraclea were also to be removed.[71] The reaction was understandably one of fury. The ambassador returned to Rome petulantly bleating that he had barely escaped alive. A second embassy was swiftly sent to pour oil on troubled waters; Polybius writes that the second ambassador was to give them a gentle reprimand for scaring the first ambassador, and that the threat to remove the cities from the League was not a real one.[72] Rome had merely attempted to scare them into behaving less aggressively, which had backfired. Truth be told, Rome had quite enough to deal with in regard to the concurrent Fourth Macedonian War and Third Punic War; the threat to effectively dissolve the League at this time was exactly that: an empty threat which hadn't had the desired effect. However, the gentle approach of the second ambassador wasn't effective either, as they reaffirmed that Sparta at least should still be allowed to secede from the League. For the Greeks in the League, this was unacceptable. When the Roman delegation sailed home at the end of the sailing season, the League spent the winter preparing for war away from prying eyes.

In 146 BCE, determined that they should manage their own internal affairs without external arbitration, the Achaean League formally declared war on Sparta and Heraclea, which also wanted to secede. What is unclear is the thought process of the League and its *strategos* for that year, Critolaus. Were they banking on the Romans being distracted by other wars so as not to intervene with theirs? Were they encouraged by Rome's admittedly inconsistent messaging on the subject? Were they simply naive about how far Rome could be pushed before it lost its temper? Or, as has been suggested, was this war against Sparta a suicide mission in the face of encroaching Roman hegemony? If Greek independence was truly going to inevitably end sooner rather than later (though arguably this was not yet inevitable at this point), perhaps the League just wanted to spend their last months of freedom doing what Greeks had always enjoyed doing most: fighting each other.

Whatever Critolaus' true motives, the Senate did indeed run out of patience, and sent a fleet commanded by consul Lucius Mummius, launching the Achaean War. Critolaus and his men seemed surprised to be challenged by a Roman army on Greek soil, and retreated as far as they could before being hunted down and killed at the Battle of Scarpheia. The League's army was all but eradicated in a single day, and they started to scramble a motley back-up force of any man, freeborn or enslaved, who would feasibly be able to fight. They mustered in Corinth. Polybius writes of widespread panic across the cities, with some committing suicide rather than face Roman retribution.[73] Mummius arrived with his army at Corinth, where he won a decisive battle against the League's hastily drawn up force. Afterwards, Mummius and his legions sacked the city, looting its treasures, pulling down its monuments and murdering or enslaving every man, woman and child who had not managed to escape the city.[74]

Everything about Rome's hot and cold approach to mainland Greece had thus far suggested that they were uninterested in direct rule, but they couldn't get the benefits of imperial rule without that degree of control; the Greeks, like the Macedonians, were not willing to do as Rome wanted when they were left to their own devices. The smouldering, silent ruins of Corinth were a stark indication that Rome had decided that direct supervision was now required. The whole of mainland Greece, not just the territory of the Achaean League, was added to the new province of Macedon, the Greeks no longer able or willing to put up further protest. Eventually, under Augustus in 27 BCE, it would become its own province, named Achaea.

The creation of subsequent provinces in western Asia was also less than enthusiastically sought after by Rome. In 133 BCE, Attalus III of Pergamon bequeathed his empire to Rome in his will, as he had no heirs. At the time, Pergamon controlled Mysia, the Troad, Aeolis, Ionia, Lydia, Caria, and parts of Pamphylia and Pisidia. Thus, the Attalid territories became the province of Asia. The move wasn't overwhelmingly popular amongst the locals, and a pretender to the Attalid throne did raise a rebellion, one which Rome saw fit to quell. Just because Rome hadn't actively sought the gift of Pergamon's territories, didn't mean they weren't willing to fight to keep them. The next Hellenistic king to bequeath territory to Rome was Ptolemy Apion, who left Cyrenaica on the North African coast to Rome when he, too, died childless in 96 BCE. This time, Rome didn't fully take over straight away, but unrest led them to put Cyrenaica under direct Roman control by 74 BCE. Rome's empire was growing and growing. At this point, only the Seleukids, Ptolemies, some minor city leagues in Anatolia, and what was left of Rhodes' territories were left standing. This was soon to change.

Chapter 5

Rome Away From Home

We have seen that Rome's empire was expanding exponentially. We know that it would eventually swallow up the rest of the Greek world, and we know that came with a lot of military violence, but, until now, we haven't seen Rome bringing gladiators along for the ride. A Hellenistic king may have beaten Rome to the first gladiatorial punch in the Greek world, but the next time we hear of gladiators in the Greek world it was firmly Romans putting on the Roman shows. In the Late Republican period, three major individuals are reported to have brought gladiation with them to Greece and Asia Minor: Lucullus, Julius Caesar and Mark Antony. To understand why they did, we need to look into the context of their presence there in the first place.

Lucius Licinius Lucullus, c.70 BCE

Lucullus was born into a prominent family in Rome in 118 BCE. As a young man, he served in the Social War against Rome's rebellious 'allies' in southern Italy, where he came to the attention of Sulla. Sulla was impressed by him, as indeed many of his peers were. He was an exceedingly clever man who had had an extensive education. He was well-versed in Greek literature and history, and an eloquent interlocutor and orator. Like most well-educated Romans of his class, he was a polymath. He favoured the arts, but was nevertheless very gifted in military matters; he combined his first experiences of war with his penchant for writing, composing a complete history of the Social War in Greek, although Cicero notes that Lucullus had a habit of throwing in deliberate minor mistakes in his Greek compositions, to reassure his readers that he was truly Roman, as philhellenism was only tolerated to an intermediate degree in Rome.[75] As a consequence of Lucullus' sophistication, Sulla found him to be both a useful military protégé and an engaging companion.

In 88 BCE, Sulla became consul for the first time, just as Lucullus first stepped onto the *cursus honorum* as quaestor, the initial junior magistracy for all aspiring politicians. Upon entering office, Sulla was given command of a conflict with the eastern empire of Pontus, on the coast of the Euxine (Black) Sea. The imperialistic, expansionist ambitions of Pontus were uncomfortably close to Rome's own goals, and at that moment the smaller kingdom of Bithynia was sandwiched between Pontus and Rome's province of Asia. Bithynia was a useful buffer zone whose independence was delaying the two larger empires sharing a border, which neither would have tolerated for long. Outright war could be prevented, or at least delayed, as long as Bithynia remained the awkward and untouched piggy in the middle.

Sulla personally had already been sent to rebuke the Pontic king Mithridates VI for his unwelcome 'interference' with smaller neighbours once before, warning him that further hostile behaviour would result in war with Rome. It was a significant threat, but Mithridates' patience for Roman meddling was finite. Soon, Bithynia, feeling smug and emboldened with the protection of Rome, followed the advice of a Roman politician named Manius Aquillius. He'd urged them to send raiding parties into Pontic territories, grab some loot, and give it to the Romans as a 'thanks' for their assistance. Mithridates was ordered not to retaliate, which understandably enraged him. He mustered his army and swept into Cappadocia, Bithynia, Asia and Cilicia in turn. He ordered the murder of all Romans in the region on sight, and the leaders of many cities were all too keen to follow his instructions, tired of Roman taxation and control. Manius Aquillius was apprehended and dragged to Pergamon, where he was executed by having molten gold poured down his throat.[76] In all, around 80,000 Romans were massacred in what became known as the Asiatic Vespers, including women and children. Rome was to retaliate with force.

It was clear to all involved that this war had been looming on the horizon for some time, and everyone knew that, for the Roman general in command, a successful victory over Mithridates would bring the victor wealth, fame and prestige. Rumours of Mithridates' increasing anger had already caused a tussle for the consulship, as, according to Roman practice, it should be a consul in command. For some time now, rival factions had been scheming to get their man in the consulship for when the crucial moment arrived. When the time came, Sulla was consul, but his rival Marius and his faction managed to wrest away command of the war from Sulla and give it to Marius himself.

Sulla faced a dilemma. He could allow it to happen and ruin his own reputation, or he could defend his honour, even when that meant marching on Rome. It was a drastic course of action that would trigger civil war: no Roman politician had marched on Rome before, no matter the stakes. This unprecedented action reflects how valuable the Greek-speaking east was seen to the Roman political class. This war required an extraordinary general, and Sulla was adamant that he was the only man for the job. He staged a military coup to prove his point and secure Roman power in the region. To back him up, he had legions of loyal troops and one loyal quaestor: Lucullus. They did indeed march on Rome itself, and Sulla successfully took back control. He then sent Lucullus to Greece ahead of him to prepare for war with Mithridates. Lucullus headed east with an extensive knowledge of its languages, history and customs. He immediately set out to garner support and ships from local allies, and started to grind down the Pontic navy. He again proved himself to be a skilled general and won a crucial naval battle at Tenedos, which was instrumental in allowing Sulla to cross the Aegean into Asia unimpeded, turning the tide on the war.

After the war, Lucullus spent half a decade in Asia Minor as an administrator. He wasn't officially in charge of the province, as he wasn't yet qualified for such a role, but Sulla charged him with pacifying the rebellious province and punishing them for their enthusiastic participation in the Vespers. He was to signal to locals that further rebellion against Rome would not be tolerated. Lucullus didn't have Sulla's vicious streak,[77] and Plutarch stresses that Lucullus was far kinder to the Greek population in Asia than perhaps Sulla wanted him to be.[78] His patience, empathy and mercy allowed him to restore a modicum of calm in the province, using force only when his diplomacy failed. The city of Mytilene on Lesbos was a long-time ally of Mithridates and hostile to Sulla.[79] They consistently refused to side with Rome, and, his patience spent, were bled dry in a brutal siege; Lucullus may have admired Greeks, but he was still more than capable of hurting them if Rome required him to.

Lucullus returned to Rome in 80 BCE to continue his political career, and became consul in 74 BCE. He wasn't involved in the fairly minor eastern campaigns in Illyria or Macedon during this period, nor was he sucked into the continuation of the civil war that was largely fought in Spain, with his fellow Sullan and rival Pompey gaining the glory there. Meanwhile, the king of Bithynia, Nicomedes III, was dying without an heir. As a final show of resistance to Mithridates, he bequeathed his kingdom to Rome in 75 BCE.[80] The buffer zone had been eliminated, and hostilities flared back up. Mithridates now had two choices: he could accept Rome's acquisition and brace himself for a tense relationship with his new neighbours, or he could take advantage of Rome's focus on internal struggles and the token force they'd sent to Bithynia by invading to block the expansion.

Rome's expansion is only now seen in hindsight as inevitable, but Mithridates knew well how empires could ebb and flow: of the three great Successor kingdoms, Macedon had been annihilated; Egypt was a weakened client state;

and the Seleukids were hanging on by a thread. Mithridates had even watched his son-in-law Tigranes II of Armenia cut the mighty Parthia down to size. Plus, Mithridates had friends in the Marian faction who were all too eager to see him bring the Sullan faction down a peg or two. In the spring of 73 BCE, Mithridates launched a swift and effective invasion of Bithynia.

At this point Lucullus and his co-consul Cotta were still in Rome, hammering out details of who would receive proconsulship where. Cotta drew Bithynia, and despite his experience in the region, Lucullus drew Cisalpine Gaul. Lucullus dearly wanted to head east again, perhaps with a feeling of unfinished business. Lucullus had made sure that Pompey was too tangled up in Spain to steal his thunder, but Lucullus wasn't going to gain much glory in Gaul. Luckily for him, the governor of Cilicia unexpectedly died, and Lucullus was able to fill the vacancy. Cilicia had nearly half of the Roman forces in the east, with two legions stationed there since Publius Servilius Vatia Isauricus' recent campaigns against local pirates. Cotta, as the first designated proconsul of Bithynia itself, headed straight to Chalcedon, a major port city in the region. Mithridates' forces swarmed the city by land and sea, and Cotta, outnumbered, saw his troops slaughtered. Local 'support' for Rome melted like snow in spring, and neighbouring cities quickly opened their gates to Mithridates with no resistance.

Meanwhile, Lucullus had arrived in Asia with a legion he'd raised in Italy, combining it with Vatia's legions from Cilicia and the two legions Sulla had left behind in Asia to guard the province after the end of the first war with Mithridates. These latter legions had, according to Plutarch, grown lazy and undisciplined, and were known to be somewhat truculent, although Lucullus was able to whip them into shape remarkably quickly, if we take Plutarch at his word.[81] This was Lucullus' moment to shine, and he immediately headed off to relieve the stranded Cotta. Mithridates' forces (including some anti-Sullan Romans sent from Spain) outnumbered Lucullus' by as many as ten to one, so Lucullus would have to think on his feet.[82] Mithridates moved to besiege Cyzicus, the only city that remained loyal to Rome. His amassed forces were huge, but this led to his downfall; enormous armies need an equally enormous amount of food and other supplies, which Mithridates could not provide. If Cyzicus fell quickly, this would not matter. Looting would refill the wagons easily. But if the city held out even for a week, then hunger would start to bite the Pontic army. Cyzicus itself was situated on a peninsula that was connected to the mainland by a narrow isthmus. All Lucullus had to do was lay a counter siege; by simply cutting off supply lines and, by setting up camp on the mainland hill to the south of that isthmus, Mithridates became trapped. The isthmus was already a bottleneck, and so easy to defend with smaller numbers.

As the weeks drew on and winter approached, Mithridates' forces succumbed to starvation and plague, and when he was finally able to escape by sea with the remaining troops with a modicum of good health, Lucullus gave chase and easily defeated the weakened troops at a battle between the Granicus and Aesopus rivers in 73 BCE. Lucullus, as a philhellene and historian, would have been well aware that he had won such a victory at the same place Alexander the Great had successfully faced the Persians in 334 BCE.

In 73 BCE, Rome had embroiled itself in the midst of multiple wars. Pompey was still dealing with the Marian forces of Sertorius in Spain, and Marcus Antonius, father of the more famous Mark Antony, was waging war against the pirates around Crete. Sulla's third mentee, Marcus Licinius Crassus, was dispatched to put down a rebellion in southern Italy led by one Spartacus, a renegade gladiator who had escaped from Capua. Many in Rome wanted Lucullus to wrap up the third war with Mithridates quickly. Lucullus, however, knew that if he persevered he could eliminate Mithridates as a threat for good. He spent months wheedling out pockets of Pontic forces across the east, picking off small units one by one before they could amalgamate into a single army. Then, Lucullus headed through Galatia, straight towards the heartlands of Pontus. Mithridates, wary of facing Lucullus in a pitched battle, began a game of cat and mouse, and attempts to starve Lucullus' army or to sneak assassins into his camp failed miserably. By 71 BCE, Mithridates was feeling increasingly pessimistic. He ordered his eunuch to kill his wives, sisters, daughters and concubines lest Romans get their hands on them.[83] This apparently disgusted many of Mithridates' commanders, who instantly defected. As for the Romans, Lucullus is said to have been devastated that the women were forced to die in such a manner. Mithridates fled to seek shelter with his son-in-law Tigranes II in Armenia (the same son-in-law that had stubbornly remained neutral thus far), and Lucullus was able to pacify the rest of Pontus with minimal effort during 70 BCE.

Satisfied (for now), Lucullus decided to spend some time in Asia. He'd been at war for four years. Mithridates was in hiding and a pariah amongst his own people, and Pontus was both conquered and ready for absorption into the Roman empire; Lucullus sent for commissioners from the Senate to prepare for the acquisition.[84] It is at this point that Lucullus decided to mark his achievements, celebrating the violence he had been wreaking with more violence.

Lucullus understood the layers of history at work here, both for his local audiences and those back home in Rome. When he reached Ephesus, he arranged many grand victory celebrations, just as Aemilius Paullus had done in Amphipolis after the Battle of Pydna nearly a century before. Lucullus was emulating Aemilius Paullus in more ways than one; Aemilius Paullus' own games had been part of an extensive campaign of demonstrating his appreciation and respect for Greek culture in order to present himself, and, by extension Rome, as a worthy and acceptable alternative to the Antigonids. When Titus Flamininus had addressed the Greek world at the Isthmian Games in 196 BCE following the Second Macedonian War and had declared that they were now liberated from the domination of Philip V of Macedon, there were surely some in the crowd that realised that this freedom was an illusion, and one that would come with a price.[85] Rome's offers to save the Greek world from various Hellenistic kings was a transactional one. Another Macedonian war later, ending Antigonid hegemony for good, Aemilius Paullus had wished to demonstrate that the cities of the Greek mainland weren't merely trading in one tyrant for another.

Plutarch tells us that, having defeated Perseus of Macedon, Aemilius Paullus had toured mainland Greece in the utmost respectful manner, visiting the great sanctuaries of Olympia and Delphi and giving gifts to the Greek cities.[86] Specifically, he says that the Greeks were both relieved and touched that Aemilius Paullus showed such attention to even the minor details of Greek culture, even though, as a powerful Roman he could have, if he'd chosen to, ride roughshod over the Greek world. Aemilius Paullus took care to demonstrate cultural sensitivity, which did as much to commend him to the Greeks as his insistence that the cities of conquered Macedon should pay less tribute to Rome than they had been paying the Antigonids. Aemilius Paullus had understood that trapping flies with honey is easier than using vinegar.

Decades later in Asia Minor, Lucullus understood the same concept. The cities of Asia Minor had been hit by a massive indemnity of 20,000 talents to be paid immediately by Sulla in 85 BCE in retribution for their participation in the Asiatic Vespers. As administrator, Lucullus had seen then that the fines were crippling, for he was the one charged with collecting them. Appian reports that many cities got themselves into significant debt in order to pay on time by taking out massive loans, with some resorting to mortgaging civic buildings.[87] It was private Roman bankers who rushed to do business with the cities of Asia Minor, like sharks smelling blood in water. Interest rates were merciless. The cities would struggle for fifteen years under the burdens placed upon them. Sulla had used the vinegar method in 85 BCE, but Lucullus in 70 BCE used honey.[88] The vinegar approach had, after all, prompted the cities to join in the

Vespers in the first place. By that point, the indemnity had been paid twice over, but outstanding debts to the moneylenders had skyrocketed to 120,000 talents.[89] Lucullus slashed interest rates to 1 per cent, wrote off any interest that exceeded the principal, and instructed creditors to collect no more than 25 per cent of a debtor's income per annum. Any banker flouting these rules was to be left with nothing. These measures were a lifeline for the cities of Asia Minor, and Lucullus happily invoked the wrath of the countrymen who had been bleeding them dry for fifteen years by implementing them.

It is no wonder, then, that Lucullus' celebrations were met with such enthusiasm from the grateful locals.[90] Lucullus held traditional regional entertainments that he knew his audience would appreciate: athletic festivals complete with foot races and combat sports, as well as the usual parades and processions to flaunt his successes. Plutarch doesn't specifically mention feasting, though we can assume they were held; feasts were an integral part of such Roman celebrations, and Lucullus was a known gourmand who would become famous for his lavish banquets.[91]

Most significant of all is Plutarch's remark that Lucullus presented gladiatorial games.[92] That's all the information Plutarch deigns to offer: Lucullus 'provided contests of athletes and gladiators'. It's a comment that nevertheless has huge significance for our study of the spread of gladiation, even if it does prompt unanswerable questions. This is our first piece of literary evidence for Romans providing Roman spectacle in the Greek world, which makes the comment significantly more important than perhaps even Plutarch realised. For him, it was a throwaway comment, but for us, this is a vital clue as to how gladiators came to the east. Plutarch is not mentioning these gladiators in a funerary context, but as part of a programme of festivities. Nobody in Rome used gladiators in this way at the time. Remember, in Rome, Julius Caesar was first using gladiatorial games for his political advantage in 65 BCE, half a decade after Lucullus presented them in Ephesus, and never managed to fully divorce them from funeral rites for his own purposes. So far, only one person had ever done so before Lucullus: Antiochus IV at the festival at Daphne, nearly a century before.

We are not told why Lucullus decided to present gladiatorial combat in Ephesus. It certainly wasn't a routine addition to such festivals, and unlike the athletic competitions was not a deferential nod to local customs and culture. Livy may have provided more context, but the relevant section of his Histories is lost. We do know that Lucullus had served as *curule aedile* in 79 BCE, and most likely had assisted wealthy men in providing gladiatorial combats at the funerals of deceased relatives. What we don't know is who the gladiators were or how Lucullus sourced them: were they professional? Were they imported from Rome?

Only two gladiatorial shows are recorded as taking place outside of the Italian peninsula at this point: those of Antiochus, and funeral games in 206 BCE, held in Carthago Nova (Cartagena, Spain) by Scipio Africanus for his father and uncle.[93] Scipio had used volunteers from the local population for his games, though we perhaps shouldn't assume they volunteered with any enthusiasm: as Futrell notes, Livy's remarks about their participation are sandwiched into a wider report of various massacres of local women, children, elderly and disabled locals.[94] The civilians of Astapa had chosen mass suicide over facing the wrath of Scipio's troops: Livy and Appian both report that the men of the town killed their wives and children with swords and then threw themselves onto the communal funeral pyre rather than meet the same fate of other towns that had been razed by Rome.[95] If victors were allowed to walk free, a volunteer gladiator's chances of survival in Scipio's games were better than those of local civilians who feared a worse fate than the citizens of Astapa.

As for Antiochus, his gladiators seem to have been locally recruited and trained, though a fragment of Livy suggests that prior to the Daphne festival, Antiochus may have been in the habit of importing gladiators from Rome, at great cost.[96] There is no evidence that gladiatorial combat continued in Syria between Antiochus' death and this point, but the concept of shipping gladiators from Rome clearly was a possibility for Lucullus if his soldiers didn't want to volunteer. A location wasn't hard to find, as Ephesus already had a stadium and a theatre (both of which would be later formally adapted to host gladiatorial spectacles regularly). So Lucullus had the means to put on a gladiatorial *munera* abroad: all we need now is a motive.

We need to look elsewhere in the sources for the motive. We know that his troops had been on constant campaign for more than three years at this point. It was normal for wars to be fought during a summer campaign season, but Lucullus had not once retreated to allied territory for rest and recuperation for two consecutive winters. His troops had instead camped in the Anatolian mountains for three years, in all seasons and all weathers.[97] Lucullus rarely permitted his soldiers to conduct raids for extra provisions, and the sacking of cities was even less common. The Pontic cities had large Greek populations, which may have influenced Lucullus' decision to discourage wanton theft, destruction, sexual assault and murder (though tactical concerns were likely a more significant reason). Roman soldiers expected to be recompensed for their arduous service and living conditions by enjoying such violence, and were accustomed to collecting piles of loot with which to garnish their salaries. Being denied such opportunities rankled, particularly since Lucullus happily liberally lined his own pockets with the contents of city treasuries. Sulla, who had understandably developed a reputation for hostility towards the Greeks, had sacked cities including Athens not just for his own enrichment, but that of his soldiers. Those soldiers then remained loyal to him throughout a civil war. In respecting the Greek cities in Pontus, Lucullus was denying his own soldiers a chance to get rich quick, and himself of a loyalty he might one day rely on. Lucullus had a morale problem that he had been ignoring for far too long, and one that, if left unchecked, had the potential to end in rebellion.

I suspect that this is a principal reason for the celebrations; the troops needed to blow off steam. Lavish parades and feasts while billeted in a beautiful city was a welcome change from endless drill and meagre provisions cooked over campsite fires, particularly when the cities of Asia Minor were so receptive after Lucullus' debt relief plans. If gladiatorial contests seem like an odd addition to the festivities from a local perspective, they make perfect sense to Roman legionaries who are finally getting to have some fun. These first gladiatorial games in the Greek world to be sponsored by a Roman were not intended for the local population, but for the tired soldiers who wanted an entertaining reminder of home. Lucullus was clearly willing to bend the rules of gladiators-as-funerary-custom if it suited his immediate need to placate his grumpy men, particularly as he was far from the judging eyes of his peers back in Rome, and so it is Lucullus, not Augustus, who is first recorded to have put on a show without a funeral. As it turns out, a single gladiator show was never going to rectify the situation, and in the following years during Lucullus' invasion of Armenia, the growing insubordination from his own troops caused him significant trouble. His command of the eastern wars was eventually given to Pompey, and Lucullus would never be remembered as one of Rome's great generals despite his numerous successes. For us, though, his impact is astonishing; the first Roman to bring gladiators to the Greek world.

Marcus Tullius Cicero, 50 BCE

By 50 BCE, much of the eastern Mediterranean was under Roman administrative control, and was split into various provinces. This meant that as well as soldiers, Roman bureaucrats, businessmen and civilians were moving in. Presumably, these Romans were as keen for a taste of home as legionaries, but the only hint of proof for this comes from a piece of gossip from Cicero. Marcus Tullius Cicero was a Roman politician who, depending on which historian you ask, was either one of the greatest orators in Roman history or a pompous blowhard. In 50 BCE he was acting as the proconsular governor of Cilicia, the coastal region north of Cyprus. He had spent a year there, managing the affairs of the province. Cilicia was, at the time, an eastern frontier zone and Cicero was concerned about neighbouring Parthia, even having to march two legions to Syria to lift a Parthian siege of Antioch in 51 BCE. He wrote dozens of letters to his friends and family during this time, as was his habit, and they have provided historians with a wealth of information. Unfortunately, I am not one of these historians, for Cicero mentions gladiators once during his governorship, and he does not go into detail.

In a letter to his dear friend Atticus, Cicero makes a passing remark about a mutual acquaintance, along the lines of: 'You'll never guess whose son I bumped into at the gladiatorial games in Laodikea, he was behaving abominably!'[98] The city of Laodikeia was usually a major city in the province of Asia, but had temporarily been shifted into Cilician jurisdiction for a short time, hence Cicero's frequent visits to oversee the courts there.

Cicero's mention of gladiators is essentially just a tidbit of gossip, so we need to consider the context he so unhelpfully fails to provide. He doesn't mention where the gladiators were exhibited, though we know that the stadium and North Theatre of Laodikeia were built over a century after Cicero's visit (though they did both host gladiatorial combats), leaving the Hellenistic West Theatre as the most likely candidate.[99] Prior to its later, permanent changes, the West Theatre might have been made suitable with the addition of wooden or rope barriers, or perhaps the agora was used, with benches brought in. Cicero also doesn't mention who was providing the games; presumably, if this was one of his duties he would have written '*my* games' and not '*the* games'; Cicero had previously discussed Atticus' own gladiatorial troupe and so one might expect Cicero to go into more detail if he was acting as *editor*. He also doesn't mention occasion; there is no reference to a funeral or otherwise, nor who made up the rest of the audience. Laodikea was not consistently garrisoned, so we don't know if the legions Cicero had taken to Syria were travelling with him or whether there was a small local force in place. All we can glean from this anecdote is that a mere two decades after Lucullus' victory festival, other Romans were following his lead in providing a taste of Rome abroad through gladiatorial games.

Gaius Julius Caesar 47–44 BCE

We next hear of gladiation in the Greek world because of a man who became arguably the most famous Roman in history. Here, we finally get some solid and significant evidence. Prior to his use of gladiators abroad, however, Julius Caesar was a junior officer who had served with Lucullus and there was no expectation that he would go on to become as famous as he did. Julius Caesar's first taste of military action was in the Greek world as a junior officer in Lucullus' pacification of Mytilene in 81 BCE, where he was awarded a civic crown for his bravery. He'd returned to Rome in 78 BCE following Sulla's death, where he'd tried his hand at the law, where he made quite the positive impression. He decided to travel to Rhodes to study with Greek tutors in 75 BCE, as many young men of privilege were wont to do at the time. A good education, especially in public speaking, was essential for a successful political career, and the best teachers of rhetoric were Greek. Many Greek tutors could be found in Rome but the very best were in Rhodes and that is where ambitious young men often went to learn. Caesar was to study with the man who had previously taught Cicero how to be such an excellent orator, named Apollonius Molon. During the voyage, Caesar was captured by pirates operating from the coast of Asia Minor. Caesar reportedly charmed his captors, particularly when he bossed them around and forced them to listen to his poetry recitals. They were apparently especially amused when Caesar protested that his ransom was set at far too low a rate and that the pirates could demand far, far more. The pirates laughed when Caesar told them that one day, when he was free, he would return to crucify them all. The exact point at which they stopped laughing when he did exactly as promised is unrecorded.[100] Caesar finally made it to Rhodes, and was studying there when Mithridates swept into Asia Minor. Entirely of his own volition, Caesar hopped onto the mainland and raised a private army using his own money to repel Mithridates as much as possible.[101] Caesar was intent on making a name for himself at home and abroad, particularly in the east, whatever the cost – financial or to the established way of doing things in Republican Rome.

He returned home to resume his political career, and the next time we see Caesar spending significant time in the Greek world it is as a former consul, Pontifex Maximus and the conqueror of Gaul, who was by this point using the Greek world as a battleground against fellow Romans. Just as four decades earlier, the wealthy and culturally prestigious Greek-speaking territories became a staging ground for Roman rivalries. This time it was Julius Caesar and his former ally Pompey who brought large-scale violence to the Greek world in their fight over leadership of the Roman empire.

At the Battle of Pharsalus in Thessaly in 48 BCE, Caesar firmly defeated the forces of his rival/former son-in-law/former colleague Pompey Magnus. Pompey survived the battle but immediately scurried around the eastern Mediterranean looking for protection from capture. He chose to head east, where fifteen years before he had forged himself a glittering career. Thanks to Pompey, the Seleukid kingdom had been ended, and its territories seized more than a decade before. Pompey had been asked to settle a squabble for the throne, and his solution was to end the monarchy and annex Syria as a new province for Rome in 64 BCE. Of the cities that he knew so well, some offered Pompey much needed shelter and provisions. In others, he found a cold reception. The ancient, famous city of Antioch in particular refused to have anything to do with him, and publicly announced that they were arming themselves in anticipation of Pompey trying to seek refuge with them, and that his life would be in danger should he attempt it.[102] Considering Pompey had brought Syria into the empire, this was embarrassing. He'd have to seek shelter somewhere else.

Meanwhile, Caesar didn't return to Italy. Instead, he sent Mark Antony there to seize control in his absence, and spent a brief couple of days in Asia Minor,[103] where Pompey had first fled to reunite with his family before heading south. Plutarch's account of the war records a number of omens across Asia Minor that could be interpreted in his favour, traditional examples of local support.[104] Caesar was happy to further stoke his popularity in the Greek world by giving citizens in Asia Minor tax breaks.[105] But he couldn't tarry, as he soon found out that Pompey had been spotted heading towards Egypt. Caesar's welcome gift in Alexandria was Pompey's severed head. He was not happy with being robbed of the opportunity to gloat over his frenemy's defeat and to appear magnanimous in showing Pompey some condescending mercy, as was Caesar's habit.[106]

Caesar found the ruling dynasty of Egypt to be a headache of an in-fighting family, just as Antiochus IV had done more than a century before. Now, Ptolemaic rulers and their rival relatives had got into the habit of imploring Rome to mediate their tussles for power. Famously, Caesar was not afraid to take on a particularly hands-on approach with the Ptolemies.[107] Here, the Greeks were more hostile to Romans.[108] The Ptolemies were the last of the successor kingdoms left standing, thanks in large part to their deference to (and reliance on) Rome. Both Crassus and Caesar had already flirted with taking Egypt as a new province, which would have finally put an end to successive generations of squabbling Ptolemaic family members beseeching Rome to wade into dynastic disputes. Many decades of invited Roman interference had nevertheless not endeared Romans to the Alexandrian population, because Roman 'help' came with so many strings attached. Caesar may have swaggered across Asia Minor, but he would receive no divine demonstrations of adoration here, particularly when he immediately held out his hand and demanded that a historic debt of ten million sesterces be paid immediately. War was expensive, and his resources were running low, it did not matter much to him that his debtor (Ptolemy XII Neos Dionysus) had been dead for several years: his heirs could pay.

Caesar's bull-in-a-china-shop arbitration led to him being besieged for nearly a year by troops invited by Egyptian politicians that resented his 'assistance.' It is not hyperbole to say that Caesar was incredibly lucky to make it out of Alexandria alive following ten months of siege warfare and riots in the city streets; at one point he was forced to swim across the harbour fully clothed, clutching vital documents. For Alexandrians, there was much at stake. They had learned from watching Rome eliminate the Antigonids and Seleukids: they knew well what their fate would be if Rome continued to poke their noses into Ptolemaic business. Caesar, a man who had already floated the idea (with Crassus) of annexing Egypt in 65 BCE,[109] was rubbing the locals up the wrong way. When relief finally came, it didn't come from Rome. Aid came from the East, when Mithridates of Pergamon[110] brought troops raised in Syria, Palestine and Arabia into Egypt via Pelusium.[111] With his troops thus supported, Caesar managed to pacify the Alexandrians following the Battle of the Nile, and left his lover Cleopatra VII on the throne alongside her young brother-husband Ptolemy XIII Theos Philopator.[112]

Caesar in Antioch

After a business-pleasure cruise along the Nile with Cleopatra to gauge the Egyptian mood outside of Alexandria, Caesar left Egypt in 47 BCE.[113] He had fires to extinguish all over the Mediterranean (many of which he had himself caused), but his first ports of call before returning to Rome were Antioch in Syria and Tarsus in Cilicia. Pompey being dead didn't mean that his faction no longer posed a threat. During Pompey's flight from Pharsalus, he'd been shown no friendship in Syria. This, coupled with post-Pharsalus omens and the aid sent from Syria during the siege of Alexandria, put Caesar in the mood to reward the city for their loyalty to him. Antioch was fortunate in their choices.

In comparison, Athens had a consistently dreadful record of backing the wrong horse and bore the scars to prove it: Sulla had sacked the city in 86 BCE as a punishment for allying with Mithridates VI of Pontus.[114] Recovery for the city was painfully slow, but Pompey had shown Athens kindness and had been very popular there. Athens backed Pompey in the civil war, and Caesar might have been tempted to let out his frustrations on the populace and buildings as Sulla had done, but apparently showed restraint and pardoned them, asking the Athenians: 'How often will the glory of your ancestors save you from self-destruction?'[115] If Athens got off lightly for backing Pompey, Antioch was to be positively spoiled for threatening to kill Pompey on sight. Hellenistic kings had long been in the habit of donating grand civic monuments to cities.[116] It demonstrated their wealth, sophistication and power, and adding their own flourish to already ancient cities bought them some cultural cachet and appreciation. At the time, Antioch was one of the largest cities in the Mediterranean, smaller only than Alexandria and Rome. Like Alexandria, it had been founded by one of Alexander's successors shortly after his death, and its excellent position in the caravan network allowed it to become vast and bustling.

Caesar lavished the city with several monuments, including a temple, an aqueduct, a basilica, a theatre and public baths. While locals would have accepted these gifts as an appropriate display of appreciation, as Greek cities had from Hellenistic kings for centuries, it is worth wondering what Caesar's peers in Rome would have thought about this behaviour. Various Romans had been conferred honours by Greek cities in the preceding decades, much as Greek cities honoured Hellenistic kings. These honours were usually graciously, if sceptically, accepted. Eventually, this honours system would morph into the Imperial Cult, where the Greek cities would compete in offering honours to Roman emperors. Pompey and Caesar both made concerted efforts to publicly refuse honours when Romans decided that they wanted to offer them;[117] and, a few years later, Caesar's unconvincing display of refusing a crown at the Lupercalia festival in Rome made his assassination all but inevitable.[118]

While abroad, Romans were happy enough to engage with foreign customs; when away from Rome, they did as the non-Romans did and accepted the adulation. However, at this point, no Roman seems to have swung so far into Greek custom that they had bestowed honours (and edifices) upon cities as Caesar was doing in Antioch. Lucius Betilienus Verus is a rare Roman exception dating from the late-second–early-first centuries BCE, having donated several civic buildings to the town of Aletrium (modern Alatri), though it should be noted that this was his hometown.[119] Caesar had no ancestral ties to Antioch, and no plans to reside there. Peers such as Pompey Magnus financed and constructed grand civic buildings, but they generally did it in Rome, where their performatively generous public donations could be best admired and appreciated. It was expected that men like Caesar should become patron to individuals, cities, or even kings, and that they would in turn become his clients in a mutually beneficial, if rigidly hierarchical, relationship. Pompey certainly had a clutch of such clients in the eastern Mediterranean, and we know he donated large amounts of cash to help Athens restore some of the buildings damaged in Sulla's attack,[120] but the sources don't suggest that his patronage extended to the erection of public buildings, and Pompey himself complained that he'd wasted his money because the Athenians had squandered it.[121] Four years before Caesar arrived in Antioch, he'd matched Pompey's 50 talents. The Athenians had specifically asked him for financial aid, and he was happy to grant it, leading to the construction of the Roman Agora.

Appius Claudius Pulcher, a former consul who had spent much of his career in the eastern Mediterranean,[122] constructed the Lesser Propylaea at the sanctuary of Eleusis in 51 BCE, partly because he was an initiate of the mystery cult there, and partly because he had promised Ceres and Proserpina (known to the Greeks as Demeter and Persephone) that he would dedicate a monument to them if they would send divine aid to end the flooding in Rome that had ruined the grain supply during his consular year three years previously.[123] Eleusis, one of their most important sanctuaries, seemed the obvious place. Cicero half-heartedly considered building a similar *propylaeon* at the Academy in Athens, specifically as a monument to himself, but ultimately decided against the idea.[124] So, a few Romans had ventured into euergetism in the Greek world for various reasons, but on a fairly small scale and with varying results.

As with so much of his extraordinary career, here we see Caesar rewriting the Roman rules. Roman benefaction in the eastern Mediterranean was clearly new, and Caesar made sure to eclipse both Pompey's 50 talents and Pulcher's *propylaea*. Moreover, even the most generous of Hellenistic kings had never donated so many buildings in one go. Even so, the sources remain relatively silent on this extremely generous display, but we should assume that donating many civic buildings would have met with raised eyebrows back in Rome. Caesar was not just acting like a foreign king; he was outdoing them, just as Antiochus IV had shown he could outdo the Romans at their own game previously. He was showing favour to a distant city; and similar accusations made a significant proportion of Octavian's smear campaign against Mark Antony in the following years.

Caesar was rushed in Antioch, as Pharnaces (another son of Mithridates IV of Pontus, and decidedly less friendly than his brother Mithridates of Pergamon), was taking advantage of the current Roman civil war by seizing cities in Armenia and Pontus, murdering (or, if Caesar is to believed, castrating) many Roman citizens in the process.[125] He left behind his relative and close friend Sextus Julius Caesar in the role of new governor of the province, who was tasked with seeing these grand architectural plans into fruition. Caesar himself would never see them completed. The reason that this generosity is so significant to this study is that Caesar ordered the construction of one more civic building: an amphitheatre. We'll discuss the form it took in a later chapter, and talk for now about the implications of its construction.

We have no literary or archaeological evidence that Antiochus IV's penchant for gladiatorial combat had survived him in Antioch by more than a century. Even if we assume that it did, to whatever extent, remain popular in sections of Antiochian society, was it produced often enough to warrant a specific venue? As we shall see in Chapter 11, Rome had no purpose-built amphitheatre at this time, and the oldest extant amphitheatre in Pompeii was only a couple of decades old. Building an amphitheatre on the Italian peninsula was incredibly new and unusual at the time; building one in Syria was astonishing. The locals don't appear to have called it an amphitheatre (Romans were calling the building type *spectacula* at the time), and John Malalas calls it a *monomacheion*, a Greek word that translates as 'place of one-on-one combat.' If Caesar's donation of many buildings was extraordinary, the inclusion of an amphitheatre is even more astounding. So, why build one?

I think we have to assume, as we have with Lucullus, that the presentation of gladiators (and in this case, a dedicated venue for them) was for the benefit of the Roman soldiers who were billeted in the local area. Having come to the region to inflict so much violence upon its occupants, the soldiers wanted to relax by watching someone else do the stabbing for a change. This was best achieved in a purpose-built location. We know that Caesar left at least one legion behind him in Antioch under the command of his relative Sextus, because we later learn that these soldiers revolted against Sextus when they were misled into thinking Caesar had been killed and that Pompey's allies now held the upper hand.[126] Antioch was a strategic place to keep troops at the time, particularly since Caesar had his eyes on Parthia to the east. His former mentor and triumvir, Crassus, had launched an invasion into Parthia from Syria in 53 BCE, lured on by the promise of glory, piles of loot and besting Pompey and Caesar (for once). It had ended with disaster; the Roman legions had been massacred at the Battle of Carrhae and Crassus killed, along with his son. The humiliating and unexpected defeat caused shockwaves in Rome (Rome always being far more intimidated by Parthians than Parthia ever was of Rome), and, ever since, Caesar had been drawn to the idea of invading Parthia himself. The idea of conquering such a ferocious rival appealed to his ego, and so he'd nurtured the ambition for several years by this point. All he had to do first was wrap up the civil war and pacify Armenia and Pontus, after which he would be free to strike into Parthia on the pretence of avenging his friend, but with the true goal of glorious one-upmanship.[127] Caesar had long known that he would need to use Syria as a springboard, just as Crassus had done, and that eventually he would need to billet far more than one or two legions there. The other buildings donated to the city served to flatter and please the locals, but the amphitheatre was clearly for the troops who would eventually swarm the city and who required entertainment when far from home.

Caesar in Corinth

Caesar built a second amphitheatre in the eastern Mediterranean, this time in the Peloponnese. Again, the location was a city that had been violently dragged into Rome's repeated interpersonal dramas. The city of Corinth had been razed by the Roman general Lucius Mummius in 146 BCE, the same year that Carthage had also been destroyed. He'd been given command over Rome's war with the Achaean League. This alliance of Peloponnesian cities had been arguing for decades over whether they should consider themselves Rome's allies or subordinates. The more Rome pushed, the more rebellious the League became, and eventually they came to the conclusion that war was preferable to subservience. The League declared war, and Mummius swept into Greece with an army behind him, swiftly defeating the Greek forces. The Senate sent a decree to Mummius ordering Corinth to be looted for everything the Romans could carry, and that anything that couldn't be moved was to be burned. Mummius massacred the men of Corinth and enslaved the women and children, he tore down the city walls and civic buildings, and desecrated temples. Statues were torn from their bases and paintings from walls, as soldiers who didn't appreciate their age or value packed them onto ships to be transported back to Rome.[128] The destruction of Corinth was a deliberate and chilling message to the Greeks, even more so than the aftermath of the Battle of Pydna some years before: Rome was no longer in the mood to tolerate dissension of any kind. Greeks could clearly not be trusted to govern themselves while acting in Rome's interest, so Rome was putting her foot down. For a century afterwards, as the archaeological record attests, a city that had been one of the great centres of the Greek world was greatly reduced. The League was dissolved, democracy banned, and mainland Greece absorbed into the Roman province of Macedonia.[129]

The refounding of Corinth is likely to have been on Roman minds quite quickly; Corinth was strategically situated to control the isthmus to the mainland, and subsequently was able to control key trading routes both on land and sea. The *diolchos*, the ship ramp that predated the Corinth Canal, was a vitally important asset, and the city was surrounded by some of the most agriculturally rich land in mainland Greece. There were many reasons why Corinth had been as influential as it had for so long, and Rome could not have been unaware that having a strong settlement on the site was strategically vital. Nevertheless, the city remained in partial ruin for 102 years, inhabited by a fraction of its previous population.[130] In the months before his assassination, the Corinth project was one of Caesar's priorities, as the refounding was an ideal opportunity to solve a problem that had plagued Roman generals for a century; veterans of Rome's many wars required homes after their service ended. The best solution, as far as the veterans were concerned, was a parcel of fertile farmland that they could cultivate in their retirement, but the problem with most Mediterranean agricultural areas was that people already owned and lived on it, and they resented being forcibly removed. On the other hand, making soldiers fight wars for two decades, risking their lives, while demanding their loyalty (particularly when asking them to fight other Romans) without ample recompense, risked leaving thousands of well-armed, well-trained killers homeless and simmering with resentment. Corinth was almost entirely empty, as its population had not come even close to recovering, and presented a solution that would please many and offend few.

Caesar set about rebuilding the city, which he renamed *Colonia Laus Iulia Corinthiensis*, though, due to his assassination mere months into the project, most of his plans were carried out by Augustus. The city was expanded and re-laid on a grid plan of streets intersecting at right angles, and its surrounding farmland divided into regular, rectangular strips. It was populated by veterans and a few locals alike. The ancient temple of Apollo was restored, and amenities were provided for the comfort and enjoyment of its new citizens. As well as the surviving Greek theatre, a brand-new circus was constructed, as well as an amphitheatre, which we will discuss further in Chapter 11.[131]

When the travel-writer Pausanias wrote about Corinth in the early second century CE, he acknowledged that much of the older, Greek sights in the city had been destroyed and that he was unable to describe them, and that the town was mostly of Roman construction. That said, he staunchly avoided writing about Roman buildings unless he absolutely had to, and concentrated on the antiquities still intact; as a Greek, he was no doubt keen to preserve and promote his Greek heritage, and must have seen the modern Roman buildings as a trifle gauche. Perhaps this is indicative of how Greeks initially viewed this first (and last) typical amphitheatre on the Greek mainland. In any event, the amphitheatre was not for them, and, in fact, it may have been a formal requirement for the colony; a surviving charter of the founding of another of Caesar's colonies the year before the refounding of Corinth gives us a tantalising clue. Caesar had defeated the town of Urso in what is now Spain in 45 BCE, and refounded it as a colony. The *Lex Ursonensis* laid out laws about how the colony was to be run, and one clause specifically states that the magistrates were obliged to stage gladiatorial and/or theatrical shows annually to honour the Capitoline trio of deities. While no charter for Corinth survives, it seems likely that an identical clause was included for the benefit not just of Jupiter, Juno and Minerva, but for the resettled Roman veterans.

Marcus Antonius, 31 BCE

Mark Antony's connections to the Greek world predate his birth. Born into a premier Roman family stacked with consuls, both his grandfather and father had served in the eastern Mediterranean (with varying degrees of success), and had forged relationships there.[132] As a young man he did what any budding politician of his rank did and got a little military experience prior to ascending the *cursus honorem*, serving under Gabinius during yet another Roman intervention over who would sit on the Ptolemaic throne of Egypt. But it is his later travels, following his career as a right-hand man of Caesar, which we are most interested in.

After the Battle of Philippi in 42 BCE, when Antony and Octavian joined forces to defeat the last of Caesar's assassins, Antony was the most powerful man in the empire. Together with Octavian and Lepidus, he was part of the Second Triumvirate. To avoid as much conflict between its members, each controlled a different sphere; Antony was the de facto ruler of the eastern Mediterranean for the next decade, returning to Italy as seldom as he feasibly could. He was a dedicated philhellene, and the role of pseudo-Hellenistic king seems to have flattered his ego. Cities tripping over themselves to proclaim him the new Dionysus and shower him with honours. Antony, having paid for an army for a large civil war, was in sore need of cash; he had no choice but to wring as much money out of cities and elites as he could, just as Sulla, Pompey, Caesar, and the Ides of March conspirators had done before him. The overt flattery of the cities can partially be attributed to trying to minimise the financial damage he threatened to wreak upon their coffers, but also because Antony was, particularly after Philippi, a genuinely impressive and intimidating figure who had eliminated (nearly) every rival. His alliance with Octavian was flimsy, and, now that they had eliminated all mutual enemies, their rivalry and mutual mistrust could easily flare up into civil war again – but at least Octavian was far away in the Italian peninsula. There was much work for Antony to do; the Roman penchant for using the Greek world as a battlefield for its civil wars had once again caused significant damage that required managing. Antony had his hands full. Various client kings and elites were removed, reaffirmed or elevated. Some cities were granted freedom; others had their autonomy revoked. In 40 BCE, the Treaty of Brundisium between the fractious triumvirs formalised Antony's dominion over the eastern Mediterranean to an even greater degree.

In the east, Antony spent significant time in cultural centres including Athens, Ephesus, Antioch and Alexandria. The latter is where he famously lived with his mistress, Cleopatra VII. Ancient sources writing about the pair largely follow the narrative of Octavian's propaganda: Cleopatra was a sly seductress, and Antony was a drunken sop in her thrall. The truth is, of course, far more complicated. Their relationship began as a pragmatic one: Cleopatra needed to protect and promote Egyptian interests to the latest dominant Roman, and Antony, who was always more than happy to enter into romantic affairs, did recognise that the Ptolemies were a valuable ally with a very useful treasury. For the first few years of their connection, it seems that both were happy to mix a little pleasure into their diplomatic dealings. Both were astute politicians, first and foremost, in the beginning. Antony was still the most formidable Roman general alive, and, while he spent winters in Alexandria with Cleopatra, he spent his summers on campaign.

As we have seen, Caesar was assassinated before he could launch a retaliatory campaign against Parthia, and Mark Antony was always keen to be seen to follow in his mentor's footsteps. For the first few years of his rule in the eastern Mediterranean, Antony had been content to entrust border incursions from hostile neighbours to trusted colleagues. But, in 36 BCE, perhaps wanting to prove that he was more than the perfect right-hand-man and a great general in his own right, Antony launched an invasion of Parthia. Just as Crassus had found in 53 BCE, Antony had underestimated what it would take to succeed, and the campaign was a disaster that led to around 32,000 Roman fatalities. During the campaign, his Armenian allies had abandoned him, so, in 34 BCE, Antony invaded Armenia in retribution, to secure some loot and to soothe his ego. This campaign was far more successful, and he brought the Armenian King Artavasdes II back to Alexandria as a hostage, along with groaning war chests of booty.

Just like Lucius Aemilius Paullus after the Battle of Pydna, Antony played the quasi-Hellenistic king with a spectacular programme of victory parades, banquets, and games. We do not have a source that tells us if gladiators performed at this point in time, though, as we shall see, Mark Antony did possess his own troupe. As part of this victory celebration, Antony also made an announcement regarding the future of the eastern Mediterranean. He declared, or rather reaffirmed, Cleopatra's position as Queen of Kings, ruling Egypt, parts of Syria, and Cyprus. Her son with Julius Caesar, Caesarion, was declared her co-ruler.

This much was fairly standard. But then, Antony made some further declarations that were not usual at all. His children by Cleopatra were also to become *de facto* monarchs. Cleopatra Selene would be Queen of Cyrene (which was by now a Roman senatorial province), and Alexander Helios would replace Artavasdes as King in Armenia, as well as becoming king of Parthia (which still remained unconquered). It was a bold statement of dynastic ambition, merging Roman with Hellenic, potentially for centuries. On the other hand, Antony was giving away territories he had no right to dispense. It was the kind of bombast that Octavian could easily exploit.

Antony soon made another declaration, and this time to the Roman Senate: he was hanging up his triumviral boots and planning a well-earned retirement, now that the eastern territories were consolidated and the Republic finally safe.[133] This put Octavian in a difficult position; he could either protest Antony's retirement, which would prolong hostilities, or he could accept that the Republic was saved – in which case, he would also have to effectively step back from the spotlight while still being seen as Antony's junior partner. Octavian refused to resign from the triumvirate. Whether or not this was a devious plan by Antony to expose his colleague's white-hot ambition to the Roman people or whether Antony truly was ready for a life of relaxation in Alexandria is unknowable, but Octavian's truculence was making it increasingly clear that the empire was no longer big enough for both men.

Their war started as one of hurling insults at each other in speeches and pamphlets. Antony was accused of being bewitched by an 'exotic' foreign queen, and of sacrificing his masculinity at the altar of decadence. In retaliation, Antony repeated rumours that Octavian had won his uncle Julius Caesar's approval via incestuous sexual favours.[134] Romans might have sneered at Greek squabbles for power, but they weren't above catty jibes themselves when it suited them. In the meantime, both sides started to build up their military forces in preparation for yet another civil war. Antony began the arduous task of mustering his enormous army in mainland Greece, anticipating using it as a Roman battlefield once again. While he was doing so, he held a massive festival on the island of Samos, drawing in athletes, actors, dancers, and musicians from across the Aegean.[135] The description of the festival by the biographer Plutarch suggests that the whole affair was incredibly Greek, and gladiators are not mentioned in the line-up. However, as we shall see, it is likely that they were there after all.

Antony brought Cleopatra with him to Athens, and made a public point of divorcing his Roman wife Octavia, who just happened to be Octavian's sister. The message couldn't have been clearer; the relationship between the two men had irrevocably broken down. In retaliation, Octavian stole Antony's will from the Vestal Virgins[136] and read it aloud to the Roman Senate, revealing clauses that included naming Antony's children with Cleopatra as his heirs, and his wish to be buried in Egypt regardless of where he died.[137] When the contents of the will became public knowledge in Rome, all sympathy for Mark Antony seems to have vanished: if this rumour had proven to be true, then all accusations against Antony must also be true. According to Cassius Dio, this included a rumour that Antony wished to give Cleopatra the Roman empire as a gift and intended to see it absorbed into the Egyptian empire, under Alexandria's jurisdiction.[138] Mark Antony wasn't a true Roman, the rumour mill ran: he wanted to be an Egyptian Pharaoh with his foreign queen and their clutch of bastard children. Cleopatra, it was alleged, had surely bewitched him for this to happen, and the misogynistic, xenophobic smear campaign instigated by Octavian has unfairly sullied Cleopatra's reputation ever since.

The Senate (at least the ones who had not travelled to join him) denounced Antony as an enemy of Rome and declared war on Egypt.[139] In the end, the war was to be short. Antony prepared for a tense winter of mobilisation and waiting, expecting the war to properly begin in the spring. Octavian's general Agrippa, however, caught Antony off-guard by sailing to the Peloponnese and besieging the city of Methone before winter had ended. While this distracted Antony,

Octavian's troops were able to cross the Adriatic Sea without opposition. Antony and Cleopatra's forces thus had to race up to Acarnania to meet the enemy in the spring of 31 BCE. Octavian had chosen to camp on one of the two promontories that narrowed the entrance to the Ambracian Gulf. Antony set up his own camp near the small town of Actium. The summer was spent fortifying these camps, sending out raiding parties, attempting blockades, but mostly in bedding in and waiting for someone to make the first major move. The actual battle didn't take place until 2 September. It isn't necessary to delve into tactics and manoeuvres here; it is enough to state that the battle did not go well for Antony and Cleopatra. Her fleet fled to Egypt and Antony abandoned his surviving troops to follow her there. Many defected to Octavian, devastated that their commander had left them to an unknown fate. Had Antony stayed with his men, he could have continued fighting in further battles; the tides of war had turned before. However, Antony would never recover from losing the loyalty of his legions. Retreating further into the Greek east, Antony spent the winter of 31 BCE in Cyrenaica, contemplating (and apparently attempting) suicide, while, in contrast, Cleopatra busied herself in Egypt with a grand scheme to evacuate her court across the Isthmus of Suez into Arabia.[140] Octavian, meanwhile, marched triumphantly to Athens, where he was met with acclaim, boasting of how he had freed them from the (evidently quite severe) obligations of feeding Antony's troops.[141]

It is only at this point that we meet Mark Antony's troupe of gladiators. Cassius Dio tells us that, upon hearing the news of the Battle of Actium, the troupe immediately left their *ludus* in Cyzicus to march down through Asia Minor and Syria to meet up with Antony in Alexandria. They, at least, remained loyal. Unfortunately for the gladiators, they were apprehended in Syria and forced to remain in Daphne, where Antiochus had first presented gladiators 135 years before.[142] This is pretty much all we know about Mark Antony's personal troupe, as they're only mentioned in this one incident. But can we read between the lines to make some guesses?

We know that Caesar and Lucullus both used gladiators to keep their troops entertained during what could frequently be uncomfortable and dangerous campaigns, so Antony had a solid example to follow (though they're not recorded as being present specifically at Actium). We know that Antony was fond of putting on lavish parades and festivals across the eastern Mediterranean, and that, while they were largely Hellenistic in nature, it is not implausible that he might have wished to have his gladiators involved in some capacity. Dio mentions that the gladiators were, at the time, stationed in Cyzicus: they were clearly intended for performances in the region. In fact, Dio states that they were due to perform in the victory games Antony was planning for when Octavian would be crushed. Were they only intended for a single performance that never ended up happening? If they were raw recruits, it is hard to imagine them breaking out and fighting their way through Asia Minor for a patron they hardly knew. The gladiators risked their lives to join Antony, and Dio does say that they fought Octavian's allies bravely en route. This loyalty suggests that their relationship with Antony was a long one, and perhaps a personal one; it would also suggest that they were seasoned arena veterans who had been with Antony and his troops for an extended period of time.

The gladiators never saw Antony again. Meanwhile, Cleopatra and Antony, reading the writing on the wall quite clearly, sent an offer to Octavian. Cleopatra would remain a docile, subordinate queen in Egypt, and Antony would retire in Alexandria – or Athens, if Octavian insisted on separating the couple.[143] The civil war would end. As far as Octavian was concerned, the war would only be over if Antony was dead, and so he marched his force to Alexandria in August 30 BCE. After a short battle which he knew he couldn't win, Antony retreated back into the city and was apparently informed that Cleopatra had already taken her own life, which was not true. Believing himself to be alone in the world, Antony died in an entirely acceptable way for a Roman general, by falling on his own sword. Cleopatra did then take her own life shortly afterwards, though ancient writers fail to agree on an exact version of events.[144] Cleopatra's death marks the end of the Hellenistic era for many historians, as the last reigning, independent Hellenistic monarch. With her death, Egypt was annexed by Octavian, who would later take the name Augustus, and become the first emperor of Rome.[145] The Greek world was now entirely under Roman control, and the imperial period had begun.

Antiochus IV had experimented with gladiators, but we have no evidence that his Roman hobby was continued in Antioch after his untimely death. It took Romans to make a Roman cultural phenomenon stick in the Greek world. Perhaps this was inevitable, given the persistent interference Rome had inflicted on the east (whether Rome claimed it had been dragged into the Greek world reluctantly or not). Rome's increasing domination over the Greeks came with an increasing presence: Roman soldiers, veterans, students, and traders poured into the region and they all wanted the creature comforts of home. Having turned the eastern Mediterranean into a massive arena of war, smaller arenas for entertainment were required. Initially, as we've seen, gladiators were not imported to entertain the Greeks themselves, but this would soon change.

Chapter 6

A Gangrene in the Greek World?

We've explored why Lucullus, Caesar, and Mark Antony spent time in the Greek world, and why they chose to bring Roman gladiators with them on their travels. They worked in a fiercely competitive political system wherein Romans were constantly fighting to acquire influence and maintain power. Whether at funerals in Rome, or keeping fractious troops happy with home comforts abroad, presenting gladiators became a part of that competitive process as the Republic crumbled around them. So what happened after the dust of Actium had settled, and Octavian's transformation into Augustus led to the Roman political system being irrevocably altered?

Where we left off in Rome at the end of Chapter 2, Augustus had brought gladiatorial shows under state control; the *praetors* whom he controlled were responsible for organising the games on his behalf, and few others were authorised to stage private shows that might compete with his own in grandeur.[146] We know a little about his games because he made sure to record them in his *Res Gestae*, his official account of the deeds he accomplished in his lifetime. He left instructions in his will that this (rather long) list of his achievements should be published on pillars in front of his mausoleum, though copies appeared in cities across the empire, too.

It features some lies amongst the truths: for example, Augustus boasts of 'Raising an army at his own expense and initiative to restore liberty to the Roman Republic, which had been in the grip of a tyrannical faction.'[147] It's fair to say that the Republic was on life support after repeated beatings from men like Sulla and Caesar, but Augustus was the one that held the pillow firmly over its face until it stopped twitching. What Augustus did do was to make the Senate terrified of a world where Antony had total control. After eliminating Antony at Actium, Augustus graciously accepted the Senate's gratitude by allowing them to give him, piece by piece, the sole power that he had accused Antony of coveting.[148]

His *Res Gestae* recounts various gifts that he gave to Rome: athletic competitions, chariot racing, beast hunting with 3,500 exotic animals,[149] and a *naumachia*, which was a re-enactment of the Battle of Salamis and featured thirty ships.[150]

He specifically mentions eight gladiatorial shows that he presented during his lifetime: three under his own name, and five on behalf of his adopted sons and grandsons, totalling 10,000 fighters.[151] Not even Caesar had produced shows on this scale. Augustus' emphasis and pride in the various spectacles he provided are illuminating: he realised that the various Games were important both for the public as a form of much-needed respite after a particularly turbulent era, but also to the public's perception of him as the man who had provided performances for the enjoyment of Rome as well as peace. We also see evidence of him following Caesar's footsteps in promoting gladiatorial fights abroad; for instance, with the grand amphitheatre that he constructed when he founded the colony of Augusta Emerita (modern Mérida in Spain), in 8 BCE.

With Augustus continuing as de facto sole ruler of the empire, the cities of the Greek world at least no longer had to worry about backing the wrong Roman horse, as so many had done in so many Roman conflicts – particularly the civil wars. However, centuries of Roman warfare on Greek battlefields (against enemies further east as well as between themselves) had taken their toll. Roman meddling had left Greek cities weaker and poorer, and their latest darling, Antony, was not only defeated, but dead and disgraced. Augustus had no appetite for wreaking revenge on such a large area, and preferred to broker peace wherever possible, even with Parthia. As far as Augustus was concerned, the Greek cities had declined in regards to their moral fibre and culture, as well as being flat broke, and his main aim (beyond restoring some stability) was to return the Greek world to its former glory days, before perceived vice and decadence had set in.[152] Such a revival of the Greek world would benefit Rome too, after all. At the same time, Romans who wished to take advantage of this new era of peace flocked to Greece to soak up the culture as tourists. Roman students continued to see an education in Greece as an indispensable feather in their caps, and even more traders than before poured into the region to take advantage of the prosperity that peace could produce.[153]

We don't see a surge of Greek gladiatorial activity in the archaeological record at this point. Caesar's amphitheatres at Antioch and Corinth would remain lonely oddities for more than a century, and there are few small finds related to gladiation from the Augustan age in the Greek world. The first point to reiterate is that securely dating small finds is almost impossible, and working out where the first gladiatorial shows were staged is difficult, particularly when viable venues were temporary or only slightly altered with the addition of fences. However, Augustus did learn a lot from Caesar, and it's possible that he also promoted games as a magisterial obligation just as Caesar did with Urso, and presumably Antioch and Corinth. Gladiators had been performing in the eastern Mediterranean for several decades before Augustus became *princeps*,[154] and it's unlikely that Roman expats and local sycophantic magistrates would need much encouragement to continue the practice. The second point is to note that archaeological evidence of the early gladiatorial shows in Rome itself is scant: tangible traces become more numerous the more bedded into culture gladiation became in both the west and the east; an absence of physical evidence does not mean an absence of early gladiators. By the second and third centuries CE we have a heaped pile of evidence for eastern gladiators in the form of inscriptions, small finds, art, and venues; gladiation had indeed bedded in. We just don't have an obvious picture of the acceleration of shows in the first century CE. It's unlikely that Augustus thought that pushing Roman cultural phenomena onto Greek cities was a priority, and there would surely be evidence of a deliberate cultural imposition if he had, but, if emigrating Romans wished for a taste of home, or locals who wished to cosy up to their new overlords wanted to demonstrate their fealty by trying out a Roman concept of a fun day out, it's equally unlikely that Augustus would have any reason to stop them.

As the Greek world continued to absorb Roman power, people and ideas, gladiatorial shows were likely to be increasingly desired by both the homesick, the curious and the sycophantic alike. As we shall see, locals soon saw the potential Greekness that could be emphasised and encapsulated in this supposedly most Roman of sports, but the first century CE (the 'Dark Ages' of eastern gladiators) only gives us glimpses of how this developed. We need to trace a line to connect the dots between Caesar's magisterial obligations in Urso to the dozens of Greek cities enjoying gladiatorial shows in the second and third centuries. We can do this by answering the question: was it Roman provincial governors or local Greek elites providing shows during the heyday of Greek gladiators?

Local Government and the Imperial Cult

The holding of gladiatorial shows was, by nature, an ephemeral gift. The public would enjoy a growing sense of anticipation from the announcement of the day of the games, then a rush of excitement during the games themselves, and then in the days that followed, the high would eventually wear off. Within a couple of years, spectators might remember the names of their favourite gladiators, but what if they forgot which local aristocrat was responsible for generously providing them with such entertainment? That simply wouldn't do, as the whole point of gifting anything to the wider populace – a library, a fountain, gladiator shows – was that the citizens would be eternally grateful and respect that politician or aristocrat for decades afterwards. It was easy enough to place an inscription on a building so that nobody forgot who paid for it, but it was much harder to inscribe a gladiator. The solution was for elites to create their own monuments that would permanently stand in the city and record their events, making sure that everyone remembered their taste and generosity. There are fragments of these memorials across the eastern Mediterranean, though we don't have a single example of a whole one. We can, however, take pieces from each partial monument, try to fit the disparate puzzle pieces together and try to recreate what a typical monument looked like.

An inscription was essential, and it needed to state the name of the elite person who had spent his own money making the lives of his fellow citizens better. Secondly, it needed a description of exactly how he had made those lives better. In this case, the *munerarius* – i.e. 'the gift-giver' – could commemorate specific shows, often with pictorial reliefs of particularly memorable fights. Blocks of stone from such a monument in Hierapolis feature a particularly dramatic fight between two fighters named Kalydon and Odysseus. In the space of three square frames the fight is recreated. In the first, the two men square off against each other. In the second, they grapple closely, and, in the third, Kalydon pushes Odysseus to the floor and holds a blade to his throat.[155] Perhaps these two were the biggest celebrities in their *ludus*, or perhaps their particular fight had been especially noteworthy for their bravery or performance.

A long list of other stones have been found featuring single gladiators in a suitably militaristic pose; they might include the name of the gladiator, but, unlike gravestones, they have no other career or personal information on them. The *munerarius* wasn't interested in the minutiae of each gladiator's life, only in the fifteen-to-twenty minutes that each gladiator fought in a show they had paid for. These stones could be inserted into a larger monument as part of a wider design, or stand in clusters in a prominent spot in the city; at Ephesus such a group was found outside the theatre. An accompanying inscription typically listed the games given by the aristocrat, with particular mention of unusual types of gladiator or exotic species of animal for the hunts. The fragments of these monuments, when found roughly *in situ*,[156] are sometimes also located in the necropolis of the town, indicating that sometimes the memorial is intended to honour the aristocrat after death. Archaeologists have also found inscriptions about elites on statue bases (without pictorial reliefs) which suggests that statues of notable citizens were erected by the city in gratitude for acts of particular generosity. Many list the provision of gladiatorial games as a reason that the populace want to signal their admiration and gratitude to the elite in question. These statues were frequently erected when the person honoured was still alive to appreciate the gesture, and surely they tacitly encouraged these men and their peers to provide yet more games.

On the Balkan peninsula, elites preferred to immortalise their games in stone before they happened, and not afterwards. This came in the form of advertisements for upcoming games, inviting people to attend 'for the health of the emperor and imperial family'.[157] Elsewhere, such notices were fairly temporary; we only have a selection of painted adverts from Pompeii because the volcanic eruption preserved them from fading or being covered with new notices. By making the announcement of games an inscription, elites could kill two birds with one stone: let everyone know when to attend, and preserve the memory of their own generosity for generations to come. Even so, these inscriptions are rarer than commemorations in the rest of the east, particularly Anatolia, which also matches the pattern of fewer venues, fewer works of art and fewer gladiatorial gravestones. On the Greek 'mainland', enthusiasm for gladiation was more restrained than elsewhere in the Greek world.

These monuments tell us important information: local elites saw value in investing in this particular type of benefaction. Rich Greeks had been in competition with their peers for centuries over who could gain the most prestige by giving the grandest and most lavish gifts to the city (a practice known as *euergetism*), and the fact that we see giving *munera* become a frequent addition to the typical list of public buildings and festivals is significant. Gladiatorial shows may have been foreign, but they weren't seen as inappropriate or repellent. Elites were able to recognise their potential as a popular entertainment, and they were willing to pay big money to provide it if it meant that they could cash in on the prestige such benevolence bought them. There was a demand for combats from the wider population that the elites were more than happy to supply. In fact, the inscriptions reveal that some elites didn't just lease troupes of gladiators, but bought their own *familia* to have on hand all the time. There are some 120 surviving inscriptions created by or for elites specifically mentioning games that they provided.[158]

Some of these elites were elected magistrates. The role of *duovir* (meaning 'two men') was, as the title suggests, a role held by two men simultaneously and lasted for a year. These officials were appointed, by election, in Roman colonies. We already know that Corinth was refounded as a Roman colony by Caesar, and several more cities were given colony status when Rome installed Roman populations and administration. These included Patrai (modern Patras),

Berytos (Beirut), Alexandria Troas (near Dalyan), and Knossos on Crete. The *duoviri* were the middlemen between the governor of each province (who was a Roman politician, either appointed by the emperor or the Senate, depending on the province) and the local population. The magistrates were therefore in charge of most of the day-to-day administration of each city. They needed to keep both the Roman provincial governor and their Greek citizens happy, while fulfilling all of their obligations. One of these obligations, if we look again to Caesar's founding charter of Urso (the *Lex Ursonensis*) was to provide either gladiatorial spectacles or a series of dramatic plays in honour of the Capitoline Triad – Jupiter, Juno and Minerva (who were the Roman versions of Zeus, Hera and Athena – with slight Roman modifications). There's no reason to believe that such an obligation wasn't common across the *coloniae*, as it meant that each city paid lip service to Roman religion (and power) while also providing locals with some much-appreciated free leisure time. *Duoviri* were elite out of necessity, because they had to pay for these festivals out of their own pockets.

In other cities, it was local elites that were the middlemen. These were elected officials whose title ended in '*arch*', a Greek suffix meaning 'leader' – *asiarch* in Asia, *helladarch* in Achaia, *macedoniarch* in Macedonia, and so on. They were also required to splash the cash on a variety of benevolent gifts that the whole city could enjoy. There was also a role called *archiereus*, which is Greek for 'chief/high priest,' and refers specifically to the high priest of the Imperial cult, whose job it was to promote loyalty to the Roman imperial family on the basis that the emperor was the glue that held the empire and its peace together; the emperor's divine authority to rule meant that his personal welfare was irrevocably tied to the welfare of the empire and its inhabitants, and so dutifully worshipping the emperor was as much a collective act of self-preservation as it was for the emperor's benefit. We also have inscriptions of these *archiereis* providing gifts including gladiatorial shows amongst other more traditional acts of civic generosity.

These two roles, leading magistrate and high priest of the Imperial cult, may have been two facets of the same job: a single magistrate with both administrative and religious responsibilities. The ancients wouldn't understand the concept of separating church and state, as religion and politics were woven tightly together. Following the lead of Caesar, Augustus and each subsequent emperor was also the Pontifex Maximus in Rome, so the idea that the local magistrate also held a prestigious priesthood was hardly alien. The magistrate's wife would also serve as high priestess. Whether or not the magistrate and the high priest were one and the same person is almost a moot point for our purposes, though the conundrum fascinates scholars of eastern Mediterranean politics. As far as we are concerned, it is enough to state that elite officials (who nevertheless relied on winning elections) were the people responsible for providing official public gladiatorial games in cities without *colonia* status, though they might also choose to fund something else instead; every magistrate and priest appeared to have options to choose from.[159] Roman officials weren't the only ones hosting the gladiatorial games, Greek ones were too.

In the western territories, providing a show was called a *munera*, meaning 'gift' or 'duty'. But just as Greek gladiators didn't like untransliterated Latin terminology and preferred to use Greek alternative words, so did the Greek *editores*. They preferred to use the word *philotimia* instead of *munera*, meaning 'for the love of honour.' Ostensibly the *philotimiai*, whether monumental or a festival with entertainments or competitions, was provided to honour the emperor, but the person providing them got a fair bit of honour themselves.[160] Any form of *philotimiai*, including gladiatorial shows, could be ruinously expensive, but many clearly felt the cost was worth it for the glory it brought them. A savvy official who wished to earn himself as much respect and prestige as possible would naturally think long and hard about what type of civic benevolence might make him the most popular. In a world where political competition had been rather dampened under Roman control, this form of euergetism also provided officials the chance to compete with each other for who could provide the most pleasing gift to the city and who would win the most gratitude from the common people. In other words, give the people what they want. Did the Greeks want gladiators?

It would be disingenuous to claim that enthusiasm for Roman gladiators was universal in the Greek world, as no form or genre of entertainment and sport has ever been universally beloved. This is as true then as it is now. That a sport as extreme as gladiatorial combat should be met with a modicum of criticism is to be expected. Gladiation didn't even receive blanket approval in Rome.

The Romans didn't invent gladiatorial combat, but they certainly refined it and turned it into a massive industry that was central to and reflective of their society. We know that gladiator shows were wildly popular, and we still conjure images of the Colosseum when we hear the word 'Rome'. We also know from our own experiences with modern pop culture that the more widely popular something becomes, a small portion of society will feel the urge to differentiate themselves from the 'common herd' by voicing their disdain for 'common, base' entertainments with increasing volume. This is particularly true of people who see themselves as educated, elite sophisticates who refuse to understand the appeal of a cultural phenomenon aimed squarely at the average citizen. We see parallels in Rome, where certain well-heeled politicians, academics, and philosophers declared that they had no interest in lowbrow performances, though Cicero observed that most of these men were merely pretending not to enjoy the shows.[161] Seneca is often presented as a strident critic of gladiatorial games, but this is, in my opinion, a misreading. In a letter to a friend, he describes going to see a spectacle and not enjoying it at all. For a start, he says that being part of a crowd is always detrimental, as it's easier to get swept up into vice. He then describes what he saw:

> *By chance I attended a mid-day exhibition, expecting some fun, wit, and relaxation, an exhibition at which men's eyes have respite from the slaughter of their fellow men. But it was quite the reverse. The previous combats were the essence of compassion; but now all the trifling is put aside and it is pure murder. The men have no defensive armour. They are exposed to blows at all points, and no one ever strikes in vain. Many persons prefer this programme to the usual pairs and to the bouts 'by request'. Of course they do; there is no helmet or shield to deflect the weapon. What is the need of defensive armour, or of skill? All these mean delaying death. In the morning, they throw men to the lions and the bears; at noon, they throw them to the spectators. The spectators demand that the slayer shall face the man who is to slay him in his turn; and they always reserve the latest conqueror for another butchering. The outcome of every fight is death, and the means are fire and sword. This sort of thing goes on while the arena is empty. You may retort: 'But he was a highway robber; he killed a man!' And what of it? Granted that, as a murderer, he deserved this punishment; what crime have you committed, poor fellow, that you should deserve to sit and see this show? In the morning they cried 'Kill him! Lash him! Burn him! Why does he meet the sword in so cowardly a way? Why does he strike so feebly? Why doesn't he die game? Whip him to meet his wounds! Let them receive blow for blow, with chests bare and exposed to the stroke!' And when the games stop for the intermission, they announce: 'A little throat-cutting in the meantime, so that there may still be something going on!'[162]*

We need to be specific about what Seneca is criticising. He is attending the midday show, the *meridiani*, which means he isn't watching gladiators at this point, but the execution of criminals. More to the point, he is criticising how his fellow spectators (at least, the ones who didn't pop out to grab lunch) are reacting to watching these executions; they aren't solemnly witnessing justice being dealt, but they are calling for the executions to be as humiliating and painful as possible, which to Seneca doesn't deem fair or necessary.

So, if this oft-used quote isn't actually condemning gladiators, what does Seneca actually have to say about them? He certainly seems familiar with the intimate workings of the arena and the *ludus*, frequently using expert terminology in his writing. Seneca, then, knew what he was talking about. In another letter, he says that while in his retirement he lives the life of a philosopher; nevertheless, he makes sure to attend every play in the theatre, regularly attends the chariot racing in the circus, and 'allows no duel to be fought to a finish without his presence.'[163] For Seneca, philosophy and spectacle needn't clash. Most of the Roman criticism we have is from early Christian writers, and we need to approach their opinions with caution as they are heavily biased. Early Christian sources were hostile to anything they perceived remotely pagan, and, if pagan Romans enjoyed going to the amphitheatre, then the amphitheatre was bad. For what it's worth, early Christians like Tertullian also criticised chariot racing and theatre, so gladiation wasn't an isolated case; any and all spectacle was considered by these thinkers to endanger the Christian soul. Greeks certainly had no issue with the theatre or racing, so do we see similar complaints?

Greek Criticism

When gladiators appeared on the Greek entertainment circuit, it is natural that they received ambivalence from some quarters and open hostility from others, which we do have evidence for; gladiators were not universally beloved. This evidence comes in the form of written accounts, including anecdotes, of certain Greeks demonstrating their disgust at the thought of gladiatorial combat. Before we continue, it is worth thinking about how historians consider written evidence. It would be easy to take everything we read at face value, and accept statements as they are given. It is natural to gravitate towards writing that aligns with our own ideals and preconceptions, and it is tempting to dismiss sources that challenge our own assumptions; the historian must learn to read between the lines to root out the biases of the writer, and to attempt to set aside biases of their own. Each historian is naturally biased; our individual experiences and beliefs inevitably affect how we view the people of the past, their actions, their ideologies, and the words that have survived for us to read.

Our concept of history is influenced by the historians who write it. Their own facets of identity and their views about race, gender, sexuality and politics seep into how they approach their topic and how they choose to interpret it. A good historian strives for transparency and an awareness of their subjectivity, and there is debate among historians about whether one should voice personal critiques on issues such as slavery, or whether this prevents us from being able to truly see issues from a purely ancient perspective.

This methodological tangent is relevant in the case of Roman spectacle in culturally Greek provinces; when presented with sources that challenge their preferred interpretation of Greek culture during the Roman period, some antiquarians sought to minimise or misrepresent those sources in order to preserve that interpretation. It's a protective response, but not good practice, because it requires an uneven presentation of the evidence we have. Criticism of gladiators by ancient writers has been used by some historians who themselves are critical of bloodsports to present an image of the ancient Greek world as a place where bloodsports were roundly condemned. Even Louis Robert, the first scholar to realise that gladiators had a significant presence in the eastern Mediterranean, called the phenomenon 'a Roman gangrene that infected the Greek world.'[164] Describing anything as a disease suggests something unwanted and unappreciated. Does this give us an accurate overview of Roman spectacle in the Greek world? Or is this a moment when the academic mask has momentarily slipped, with the historian projecting his own belief system onto a society he has idealised? It is not my wish to mould antiquity into a form I approve of and admire, and it is not my job to excise what I do not want to speak of from my presentation of this topic. The following discussion of ancient sources has often been used by the 'prosecution' in this case as evidence that Rome foisted gladiators onto unimpressed Greeks. I could, in presenting this 'defence' case, skip this next section if I thought it detrimental to my argument, but why gloss over a pile of evidence when I could cross-examine it? It is my job to present all the sources I can, without giving one type of evidence preferential treatment, or failing to provide critical analysis. So let us review these ancient Greek critiques, and see if we can't read between the lines.

The first thing to note is that the literary evidence is heavily Athenocentric. This is the case for nearly all aspects of the ancient Greek world. Athens was one of the largest Greek cities and not only did the city produce some exemplary historical figures, but it also drew in prolific writers and experts from around the Mediterranean. The Athenians were also more devoted than most to inscribing anything and everything they deemed important onto stone, meaning that we have an astonishing volume of literary and archaeological evidence from this one city. But we should hesitate before we apply Athenian ideas to the rest of the Greek world, particularly in the Roman period. At that point, Athens was not the powerhouse it had been in the fifth century BCE, and was reliant on trading on its golden past for tourists and history buffs. Its population had shrunk dramatically, and Greek cities like Alexandria, Antioch, Pergamon, Ephesus, Hierapolis, and Byzantium were much larger, richer, and more vibrant. In other words, Athens was a bit of a relic, clinging on to the memories of its heyday, and the conservative writers there may well have been a little out of touch with the modern, increasingly Roman world around them. These are the men who left behind written evidence: the average working-class Athenian in the Roman period did not. They were men clinging on to their own idealised concept of a period they had no personal experience of, and such people often mistake their own opinions for general consensus, even now. We should not wander into the same trap.

We are then left to weigh the literary evidence of the writers and the archaeological evidence left by the average Athenian and try to marry the two pictures they give together to work out what was really happening in Athens and beyond.

Dio Chrysostom

Dio Chrysostom was originally from Prusa in Bithynia, but travelled extensively and spent a great deal of time in Athens. He was active in the second half of the first century CE, and worked as a philosopher and orator. He was heavily influenced by Stoic philosophy, and believed that a lack of restraint in general and the pursuit of luxury and pleasure specifically robbed a person of virtue; in other words, he's not the target demographic of gladiatorial shows. He says:

If you were no whit superior to the Athenians in other respects, perhaps you would not find it necessary to feel any jealousy of them in this one matter and to consider how you might have a reputation better than theirs. But as matters now stand, there is no practice current in Athens which would not cause any man to feel ashamed. For instance, in regard to the gladiatorial shows the Athenians have so zealously emulated the Corinthians, or rather, have so surpassed both them and all others in their mad infatuation, that whereas the Corinthians watch these combats outside the city in a glen, a place that is able to hold a crowd but otherwise is dirty and such that no one would even bury there any freeborn citizen, the Athenians look on at this fine spectacle in their theatre under the very walls of the Acropolis, in the place where they bring their Dionysus into the orchestra and stand him up, so that often a fighter is slaughtered among the very seats in which the Hierophant and the other priests must sit. And the philosopher who spoke about this matter and rebuked them they refused to obey and did not even applaud; on the contrary, they were so incensed that, although in blood he was inferior to no Roman, but enjoyed a reputation greater than any one man has attained for generations, and was admittedly the only man who since the time of the ancients had lived most nearly in conformity with reason, this man was forced to leave the city and preferred to go and live somewhere else in Greece.[165]

In this extract, Dio Chrysostom is roundly criticising the Athenians, but not to the Athenians themselves. He is talking to the assembly at Rhodes, and using Athens as a cautionary tale of how not to behave. As far as he is concerned, the Athenians have thoroughly fallen into disgrace, and their penchant for gladiators is his chosen example. He mentions Corinthians watching gladiators in a dirty glen outside the city, by which he must surely be referring to the amphitheatre there.[166] In contrast, he describes Athenians as watching combats in the Theatre of Dionysus on the slopes of the acropolis, and we can confirm this because the safety wall built around the *orchestra* in the Roman period is still in place today.[167] The unnamed philosopher who was so disgusted with gladiators in the theatre that he moved away is believed to be either Apollonius of Tyana or Musonius Rufus.

So why is Dio Chrysostom complaining about Athenian gladiators to people in Rhodes? We need to step back from the excerpt and look at the entire speech, called the Rhodian Discourse. The main thrust of the speech is that Rhodians, who famously had more than 3,000 statues in their city, were now cutting corners. Statues were very expensive and, since the city was already a veritable forest of them, the Rhodians had started recycling old statues whenever someone new was honoured: they chipped away the existing inscriptions and slapped a new name and inscription on an old statue. No eminent citizen wanted a second-hand statue; having a statue of yourself erected in public was the very height of honour in the ancient world. This, of course, is not directly connected with gladiators, but Dio is comparing the damage the Rhodians risk to their reputation with this shady practice as equal to the damage Athens has done to her own reputation by embracing gladiatorial combat.

What is important here is Dio's audience. He is speaking to the assembly, i.e. the male citizens who determined policy (as far as the Romans would allow), and he is discussing how civic honours are bestowed.[168] His criticism of gladiators is a personal one, and the fact that he describes Athenians as such enthusiastic gladiator fans suggests that his distaste of spectacle might put him in a distinct minority in that city. Would the average Rhodian know or care if the odd statue got reused? Would the average Athenian care much if a pompous philosopher or some Rhodians didn't like that they were gladiator fans? We cannot assume that Dio Chrysostom's opinions reflect that of the Athenian or even Rhodian population, though it is true that archaeological evidence of gladiators from the island is incredibly scant, perhaps indicating that Rhodes did not adopt gladiatorial spectacle with the same vim as their close neighbours in Asia Minor and Crete. If this is indeed the case, Dio Chrysostom is savvily using exactly an example of 'bad' civic practice that he knows will best persuade the Rhodians to take his advice about their own negative habit.

Apollonius of Tyana

Apollonius was about a generation older than Dio Chrysostom, and was born around 15 CE in Cappadocia. He too was a philosopher, and spent his life travelling, spending considerable time in Athens. An anecdote about Apollonius of Tyana survives in his biography, written by Philostratus in the second century CE. It says:

> *The Athenians used to assemble in the theatre below the acropolis and watch human slaughter, so that it was more popular there than it now is in Corinth. Paying large sums of money, they assembled adulterers, pimps, burglars, cutpurses, slave dealers, and types like that, and then armed them and told them to enter combat. This too Apollonius denounced, and when the Athenians summoned him to the assembly, he said he would not enter a place that was impure and full of gore. This he said in a letter, and added: 'I am surprised that the goddess has not already left the acropolis when you pour out blood of this kind for her. At this rate, it seems to me, you will no longer sacrifice oxen when you celebrate the Panathenaea, but human hecatombs in the goddess's honour. And you, Dionysus, do you frequent the theatre after so much blood? And do the wise Athenians pour libations to you here? You too must leave, Dionysus: Cithaeron is purer.*[169]

So the relevant discernible points are that Apollonius is upset that Athenians are choosing to spend large amounts of money on these games, which he clearly deems to be immoral. The goddess he refers to is Athena herself, as the kind of blood sacrifices she was accustomed to were animals like bulls. This comment should not be taken to mean that gladiators were some sort of blood sacrifice (and they were not), but that Apollonius considers only one form of bloodshed to be appropriate given the sacred location. Dionysus is mentioned, just as he is by Dio Chrysostom, and Apollonius is urging the god to vacate Athens for Mount Cithaeron, which was also sacred to his cult and was presumably not a place contaminated with combats. This is the main crux of Apollonius' tirade: the choice of location. His criticism echoes what Dio Chrysostom had to say when he referenced the statue of Dionysus, which was brought into the theatre during the sacred drama festivals. Neither philosopher could stomach that the theatre was used as a gladiatorial venue, because the theatre itself was a sacred space.

Multifunctionality itself wasn't an issue; Greek theatres were often used for general assemblies like the one Apollonius was invited to. They provided comfortable seating for large numbers of citizens, excellent acoustics for discussions, and were frequently placed conveniently close to the civic heart of cities. The Theatre of Dionysus was no exception. Now, the civic assembly would not meet during a gladiatorial *munera*, nor immediately after one, and so the theatre would have been neat and tidy when Apollonius refused to enter, and we shouldn't consider visible viscera strewn across the floor to be the cause of Apollonius' ire. One might argue that assemblies were a secular event, and so it was entirely fair to have other secular events taking place in a sacred area, but that is a very (subjective) debate around what an individual deems appropriate. For example, we can easily accept concerts of classical music being performed in a cathedral, but a burlesque show in the same building would likely draw criticism.

In the Greek world, a theatre was much more than a place to see a play for light entertainment. This was perhaps most true for the highly educated elite class in Athens and the Theatre of Dionysus, the very place where tragedy was first produced. In this theatre, the citizens of Athens gathered to hear plays that spoke of what it meant to be human, and how one should live life. These plays challenged society by interrogating its ideals. More than any other theatre, the Theatre of Dionysus was an icon of cultural brilliance. This was the view of ancient elites, and the view of many archaeologists and academics now, some of whom try to brush gladiators fighting in that very theatre under the scholarly carpet.

However, I propose a counterargument: if we look at gladiatorial fights through the lens of Roman ideology, the combats also had a lot to say about how to live life and what it means to be human, just in a very different voice. While some refused to listen, it seems that many Greeks did. We cannot use these sources as proof that ancient Greeks didn't want gladiatorial combats performed in their cities, as the ancient critics are bitterly complaining that the majority of Athenians were regular and enthusiastic spectators. The Theatre of Dionysus must have indeed seen fighting on a regular basis, but the fans in the seats did not write accounts of their appreciation. The educated elites had become a very vocal minority.

So why were these philosophers so hostile to gladiators? I suspect that this hostility runs deeper than an aversion to bloodshed. They belonged to a tradition known as the Second Sophistic, named because the members of this unofficial group wanted to emulate the sophists (teachers of rhetoric and philosophy) of the fifth century BCE. They were admirers of Homeric literature, the old tragedies, orators like Demosthenes, and they celebrated the art and architecture of the Classical era. They wanted to create the next generation of superstar philosophers.

It's no coincidence that this movement began in the first century CE under Roman occupation, because its core aims were the preservation and promotion of traditional Greek culture and customs. The Second Sophistic was a protest and a renaissance wrapped up into a single cause: maintaining cultural superiority, even as political independence was eroded. If a custom wasn't Greek, the philosophers wanted nothing to do with it, and if it was Roman, they had all the more reason to detest it. In Athens, the Second Sophistic was interested in the Greek world of yesteryear, and modern Roman gladiation simply was not compatible. Whereas the original sophists in Athens were deeply engaged with politics (as this was the century of Athenian radical democracy, as well as the brief Athenian empire), the Second Sophistic had little opportunity to influence politics in the imperial period—the Romans may have taken a relatively hands-off approach to individual Greek cities, but only if the cities each acted in exactly the manner Rome was willing to tolerate. This new movement was more focused on aesthetics, and the sophists' speciality was public speaking. Excellent at extemporised oratory, the sophists drew legions of admirers who would gather to hear them speak, and it seems that, on occasion, the sophists did speak about gladiators. However powerful their rhetoric may have been, our archaeological evidence reveals widespread adoption of Roman spectacle and suggests that, for many, the expert rhetoric of the sophists fell on deaf ears.

I do wonder, particularly given the emphasis on the Theatre of Dionysus, whether the Second Sophists would have been quite so vocally opposed to gladiators had they performed anywhere else. To return to our modern analogy, far fewer people would protest if a burlesque show was hosted in a nightclub three streets away from the church. In ancient Athens, the Panathenaic Stadium was home to the athletic festival sacred to Athena and was, like the Theatre of Dionysus, converted to stage combats despite its sacred status.[170] This is not mentioned by the philosophers: perhaps the literary festival was deemed more culturally significant by them than the athletic festival. Or, perhaps, the philosophers would have been able to tolerate gladiator shows outside the city walls in a Roman amphitheatre, even if it would be 'dirty' like the one in Corinth. Is the point less about the performance, and more about the performance space? Is it less about keeping the Theatre of Dionysus sacrosanct, and more about reserving it for Greek forms of entertainment only? Was it the religious aspect of the theatre that the sophists wanted to keep pure, or the ideal of Greekness?

Lucian of Samosata

Our next criticism is again Athenocentric, but this time from the second century CE. It comes from the works of Lucian of Samosata (modern Samsat in Türkiye), which was a city in Commagene. When Lucian was born in around 125 CE, the region was part of the Roman province of Syria. After an itinerant life of teaching across the eastern Mediterranean, Lucian settled down in Athens for a decade devoted to writing, and one of his works was a biography of a philosopher who had also been his own teacher, named Demonax. Lucian is our only surviving source for Demonax, leading some to believe that he'd made him up (because Lucian was a satirist). However, it's more likely that Demonax was a real figure and that Lucian's biography of him was simply rather idealised and may have exaggerated the truth a little.[171] Most of the biography is actually a collection of Demonax's witty quips, which Lucian clearly takes delight in. The relevant pun for us is this:

> *When the Athenians, out of rivalry with the Corinthians, were thinking of holding a gladiatorial show, he came before them and said: 'Don't pass this resolution, men of Athens, without first pulling down the altar of Mercy!'*[172]

Pausanias mentions an altar to Eleos, the goddess of mercy, pity and compassion, placed in the Athenian agora.[173] The meaning behind this bon mot is fairly clear: as far as Demonax is concerned, one cannot care about mercy if one is simultaneously hosting bloodsports. The city has room for compassion or cruelty, but not for both. As criticisms go, this is a sympathetic one, and it reminds us that for all of its popularity, the profession of gladiators was a hard one and had significant risks, particularly for the combatants who'd had no agency in choosing that career. In subsequent chapters of this book, I will explore exactly why a large number of ordinary Greeks *did* consider Roman gladiation to not only be morally acceptable, but congruent with the Greek culture the Second Sophistic philosophers championed. I will also talk about the clear pride displayed when some of the gladiators discuss their profession. Still, it is perhaps pertinent to keep Demonax's little pun in the back of our minds as we continue, and to remember that the gladiators were real people in an extraordinary and precarious situation.

So there was some Greek pushback to Roman gladiation, but of a character that is entirely to be expected and from people that do not seem to represent the view of the average Greek. We have seen that colonies such as Caesar's likely had the provision of gladiatorial games written into their charters, and we do have a handful of inscriptions from the first century CE suggesting that local magistrates and priests were providing gladiatorial shows in the very early imperial period. By the second century CE, there had been plenty of time for the Greeks to get acquainted and familiarised with gladiation, and we see evidence that the frequency of shows crescendoed across the Greek world, with some cities making sure that gladiatorial shows were an annual event.[174] In cities such as Pergamon, the office of high priest even came with a dedicated gladiatorial *familia*, who would be inherited each year by the next priest who took up the post. There was no point keeping a fully staffed *familia* with its stable of fighters, its trainers, medics, and auxiliary staff, if games weren't a regular occurrence, and high priests could recoup some of the costs of maintaining the *familia* for twelve months by leasing them to smaller cities without their own troupe. The increase in local officials giving gladiation as their *philotimiai*, combined with the expanding number of venues being altered to make them safe for hosting fights and the growing amount of gladiatorial art as we move from the first to the third centuries CE, all point to Greeks responding positively to the combats they were provided with and coming to expect them as the decades wore on. It's hard to understand this in any way other than that the officials were simply giving the Greeks a Roman form of entertainment because the Greeks wanted that entertainment.[175]

An Aqueduct for Aphrodisias

The emperor could be consulted on certain affairs if deemed important enough, and when this happened the emperor's decisions were, in typical Greek fashion, inscribed in stone for every (literate) citizen of the city to read. One such letter from the emperor Hadrian was found on a stone in Aphrodisias, preserved thanks to it being repurposed as a paving slab.[176] It reads, if you'll allow me to paraphrase:

> I approve the funds that you have allocated for the construction of a new aqueduct. As for certain citizens who have been nominated for the high priesthood and say they can't afford to take up the post, their finances should be examined to determine if they are telling the truth or evading their duties; if the latter, they

should be the first to serve as high priest, as the fairest course of action. Not only do I agree with your proposal to take money from the high priests for the aqueduct instead of gladiatorial shows, I praise the idea.

Reading between the lines, this letter from Hadrian is a response to a lost missive to him from the Aphrodisian magistrates, who seem to have appealed to him for advice: they could afford an aqueduct or gladiatorial shows, but not both; which should they pick? Hadrian is agreeing with their suggestion that an aqueduct was the better bet, which is unsurprising: aqueducts were incredibly beneficial to daily life and health, providing clean, potable water for public fountains and baths, and were built with longevity in mind. Gladiatorial shows, while fun, just weren't as practical. Hadrian has also been told that a few rich Aphrodisians had been trying to avoid serving as high priest of the Imperial cult, claiming that they simply couldn't afford the *philotimiai* that were an obligation of the post. It is true that the costs of *philotimiai* were considerable, but it was considered shameful to avoid paying if one was able to do so; wealth was to be shared with the populace in some way or other. This reluctance has been read in two ways. Firstly, that potential high priests were reluctant to spend their money on something as (comparatively) boring as an aqueduct when gladiators would provide rather more glamour.[177]

Alternatively, it can be read as saying that gladiator shows were becoming so ruinously expensive that nobody wanted to spend money on them and would much rather use their money on something tangibly useful.[178] The letter is dated to 125 CE, so before Marcus Aurelius' 177 CE decree that regulated the price of gladiator shows, curbing the exorbitant costs across the empire. There was clearly a need for such regulations if potential priests were so hesitant to serve, but it's also obvious that gladiator prices were spiralling because they were in high demand, particularly if such a large monument as an aqueduct was seen as a more affordable alternative. So, whichever way we interpret this letter, we can ascertain that normal Aphrodisians were loudly clamouring for gladiatorial shows, and officials needed the emperor to rubber stamp plans for the aqueduct. This way, no locals could complain when they didn't get their spectacles, because the decision was technically not in the hands of local officials anymore.[179]

From the evidence presented here, it seems like the local magistrates and high priests were responding to a desire for gladiation by increasing the number of shows, rather than being forced to provide gladiators by the Roman provincial governors. But can we be confident of that? It's time for our first case study.

Chapter 7

CSI Case study: Romanisation?

We've seen that there was, in the past, a general consensus that Romans must have forced gladiators on to the Greek world, shoving combats down their unwilling throats. This theory falls under the old idea of 'Romanisation', the idea that Romans forced Romanness in all aspects of life upon unwilling provinces. In the previous chapter I've shown a lot of evidence that suggests this wasn't the case, and instead that Greek elites were hosting gladiator shows in response to demand from local populations. A great way to check this is to compare the development of gladiation in the Greek world to its development with their close neighbours, to see how other provinces responded to Roman rule and the cultural sensation of gladiators. For our first case study, then, we need to travel to the province of Judaea and examine the evidence there.

Judaea and the larger region of Palestine had been part of the wider Greek world since at least as early as the Wars of the Diadochi, first under the Ptolemies and then under the Seleukids. As such, there were Greeks living in the area, particularly along the coast and in cities, but they were a minority among other local groups, including Jews. Ancient Palestine was a multicultural place, with several languages spoken, religions practised, and different cultural events observed. One of its most famous kings was Herod I, also known as Herod the Great. He was the son of Antipater the Idumaean, a great friend of Julius Caesar, who had granted Antipater Roman citizenship and the position of chief minister of Judaea. This allowed Antipater to found a new ruling dynasty. Herod started his own career as a provincial governor of Galilee, and was later promoted by Mark Antony. With Antony's encouragement and assistance, Herod marched on Jerusalem in 37 BCE and deposed the last of the Hasmonean kings, Antigonus II Mattathias. Herod thus became king of Judaea. He is undoubtedly most famous for his antagonistic role in the nativity story, wherein he attempts to murder the newborn Jesus Christ.[180] While this story is almost undoubtedly a fabrication (though admittedly Herod could be cruel), this particular book is not the right place for trying to salvage Herod's biblical reputation. Rather, we're interested in his passion for both Greek and Roman cultural institutions.

Herod was an unabashed philhellene; he was a huge fan of Greek art, architecture, literature, and performance. The Jewish historian Flavius Josephus gives us some examples of Herod's love of Greek culture: Herod bestowed so many buildings and statues to various Greek cities that Josephus says it would take up much of his book to list them, but gives restoring the Temple of Apollo in Rhodes as a good example of his largesse. Josephus also records that the sanctuary of Olympia, experts at hosting the largest athletic festival in the Greek world, were nonetheless a bit rubbish at managing their finances and were on the verge of cancelling the 192nd Olympiad in 12 BCE – an unprecedented move. Herod swooped in to save the day with a big pile of cash, and the Olympics were able to go ahead as normal.[181] In gratitude, Herod was named an *agonothetes*, or 'president/sponsor', not just for the 192nd Olympiad, but for life. To be declared *agonothetes* in perpetuity was rare enough, but for the title to be conferred upon a non-Greek like Herod was entirely unprecedented.

Herod clearly loved Greek athletics, and instituted his own festivals back in Judaea, including a festival held every fifth year at Caesarea Maritima and Jerusalem, which was no doubt popular with the Greek residents living there. And if Herod was going to host events for an international audience that could compete with anything on the Greek mainland or in Asia and Syria, he needed impressive venues. In fact, if Herod has a reputation for two things, they are his cruelty and his vast building programme. We are interested in the latter. As well as temples, theatres, fountains, baths, gymnasia and colonnades, Josephus tells us that Herod built 'amphitheatres'. The problem with this term is that Herod didn't build anything that looked like the Colosseum, or even Caesar's rock cut arena in Corinth. Herod built hybrid venues that could host many types of contests and performance, and since nobody had a term for that, Josephus chose to use 'amphitheatre' as an umbrella term because etymologically it made logical sense. Herod was able to combine elements of many Greek and Roman building styles into his own blended edifices to create truly multifunctional venues. Hippodromes were built in Jerusalem, Jericho, and Caesarea Maritima, the latter of which also boasted an *amphistadium*.[182]

Multifunctionality came in very useful, because, unlike the Greeks, Herod was happy to combine Greek theatre, musical contests, chariot racing and athletics competitions into the same festival programme as Roman *venationes* and gladiatorial shows.[183] Josephus makes a point of noting that, while foreigners were very impressed with the grandiosity of Herod's shows, the locals were not impressed at all. In particular, they considered seeing men fighting (and being killed by) animals to be a 'foreign practice' and resented it. Herod was undeterred, however. He was a great admirer of the Romans and had visited Rome more than once: it's plausible that he witnessed a Roman show first hand and was impressed by what he'd seen, not to mention his desire to impress Augustus and Marcus Agrippa, whom he counted as friends. Herod was the kind of cosmopolitan king who looked outside of his borders to find styles of art, architecture and entertainment that he could introduce back home. However, in Judaea we don't see this explosion of Roman spectacle continuing much past Herod's death (in either 4 or 1 BCE). We don't see the same gradual development of hybrid venues in Palestine as we do in the Greek mainland, Asia Minor and Syria. The stadiums, theatres and hippodromes continued to be used for athletics, plays and horse racing, but gladiators fall off the literary and archaeological records from here until much later in the Roman imperial period.

Judaea was annexed by Augustus less than a decade after Herod died. August considered Herod's sons to be less than competent rulers, and so Judaea became an official Roman province. The first few decades of direct Roman rule were decidedly turbulent, eventually leading to a revolt and war with Rome in 66 CE. The future emperor Titus crushed the rebellion and ended the war in 70 CE by razing Jerusalem to the ground, massacring its inhabitants, and desecrating the Jewish Temple. The loot Titus hauled back to Rome was put to good use as far as Romans were concerned; the treasure funded the construction of the Flavian Amphitheatre (the Colosseum), using the slave labour of captured Jews. In the interim, between becoming a province and the siege of Jerusalem, we don't see evidence for gladiatorial shows being presented by Roman officials nor local magistrates and priests. The number of Roman soldiers stationed in the Levant increased following the Bar Kokhba revolt in the 130s CE, during which the Jewish population was severely depleted. More legionaries led to a greater demand for gladiatorial games, and a large amphitheatre was built shortly afterwards in Maresha/Betaris (now known as Beit Guvrin). More spectacular buildings were constructed or adapted in the Levant during the following centuries to cater to Roman legionaries.[184] Even so, there is no concrete evidence for a single Jewish gladiator, and few seemed to attend and enjoy the games. The Jerusalem Talmud specifically forbids Jews from attending, lest they be complicit in murder. The Babylonian Talmud allows Jews to attend for two reasons only: to loudly shout 'mercy' when Jews were to be executed in the arena to try to prevent their deaths; or so that there would be witnesses to Jewish deaths, allowing widows to legally remarry. These texts were written to help Jews navigate their daily lives but nowhere is it mentioned that they might be compelled by their Roman conquerors to attend gladiatorial games by Romans, who did not seem remotely bothered that their favourite pastime was not welcomed by the local population.

Why would the Romans have pushed a cultural institution onto one province and not the neighbouring province? After all, it seems perfectly possible for the inhabitants of the province of Judea to, at the very least, avoid participating. In the Greek cities just down the coast, however, we have seen enthusiastic attendance, participation, and sponsorship.

I think, if we weigh the evidence, we see that gladiators cannot have been forced upon an unwilling Greek population. Rather, it seems, Greek cities wanted Roman spectacle because they enjoyed it on merit, and their local magistrates were usually happy, purses willing, to provide the populace with the shows that they craved. Moreover, the surviving fragments of commemorations attest that many priests and officials wanted to immortalise their provisions of gladiators in stone because it brought them honour and glory.

Romans brought gladiators to the Greek world for the benefit of the Romans who worked and lived there, just as they did in Judea. It doesn't seem to have been any part of their plan to include the locals in their favourite entertainment. Indeed, they may well have been ambivalent or even bemused about how fervently the Greek locals adopted this entertainment. Either way, the idea that gladiation was a polluting infection that Rome inflicted on the Greek world is not a conclusion that many Greeks would have agreed with.

Chapter 8

A Day at the Games

The programme of average games in the Colosseum or similar western amphitheatres was at least one full day of dramatic and compelling events that Romans found irresistible. We won't be able to understand what attracted Greeks to the arena if we don't first understand why Romans were obsessed first, so let's dive into how a day at the amphitheatre worked on the Italian peninsula.

The first thing required for a show was marketing. In the town of Pompeii, several adverts for upcoming games were found painted on the exterior walls of buildings, preserved in the eruption of 79 CE. They typically told passers-by everything they needed to know: the reason the games were being put on, how many gladiators would be competing, the name of the person paying for the event and the date and location. As well as local games, adverts were found promoting games in nearby towns such as Nola and Cumae, because spectators were willing to travel to neighbouring towns to watch the Games, particularly if their favourite gladiators were competing, in much the same way that modern football fans attend 'home' and 'away' matches. And, just like with modern football, spectators could get rowdy when local rivalries got tense: a riot between local Pompeiians and visiting fans from Nuceria resulted in Pompeii being slapped with a ten-year ban on all arena spectacles by the Roman Senate.[185]

Entry to amphitheatres like the Colosseum was free, because the emperors (or local magistrates) were providing the spectacle as an act of benevolence. All a fan had to do was obtain their entry token, called a *tessera*. There were different *tesserae* for the circus and theatre, as well as grain doles and festival banquets. It is frustrating that none of these tokens for the Colosseum survive, but the surviving examples of other *tesserae* give us clues as to what they were like: they could be small circles or oblongs made from clay, stone, glass or metal. We can imagine that the tokens for the VIP seats were likely made of more expensive materials, and perhaps decorated on one side with an image. The same process was used to get into the theatres and circuses. Tokens were coveted, as demand far outstripped supply. This was particularly true for the gladiatorial games, which were staged with far less frequency than plays and chariot races.[186] In other words, even if the Colosseum held huge amounts of people (and estimates range between 50,000–87,000), tokens were highly sought-after. As to exactly how one got their hands on tickets, we can't really say for certain.

What we do know is that seating was carefully organised from Augustus onwards, as he'd decided it was no longer enough to merely reserve front rows for senators.[187] The *cavea*, or seating area, was split into three horizontal bands:

- The *ima cavea*: '*ima*' means lowest, and this level of seating was closest to the arena.
- The *media cavea*: '*media*' (think: medium) formed the middle band of seating.
- The *summa cavea*: '*summa*' means upper or highest. At the very top was a colonnade called the *summum maenianum in ligneis* where ladies sat, shielded from the urban poor.

Each of these horizontal bands, or *maeniana*, were usually separated from each other by a walkway (*praecinctio*) backed by a *podium* wall, or maybe a high balustrade. Each of the levels were cut into distinct vertical wedges called *cunei*, like a pizza. Stairways from the seating to the warren of passages below made for convenient gaps, but richer amphitheatres also had wonderfully decorated balustrades between *cunei*.[188] It's not so easy to see from what's left of the Colosseum, but it's still clear at amphitheatres such as Arles that trying to switch seats from *summa* to *ima* without using several staircases or jumping over a wall would have been deliberately difficult. Where each person sat mattered a great deal, and each seat had societal structuring as a built-in feature.

The seven front rows of the *ima cavea* were called the *podium* and were reserved for senators, priests, military heroes and foreign dignitaries. This most prestigious seating was carefully organised by rank. Senators of patrician status with consuls among their ancestors were given better seats, away from senators with plebeian ancestry. Fourteen wedges separated the uppermost crust from the *homines novi*. The top of the lowest band had twelve rows split into sixteen wedges and were allocated to men of equestrian rank. Equestrian rank had strata of its own, and Bomgardner makes a suggestion that one might chart the highs and lows of a knight's career by noting his changing seat allocation over time.[189]

The middle bank of seating had nineteen rows in sixteen wedges. Male citizens would be seated here if they had enough wealth to wear a toga. The subdivisions here were categorised by profession, wealth and age. The *summa cavea* at the top was for plebs, slaves, poor immigrants and women. While individual seats may not have been as closely allocated here as below, separation was still the order of the day. At the very top, there were boxes for rich women, out of view from the urban poor.

Spectators were seated according to a myriad of social factors, and most of them sat with their peers, in close proximity to those ahead and behind them on the social ladder. Potentially, one could look at a seat by tier (*maenianum*), wedge (*cuneus*), and row (*gradus*), and this could tell you a dizzying amount of information about who was to sit there. A specific seat revealed much of one's identity, and was a very public statement of your place in society.[190] Half of the amphitheatre experience was seeing, and the other half was being seen.

The token would therefore need to specify your seat number, section, which entrance you were to use, and the date of the performance. The system worked very efficiently, because imperial amphitheatres had dozens of numbered entrances,[191] corridors, and staircases underneath the seating, meaning there were many efficient routes to guide each token holder to their seat with minimum crowding. With each person following their assigned route, even the Colosseum could be fully seated or emptied in ten to twenty minutes,[192] a feat many modern stadiums cannot manage today.

It has been suggested that entrance tokens might have been distributed by ballots, with separate ballots needed for each section of seating. It's also possible that seating blocks designated for particular groups might have been given out in blocks for guilds and societies to hand out as they saw fit, or distributed through the patronage system that was so integral to Roman society. Either way, for many people a day at the amphitheatre was a very special day out indeed.

The popularity of the games meant economic opportunities. There would have been temporary market stalls selling various souvenirs to fans, such as the dozens of terracotta figurines and lamps with gladiators on them that survive to this day. These were mass-produced, as some of the moulds that have been excavated attest. Other canny vendors might sell cushions or fans for spectators who were willing to pay for a little comfort. For those who forgot a packed lunch, it was worth grabbing some food and drink from the snack stalls because the entertainments went on all day. Multiple amphitheatre excavations have found deposits containing the remains of various snacks, including nut shells, chewed chicken and pork bones, fruit stones and fish bones. It turns out that bloodsports had no effect on the average Roman appetite.

Venationes

The morning was devoted to animals. A huge import industry grew around the Roman desire to see animals in the arena, involving expert hunters, specialised transportation and animal handlers who kept the animals in captivity until they were needed. *Venationes* initially developed separately from gladiatorial events: before the construction of the Colosseum, they were more likely to be seen in large venues like the Circus Maximus as part of the *ludi circenses* or for a victorious general's ostentatious triumph. Some animals were displayed purely as exotic marvels, turning the arena into a temporary zoo. Some tamed species were even taught how to perform tricks; Pliny the Elder describes an elephant walking a tightrope.[193] Others would be forced to fight other animals, so that spectators could witness what a fight in the wild might look like, or watch trained hunters (*venatores* and *bestiarii*) hunt on horseback with packs of hunting dogs. Other *venatores* specialised in fighting animals on foot, usually with spears.

The most popular species of arena animal were bears, bulls and big cats (who were referred to under the umbrella term *africanae*, regardless of origin), though rhinoceroses, wolves, hippopotami, giraffes, crocodiles, ostriches and the aforementioned elephants are also attested in archaeology, art and literature. It has been previously assumed that 'big ticket' species were reserved for the grandest amphitheatres in the most important towns and that smaller Games relied on indigenous species, but recent research has proven that even small towns on the edge of empire witnessed incredible animals from opposite territories of Rome's influence; the skeleton of a *venator* was excavated in the English city of York, and his pelvis showed deep bite marks.[194] Osteoarchaeologists measured the size and shape of the depressions in the bone, and determined that the wound was caused by a large feline, probably a lion.

We know that Greek spectacles also had *venationes* thanks to art and epigraphy. Greeks also used the word 'hunt' for the morning show, but they used their own Greek word κυνηγέσιον (kynēgesion) rather than *venatio*. Animals displayed in eastern Games include lions, panthers, leopards, bulls, boars, ibex, gazelles, bears, ostriches and deer. It's interesting to note that there are far fewer gravestones of eastern beast hunters than gladiators. We cannot confirm if this means that they were simply less numerous, or less likely to purchase memorials for themselves.

Meridiani

Meridiani means noon, the time when the beast hunts would wind down. At this point in the Games, there was often a display of public executions. It used to be the consensus among scholars that the Roman world didn't use prison systems as a form of punishment itself, although exciting new research is challenging both that idea and the assumptions that underpinned those assumptions in previous scholarship.[195] It now seems likely that ancient Roman society had a range of carceral practices and that prisons were integral to its economic, political and social life. We remain confident, however, that public executions were a key element of ancient systems of punishment. The methods of execution, known as *summa supplicia*, were mainly beheading if the accused was a Roman citizen, but became demonstrably more imaginative, prolonged, and brutal when applied to foreigners and the enslaved. These executions in particular were deemed appropriate to stage in front of large crowds, for two main reasons: firstly, horrific executions were intended to serve as a deterrent to those tempted to commit a crime; and secondly, the population of each city needed to see that justice was being meted out. Public executions were a way for the populations to collectively see that anti-social behaviour had severe consequences.

Beasts from the morning shows could be used for a particular kind of execution; being killed by a wild animal in an arena falls under the method of capital punishment known as *damnatio ad bestias,* or 'condemnation by beast'. This was one form of *summa supplicia*: the severest methods of capital punishment for *noxii* (condemned criminals). Other methods included crucifixion (*damnatio in crucem*), being burnt (*vivi crematio*; literally 'living cremation'), beheading (*capitis amputatio*), and hanging (from a fork shaped pole: *furcam damnatio*). Other criminals were condemned *ad gladium*, and would be handed a wooden sword and forced to fight a professional gladiator. Many of these methods fell in and out of fashion over the centuries and were mostly reserved for slaves and foreigners. Free citizens could also be executed in a similar manner if their crime demanded a severe penalty, but they were usually punished less brutally.

After the criminals were all definitely dispatched, the arena was cleared of corpses and debris in preparation for the main event: gladiators.

Gladiatorial Combat: The Rules

Far from the frenzied battles that Hollywood's arenas provide, gladiatorial combat in the amphitheatre was far more structured. We know that combats had rules, although unfortunately we are unable to reconstruct exactly what they were as no gladiatorial manual survives. Frescoes and mosaics confirm that most fights were closely monitored by two referees: the *summa rudis* and *secunda rudis*. It's likely that the roles went to former gladiators who were intimately familiar with how a combat should be fought. We also know from artwork that the referees carried long rods which they held out between the fighters to pause the duel. This could have been because there were illegal manoeuvres that went against the enforced spirit of fairness, but also to ensure that the fight didn't descend into unregulated carnage. The Romans appreciated a fair, evenly matched fight between gladiators because it made the bout more technically interesting. Dirty tactics might be attempted, but would be quickly shut down by the referees. Referees were also on hand if the fight needed to be stopped for any reason. A snippet from Suetonius gives one clue about this. It seems that if a gladiator fell over, the fight would be paused so that he could get back onto his feet safely before the fight could be resumed. Suetonius recounts that Claudius, whom he describes as enjoying gladiatorial fights like common men did, insisted that, if a gladiator fell, he should be killed.[196] This anecdote comes from a section specifically designed by Suetonius to demonstrate that Claudius was unusually cruel so we can assume that, outside of his reign (41–54 CE), falls were not something a gladiator need be too concerned about.

Artistic depictions of referees also suggest that arena officials stepped in to pause their fight if a serious blow was struck, and a decision would be made before it could continue. Certain bouts were fought *ad digitum*, meaning 'to the finger.' Again, artwork gives us precious clues that this involved a gladiator holding up his arm with his index finger outstretched. It was how a gladiator indicated that he was yielding to his opponent because he was too injured or exhausted to continue, and no blows were allowed to be struck after the finger was extended. The fight would then end, and, in some cases, the loser's fate would be in the hands of the *editor*. The crowd would be yelling their opinions on what should happen next, whether the loser should live to fight another day, or whether he had performed poorly enough to forfeit his life. It was common for losers to walk out of the arena, if they had still managed to win over the crowd. It is also likely that referees paused the match upon significant injury, making the call on whether the fight could or should continue. Other fights were fought *sine missione*, without mercy. No reprieve was granted to the losers in this case, and, if they hadn't already been killed during the actual bout, they would be quickly dispatched by their opponent using a single thrust of the sword. This sort of match was actually banned by Augustus, though the ban didn't prove permanent. In extraordinary circumstances, a tie might be declared, as in the case of Priscus and Verus at the inaugural games in the Colosseum.[197]

Surprisingly few fights ended with death. Depending on the century and location, it is estimated that a gladiator had between a one-in-five to a one-in-ten chance of a fatal outcome. In the Greek world, this is confirmed by gravestones which mention both the number of victories won and the larger numbers of total bouts fought. Death could result in several ways: a well-placed injury could kill a gladiator mid-fight, but it's debatable whether many gladiators would deliberately attempt to kill knowing that the *editor* would have to compensate the owner of his opponent and might be very put out at having his hand (and purse) forced. In a *sine missione* (without mercy) match, this would not be a concern as someone was required to die. In other matches, which were far more common, death could be decided for the loser if he had failed to put on a good show or if he was so injured that a quick death would be a mercy. The exact method of dispatching doomed gladiators seems to vary by region, both in artwork and osteo-archaeological evidence. The death-blow was designed to deal death quickly, and the gladiator was expected to remain stoic throughout, showing contempt for death in the face of his demise. Common methods included cuts to the throat, or a blade driven down into the ribcage from the shoulder, so that suffering was minimal, as suffering wasn't the point once the decision had been made. It can't have been easy for the victor to execute his opponent. In smaller shows, there may have only been one gladiatorial *familia* hired, which would mean that gladiators were fighting the same men they trained, ate and lived with every day. This was another reason to make the death blow quick. There is some evidence that gladiators resented this part of the Games; when some victors hesitated to kill their opponents, the emperor Commodus punished them by having them executed too.[198]

Death wasn't guaranteed but, as the osteo-archaeological evidence from Ephesus attests, gladiatorial bouts could still be incredibly dangerous. Multiple healed wounds confirm that gladiators were given exemplary medical care and were able to continue in their careers, and the most famous Roman physician, Galen, earned his exemplary reputation after his service as *ludus* surgeon in his hometown of Pergamon. Gladiators were a valuable commodity who had significant amounts of money invested in their upkeep: most *lanistae* were keen to protect such investments by providing nutritional food and expert medical care. Both epitaphs and skeletal remains do confirm, however, that death was not entirely preventable in the arena. The largest percentage of wounds in the Ephesus gladiators were found on the skull, which we would be too quick to assume is explained by the head being a main target. Rather, we should bear in mind that cuts that sever arteries or puncture vital organs do not necessarily reach the bone. These were the types of injuries that even the best physicians were powerless to help.

The Appeal

Why did Romans enjoy watching the gladiators fight? That's a question on which historians can never quite agree, but it's worth dispelling one prevalent misunderstanding straight away. The Romans did not watch gladiators because they had a collective insatiable bloodlust. It's a common misconception that, while it is slowly becoming less prevalent, isn't helped by Hollywood swords 'n' sandals movies that insist on depicting Roman spectators as a mindless, savage mass. The reality is far more complicated, but if we try to truly understand why Romans enjoyed watching men fight, we end up learning so much more about their culture.

Various historians have put forward their own theories, and I believe that the arena was a multi-faceted place in which many of these theories can co-exist.[199] As with modern forms of entertainment, individuals within the mass of spectators had certain aspects of that entertainment that they favoured over others, and personal, emotional responses to different elements of each fight. A thousand people can attend the same event, but none have an identical experience or emotional response because each person has a unique identity. It is for this reason that many explanations for the Roman fascination can comfortably co-exist, and why we should be hesitant to homogenise the spectators too much. Historians are at a disadvantage, simply because we have no written accounts of attending games from a fan's point of view. All we have are critiques from writers who were either ambivalent or openly hostile towards the phenomenon.[200] We can't take these accounts at face value, so speculation is unavoidable.

The first theory is that life in Rome was often unpleasant. The vast majority of the city population was poor, and worked incredibly hard out of financial necessity. For many, home was a cramped apartment with poor ventilation, little natural light and no plumbing, in crowded tenements where landlords could charge eye-watering rents. The city was rife with crime, with no police force to inhibit it. Life would be more comfortable for those who could afford to purchase an enslaved person, for whom life was generally far worse than being poor and free. Infant mortality was high, and diseases that are easily medicated with modern medicine meant that for many, life was painful and short. Festival days were an essential respite from the mundanity and frustration of living hand to mouth. Alongside the chariot racing in the Circus Maximus, a day at the Colosseum could be seen as a much-needed safe space to let off some steam. The entertainments offered diversion, but also a chance to revel in aggression, albeit vicariously. It would be inappropriate to take out latent rage on an annoying neighbour or a swindling shopkeeper, but watching extreme violence in a controlled environment was a socially acceptable method of expelling some tension. Just as modern society produces hyper-violent movies, video games, and television shows, Romans in the amphitheatre felt comfortable watching violence that they knew was unacceptable for themselves in 'real' life to indulge in. With this 'safety valve' in place, it was hoped that citizens would release enough pent-up stress watching gladiators in the Colosseum that they wouldn't resort to rioting because of their harsh living conditions outside of it.

The theory has its issues: for many of the upper and middle classes in the *ima* and *media cavea*, life was in fact rather comfortable. More than this, Rome remained a violent place outside of the arena. Domestic violence was a common issue across the social spectrum,[201] and robberies and assaults seem commonplace, particularly at night. If watching gladiators was supposed to be a cathartic purging of emotional frustration before that frustration erupted into a physical, violent release, it doesn't seem to have worked. As with modern discussions about violent video games, it could be asked whether the arena even gave a sense of permission to certain spectators with violent tendencies, rather than acting as a safe outlet for rough urges. It could also be suggested, though, that exposure to gladiatorial combat served as a kind of inoculation against the violence of daily life, which was seen as helpful for coping with life in the city as well as a battlefield.

Another idea centres on the gladiator as the ideal alpha male. Romans had a concept called *virtus*, or virtue,[202] which was a set of attributes that all men should possess to be excellent.[203] The attributes included physical courage, mental fortitude, discipline and self-control. The term had several applications, from an ideal soldier on the battlefield to an exemplary politician in the Senate; men could demonstrate *virtus* in any walk of life. It's a complex, fluid and loaded term. It's also a term that was normally only applied to citizen males. Gladiators were not citizens; prisoners of war and men bought at slave markets were already low in Roman society, but even a free citizen who volunteered for the gladiatorial career (known as *auctorati*, literally 'men who had hired themselves out') was stripped of some of their civic rights when they signed up. They became *infamia*, from which we get our word infamy. This was an irreversible reduction of civic status and social standing, inflicted upon perpetrators of certain crimes as well as those in professions including sex workers, actors, dancers, executioners, undertakers and gladiators. It came with social stigma; few respectable people would want to be associated with *infames*, though there are exceptions to every rule.[204]

This theory suggests that the gladiator was the ultimate teaching tool of *virtus*. Under the premise of a day of entertainment, Romans would receive an educational demonstration of what it meant to be a man. Gladiators were tough, they were brave and they were experts in their skillset. An ordinary Roman could watch an impressive gladiator and want to emulate the qualities they displayed on the arena floor, because the attributes of *virtus* were transferable to other walks of life. If we use a modern equivalent, the prevalence of Hollywood movies based on the American military perform a similar role; on a surface level the movies are popcorn entertainment, but they also communicate the ideal attributes of a soldier, and present being an exemplary soldier as aspirational. Few in the cinema will experience combat, but they can imagine themselves in a character's shoes, and consider how they might conduct themselves in similar circumstances. In this theory, the arena asks: 'This is what it takes to be a man – would you measure up?' Romans were proud to see themselves as a military society, even if, by the imperial period, few citizens in the city had ever set foot on a battlefield. By creating a form of mass entertainment that was so militarily coded, ordinary Romans could still engage with battle (from the safety of their seats) and consider themselves connoisseurs of combat.

The arena, much like Second World War movies, also presents an idealised death. Gladiators were taught to accept death without obvious emotion and to remain calm as their opponent struck a killing blow. Losing composure by screaming, begging, sobbing or attempting to flee was unthinkable. This was the ultimate lesson; a true man of *virtus* controlled himself until the very end, and didn't let any weakness consume him. In a war movie, that would be the doomed soldier who never stops firing his weapon, even when wounded and dying. Expectations around the behaviour of men in situations of extreme stress have long been formed around an idealised concept of properly masculine conduct. Gladiators, then, served to demonstrate both how to live, and how to die. This is where their status as *infames* becomes particularly interesting:

it has been suggested that their inferior status was necessary to allow Romans to watch their deaths without feeling nagging pangs of guilt. The Romans were very well aware that they dehumanised gladiators, it wasn't a subconscious phenomenon; there was no room for sympathy in the arena stalls. For the gladiator himself, embodying *virtus* through his own excellence and eventually the manner in which he approached his own mortality may have been a way to regain some of the dignity he'd had stripped from him. Regardless of *infamia*, a degree of respect might be earned.

A third proposed explanation relates to Rome as an imperial power, with an awareness and anxiety about what that meant for the citizens of the city itself. Erik Gunderson's theory suggests that the Colosseum functioned as a kind of empire in reverse.[205] In day-to-day life, Rome (despite being the largest city in the world at the time) was a tiny pinprick on the map in comparison to the vast territories it controlled. Rome itself was surrounded by provinces it had conquered and taken by force, filled with millions of people who lived under Roman rule who could (and frequently did) revolt at any given time, and, beyond the provinces, more than 3,000 miles of borders needed constant protection from foreign kings and tribes. It took a lot of concerted effort, money and troops to keep the provinces ticking over quietly, and to keep the borders secure. Despite its outwardly cocky displays of dominance, Rome itself plausibly had good reason to feel a little anxious.[206]

However, Gunderson invites us to think of the amphitheatre as the opposite; the arena is the tiny speck in the centre, populated with gladiators dressed as historic foes and barbarians and animals imported from all over the empire and beyond. The population of the city was, in the *cavea*, a huge mass of people that completely surrounded the arena. Now, the city was the majority, and, to soothe its anxieties, it wielded tight control over the arena, which was far easier to manage than the empire itself. The Colosseum was therefore a place where Romans could be reassured that everything was fine. What better way to demonstrate that Rome had everything under control than seeing thousands of animals from the farthest corners of its dominions; Rome could even bend nature to her will. As for the gladiators, the citizens (through their chants) had a say in whether human beings lived or died. Even the poorest plebeians could yell '*mitte!*' ('spare him!') or '*iugula!*' ('kill him!') and a sensible emperor took the crowd's chants in mind before announcing the fate of a defeated fighter. There would be no revolts or dissension from the arena; Rome might struggle to keep an empire calm, but it micromanaged the Colosseum with startling efficiency. Whether or not this theory is applicable to the amphitheatres of the provinces is debatable; while some may have been comforted by the protection offered by Rome and considered it a good trade-off for autonomy, others may have considered such a distillation of imperialist authority a little too close to the bone.

A final compelling theory, and one that I believe is fundamental to understanding the gladiatorial phenomenon, is simply that humans often seem compelled to watch violence – in both the past and the present. There is a popular saying that 'the past is a foreign country, they do things differently there'. Older scholarship has often used this concept to denounce gladiatorial combat as brutishly alien, so wicked that the scholars felt compelled to turn away from the topic as much as possible. The idea of making men fight to the death was simply too horrific to comprehend. It threatened to topple the interest, and in some corners of academia, the respect these scholars held for ancient Rome. I have two issues with this moralistic handwringing.

My first is that any Roman scholar should be easily able to identify plenty to disgust them about the ancient Roman world outside of the arena, but we find few similarly emotional condemnations for, say, the cruelties of Roman imperialism or slavery. Imperialism and slavery are still very much concerns in the modern world,[207] which might lead one to wonder why scholars have reserved their condemnation (and their florid use of emotive adjectives) for gladiators over issues more directly applicable to modern life. This tide is turning, but slowly and not without pushback. For some for whom Rome remains an ideal, it remains more comfortable to treat gladiation as an oddly inhumane quirk of Roman society, rather than a logical product of its inherent callousness in other spheres of daily life.

My second is that when gladiation is approached as a unique and inexplicable phenomenon, it doesn't just provide an opportunity to downplay other Roman oppressions in comparison; it also fails to attempt to understand the human fascination with violence. Garrett Fagan explored this in his book *The Lure of the Arena*, noting that public executions have been a feature of many societies since the Mesopotamians through to several modern states.[208] He argues that, even when the methods of execution were sickening in their creativity, hundreds or even thousands of people were still drawn to witness them, which suggests a morbid curiosity and involuntary thrill that humans experience when witnessing violence being inflicted, as well as from inflicting it. Violent sports are not unique to the Romans. Hunting and contact sports existed long before Rome, and still exist in many forms today.

Even if death were not the point of a gladiatorial combat, it remains true that the fatality rate of gladiators was far higher than modern boxers, wrestlers and bullfighters. Does this suggest that modern society does not have the same propensity for enjoying watching violence? I would hesitate to make this conclusion, because we still ingest an enormous amount of violence for our entertainment – we just mostly simulate it now. Humans are clearly curious about witnessing violence, but have usually required a justification for feeding the fascination. Often, we have invented a long list of 'get out of jail free cards' to absolve us from guilt. Watching an execution is excusable, because the condemned strayed from the agreed bonds of society and thus 'deserves' the pain and spectacle of the execution. Watching footage of fatal accidents on the news is OK, because we are informing ourselves of current events, and accidents happen. Watching athletes or performers risk death in perilous sports or stunts is fine, because if the worst happens, we can tell ourselves that they 'knew what they were getting into'. Humans still retain the capacity to tolerate, or even derive pleasure, from pain and death on a mass scale. In the genocide of Palestinians in Gaza (still ongoing at the time of writing), some Israeli civilians have set up viewing platforms where they can picnic while surveying bombs being dropped on the people they believe have no right to exist on that land. Justifying violence, both perpetrating and bearing witness to, has always existed and continues to exist in society on both micro and macro levels.

For many of us, the justification we use to soothe our niggling guilt about consuming violence is to keep it fictional. We are content to read murder mystery novels in the comfort of armchairs. We can happily watch actors simulate brutal acts on stage and screen, particularly when theatre props or special effects create realistic bloody wounds. Video games can be notoriously and gratuitously violent (and with arguably less ideological justification) and yet remain one of the most common forms of entertainment. On any given day, gaming consoles, movies, television and novels expose us to imaginative forms of violence in a volume that even Romans couldn't conceive. We happily pay significant amounts of money to watch depictions of wars (both real and fictive), people getting eaten alive by dinosaurs or aliens, serial killers hunting down high schoolers, women getting brutalised before we see detectives attempt to solve the case and mafiosos torture spies. These scenes are unfalteringly graphic, but we rarely switch off. We should bear this in mind before we judge Romans too harshly: I suspect that some corners of modern society would once again accept unsimulated gladiators if enough manufactured consent (and money) could be made. All that the Romans required was dehumanisation, and we're still very adept at that.

In conclusion, perhaps the main appeal of gladiation was that it was, in its simplest form, thrilling. Each match had an uncertain outcome, the stakes were high, and spectators were easily drawn into becoming emotionally invested in the events. Spectating was a communal activity that fostered a sense of community and belonging, as with any other large-scale entertainment event. Adrenaline was pumping for gladiators and spectators alike. For gladiators, it was imperative that they put on a good show and use every single manoeuvre and tactic they'd learned in training. For spectators, there was the permissive rush that came from being in a huge crowd, part of a community coming together for a single purpose. Far from a day of chaos and carnage, the programme was a day of carefully regulated violence that served an ideological purpose: promotion of masculine ideals, promotion of Roman imperialism and a demonstration of Roman dominion over both humans and nature. As we move to discuss how gladiators were received by Greeks, it will be interesting to see if ideology was exported as successfully as *armaturae* were.

Chapter 9

Life in the Ludus

It's important to understand exactly what a gladiator actually was, particularly as we've just learned that they shared an arena with beast hunters and condemned criminals. *Venators* and *bestiarii*, the beast hunters, were not interchangeable with gladiators. They were trained separately, and, in Rome, had their own training school and accommodation in the *Ludus Matutinus* (which replaced an earlier *Ludus Bestiarius*).[209] Gladiators never fought animals, only each other. The word that Greek intellectuals used for gladiators was *monomachoi*, meaning one-on-one fighters, which further illustrates this point.

Gladiators were professionals, in the sense that they were all working under a contract. For enslaved gladiators, this meant that their *lanista* legally owned them. Sometimes condemned criminals were sold to the *lanista* on the assumption that death would find them eventually. For freeborn citizens or freedmen, their contract with the *lanista* was slightly different; their time in the *ludus* could be specified in their contract as a certain number of years to be served or the number of fights to be performed. All gladiators were paid for each match, regardless of their status, and the *lanista* took a cut to cover their purchase, training, and accommodation costs. Earning money meant that gladiators could potentially buy out their contracts or buy their freedom, and additional prize money from victories allowed those who survived the arena to potentially retire quite comfortably. In some cases, even some condemned criminals could earn their freedom if they fought successfully enough times, with the hardships of the profession perhaps seen as penance enough and redemption a suitable reward for exemplary performances. The final aspect of gladiators that separated them from the men sent out to die during the lunchtime break was their training. Gladiators were not men who had wooden swords pushed into their hands moments before being thrown into an arena, otherwise entirely unprepared. Those men were not gladiators; they were a sideshow. Gladiators were highly trained, highly specialised experts in their craft. They lived (at least in their initial training) in the *ludus* in which they trained, bunking in cells.[210] They spent every day training with wooden weapons (partly to prevent unnecessary injuries but also to prevent rebellion), mainly practising weapons manoeuvres against a wooden post called a *palus*.

Gladiators were ranked according to their skill level, and the system was named after this training; a top gladiator was a *primus palus*, below him was the *secundus palus,* and so on. A gladiator's *palus* ranking directly determined his performance fee and prize amounts, which were eventually capped to prevent gladiatorial shows bankrupting their sponsors. Every gladiator wanted to work and live long enough to ascend this hierarchy – not just for glory, but for the earning potential. Daily training continued throughout a gladiator's career, allowing him to master his skills and keep in peak physical condition. A gladiator might have resided in the *ludus* for many months before he ever entered the arena because spectators expected a decent show and weren't impressed by amateurish performances. In fact, clumsy fighting was enough to turn a crowd against a gladiator, and they would likely call for his death if he disappointed them. Initial training was essential to survive the early stages of a career, and the hard-won experience of multiple combats with real weapons in front of a crowd allowed men to progress into top fighters.

Gladiatorial Types

When gladiation was first developing in Rome, early combatants were frequently prisoners of war. Making these prisoners fight to the death was useful in several ways: the combatants were conveniently captured already bearing arms and armour, meaning that there were no costs to kit them out; they were usually trained enough in warfare to put on a decent show with minimal cowardice and clumsiness; and it was an effective way to humiliate the defeated enemy. It could boost morale amongst Rome's own survivors who had just experienced the horrors of the battlefield or citizens who wanted some closure after having lost brothers, sons and husbands in war; they got to see the 'perpetrators' of their pain being punished in front of them. Alternatively, men enslaved, both at home and abroad, were plentiful and inexpensive, meaning that they were both affordable and considered to be expendable. The enslaved were considered the lowest class, worth less even than a foreign captive, and Rome frequently had an almost inexhaustible supply of both. Enslaved men would be equipped with whatever was lying around, resulting in some hodge podge combinations of arms and armour. It took a while for gladiatorial types, known as armatures or *armaturae*, to develop and become standardised. A number of styles became popular, each with their own distinctive arms and armour.

Initially, in keeping with the habit of making prisoners of war fight for their entertainment, Romans developed these early *armaturae* based on their historical enemies and rivals. One of these *armaturae*, the *samnite*, was apparently inherited from Rome's allies in Campania,[211] a coastal region that included the cities of Capua, Naples, and Pompeii, which had a long rivalry with their neighbours in the mountainous region of Samnium. As Rome swallowed up its neighbours into its empire, it became a bit of a touchy subject to have gladiators named after peoples who were now part of the wider culture. The *samnite* and *gallus* types were quietly rebranded into geographically 'neutral' types, though the *thraex* was never renamed. By the Late Republican and Early Imperial period, the categories of gladiator were diverse. These categories were now split into three groups:

- *scutarii*, those who wielded a large shield called a *scutum*.
- *parmularii*, who carried a smaller shield of which the *parma* type was common; and
- a third group, who used no shield at all, and seem to have had no common collective name.

Early in their training, before they ever entered an arena, novice gladiators would be assessed according to their build and agility, and then would be assigned to the *armature* they were most suited to. Each *armature* had its own distinctive kit and fighting style, and typically there were traditional opponents for each type. This diversity ensured that a programme of several fights over an afternoon would each be different and that the audience would not get bored. The specialised expertise of each *armature* was a great source of professional pride, and few gladiators (east or west) called themselves such, they referred to themselves by their specialisation.

All gladiators wore a base outfit of a *subligaculum*, or loincloth. That was secured in place by a *balteus*, a thick leather belt. Different pieces of arms and armour were then added to each *armaturae* to build up their defences. Basic armour included greaves for leg protection, known as an *ocrea* (pl. *ocreae*) typically worn over leg padding. Arms could also be padded, which could then be covered by a *manica* (pl. *manicae*) on the forearms or a *galerus* that protected the shoulder. The extremities were well protected, but the torso was always bare. This is one of the key differences between ancient gladiators and soldiers, who depended on protecting their chests with breastplates or chainmail tunics. The exclusion of torso protection lent gladiatorial bouts an extra layer of difficulty for the fighters, and gladiatorial fighting styles developed to take torso protection into account. Shields became crucial.

Scutarii

These gladiators were the heavyweights, the armoured tanks of the arena. They each carried a *scutum*. These shields weren't exclusive to gladiators; many different types of ancient warrior used a version of it, including Roman legionaries. They were rectangular and semi cylindrical, weighing around 10kg, and, if held in the correct position, should sit with the uppermost edge just above the bottom of the helmet, and the bottom edge sitting just below the top rim of the leg protection. The semi-cylindrical curves served to wrap around the front of the body. As such, in a proper defensive stance, there should be very little skin showing, leaving not much for an opponent to aim for. If the gladiator's arm got tired and he let the shield drop down even slightly, he left himself vulnerable. The most interesting thing about this shield is that a gladiator could do some serious damage with it in attack; it had a metal boss in the centre to protect the hand that he was holding it with which he could use to push into his opponent. Alternatively, he could bring the bottom edge of the shield down onto his opponent's foot, or the upper edge up beneath his chin to try and dislodge the helmet. Far from the sword-on-sword clanging that we see in cinematic gladiator fights, we should imagine shield on shield pushing as *scutarii* pairings sought to knock each other off balance in order to expose some vulnerable skin. The *scutarii* relied on their shields for protection, but also had helmets and some protection for their limbs.

All the *scutarii* also carried a *gladius*, the sword that gave gladiators their name. Again, these weren't exclusive to gladiators; it was a standard issue weapon for legionaries. Until the early first century CE, the blade was typically 50cm in length, but was shortened down to around 35cm in the following centuries; the early sword was excellent for both slashing motions as well as stabbing, while the shorter version was only really useful for jabbing motions.[212] This jabbing method conserved a lot of energy, and a seasoned fighter would be able to aim his jabs very carefully to find the miniscule gaps between shield and armour.

Interestingly, we know about the jabbing approach to gladiatorial fighting because of the popularity of gladiators in the Greek east. We have a lot of art from the eastern Mediterranean featuring gladiators, and how they're depicted can tell us a lot. For instance, a majority of *scutarii* there are depicted with a different weapon. Instead of a *gladius*, Greeks seem to have preferred the *pugio*, a triangular shaped blade that was much shorter than a *gladius*, and is classed by some as a dagger rather than a sword. Because the blade was about half the length of a *gladius*, the *pugio* was even less likely to be used for slashing and cutting. It was really great for jabbing though, which is how it gets its name; *pugio* comes from the Proto-Indo-European root *pewǵ*, meaning 'punch' or 'fist'. The Greek word for boxing uses the same root, and is called *pygmachia*, which means 'fist fighting'. The Greeks may have preferred to use the *pugio* simply because it suited their gladiatorial style better.

The second set of evidence relates to gladiatorial epigraphy. Michael Carter has carefully studied the language used in six inscriptions from Sagalassos, Thyateira, Gortyn, Smyrna, Ephesus, and Miletus.[213] They are all commemorations of specific Games given by a named *editor* (usually an *asiarch* or priest of the imperial cult) in order to boost their prestige. After all, what was the point of giving a grand Games if nobody recorded such generosity for posterity? These six stones have the same unexpected statement: the weapons used by the gladiators of these specific Games were sharp. This might come as a surprise – after all, swords and daggers are famously designed to be sharp so why is this worth mentioning? A swimming competition would never be advertised as taking place in a wet pool. The answer can only be that sharpened weapons were actually not the arena norm. Carter notes that the Greek word used is οξύς (oxys), which can be translated as 'sharp' but is more specifically translated as 'pointy'. He therefore hypothesises that the lengths of the blade were still sharp, but that the tip of the blade was usually blunted except on these rare occasions. These blunted tips are only effective as a safety measure if the main technique is stabbing, rather than slashing, otherwise the blades would be dulled as well. Of course, cuts from a slash are easier to survive and medically treat than a punching stab to the abdomen.[214]

The *scutarii* were divided as a category into the *provocator* (the 'challenger'), the *secutor* (the 'chaser'), and the *murmillo* (the 'fish man'). Because the *scutum* was large, the *scutarii* only needed one *manica* on the sword arm. The *provocatores* fought other *provocatores*, armoured tank versus armoured tank. For this reason, they protected both legs with greaves that reached to the knee. *Murmillones* and *secutores*, however, fought *parmularii*, who were lightly armoured and quicker on their feet. A higher degree of agility was required to deal with nimble opponents, so only the forward leg was protected by a greave. Helmets were also designed with opponents in mind: the *provocatores* wore one that flared down around the neck, deflecting blows, and, if the restricted vision of the protective visor was a problem, at least it was the same for their opponent. The *murmillo*, whose traditional opponents had curved swords or spears, needed a large peak over their face for protection, and the helmet also had a distinctive 'fin' as a crest. In contrast, the *secutores* fought *retiarii* armed with tridents and nets, so their helmets were completely smooth to prevent the *secutor* getting snagged, and two tiny eye holes that a trident would (hopefully) fail to penetrate. With helmets clocking in at nearly 3kg, the sword at 1kg, and the shield at 10kg (not to mention the greave and arm guards), *scutarii* needed to be muscular, with considerable stamina. Their best tactic was to stand firm and defensive while allowing their opponent to tire, before dealing a carefully aimed blow.

Parmularii

With smaller shields, *parmularii* were more agile but they needed to be: protecting the torso required more effort and *parmularii* needed to be able to dodge blows quickly. The two main *armaturae* were both particularly relevant to the Greek world, because they had inspiration from the same region. The *thraex* was one of the early *armaturae* that had a faintly xenophobic tinge, as they were supposed to represent Thracian warriors. Interestingly, this *armature* was never rebranded like the *samnite* or *gallus*, who were morphed into *secutor* and *murmillo*. The name and the xenophobia remained. The *thraex* was armed with a small shield that could be square, oval, rectangular, or circular. Because the shield was small, he wore *ocreae* on both legs, and they reached up past the mid-thigh instead of stopping at the top of the knee cap. The sword arm was protected with a *manica*, and the helmet had a wide brim and a visor to protect the face, topped with a distinctive crest in the shape of a griffon. The sword of the *thraex* was known as a *sica*, and the blade was bent in the middle so that it almost resembled a boomerang. This allowed for a unique fighting style that encouraged curving slashes aimed at the sides and back of an opponent. The *sica* was the only part of this *armature* that had any authentic connection to Thracian warfare at all, and, to the population of Thrace, this gladiator must have been seen as a bit of a parody, if not a derogatory caricature.

When we plot our evidence for the existence of *thraeces* onto a map, we see some very interesting information that suggests this to be true. A collection of volumes named *Epigrafia Anfiteatrale dell'Occidente Romano* (Amphitheatre Epigraphy of the Roman West, which I'll abbreviate to *EAOR*) is an exhaustive collection of every known inscription regarding gladiators in the western

European provinces, organised by region. The evidence from the rest of the empire is not included, as most of it was catalogued by Louis Robert in 1940, and gladiatorial inscriptions from African provinces have yet to be collated and published at all. However, even if we just focus on western Europe, the evidence in the *EAOR* tells us that the *thraex* is the second most attested *armature* in the west. They were clearly wildly popular. Having mapped references to *thraeces* in the eastern half of the empire, they remain popular, if not to the same extent. They are attested in nearly every region we cover in this book, but there is not a single sign of them in Thrace. We know that Thracians embraced gladiation as an entertainment, because they adapted several venues in the region in order to host it, and we have evidence of other types of gladiator being present as well, but Thracians seem to have roundly rejected the *thraex*. Of course, we're working with an incomplete set of evidence, but compared with the even distributions of other *armaturae* across neighbouring areas, the absence of any *thraex* in Thrace is noteworthy, and potentially signals a boycott of an *armature* deemed culturally insensitive.

We should, then, ask if the pattern is also true for the *hoplomachos*, which was another *parmularii* and this time one that was based on a Greek hoplite. The *hoplomachos* doesn't appear very often in evidence within the *EAOR*, and only once after the first century CE. In the west, it seems like the *hoplomachos* was a niche *armature* that fell out of favour. The eastern evidence for the *hoplomachos* isn't exactly overwhelming either, but there is definitely a presence. Reliefs of *hoplomachi* have been found in Ephesus, Aphrodisias and Halicarnassus.[215] While this seems scant, Asia Minor was home to nearly a quarter of attested *hoplomachi* reliefs and inscriptions recorded across the entire empire. There are also several *hoplomachi* depicted on terracotta lamps that were produced en masse in Cyprus and Asia Minor; the *hoplomachos*, even if niche, was recognisable enough to warrant mass production of memorabilia. So why was the *thraex* rejected in Thrace, but the *hoplomachos* was welcome in Asia Minor?

The *hoplomachos* should, theoretically, have been far more popular across the entire empire. The *hoplomachos* was armed to the teeth, starting the fight with a spear, known as a *dory*, as his primary weapon. This was a one-handed thrusting weapon, to be used at a distance. From art, we know that they ranged between around 6-7ft long. A *hoplomachos* could wield it overarm, aiming at the head or shoulders of his opponent, though this left his side dangerously exposed. An alternative was to tuck it underarm, close to the body, to thrust into the belly. He'd likely be facing a *murmillo*, and we know that they had pretty much full armour coverage, so accuracy with the spear would be key.

A good tactic might be to harass the shoulders of the opponent, to wear him out and make his defensive arm droop or weaken his sword arm. Another sensible ploy would be to goad the *murmillo*, weighed down with all that armour, into going on the offensive, tiring him out. Once the opponent tired, the game became far easier as the *hoplomachos* had a secondary weapon. If the *murmillo* managed to get within striking distance, or the *hoplomachos* dropped the spear, he could switch to his *gladius* or *pugio*. Rather than grip his shield handle with his hand, it would be strapped to his arm leaving his defensive hand free to grip the sword, making the switch quick and fluid.

At these close quarters, weaponry between the two *armaturae* was evenly matched, but the shields varied in size, leaving the *hoplomachos* vulnerable in comparison. Then again, the *parma* shield weighed about a fifth of a *scutum*, so the *hoplomachos* would not tire as quickly. The differing kit of a *hoplomachos* was also designed to compensate for less shield cover. Like the *thraex*, their greaves came further up the leg. Worn correctly, these didn't impede movement too much. The *hoplomachos* also had the standard *manica* protecting his offensive arm, and his torso was completely bare. From artwork, we know that the standard helmet had a face visor protecting the eyes but limiting vision. It was augmented with a broad brim that would hopefully deflect blows, and came with the most elaborate crest possible, frequently topped with a plume of large, dramatic feathers.

The agility and multi-weapon fighting style of the *hoplomachos* may not have been the sole reason that Greeks nearly single-handedly made sure that their existence carried over into the second and third centuries, however. Nearly all Greeks knew the stories most famously recounted in the *Iliad* in the Roman period and were familiar with key scenes of the epic poem. In analysis of the text, just over 80 per cent of all injuries in the *Iliad* where the weapon is specified are caused by spears, followed by swords at just over 9 per cent.[216] The Homeric language is stark in its descriptions of the kind of injuries one would inflict with a spear, and it's clear that it was an effective weapon in experienced hands. For Greeks wishing to witness or participate in combats similar to the iconic battles they grew up listening to in stories, the *hoplomachos* would have been the ideal solution as the only gladiatorial class using the spear, the quintessential weapon of the *Iliad*. This likely explains the wider popularity of the *hoplomachos*.

Some of the most exciting fighting techniques came from gladiators with no shields. The *retiarius*, or 'net man', was the only gladiator not permitted a helmet, and he had no protection on either of his legs. One arm was padded from wrist to shoulder, where a metal *galerus* acted as a shield to protect the neck. As such, they were the least protected gladiator class. Their main defence was the speed, stamina and agility that came with unimpaired vision and nothing heavy weighing them down. For an *armature* so vulnerable, it may seem strange that they are the most prevalently attested class in both halves of the empire. The answer lies in their weaponry, which ensured a tense and compelling fight. Against the armoured tank of a *murmillo* or *secutor*, the *retiarius* was armed with a long trident (*fuscina*) and a weighted rope net (*rete*, which gives the *retiarius* his name). He was the fisherman of the arena. A *retiarius* was practised in hurling his net just so, expertly tripping up opponents, yanking shields and weapons out of their hands, or toppling an opponent by pulling the net down over his head. Only those ignorant of arena tactics underestimated the *retiarius*, and osteo-archaeological evidence from Ephesus shows exactly how dangerous a net fighter could be. A cemetery in the city was discovered to contain the burials of at least sixty-six gladiators; this conclusion was drawn not only by their *in-situ* gravestones detailing their identities, but by the extensive wounds noticeable on their bones. At least one individual skull shows two puncture wounds that go straight through the bone, 5cm apart. Specialist archaeologists determined that the wound was caused by a powerful blow from a trident, particularly since a fishing trident from the same period found in Ephesus harbour had prongs exactly 5cm apart. They were even able to determine that the central prong was barbed, which not only made the trident more fearsome, but was theorised to be a helpful addition if used as a hook to dislodge a helmet or shield.[217]

One issue that scholars have repeatedly found specifically with Greek gladiators is that sometimes when a gladiator's type is stated on a gravestone or in art, the figure doesn't have exactly the pieces of arms and armour we consider to be correct for that type. For instance, a Greek *secutor* might be wearing the wrong helmet, or a *murmillo* might be wearing the wrong greaves. This sometimes means that the best attempt of categorisation we can make is 'scutarius' or 'parmularius'. However, these distinctions were important. We don't have a single gladiatorial tombstone where a fighter calls themselves a 'gladiator', they referred to themselves very specifically by their fighting style.

There are many possible explanations for why Greek gladiators didn't always have exactly the same armour that their Roman counterparts had. It might be that gladiatorial troupes were forced to share arms and armour in common. The *familia* might not have enough funds to create a bespoke set of arms and armour for each fighter, particularly given that most fighters might only have used their equipment once or twice.[218] For shows with a long list of fighting pairs, multiple men could have been sharing equipment throughout the day. Having an armoury of shared equipment might have affected whether each gladiator wore armour that completely matched western expectations. Another possible explanation is that figurines and lamps that depict Greek gladiators were made by ceramicists who weren't completely versed in *armaturae*, and that sculptors may have had pre-made gravestones available for purchase; a *provocator* without the cash for a bespoke design might have had to make do with an 'off the rack' gravestone depicting an amalgamation of *scutarii*, and use the epitaph (which was not pre-carved) to specify his actual fighting class. Perhaps Greek gladiators were simply more relaxed about their equipment, as long as it was usable: simple pragmatism and different priorities are often an explanation. People rarely fit neatly into categories, even when the names of those categories are important to them.

A Day in the Life

So, once a rookie was categorised and settled into training, what was the life of a Greek gladiator like? The best evidence to give us answers would be to look at where they lived, a *ludus*. This was the building where gladiators ate, slept, and trained together. Archaeologists have found *ludi* before; the largest one in Rome, named the *Ludus Magnus* ('Great Training School'), has been excavated and its ruins are visible next to the Colosseum. Another gladiator barracks was found in Pompeii, and, most recently, the remains of a large *ludus* were identified and excavated in Carnuntum (Vienna). In the Greek part of the empire, we have enormous amounts of gladiatorial evidence like gravestones and inscriptions, sometimes more than multiple western provinces put together, but a confirmed *ludus* site is yet to be found, even though we know that cities like Pergamon and Cyzicus had them. If we were to win the archaeological lottery, we would find a building with a clear floor plan, covered in helpful graffiti and inscriptions, with pristine armour, weapons and various personal possessions hidden underneath a wonderfully shallow, undisturbed layer of easily removed dirt. Alas, so far this has not happened.[219]

Thankfully, we have other forms of evidence, but they require careful assessment. If we fail to be diligent, misunderstandings can easily arise. For instance, there are two such misunderstandings that have become 'fact' and now get repeated on the internet *ad infinitum*; gladiators ate nothing but beans, and they ate to get fat. Where have these misconceptions come from?

Flabiators

The idea that gladiators were purposefully obese is relatively new and it can be traced to the Ephesus excavations, where an intact gladiator cemetery was found with dozens of skeletons for archaeologists to study: DNA, stable isotopes and the radiocarbon that can survive in bones can give a wealth of information about the deceased, including where they grew up, when they died, what they ate and whether they were healthy. The cemetery discovery and the scientific study on the bones of the gladiators made the news headlines worldwide.

During the press frenzy, one of the paleopathologists involved in their study gave an interview to a magazine, making a pretty generalised statement based on the results of stable isotope testing on the bones. The tests suggested that most of the Ephesian gladiators had a largely vegetarian diet with large amounts of barley and beans. Recalling a quote from Pliny the Elder that mentions gladiators and barley, the conclusion given in the interview was that gladiators were deliberately fat.

> Gladiators needed subcutaneous fat. A fat cushion protects you from cut wounds and shields nerves and blood vessels in a fight. Not only would a lean gladiator have been dead meat, but he would also have made for a bad show. Surface wounds look more spectacular. If I get wounded but just in the fatty layer, I can fight on, it doesn't hurt much, and it looks great for the spectators.

The problem with this interview is that it has been heavily misinterpreted; the paleopathologists' assertion was that gladiators needed to have a reasonable amount of body fat, but misquotations have twisted his words to mean 'gladiators were ideally obese'. This assertion has remained largely unchallenged but often repeated, making its way into many documentaries and magazine articles, but there are several issues with assuming that gladiators were flabby.

Firstly, gladiators were intensively trained with specialised instructors who prescribed hours of daily physical exercise. Such a regimen would make it very difficult to put on excessive weight that was not pure muscle. Secondly, we have dozens of examples of gladiators in art, and none of them could be classed as obese. Lastly, there wasn't much point in having what we would now deem an unhealthy amount of body fat, because, while subcutaneous fat does indeed act as a protective layer, this protection is minimal at best given the size of blades gladiators fought with.

As we have seen, most gladiators fought with the *gladius*, a short sword which was also used by the army. It was primarily a stabbing weapon, the point of which could prove fatal at a mere 5cm of penetration.[220] Extra subcutaneous fat, even in the obese, is not going to prevent a fatality from a *gladius* thrust. As we learned, there is compelling evidence from the Greek world suggesting that most of the time the point of gladiatorial swords must have been blunted. When we consider the nature of gladiatorial combat, this makes a lot of sense. Legionaries in tightly packed formations used short swords in a thrusting manner to methodically deliver fatal blows to as many enemies as possible in a short space of time. Gladiatorial fights, however, were one-on-one in a vast space, and designed to be as entertaining as possible for a prolonged length of time: most fights are estimated to have lasted on average between ten and fifteen minutes.[221] Blunting the points of swords reduced (but did not eliminate) the probability of fatalities, which, as we will see in Chapter 18, were incredibly expensive for the magistrates footing the bill. But did a blunted tip change how gladiators fought, and inspire them to get fat as a form of defence?

The *gladius* could be used in a slicing, slashing motion, but the Romans knew it was a reckless technique. The idea that a few shallow slashes with the long edge of a sword could produce safe spurts of blood to entertain the crowds doesn't particularly align with how the Romans saw using the sword in that way. Vegetius writes:

> The Romans not only easily conquered those who fought with cutting motions, they even ridiculed them for doing so... When a cut is delivered, the right arm and side are exposed, but the stabbing point is delivered with the body protected and wounds the enemy before he sees it. This is what characterises Roman practice with respect to combat.[222]

Gladiators wore less armour on the torso than legionaries, so it does not make sense for them to regularly raise their arms to slice, leaving so much of themselves exposed. But, if points of swords were usually blunted, how *did* gladiators fight?

We don't have a surviving ancient manual to reveal the rules of combat, though we know they existed. What we do know is that gladiatorial bouts were carefully controlled by referees, and that fighters were placed in traditional pairings according to their armature and fighting style – for instance *retiarius* versus *secutor* or *murmillo* versus *hoplomachus*. Fighters were given their speciality early in their career, and their training would have been specific both to their style and to defending themselves from the style of their normal opponent types. Beyond this, much is a mystery.

An archaeologist named Marcus Junkelmann, having studied gladiatorial arms and armour and artistic depictions, decided that the best way to fill in the gaps in our knowledge was with practical experimentation, and so formed his own modern gladiatorial *familia* to test out various techniques and theories.[223] He gathered together a group of volunteers who for months trained with replica arms and armour and fought in countless mock combats to see which techniques won the upper hand, and which turned out to be useless. The results of years of this experimental archaeology are fascinating.

Firstly, we must forget the cinematic hacks and slashes we're accustomed to; the swords are too short for the constant clanging we see in movies. Junkelmann's heavyweight gladiators found that it was their shield, the *scutum*, that was the primary piece of kit with which to parry a sword. The *scutum* is a large shield that protected most of the body. Slashing blows with a sword would often do little more than produce a loud clang, and such ineffective manoeuvres in heavy gear were too tiring to waste time performing. Not only this, but a hacking slash leaves the side of the attacker's torso dangerously vulnerable. However, careful thrusts aimed at gaps between sword and armour were more effective, and as we've seen, thrusting blows are dangerous at any percentage of body fat. This aligns with the theory that sword tips were frequently blunted to minimise physical damage to the gladiator's bodies.

None of Junkelmann's conclusions indicate that a gladiator would have benefitted in any way from being fat. Galen, the famous doctor of the Roman world who began his career as physician to Pergamene gladiators, witnessed the damage a slashing injury could make first hand. He mentioned that most of his fellow gladiatorial medics found these cuts difficult to treat and that they involved long periods of recovery. In one example, Galen talks about a blow to the upper thigh that had sliced deep into muscle.[224] Against a *gladius*, thick subcutaneous fat is simply no substitute for a shield or armour. A gladiator's armature was his primary protection, and a second layer of defence, such as obesity, would be superfluous at best and a hindrance at worst.

The misconception boils down to confusing a stocky physique with a morbidly obese one, which comes down to the paleopathologist being misunderstood; he didn't claim that gladiators were fat, just that they had, as all but the leanest people do, a layer of fat on their bodies. If we take the same paleopathology team's assessment that the Ephesus gladiators were heavily muscled and pair it with the portrayals of gladiatorial physiques that we have, I think the best comparison we can make with a modern athlete would be to a professional rugby player. These men can't exactly be considered small; many rugby players have broad shoulders, strong legs and barrel chests.

But they're not all the same, because each position on the team has a different role requiring its own physicality.

Let's consider the rugby players who are frequently in a scrum or a ruck, known as the forwards. They're the biggest players on the pitch, and need to be very strong. Ideally, they're built to make it very difficult to push them onto the ground, so being heavy is a bonus. The other players, known as backs, are required to do more running as they seek to carry or chase the ball over long distances. These players, then, tend to be leaner. No position on a rugby team requires a player to be as lithe as, say, a professional footballer. A layer of fat helps to provide the energy required for the explosive bursts of activity and the endurance needed to perform, but rugby players train too hard and eat too carefully to become morbidly obese, while making sure they're also not unhealthily lean. The modern obsession with less than 3 per cent body fat is purely about aesthetics, not athletic potential.[225]

So let's take our hypothetical professional rugby players and put them in a hypothetical arena. The forwards would make excellent *scutarii*, heavy enough that the larger shield won't weigh them down and with enough heft to knock an opponent to the sand. Our backs, faster and lighter, would excel as *parmularii* or *retiarii*, roles which required fast and nimble feet, but enough strength to face off against a *scutarius* and enough stamina for a prolonged combat.

Diet

Gladiators needed to eat, and, as professional athletes, they needed to eat a lot. We know that the best *familia* employed doctors like Galen who would have been able to advise on the ideal diet for training, but at the same time it's unlikely that even a very rich *lanista* would be able or willing to provide gourmet food to fighters year-round. In fact, we know that gladiators had a feast with indulgent food the night before any Games, as a special treat; usually the fare was plain and cheaply filling. The good news for us is that diet leaves its traces in bone, long after we've gone. So we can ask: did gladiators have a different diet to civilians?

The gladiators excavated in Ephesus were found within a cemetery that also contained civilians who lived and died at the same time, in the same place, making the ideal pool of subjects to study for comparative purposes. The best test is isotope analysis, which can determine the amounts of things like carbon, nitrogen and oxygen present in the bone. Different ratios can indicate if someone ate a lot of animal protein or were vegetarian. Isotope analysis at the Ephesus cemetery revealed that the civilians had practically the same diet as gladiators: largely vegetarian food heavily featuring barley and legumes.[226] The only difference scientists found between gladiators and civilians was that the gladiators had higher strontium levels, which could be attributed to either increased dairy intake or a diet featuring a lot of seafood. However, a clue in ancient literature gives us an alternative cause of elevated strontium: a Roman sports drink.

Quoting Marcus Varro, Pliny the Elder says: 'Your hearth should be your medicine chest. Drink lye made from its ashes, and you will be cured. One can see how gladiators after a combat are helped by drinking this.'[227] Pliny suggests ash as a cure for a lot of different ailments in his writings, but there is evidence that this particular drink was indeed beneficial for bone strength, which for gladiators would have been a priority. It is possible, then, that the gladiators of Ephesus were prescribed a smoothie with ashes mixed into it.[228]

It perhaps shouldn't surprise us that the Ephesian gladiators were eating barley, as Pliny's writing is frequently quoted on the internet in discussions about gladiators. He uses the word *hordearii*, which means 'the barley men', and states that gladiators got that nickname because they ate so much of it. This word has become so well known that certain websites include barley recipes for modern people to experience 'the gladiator diet'. Again, we need to exercise some caution here, because suggesting that barley was so tightly associated with gladiators simultaneously implies that few other people ate it. Using a single phrase from a text isn't good historical practice, so let's take a step back to examine Pliny's wider point. He says:

> Barley is the oldest among human foods, as uses of barley is proved by the Athenian ceremony [at Eleusis] recorded by Menander, and by the name given to gladiators, who used to be called 'barley-men'. Also the Greeks prefer it to any other grain for porridge. There are several ways of making barley porridge: the Greeks soak some barley in water and then leave it for a night to dry, and next day dry it by the fire and then grind it in a mill. Some after roasting it more thoroughly sprinkle it again with a small amount of water and dry it before milling; others however shake the young barley out of the ears while green, clean it and while it is wet pound it in a mortar, and wash it of husk in baskets and then dry it in the sun and again pound it, clean it and grind it. But whatever kind of barley is used, when it has been got ready, in the mill they mix in three pounds of flax seed, half a pound of coriander seed, and an eighth of a pint of salt, previously roasting them all. Those who want to keep it for some time in store put it away in new earthenware jars with fine flour and its own bran. Italians bake it without steeping

it in water and grind it into fine meal, with the addition of the same ingredients and millet as well.[229]

First of all, let's note that, by the sounds of it, all Greeks made a habit out of eating barley porridge, not just gladiators. This is backed up by the isotope analysis. Barley was a staple of Greek cuisine, and would have been a frequent ingredient in all sorts of meals. The second thing to note is the tenses that Pliny uses. The Greeks are still soaking barley when he is writing in the 70s CE, but the gladiator's nickname of 'barley-men' is firmly in the past tense; gladiators *used to* be called barley-men. Had the name fallen out of common parlance? Galen, our gladiator doctor extraordinaire, provides even more context. He was writing around a century after Pliny, and not only confirms that gladiators used to be called barley-men, implying that they no longer were, but that it seems to have been a localised nickname in Athens. So not only was the term *hordearii* outdated by the 70s CE, but it may also well have been only used in a small area. Lastly, we should not overlook the most important part of the report: apart from the ash drink, the diets of gladiators and civilians seem to be almost identical.

As for Galen's gladiators in Pergamon, he describes a diet rich in fava beans, which he notes not only made the gladiators rather windy, but made them 'fleshy rather than firm'.[230] This rather suggests that his gladiators had some padding that obscured their six packs, similar to some of the heftier rugby players we discussed above. We shouldn't assume that 'fleshy' means 'fat'. Galen is specific with his terms, and if Galen meant 'fat' he could have used the appropriate words he uses elsewhere in his medical texts; the word he uses for obese is 'polisarkos' and it is not used for gladiators. Instead he clarifies that the gladiatorial body type in Pergamon was not rock hard, but softer and less dense. Gladiators could perhaps pinch an inch, but their rigorous training ensured that they remained mainly muscle.

Our evidence may be limited to osteoarchaeological evidence in Ephesus and the writings of a doctor in Pergamon, but we see the beginnings of a pattern. The gladiators were fed on a diet of cheap and filling food that nevertheless provided them with a lot of carbohydrates and protein. Their diet was rich in grains, beans, lentils and peas, cooked in various forms, and flavoured with nutritious vegetables. This is in direct contrast to Greek contact athletes like boxers and wrestlers, who were fed a very bread and meat heavy diet.[231] In the Greek world, meat was very expensive and reserved for special occasions, so while it's unlikely that gladiators were being fed such costly food, most of the populace who came to watch them fight would also be eating a very similar diet of porridges and stews, perhaps with the occasional fish dish if by the coast, or meat on festival days.

Medicine

We know the most about gladiatorial health from the writings of Galen. A Pergamon native, he travelled to Alexandria, Smyrna, Corinth, Palestine, Syria and Cyprus for nearly a decade to study medicine under the best teachers available. When he came home, he got a job at the High Priest's *familia*, becoming responsible for the well-being of the gladiators there. It was in Pergamon that he really became a master of anatomy, for where else would a doctor have such regular access to such grisly wounds? Here, Galen got some serious hands-on experience in what we'd now call trauma surgery: learning on the job, operating on men suffering from massive injuries with only herbal remedies to numb the agony.

The quality of the *ludus* doctor varied largely according to local availability and affordability. The gladiators of Pergamon were lucky, their *familia* was exceptionally well funded and Galen was a genius at the beginning of an illustrious career; his experience and talent would eventually lead to him becoming the personal physician to emperors Marcus Aurelius, Commodus and Septimius Severus. Sensible *lanistae* would hire the best doctors available, simply because, as we've seen, gladiators were an expensive long-term investment, and keeping them alive and fighting fit was a financial, if not humanitarian, priority.

Galen boasted that he saved more lives than any other gladiatorial physician, and the osteoarchaeological evidence from Ephesus suggests that their doctors were talented too: many of the skeletons displayed fractures and cuts that had fully healed,[232] which would be impossible without the utmost medical care.

Training

As far as we can tell, training didn't differ between the *ludi* of the eastern and western Mediterranean. Expert coaches would train recruits using wooden weapons, and the recruits would practise manoeuvres by striking their swords on a wooden upright post called a *palus*. The *palus* became a symbol, and the gladiators were ranked by a *palus* number; the very best veterans were called the *first palus*, and so on and so on. When the recruits had learned a few different techniques, they would be allowed to use their training swords in practice fights against their peers in the *familia*. The only time a gladiator was permitted to use a metal weapon was when he was fighting for real in front of the public; nobody wanted unnecessary injury, or worse, an uprising. Once trainers had got a feel of each recruit's strengths and style, the rookies would be sorted into their *armaturae: murmillo, thraex, provocator, retiarius,* et cetera. Each type would then move on to train with a more specialised coach, who were most likely retired arena veterans themselves. Training was a daily occurrence, and getting arena-ready took months of constant practice. Each move needed to be rehearsed again and again, the tactics of opponents studied, and strength had to be built up so that each man could withstand their first bout. If a rookie could survive that first fight, then a potentially long career and perhaps even retirement opened up for them. All they had to do was survive as long as possible.

Chapter 10

A Picture Paints a Thousand Wounds

We've seen how the Romans first got involved fighting, conquering, and finally, ruling the Greek world, and the various ways that this ongoing violent military process introduced gladiator games to the region. We've also seen some pushback from certain elite Greeks to this cultural trend, and tested that limited set of evidence against our first proper case study: the evidence from the neighbouring province of Judea. We also know a bit more about how gladiators trained and fought, and how a day at the Games might proceed for spectators.

Now seems like a good opportunity to get really stuck into a case study using one of the most important pieces of evidence we have: art. More specifically, the visual representations of gladiators in everyday souvenirs, graffiti, mosaics, and more. Most Greeks simply didn't write a lot down, and we have a tiny fraction of the writings from the few Greeks who did. Luckily, even if the average Greek didn't write many essays, they did leave us valuable clues as to their interest in gladiators through a very significant medium: art.

Gladiators were a common feature in artworks found across the empire, but the artworks found in the Greek territories are an important counterargument to the view that Greeks didn't really enjoy Roman spectacle. This isn't typically a hypothesis pushed onto provinces in the west where gladiatorial artwork is found, where archaeologists seem more ready to accept that gladiation was enjoyed by locals and Roman alike. My argument is that Greeks took gladiation to their hearts because they could view it from their own cultural perspective, and one way to see that is in the artwork made by and for gladiator fans in the eastern Mediterranean.

Souvenirs

Any large modern entertainment event aims to extract as much money from the audience as possible. On top of ticket prices, spectators might need to book a hotel to stay at, and they'll need to buy food and drinks either at nearby restaurants or at concession stands strategically dotted around the entertainment venue.

Each entertainment performance, then as now, creates its own network of supply and demand. We can easily imagine enterprising locals seeking to earn some cash by looking after the daily needs of the out-of-towners who would travel to the Big City to see a gladiatorial show. Unfortunately, they don't leave much trace. What about the other things for sale at big shows? At modern concerts, sports games, cinemas and theatres you'll find all kinds of souvenirs on sale: T shirts, CDs, programmes, action figures, themed plastic cups and popcorn buckets, and more. Do we see equivalent memorabilia in the archaeological record?

Not only do we have some excellent examples of keepsakes, but we also have piles of them.

Lamps and Figurines

Most of the souvenirs excavated by archaeologists are made of terracotta. This is for two reasons: firstly, clay was easily available and relatively easy to mould and fire in comparison to, for instance, sculpting small figurines from marble. Secondly, once fired, terracotta doesn't decay. Wood was as accessible and easily carved, but, if souvenirs were made this way, it's unlikely that the wood would survive for centuries without rotting as wood is only preserved in exceptional conditions. We can't discount the production of wooden souvenirs, but we don't have any to prove the theory. Terracotta, if it isn't crushed to dust, is a different story: it is remarkably durable, and some items are excavated from the ground looking like they were fresh from the kiln.

One of the most popular and common types of terracotta artefact is the lamp. A common alternative to candles, lamps were usually in the form of an enclosed dish that contained oil, with a nozzle on one side with a hole for the wick. The circular top of the lamp could be left plain, but the vast majority featured some form of decoration. Popular images included mythical scenes, erotica, flora and fauna, and gladiators. Most were sized to easily fit into the palm of the hand, so that they could be carried around at night. They were fairly cheap to manufacture and could be easily mass-produced; archaeologists have found moulds that the clay could be pressed into to produce exact copies of popular images. In short, it was the kind of object that was an essential item, inexpensive to purchase, and everyone would have owned at least a couple. Because they could be broken easily if dropped, the average person would buy dozens in their lifetime.

Lamps specifically decorated with gladiators aren't unique to the Greek world, but they are found in significantly high numbers there. In fact, some of the major hubs of lamp production are found in the Greek world, including Cyprus and Knidos, leading to a staggering number of gladiator lamps being produced locally. Some depict a single fighter in a pensive pose, but most show the particularly memorable moments of fights between two combatants, including the victor preparing to deal a fatal blow to the loser. Like with every knick-knack in our modern lives, designs of lamps were chosen by individuals to reflect their personal interests, and the number of gladiatorial lamps found across the empire does suggest that there were a large number of gladiator fans who liked to own a little tangible connection to their favourite hobby, in the same way we might wear the shirts of our favourite sports teams or bands today.

To me, it's really indicative of the Greek acceptance and enthusiasm for gladiator spectacles that local pottery manufacturers decided to produce arena memorabilia in such large quantities. One particular site exemplifies this, I think.

Knidos Sanctuary

Mass-produced lamps were, as we've seen, easily available and easily disposable, given their cheapness and relative fragility. They were an everyday, mundane item. But that doesn't mean that they couldn't be imbued with meaning in specific circumstances. In the Victorian period, an archaeologist named Charles Thomas Newton was working for the British Museum. He led a particularly ambitious project in Asia Minor in the 1850s, during which his most famous achievement was locating and excavating the remains of one of the Seven Wonders of the World: the Mausoleum of Halicarnassus (in modern Bodrum).[233] During this trip, he also excavated other ancient towns nearby, including the beautiful site of Knidos, which sits on a hillside next to the sea.

On a high terrace at Knidos, set a little way away from the main town, he found a fragmentary statue of the goddess Demeter, whose head had been separated from the body. Moreover, the head was lying on a pile of black terracotta lamps. Curious, and keen to find more statues, Newton decided to excavate the entire terrace. He did indeed find more pieces of various statues, which he identified as Demeter and her daughter Persephone. He also found several sheets of lead, which had been rolled up; when he unfurled them he found that they were curse tablets, pleading to Demeter, Persephone and the myriad gods of the Underworld to intercede on their behalf. One woman named Antigone claimed she had been unjustly accused of attempted murder using poison, another named Prosodion cursed an unnamed woman who seduced her husband. But what Newton found in the greatest volume was lamps. Hundreds of terracotta lamps. They were placed in subterranean chambers that he initially mistook for graves, until he found no trace of human remains. The chambers had brick walls and had been roofed over with tiles. He also found some little figurines and the skeletal remains of what he guessed were animal sacrifices. Newton had enough evidence to suggest that he had found a sanctuary of Demeter and Persephone, and that these chambers formed the foundations of what may have been a small temple or temples dedicated to them, of which there was now almost no trace.

The oldest lamps came from long before the Roman occupation, and were usually elaborate and of excellent quality, decorated with girls carrying water jugs, theatre masks, or plants. But there were also lamps dating from the imperial period, not quite as fine, and rather cheaply made in comparison. Newton discovered that though he had easily more than a hundred Roman lamps, their decorations weren't particularly diverse, if they even had a decoration at all. He found lamps with birds, animals, and plants, but the most striking collection featured gladiators.

So, why were hundreds of lamps buried beneath a temple over the course of hundreds of years? Lamps were a common form of votive offering, as they were affordable and easily available, but having such large numbers in special chambers was unusual. Newton recalled a snippet he'd read in Pausanias, about a similar sanctuary of Demeter and Persephone in Argos where lighted lamps were lowered into dark chasms as votive gifts to the goddesses,[234] and it does seem that the lamps at Knidos were indeed deposited very carefully in specific structures within the *temenos*, rather than being thrown into a messy heap like discarded trash. The votive hypothesis is a strong one. The next question is, why were gladiator lamps there?

On one hand, lamps of all kinds of designs were mass-produced and marketed, as we've seen. It might be that not a lot of thought was put into lamps at the time of purchase, in the same way one probably wouldn't spend hours deliberating over which novelty coffee mug to buy for someone today. On the other hand, Newton specifically says that when he looks at the Knidos lamps, there are a small number of very specific decoration categories that they fall into.[235] If any old lamp would suit the votive purpose, we might expect to see many more themes of decoration. Could it be that the gladiator lamps were chosen specifically because they were deemed particularly appropriate? Persephone was the queen of the Underworld, so the act of gifting her with lamps had an association with death, just as gladiatorial combat did. Perhaps it was the very fact that gladiators faced death without fear that made the lamps such an appropriate gift for Persephone. We can't know for sure, but it does seem like another example of how gladiator culture more broadly could fit into the existing customs and culture of the Greek world.

Canteens and Dolls

Aside from lamps, other day-to-day items were also made from terracotta. Lots of people would have gone about their days carrying an *oinophoros*, a kind of canteen or hip flask that in the Roman period was usually circular in shape, with a short, flared neck at the top and perhaps some small handles on each side. They were made by two halves being moulded into the shape of shallow bowls which were stuck together along the rims before firing in the kiln. They were sized to be easily held in one hand, or to fit inside a small bag or be hung from a belt. This way, as ancient people went about their day they could carry a drink of wine with them as they moved around the city, and perhaps refill them at bars throughout the day. As another easily breakable item, they were often fairly cheap and mass-produced, but, as with lamps, many people were happy to pay a little extra for a decoration: moulds and stamps have been found that demonstrate how simple it was to make dozens of copies of a particular design. There is usually a circular frame, sometimes made to look like a wreath, with a medallion style image inside. The size of the *oinophoroi* allowed the potters to make images with more content and detail than a smaller lamp. Mythical characters and animals were popular, but gladiators and beast hunts are one of the most commonly attested themes.[236] Sherds have been found across the eastern Mediterranean. Again the premier manufacturing workshops were based in Pergamon and Knidos.

One hip flask has an erotic scene on one side and a gladiatorial duel on the other.[237] This might be a meaningful contrast between the life-affirming, and, indeed, life-creating act of sexual intercourse, cleverly and poignantly compared to the violence and death of the arena; the creation of life and the manufacture of death. It may also, of course, reference the documented sex appeal of the gladiators themselves, who were the heart throbs of their day. Others have different stages of a fight depicted on each side of the flask; it wasn't uncommon to have images of the last moment of a gladiator's life pressed into wet clay with stamps so that a constant reminder of death could be sold to eager fans.

As well as lamps and flasks, terracotta was used to make little gladiatorial terracotta dolls, which archaeologists have found in several places around the eastern Mediterranean. Excellent examples come from collections found in Pergamon[238] and the theatre of Parion,[239] a port city on the south coast of the Sea of Marmara. Archaeologists have excavated multiple fragments of pottery dolls, and several of them are dressed as gladiators. What's particularly interesting about these dolls is that the torso and limbs are separate pieces, each with small holes so that the limbs could be attached to the torso with short lengths of string. In other words, these dolls had articulated limbs that could be moved around. The heads even show grooves where removable helmets could be fitted on, and there are holes in the hand where miniature replica weapons could be slotted in, though these have not survived. Gladiatorial statuettes were decorative, but these were also action figures, designed to be held and played with. It also raises the interesting question about who their target demographic was? Were children being bought these action figures to play with, re-enacting the scenes they were allowed to watch in the theatre or arena? Were they begging their parents for full sets of interchangeable miniature helmets and weapons so that they could dress their doll as different types of gladiator? That so many were found at Parion theatre itself suggests that an enterprising potter had set up a merchandise stand on days when gladiators used the theatre, taking advantage of children tugging on their parents' tunics and pleading incessantly for a new toy.[240]

Again, we can't say for sure – and these case studies are for you to decide – but the presence of cheap, mass-produced, everyday items like canteens and dolls in the archaeological record really does seem to me like enthusiasm for gladiators had permeated wider society to the point that economies thrived on that popularity.

Graffiti

Graffiti was as ubiquitous in the ancient world as it is today, and as comparatively diverse. Graffiti captures what the ancient people who created it were thinking about at a specific moment: what they found appealing, what they deemed important, or, as was often the case, featuring a phallus. Needless to say, if gladiators were accepted into Greek culture, we should expect to see them in the graffiti we find.

When archaeologists of the Roman period talk about graffiti, we usually default to talking about examples from Pompeii. That town had graffiti scrawled or painted onto practically every wall. The problem is, we only know this because the Vesuvian eruption buried the entire town in volcanic ash, preserving even scribbles made with charcoal. That kind of preservation is really rare, so we won't have such a good set of data to work with in the eastern Mediterranean.[241] Instead, we have a small collection of surviving graffiti which, if we take Pompeii as a good indicator of how much the ancients loved to doodle, is a miniscule percentage of the scribbles that ancient Greek and Romans made there that have been lost to time.

We'll be talking about two different types of graffiti; those that are scratched into stone or plaster using some kind of tool, and those that are painted (which are technically known as *dipinti*, not graffiti). We may not have as many examples as the town 'frozen in time', but, once we start looking, we do find gladiator sketches in all kinds of places.

Ephesus

Ephesus was one of the major cities of the ancient world, and reached its peak in the Roman imperial period when its population was nearly a quarter of a million people. It was even home to one of the Seven Wonders of the World, its magnificent Temple of Artemis. We know a lot about the gladiators of Ephesus; we still have the massive theatre and stadium that each sat 25,000 spectators at a time and were both architecturally adapted to make it safe for gladiator shows.[242] We also have a collection of gladiatorial inscriptions and one of only two confirmed gladiatorial graveyards.[243] We discuss both these types of evidence elsewhere in our study; for now, our focus in this case study is the graffiti.

Art fans may have heard of the Borghese Gladiator, a two-metre marble statue dating from around 100 BCE and made, if not in Ephesus, by an Ephesian sculptor named Agasias. A well-muscled, handsome man stands in a defiantly defensive pose, holding his arm in front of him as if to repel an attack coming from above. At some point in its history, the statue was taken to Italy where it decorated Nero's seaside palace at Antium (modern Anzio). Rediscovered in the 1600s, it was added first to the Borghese collection in Rome, and then later sold to Napoleon Bonaparte in 1807, who put it in the Louvre where it still stands today. It's a marvellous statue, and a rare Greek original (Romans typically commissioned themselves copies of original statues they admired). I would love to say that this was an example of gladiatorial fandom in the first century BCE Ephesus, but there are problems. Firstly, 100 BCE is a little too early for Agasias to have been inspired by the gladiator troupes of various Republican Roman generals.[244] Secondly, the statue is almost entirely nude, and has none of the accoutrements we'd expect a gladiator to be wearing or holding. In the 1800s, a scholar named Friedrich Wilhelm Thiersch suggested it was instead a warrior whose opponent was mounted on a horse, which would explain the pose. He even suggested it might represent Achilles, possibly facing off the Amazon Penthesilea, the famed horsewoman of myth. This would also explain why the statue is portrayed as heroically nude, the standard outfit for heroes immortalised in stone or bronze. The Borghese Gladiator is, therefore, very unlikely to be an example of true gladiatorial art from Ephesus. To find the real deal, we have to think slightly smaller.

The first place to logically look would be close to where gladiators performed. Ephesus had two venues it used for shows: the theatre and the stadium. At the theatre, several big blocks of stone featuring figures of gladiators carved in relief were found close to its entrances, like posters advertising the shows inside. But, if we want to find gladiatorial art made by a fan, we need to think even smaller.

Luckily, Ephesus boasts an extraordinarily well-preserved section of housing, known as the Terrace Houses. They are situated close to the famous Library of Celsus (the subject of many a postcard) and consist of two blocks of houses. The Terrace Houses date to the Roman period, and are strikingly opulent; it was the middle and upper classes who lived in this part of town. Luckily for us, if not the residents, the houses were eventually buried under a thick layer of sediment, preserving them at a comparable level to Pompeii. Excavated since the 1960s, modern techniques have even revealed that the Terrace Houses aren't deteriorating as much as those in Pompeii. The Terrace Houses thus provide a snapshot of well-heeled life in the city, with mosaics on the floors and frescoes on the walls intact. And just as in Pompeii, where there is a wall, there is graffiti. Archaeologists have found doodles of animals, ships, and even shopping lists complete with prices. But, of all the subjects, gladiators are the most common across all houses.[245] These scratchings into painted plaster represent snapshots of what was on a person's mind when they found themselves at a loose end, and evidently more than one resident was thinking about gladiatorial fights long after they left a show.

Smyrna

And it wasn't just in Ephesus that idle people chose to doodle on walls. Smyrna (modern Izmir) was a small town on the Aegean coast of Anatolia until Alexander the Great visited and, seeing its potential, invested heavily in the city; it soon became a vibrant, thriving hub. Smyrna remained one of the most significant cities in Anatolia right through to the Roman period, where it rivalled Ephesus and Pergamon, and has been continually inhabited ever since, remaining one of the most important cities in Türkiye today.

Centuries of occupation does mean that, unlike Ephesus, it's not possible to excavate or reconstruct whole buildings, boulevards, and city blocks. Digging down to entire ancient monuments is difficult, as most are covered with modern houses or have had their stone taken away for reuse elsewhere. That said, the stadium has been located, if not extensively investigated, and excavations are underway at the theatre in the hopes of restoring it and turning it into a heritage site. The stadium was definitely used for Roman spectacle – we have testimony of Christians being martyred there – and it's likely that excavation of both buildings will reveal physical evidence for gladiatorial shows. We know that residents of Smyrna must have staged such spectacles rather often, as it is the location of the biggest collection of gladiatorial gravestones yet found in the Greek world. Smyrna was clearly an excellent location for catching a spectacular show.

Elsewhere, among the modern buildings, there are other ancient ruins to be found. They mostly date to the later imperial period as Smyrna suffered a catastrophic earthquake in the second century CE. One area that has been excavated and preserved is the ancient agora, which is now an archaeological park. The agora of any ancient Greek city was its hub, being the main location for markets, courts and administration. Smyrna was no exception, and visitors can still see the remains of markets, offices, various council buildings, a bathhouse, and even the public toilets. The agora itself was laid out by Alexander or his generals, and was restored many times over the centuries due to earthquakes in the area. The main open space is rectangular, with porticoes on its long sides and a grand basilica running along its northern side. For Romans, the basilica's main purpose was as a courthouse.[246] Because the agora was built on a gentle slope, the basilica was built upon a *cryptoporticus* (a covered corridor or passageway) to level the ground, and the *cryptoporticus* was used as a basement. Not much of the basilica itself survives today, but the *cryptoporticus* is very well preserved. It is a warren of corridors and rooms, with half apparently used for storage, shops, workshops and offices, and half as a covered area for the public to use in inclement weather. The *cryptoporticus*, then, was a busy building in the centre of town, frequented by any number of Smyrna's citizens. It was the ideal location for graffiti artists, and archaeologists were stunned to find that dozens and dozens of individual drawings had survived there for nearly two millennia.

Mostly the drawings are *dipinti*, i.e. painted pictures using black soot or red brick dust mixed with fat, oil, or resin to make paint: there are some incised graffiti that can be seen on surviving plaster as well.[247] Again, as with

Ephesus, there are the usual drawings of animals, birds, and – both naturally and timelessly – quite a few phallic doodles as well. As Smyrna was a bustling port, it's not surprising that ships are the most popular category of graffiti, but there are 31 graffiti that are identifiably gladiatorial, making this the second most prevalent theme and 20 per cent of all pictorial doodles. There isn't any text connected to the figures; no names, fight records or dates. This makes it difficult to determine whether these gladiator images are adverts for upcoming games or memories of past combats. Either is very possible, and we have precedents for both.

We also can't tell who drew them. Was it fans? Proud gladiators? Or were they commissioned by the gladiatorial *familia* in the town to promote their troupe? In Pompeii, the gladiator graffiti were mostly scratched into plaster, and rather crudely made, suggesting they were off the cuff. We know that Greek gladiator fans scored lines into plaster because of the Ephesus Terrace Houses, and as plaster rarely survives well, I think it's safe to assume that houses across the eastern Mediterranean had similar gladiator sketches that have simply been destroyed, including in Smyrnaean houses. However, the basilica drawings are very different. All but two of the Smyrna drawings are painted, showing a comparatively elevated level of technique and skill.[248] Somebody deliberately took the time to make or acquire paints and brushes, take them to the basilica, and daub pictures they'd put thought into. We tend to assume that all graffiti is haphazard, impetuous vandalism, because that's what modern society considers modern graffiti to be, but we shouldn't assume that all ancient graffiti was created for the same reason; the volume and quality of some of the Smyrna gladiator paintings suggest that they were designed, planned, and created with care, unlike the idle graffiti in, say, the Ephesus Terrace Houses. However, without any accompanying text, we simply don't have as much context as we'd need to make a firm theory.[249]

Even if we can't reconstruct exactly who drew the *dipinti* and why, there is still interesting information to learn. For instance, *provocatores* are far and away the most popular *armature* in Smyrna, with eighteen drawings dedicated to them. The gravestones from Smyrna suggest that there was a fairly even distribution of gladiatorial types performing in the city, but the graffiti definitely reveals a preference for the *provocator*. The drawings typically show combats in progress, but, interestingly, only one depicts a death. Perhaps it records a specific combat; the gladiator is drawn as having been decapitated, which would have definitely been a memorable and powerful experience for anyone watching. Otherwise, it's the process of the combat that's interesting, rather than a negative result.

Nothing quite like the Smyrna Basilica graffiti collection has ever been found in the western parts of the empire for us to make a thorough comparison, though there is a hint that a comparable group once existed in Aphrodisias.

Aphrodisias

Aphrodisias, named for the city's patron deity Aphrodite, was once the main city in the region of Caria, western Anatolia. Smaller than Ephesus or Smyrna, it was nevertheless a town that punched above its weight, and was famed for the sophisticated elegance of its architecture and for its peerless sculptors. A Seleukid town founded in the second century BCE, Aphrodisias truly reached its peak in the Roman period. The city boasted both a stadium and a theatre adapted to host gladiators, and the twenty-five gladiatorial gravestones we know of speak to the popularity of Roman gladiator spectacle there.

More specifically, for our purposes right now, so does the volume of related graffiti, much of which is to be found in the northwestern corner of the 'South Agora' (or more correctly, the Urban Park). This wasn't an agora at all, but was a long colonnaded rectangular public space surrounded by porticoes, with a long pool running down the centre and ornamental palm trees. It was definitely a public space, but seems to have been more of a pleasure plaza for promenading, rather than a commercial and civic hub. It has only recently been fully excavated, and archaeologists found hundreds of pieces of graffiti. Here, gladiator figures and animals from *venationes* have been scratched straight into marble columns on the northern portico, perhaps as they sat with their friends having a chat about recent spectacles. It wasn't just central locations where gladiatorial graffiti was found either, for someone has carved a comic strip-style battle between some *retiarii* and (presumably) *secutores* into a block of stone found by the city's West Gate. In other words, graffiti is found, unsurprisingly, where people congregated or passed by frequently. The location attracted scribblers, but also ensured that their scribbles would be seen by a large number of other people.

Predictably, there are lots of gladiatorial graffiti where gladiators were performing: the stadium and theatre. Both monuments have little sketches of gladiators carved directly into the seating blocks, suggesting that some enthusiastic fans spent their time between combats scratching their favourite fighters into the seat right next to their leg. I've never carved a picture into solid stone using whatever I have in my pocket, but I'm going to guess that each graffiti took quite a while to make, and the difficulty might explain why they best resemble a child's stick man drawing. In the theatre, a fan has inscribed a crudely drawn little *thraex* into his seat, revealing himself to be particularly fond of the lighter style of fighter. A few rows further towards the front, there is a crude sketch of a *retiarius*, and what seems to be a *hoplomachus* close by. Similarly, someone has carved a *retiarius* into their stadium seat, complete with trident and net. Seating was assigned for these shows, so the graffiti may actually be little unofficial seat markers, a way that the artist could easily claim ownership of the seat at the next show: 'It's mine, see – I carved this gladiator here last time!'

Parion

Let's briefly return to Parion, where we talked about the gladiator dolls. That is evidence for enthusiasm for Roman spectacle already, and we know that gladiator games were performed here, as an honorific inscription dating to the reign of Commodus (180–192 CE) states that gladiator fights were to be held there every five years following a restoration of the theatre.[250] We will return to the theatre itself later; for now, there is a further clue to gladiator fandom hidden in the theatre itself: more graffiti.

What makes the Parion graffiti particularly interesting is its location. It's not in a public space like an agora, and it's not carved onto seats in the theatre. Instead, the graffiti has been carved into the façade of the *proskenion* wall, i.e. the wall that holds up the stage above the level of the *orchestra*. In other words, the graffiti artist would have had to kneel on the floor of the *orchestra/ arena* itself to access the wall. Clearly this wasn't undertaken during the show itself, so who was entering an empty theatre to scratch gladiators onto what was essentially the arena wall? It certainly doesn't seem that the pictures were officially commissioned in lieu of more expensive reliefs, as the design isn't regular and shows little sign of planning. On the other hand, the quality is certainly much better than the stick men at Aphrodisias and other cities, with properly proportioned figures depicted in authentic poses and with accurate arms and armour. The graffiti can be found on two blocks, one above the other. The lower block features two *thraeces*, easily identified by the gryphons on their helmet crests, ganging up on a single *murmillo*. Above is another *murmillo*, along with a *bestiarius* carrying a whip. It's unclear whether both levels were completed at the same time, or by the same person. Perhaps this was a sly advert for the local gladiatorial troupe, cheekily added to their workplace, or a dedicated gladiator fan who hoped that their art may inspire the authorities to put on games with more frequency.

Evidence like this is especially interesting to consider. We can't say for certain who made it, when, or why – and that uncertainty can be frustrating for historians as well as readers. It would make presenting this argument so much easier if these case studies were more straightforward. However, I think we can say that it makes the theory that imperial Roman administrators were forcing gladiators onto local Greek populations seem less likely, at the very least.

Mosaics

So far in this case study, I've presented you with evidence of mass-produced or ad hoc visual culture, representing engagement from the types of people who were unlikely to have their words preserved for posterity (if they wrote their thoughts down at all). The final group of visual culture to examine here, however, might be the most interesting of all because they reflect the tastes and expenditure of wealthier fans: those who we might otherwise assume were represented by the texts recording the thoughts of men like Dio Chrysostom and Apollonius of Tyana, who we encountered previously.

These gladiator fans were wealthy enough to afford something larger and more permanent than a figurine or lamp and they certainly wanted something more sophisticated than a graffito. They turned to home décor, a trend that is common in both the eastern Mediterranean and the western territories of the empire. And not just any old home décor: several mosaics have been discovered that feature gladiators, and all are in domestic spaces.

Mosaics were a popular flooring solution, being durable but also elegant. The ancient Greeks in previous centuries had made their mosaics with coloured pebbles, which could make a nice visual effect but often created quite an uneven surface. From the Hellenistic period onwards, mosaics had developed into quite the art form, and their popularity spread across the Mediterranean. Slabs of different stones were carefully cut into small, regular squares, called *tesserae*. The floor to be decorated would be covered with a layer of mortar, and the *tesserae* gently pressed into it when the cement was still slightly wet. Poorer families would have to make do with coarse, uneven *tesserae* in a single colour, but flooring was considered an excellent method of flaunting wealth and taste: if you wanted to show off your fortune and your character, you paid extra for a mosaicist to design a floor to impress. Mosaics were primarily designed to be hard-wearing and long-lasting, so why waste the opportunity to push the boat out a little? The richer someone was, the more colourful and elaborate they frequently wanted their mosaics. The choice of designs was staggering, with different colours of stone (and sometimes even *tesserae* made of ceramic or glass) used to make various patterns and pictures. Each mosaicist would have a pattern-book of popular designs to choose from, but the really rich could afford something bespoke.

For the rich in the ancient world, the home was not as private as it often is today. The house of a powerful person needed grand reception rooms for welcoming associates and clients, as well as large studies for doing business and additional large rooms for entertaining and dining. Up to half of the house was considered to be public, as many people from outside the household would be visiting throughout the day, every day. Home décor was therefore a public presentation of the family and its social standing. Wealth, class and sophistication were communicated through the tasteful furniture and antique ornaments: there was a reason the Romans looted so many vases, paintings and statues from Greek cities after all, but refinement wasn't just telegraphed in portable goods. Every surface, often left a monochrome blank in modern houses, was a potential canvas for decoration. Ceilings were coffered, walls covered in frescoes, and floors with mosaics. The floor became more than something to walk on, it became an opportunity to signal social clues to one's wider network. And as a costly investment that was intended to be in place for a significant period of time, the design of a mosaic was something a homeowner would naturally put a lot of thought into. They wanted the mosaic to reflect who they were, and their lifestyle and preferences. Hence, we find a lot of mosaics featuring gods and heroes from popular myths, bucolic or maritime scenes, hunts or even visual puns, like mosaics of dropped food placed on a dining room floor.[251] One could also install a permanent reminder of their favourite pieces of popular culture, in the same way that many modern people might frame a favourite movie poster or album cover, or display paraphernalia associated with their chosen sports team.

So the surviving examples of gladiatorial mosaics in the Greek world are significant. They challenge the notion that it was only the poor, uneducated, and unrefined Greeks who could possibly enjoy Roman spectacle. Clearly, upper-class Greeks valued gladiation highly enough that they wanted to create a permanent, public declaration of their enthusiasm in their own homes. More than that, they deemed these not only appropriate, but important enough to eschew more traditional subjects. Not all mosaics survive, as they are susceptible to environmental changes like moisture and temperature, and can be easily damaged or destroyed by agricultural practices, plant roots or successive buildings. Some simply haven't been excavated yet. Nevertheless, in our partial sample, there are Greek gladiatorial mosaics. Excellent examples are on the islands of Kos and Cyprus, and have been left *in situ*. This makes putting them into the context of the building so much easier, and both are easily accessible to visitors.

Kos

The main town on Kos (also called Kos) has numerous archaeological sites, and its gladiatorial mosaics are found in the area known as the Western Archaeological Zone, close to the Odeon. This was a bustling area of the ancient town, close to the harbour, and boasting baths, a stadium and a gymnasium. It was the kind of neighbourhood where houses were grander than usual. One is known by archaeologists as the House of Silenus, named after the mythological subject in one of the many mosaics in the house. The mosaic that we're interested in had three panels. One features a man on a horse, the other features an animal hunt, and the final panel depicts two gladiator combats. On the left, two *scutarii* face off. They seem to be *murmillones*, though their helmets have no crest, making them a kind of hybrid *murmillo/secutor* helmet type. They're both holding their large shields up, and the figure on the left extends his sword arm. The tip of his sword is depicted dripping with blood. Oddly, only the stabbed gladiator of the pair is named; he is called Aigialos, which may mean 'crashing waves'. Between the two fights is a referee, who appears to be preoccupied with the fight on the right. A *retiarius* with curling golden hair is named Zephyros. He's holding his trident and leaning towards his opponent Hylas, another *scutarius*, who is pointing a dagger at Zephyros' throat. Zephyros is named after the god of the western wind, a suitable epithet for a nimble net-fighter, and Hylas is named for Heracles' loyal companion and arms bearer.

Louis Robert, the first person to collect gladiatorial artefacts in this region, doesn't believe that the mosaicist could possibly have created the designs of gladiators from his own experiences and must have been copying designs from elsewhere, presumably in the western territories of the empire.[252] If that were true, I'd question why the names of three of the gladiators have been included: that would seem to suggest that the mosaics are depicting real fights that the homeowner particularly enjoyed—or, at least, real gladiators they were familiar with. Besides, we have gravestones and memorials of gladiators present on Kos, suggesting that fights occurred on the island, even if we can't pin down where they happened yet. There's no reason to suppose that local mosaicists would not have seen enough combats to be able to design a picture of one. Furthermore, on the mainland, Halicarnassus and Knidos were both cities with confirmed gladiatorial venues, and they were each a mere half day's sail away. Special events like games were a good reason for people to travel to neighbouring communities; someone local was perfectly capable of designing a gladiatorial image from scratch. Unfortunately, it's difficult to ascertain what the room was used for, but such a mosaic would certainly have been intended for a room that visitors to the house would visit, notice, and admire. Mosaics were meant to be seen.

Cyprus

Cyprus was a small province that was generally not paid a great amount of attention by Rome, but it boasted significant religious sanctuaries that helped it stay relevant and prosperous. A town named Kourion lay on the southwest coast of the island, at a place now known as Episkopi. We know Kourion's theatre was adapted for gladiatorial shows sometime between 210 and 250 CE, when it appears to have been changed back. A mosaic found in Kourion dates to the decades after the theatre was changed back, which suggests that some locals still had a distinct taste for spectacle, so perhaps at this point it had moved to the town's stadium. When the mosaics were found, they were so significant that archaeologists named the building for it, and it is now known as the House of the Gladiators (even though some scholars suggest it may have been a *palaestra*, rather than a villa). The two mosaics were found in the same room, which has been identified as an atrium. The atrium of a Roman house was an internal court, with a skylight opening in the roof (*compluvium*) set above a shallow, ornamental pool that caught rainwater (*impluvium*). The atrium was one of the public rooms in the house, so we can assume that the owner wanted these specific mosaics to be seen by all of his guests and associates.

There are two scenes of gladiators in the atrium around the *impluvium*. The first shows a set of opponents facing each other, though neither is dealing a blow. Their names are given as Margarites and Hellenikos. They wear the smooth helmets of *secutores*, who weren't typically paired off against other *secutores*. They have the requisite large shields, but these are rounded ovals, not curved and rectangular as we may expect. In the second image, a *thraex* named Lytras is separated from his *provocator* opponent, whose name is lost, by a referee named Darios stepping in between them to pause the fight.

Again, this is just one piece of evidence and it doesn't tell us everything we might want to know about gladiators in Cyprus. But it does tell us that one member of the local Greek elite thought that gladiators were an appropriate way to decorate one of the most public spaces of his home. Presumably, he felt his many likely guests would share that feeling.

Conclusion

Together, the surviving artworks made for and by gladiator fans offer a tantalising glimpse of a world with a vibrant memorabilia trade and famous fighters etched onto walls both private and public. In most cities, gladiatorial *munera* might be only hosted on one or two occasions a year, and in some cities, like Parion, that they may have been even less frequent. Despite this, I think the visual culture we have remaining, presented here, suggests that many Greeks had gladiators on their minds year-round, and liked to have reminders of their favourite fighters and combats to look at during the long months between shows. This evidence suggests that's true for the wealthy as well as those less well-off, and it's a testament to enthusiasm and acceptance of a foreign cultural custom made their own, in direct contrast to the protestations of a minority of haughty philosophers.

This case study is important in its own right. But I think it also helps us ask the next essential question: where were people seeing the gladiatorial combats that they were seemingly so fond of?

Chapter 11

The Aversion to Amphitheatres

It is a truth universally acknowledged that an entertainment phenomenon in possession of a large fanbase must be in want of a suitable performance venue. In the Greek world, every self-respecting city had a theatre for plays and poetry recitals, and possibly a stadium or hippodrome to host one of the hundreds of athletic competitions held across the region. Their designs were fine-tuned over centuries until perfected while appearing deceptively simple. Theatres had acoustics so precisely engineered that audience members in the very highest seats could still hear actors whisper, stadiums hosted multiple athletic events – and both could seat thousands of spectators who all had an unrestricted view. By the time the Romans started throwing their weight around the Greek world, these monuments were already ancient. And yet, we have very few ancient amphitheatres in this region. We know gladiator combats were immensely popular in much of the Greek world and we know they took their performance venues seriously. What, then, explains this absence?

As we will discover in this and the following two chapters, it is not an absence of evidence; in fact, there is plenty of evidence. We just haven't been looking at it properly. We start with Rome, to get an idea of what people have traditionally been looking for. In Rome, the situation was slightly different than the Greek world. Historically, the city hadn't featured many big permanent entertainment structures. The Circus Maximus was the exception to this rule, almost as old as the city itself. The Romans adored chariot racing, which remained the foremost mode of entertainment for centuries. It was also the only mode of entertainment that was deemed worthy of a permanent venue from the Kings of Rome until the Late Republic period.

Rome caught the theatre bug early (Livy hazards to date the first rudimentary performances in the city to 364 BCE),[253] and yet the first (successful) attempt to build a permanent theatre was that of Pompey the Great in 55 BCE. Up until this point, permanent theatres had been avoided: the aristocracy weren't fond of the idea of the populace wasting good working hours by watching plays; neither were they comfortable with potentially unruly citizens using permanent theatres as the Greeks did, to meet up in large numbers and discuss politics. As such, the plays and pantomimes that grew so popular in the city were staged in temporary theatres built out of wood, erected for specific occasions and torn down straight afterwards. Despite their temporary nature, these theatres were increasingly large and elaborate.[254] In fact, Pompey only circumvented this tradition by claiming that his theatre was merely the elaborate steps of the temple of Venus that he had perched above the highest row. The theatre was immense, and it's still possible to trace its dimensions in the map of Rome's modern streets.

The Romans also came into contact with Greek athletic festivals as they ventured further from Latium. Again, while athletic competition was readily absorbed into the city's cultural programme, events were held in temporary venues or the Circus until a permanent stadium was constructed in around 80 CE by Domitian. From 217 BCE, when curious Romans witnessed their Greek neighbours in the south of the Italian peninsula put on athletic contests, they began to incorporate footraces and contact sports performed by Greek athletes into wider spectacles for the public, alongside chariot racing and beast hunts.[255] Athletics came to Rome in a similar way to theatre; a slow process that was gradually absorbed into the city's cultural programme, but without a permanent structure to call home for several centuries.

Forums

The amphitheatre, now an iconic image of ancient Rome, was the solution to Rome's need for a building that could house huge spectacles while entertaining as many spectators as possible. But for all its fame as an emblem of 'Roman-ness', the most iconic example, the Colosseum, wasn't constructed until the 70s CE. This means a gap of three and a half centuries between the first fight in Rome and the opening of the Colosseum. With athletics and theatre in mind, we begin to understand why no amphitheatres were developed when gladiation began in the 200s BCE. All forms of spectacle, apart from chariot racing, were staged in temporary venues until the last decades of the Republic. Exploring where gladiators were fighting in the western Roman empire before the Colosseum was built can help us see their Greek-speaking counterparts more clearly.

Early examples of amphitheatres, theatres, and stadia were mainly temporary wooden structures in fora. Valerius Maximus places the first fight in Rome in 264 BCE at the Forum Boarium, a commercial hub that was mainly used as a cattle market where it would have been easy enough to bring in some benches for spectators, if they needed to sit at all. With only three pairs of gladiators, the spectacle would hardly fill a full day like later Games in the Colosseum. The next fight (or the next considered worth recording by Livy, at least) took place in the Forum Romanum, which continued to be used for gladiatorial games until the late-20s BCE. Here, seating solutions were more elaborate, including temporary balconies that could be added to the exteriors of the basilicas lining the forum during the Middle Republic.[256] Bleacher-style seating was also erected at ground level, and, while no writer describes their exact form, the best interpretation is that of an oval structure placed between the basilicas Aemilia and Sempronia.[257] There is a reason why this shape was needed; the Forum buildings were erected by competing aristocrats with little thought to architectural harmony; the Roman Forum is a hodgepodge of buildings plonked somewhat haphazardly around a (mostly) open space, and not the neat and tidy rectangle-surrounded-by-buildings of fora such as Pompeii. And so, the oval shape fits into the space harmoniously while allowing for a clear view from every spectator seat, and is likely the inspiration of permanent amphitheatre designs. It is estimated that the wooden structure could be erected in the Forum in about a week, and dismantled after a Games in even less time, allowing for the commercial and political activities of the Forum to continue mostly unimpeded.[258]

For more than two centuries, these temporary gladiatorial venues were deemed preferable to a permanent structure, in exactly the same way as theatres and stadiums. The first permanent amphitheatres were actually built outside of Rome, usually on the edges of towns and close to arterial roads. Most were built in Campania, which makes sense considering the established popularity of gladiators in the region. The first securely dated amphitheatre is that of Pompeii, which opened in 70 BCE. In the already crowded city of Rome, the Forum Romanum was gaining new additions as fast as wealthy citizens with a craving for prestige could build them, and the space available for temporary arenas was shrinking. Augustus, the man who claimed to have found a city of brick and left it a city of marble, soon rectified the situation. The Forum was becoming claustrophobic, but the Campus Martius (the Field of Mars) was still almost entirely undeveloped. A flat plain between the River Tiber and Rome's civic centre, the Campus Martius had been so prone to flooding that it wasn't even cultivated for crops during the time of Rome's kings and the subsequent Republic. It was just outside of the *pomerium*, the official legal boundary of Rome, which meant it had a slightly different status than the land inside the boundary in some important ways. It was where Rome's armies assembled before officially beginning and ending campaigns, and many of the temples and monuments there had an overt military nature. It also held the Circus Flaminius (which, despite its name, was technically a hippodrome). It was not used for chariot racing like the Circus Maximus, but for horse racing during the Taurian Games, held in honour of the infernal deities, the gods of the underworld. The space for the Circus Flaminius was sectioned off in 220 BCE by Gaius Flaminius Nepos, but throughout its entire history was never truly permanent. Its seating was wooden and supported by vaulting, the benches erected and dismantled as required, and the Taurian Games only sporadically held in times of religious anxiety. It was also used for military parades.

In the final, turbulent years of the Republic, the Campus Martius had become a battlefield between political rivals who hoped to score points with the populace by building impressively grandiose monuments. Pompey Magnus, Julius Caesar and Augustus and their respective allies and rivals all built on a monumental scale to court the favour of the Roman people, and the Campus Martius was the main stage for their efforts. As we've seen elsewhere in the Roman empire during this period, many of the events and buildings (temporary or permanent) were explicitly martial. To take just one year as an example, 46 BCE saw Julius Caesar build a temporary stadium to host triumphal games of athletics after campaigning in Gaul, Egypt, Syria, and North Africa.[259] More audaciously, in the same year Caesar excavated a large hole close to the river, flooded it, and hosted the first documented mock naval battles in the city, called *naumachia*.[260] Though the battle was orchestrated, the participants were prisoners of war and were not intended to survive the spectacle. As always, Augustus surpassed his predecessors. One of his key generals, Titus Statilius Taurus, was crucial to the final military victory over Mark Antony. Statilius Taurus used his financial rewards and the prestige of this victory to inaugurate the first permanent amphitheatre in the city of Rome in 29 BCE, and hosted gladiatorial contests in celebration. The citizens of Rome were ecstatic, and reportedly thanked him by allowing him to choose one of the *praetors* every year.[261] Unfortunately, nothing survives of the monument today and even its location in the Campus Martius is uncertain. A likely spot was between the River Tiber and the Circus Flaminius, which as we have seen was already the traditional place to erect buildings to give thanks for military victories.

We cannot be sure of its exact design, though amphitheatre expert Katherine Welch suggests that it likely had a stone exterior in the Tuscan style, with wooden seating inside.[262] Compared with the later Colosseum, it was decidedly modest, though comparable in size perhaps to other Republican amphitheatres. It never became the sole locale for spectacle in the city, with Augustus and his heir Tiberius both choosing to use the traditional temporary seating in the Forum.[263] It was soon eclipsed by the amphitheatres that followed elsewhere on the Italian peninsula, and must have rather quickly looked dated and insufficient.

Throughout the reigns of the Julio-Claudian dynasty, the progress of amphitheatres was inconsistent. Each emperor and his allies held gladiator games but there was no consistent policy around venues. During the Great Fire of Rome in 64 CE, the Amphitheatre of Statilius Taurus burned down, leaving the city without a permanent amphitheatre. A few years later, a new dynasty ruled Rome, the Flavians, founded by Vespasian in 69 CE.

In 70 CE, Vespasian's son Titus besieged and conquered Jerusalem, sacking the city and desecrating the Second Temple. Tens of thousands of Jews were killed or enslaved. The loot Titus seized from Judaea was brought back to Rome, and funded the greatest amphitheatre in the entire empire. The amphitheatre was originally known as the Flavian Amphitheatre after the dynasty who built it.

The name we know this venue by came from association: the new amphitheatre was constructed next to a colossal statue of Nero, and the location was deliberate. Nero had surveyed the devastation of the Great Fire and seen an opportunity. He built the Domus Aurea, or Golden House, on some of the land that had burned. His new palace was truly extravagant, estimated to cover between 100 and 300 acres of central Rome between the Palatine, Caelian, Oppian and Esquiline hills. The area had been largely residential, interspersed with commercial properties, but survivors of the fire, both rich and poor, were unceremoniously informed that they would not live or work there again. The Domus Aurea complex boasted villas, baths and gardens, fountains, statues, pavilions, orchards and even a decorative forest, creating a luxurious countryside estate where city blocks had once stood. Dining rooms were fitted with mechanisms that sprayed perfumes and released clouds of flower petals above the heads of guests. One dining room rotated day and night as if enchanted. The aforementioned bronze Colossus, at least ninety-nine feet tall, stood in a vestibule near to an ornamental artificial lake. When his new palace was complete, says Suetonius, Nero mildly remarked that finally, he could live in a house fit for a human being.[264] Historians at the time and ever since have been hostile towards this grand scheme, despite the fact that Nero had already been in the habit of constructing buildings for the public, opening his private buildings and gardens to the public, and that archaeological evidence supports the idea that many areas of the Domus were designed with similar intentions.[265]

Vespasian wasted no time in dismantling the Domus Aurea complex, leaving only a villa behind.[266] Eventually, emperors would build temples around the site, but the first monument to be built there was Vespasian's amphitheatre. Its location was where Nero's artificial lake had once stood. Vespasian and Titus were making a grand show of dismantling the private pleasure palace of a bad emperor, and giving the site back to the citizens of Rome in the form of an ostentatious monument for the public, the largest amphitheatre they had ever seen. The Flavian Amphitheatre was never surpassed during the Roman empire; no amphitheatre afterwards was larger, more intricately designed, or as highly decorated. The Colossus of Nero was allowed to remain, but altered to depict Sol, God of the Sun. Nero was erased.

Even a narrative of Nero as a semi-competent emperor would not suit Vespasian's purposes. Nero was the last of the Julio-Claudian emperors, and his death had been followed by the tumult of multiple men competing to found a new dynasty. The whole affair was unprecedented. Vespasian was a general. He wasn't even from the patrician class. To secure his dynasty, he must do everything right while reminding Rome of everything Nero had got wrong. Nero was presented as a megalomaniac, and constructing the Colosseum on top of his private lake was part of the Flavian masterclass in political propaganda. As far as Vespasian was concerned, Nero himself had provided a lot of ammunition with which to tarnish Nero's reputation. Nero, the emperor who had abandoned Rome for an entire year to tour Greece, strumming his lyre and singing to captive audiences, winning Olympic chariot races he didn't even finish, was entitled and egomaniacal. Vespasian and his son Titus, who had left Rome to go conquering with the legions they commanded, promised to return (some) of the land Nero had seized and munificently handed it straight back to the populace in the form of a great monument designed for their pleasure. The dichotomy was stark, if exaggerated; Nero had been selfish, narcissistic and entitled. Vespasian and his family lived to serve, were generous with their wealth and their middle-class heritage ensured that they would not be entirely out of touch with ordinary Roman citizens. Closely examining the context in which the Colosseum was built like this helps us see both the historical context more clearly and understand how popular gladiator games were in this period: popular enough to help a new dynasty establish itself.

Vespasian died less than a year before the amphitheatre's completion, leaving his son Titus to finish the project in 80 CE. Its seating capacity is estimated to be around 50,000, though some have claimed 87,000 to be its maximum. While considerable, this is still only 5-8 per cent of the estimated population at the time, which stood at around one million inhabitants.[267] To ensure that everyone got to experience the lavish inaugural games within, Titus arranged for them to last more than 100 days. The young writer Martial, reliant on the benevolent support of patrons, sycophantically toadied up to Titus by publishing *Liber Spectaculorum*, a series of epigrams that gushingly describe the amphitheatre and those first Games within. The first epigram lists wonders of the world including the Pyramids of Giza, the Temple of Artemis at Ephesus and the Mausoleum of Halicarnassus, and states that the fame of the Flavian Amphitheatre will eclipse them all. The second, to really drive the Flavian propaganda home, recalls the 'despised halls of that cruel king' that once stood on the site.[268] When Hadrian moved the Colossus closer to the Flavian Amphitheatre so that he could build a massive new temple to Venus and Roma in 135 CE, he took the opportunity of adding a crown to the statue and declaring that it now depicted the God of the Sun, Sol.[269] It was this adjacency of the 'Colossus Solis' that eventually led to the amphitheatre being coined the 'Colosseum' in around 1,000 CE, a name that has stuck.[270]

Built to mark a military victory and paid for by the spoils of war, like so many Roman monuments, the Colosseum was a testament in concrete and marble to militarism, imperialism and testosterone. It was also the result of decades of amphitheatre development and an ongoing negotiation between popular tastes and elite ideals. In the 109 years between the inaugural Games in Rome's first and largest (if not last) amphitheatre, we still see the widespread use of temporary arenas, constructed of wood, utilising existing buildings. This is a phenomenon that we will see repeated when we examine Roman spectacle in the Greek world.

Early Amphitheatres in the Greek World

We do have literary evidence for wooden amphitheatres being erected in cities including Berenike and Berytos, which is lucky, as they would leave little archaeological trace. We will never know how many temporary amphitheatres were actually built in the Greek world, nor how many benches or *maeniana* were erected in various agoras. An inscription from Delos commemorating a gladiator named Epagathus specifically records that he won eight victories on Delos, which does have a theatre, albeit unadapted. However, there is a compelling case for the locale of Delian gladiation being the Agora of the Italians. Evidence suggests that this Agora was specifically constructed as a multifunctional space, noting that the unpaved courtyard and quadrilateral two-storey porticoes surrounding it lend themselves perfectly to the *maeniana* style benches and balconies that Vitruvius advised for makeshift gladiatorial displays in the forum of Rome in *De Architectura*. The ample epigraphic evidence for gladiation in Thracian Beroe/Ulpa Augusta Traiana, now Stara Zagora, is the greatest concentration in Bulgaria,[271] and has prompted the search for a venue. Neither a theatre nor amphitheatre has yet been identified, though one is believed to have been present,[272] particularly since nearby Serdica had an amphitheatre, and Philippopolis had both a stadium with podium wall and a converted theatre. In fact, the weight of the evidence in Augusta Traiana may suggest the location of the region's *ludus*.[273] Physical evidence for an amphitheatre remains elusive, however, a venue suitable for gladiation has been identified in Augusta Traiana, and it is one that also has ties to dramatic performance and athletic competition. A complex of *thermae-gymnasion* and a *theatron* were already the locale for recitals and athletic competition. The addition of some stone safety barriers in the complex piazza, decorated with gladiatorial relief, point to combats being staged here. It is not inconceivable that *maeniana* in the form of wooden bleacher style benches could have been erected here on an *ad hoc* basis.

Could other *poleis* have used agoras or other open spaces to similarly stage gladiatorial combat? Stone parapet wall adaptations like those at Stara Zagora have not been found elsewhere outside of theatres, but less permanent safety arrangements could easily have been substituted, particularly in *poleis* who staged gladiation with less frequency. Could other *poleis* have used agoras or other open spaces to similarly stage gladiatorial combat? Stone parapet wall adaptations like those at Stara Zagora have not been found elsewhere outside of theatres, but less permanent safety arrangements could easily have been substituted, particularly in *poleis* who staged gladiation with less frequency. We should consider that open, urban areas being temporarily used for gladiation to be more common than thus far assumed, particularly when benches could be so cheaply and swiftly erected. Indeed, I find this ad hoc use of agoras to be a likely solution in the early adoption of gladiation in the east in poleis that would later find Roman bloodsports popular enough to invest in a permanent alteration to a theatre or stadium, as we'll investigate in Chapters 13 and 14.

As we have seen, Julius Caesar, who was so quick to recognise the political potential of harnessing spectacle in Rome, was also responsible for the first gladiatorial venues in the eastern provinces – in Corinth and Antioch. However, in both these examples, we immediately run into the same problem; we know hardly anything about them. At Corinth, the unexcavated amphitheatre lies far away from the tourist trail, unsignposted and unloved. It's easy to miss from the road, but its telltale oval shape is clear to see on satellite imagery websites, nestled between agricultural fields and an olive grove. As these aerial images suggest, the site is largely forgotten and unkempt, with few people paying it much mind. Antiquarians have made basic plans of the monument of what they could observe from wandering around the site, but it's never been excavated. It's an early and important site nevertheless, and there are still opportunities to learn something. What can we tell from the parts of the structure that are visible?

The amphitheatre sits in a natural depression, which its architects exploited. They carved out the living rock to create the arena and *cavea* seating, which is the same method we see at the contemporary amphitheatres at Sutrium in Etruria and Carmo in Spain. Left open to the elements for two millennia, the *cavea* rock is somewhat weathered, which makes accurate measurements of the arena size somewhat difficult to ascertain. It does appear to be slightly larger than the other fifteen or so amphitheatres constructed in the first century CE.[274]

Another question that could be answered by an archaeological dig is whether the *cavea* was extended at the top using wooden bleachers, as at Sutrium and Carmo. Geographically, it's exactly where we would expect an amphitheatre to be. When the city was rebuilt as a Caesarian colony, Roman urban planners organised the street plan into a blanket of neat and even rectangular city blocks with criss-crossing streets, much like Manhattan.[275] The amphitheatre, like the circus built in the town at the same time, is sized and located to seamlessly fit into this pattern. The amphitheatre is a whole kilometre away from the ancient forum (which sat on the site of the Greek agora), but this was not unusual. Large scale entertainment venues were rarely situated near the civic centre, and, as at Pompeii, Corinth's amphitheatre sat in a corner of the town tucked just inside the city wall. That way, on days where the amphitheatre was in use, the scores of visitors from the countryside and neighbouring towns wouldn't clog up the downtown area. In short, we don't know much, but we can be fairly certain that Corinth's amphitheatre was no-frills, which may be why the city decided to radically overhaul its theatre to host gladiators a couple of centuries later.[276] It's sometimes claimed that the amphitheatre can't have been in use for very long, though the city's famed penchant for gladiators was often commented on in Athens, which suggests that shows at the amphitheatre were actually rather common to keep up with demand.

In Antioch, now known as Antakya, the amphitheatre is not even firmly located. Early antiquarians exploring the city in previous centuries marked an oval-shaped ruin on maps, but the city has grown immensely since then and the rough location of what was only assumed to be an amphitheatre has been covered by modern building developments. There are some curved walls still visible in the rough place that the antique maps suggest, but they have never been excavated, and excavation is the only way to confirm what the structure is. As such, the amphitheatre is only sometimes present on modern archaeological plans of the ancient city and is mentioned in most books on the city only in passing. We know nothing about its construction, though the chronicler

John Malalas mentions blocks of its stone being repurposed into city walls under Theodosius.[277] Malalas doesn't strike me as the most reliable witness at times, his description of the amphitheatre being close to Caesar's theatre on the slopes of the acropolis is suspect, as the theatre is half a city away from the oval structure noted by antiquarians.[278]

Both these amphitheatres were ordered by Julius Caesar himself, a man who has been the focus of so much research into the ancient world. Yet both remain unexcavated. Why? The first answer is that excavation is time consuming and expensive, and digs are targeted at certain sites accordingly. Priority in the earliest archaeological digs was usually given to famed sites that scholars had read about in ancient literature. Antiquarians such as Heinrich Schliemann were drawn to noteworthy sites like moths to a flame, and they excavated in search of what might be described as 'Cool Stuff'. As archaeology became more methodical in the late-nineteenth century, countries including Britain, France, Germany and the United States rushed to found archaeological institutes (often known as Schools) in Greece, and jostled over which institute got to excavate which site. They were in search of the most famous sites in Greek history; and, while they showed more interest in architecture than antiquarians, a lot of their motives were also fuelled by Cool Stuff, the portable treasures that they could take home and fill their own archaeological museums with. Athens, Delphi, Olympia and others were obvious targets.

The American School of Classical Studies at Athens secured the right to excavate Corinth in 1896, and they have been actively excavating the site ever since. Despite the amphitheatre being identified in the 1700s, ASCSA have yet to go anywhere near it. The excavations of most foreign archaeological institutes in Greece have (until recently) been unabashedly focussed on the Classical period (roughly between 510 BCE and the death of Alexander the Great in 323 BCE). The Archaic period, just before the Classical, occasionally draws interest, and the Hellenistic period which followed it fares a little better. For archaeologists in Greece, the period of Roman occupation has very rarely been a priority, though this is (very slowly) changing.[279] In many ways, archaeologists are taking their lead from Pausanias, the travel writer of the second century CE. His detailed descriptions of the towns, cities and shrines of the Greek mainland have acted as a treasure map for archaeologists for centuries, and even he, living in the Roman period, can't be bothered to include Roman buildings in his writing. It is the classical that is the most respected, admired, and worthy of commemoration.[280] For him, the Roman monuments were garishly modern, a little gauche, and not worth the papyri it would take to record them on. Archaeologists have often seemed to agree. A stark exception to this indifference is any place specifically mentioned in the New Testament, such as the Corinthian forum where Paul preached. Fame, be it literary or biblical, secures interest, and interest secures funding. Caesar's amphitheatre doesn't get much of a mention in ancient literature, and Paul isn't described as speaking there. No Christians are recorded as being martyred inside it. The amphitheatre remains neglected. As a Roman ruin in a Greek city, set apart from the temples of the centre, it sits on the periphery waiting for some attention.

After Corinth and Antioch, there appears to be a pause in the buildings of amphitheatres in the Greek-speaking territories. Amphitheatre design had accelerated rapidly in the decades between the rock-cut amphitheatre at Corinth and the Flavian Amphitheatre in Rome, and so one might expect the next amphitheatres in the Greek world to resemble sophisticated contemporary examples such as Verona (built in 30 CE) or Arles (built in 90 CE). This doesn't seem to have been the case, though lots of evidence has not yet been investigated. The ambivalence towards Roman monuments by archaeologists might explain this: in the western territories, the discovery of an amphitheatre can make headlines and attract a lot of excavation funding; elsewhere, several amphitheatres have never been excavated. There are, however, several instances of unexcavated Greek amphitheatres that have nothing to do with disinterest. A brief survey of these unexcavated sites, and what we know of their history, helps fill in the blanks in our pile of evidence a little.

Hierapytna, Crete

Hierapytna was a thriving port city on the island of Crete, conquered by the Romans in 67 BCE. Aware of its strategic importance, the Romans heavily invested in the town, especially to improve its harbour. The fruits of this Roman labour were still clearly visible until recently; several foreign travellers to Crete reported seeing ruins that were recognisable. The city (now known as Ierapetra) was also later recognised for its maritime potential by the Venetians, whose own empire controlled the island through the thirteenth to the seventeenth centuries CE. Much of what we know of the Roman city comes from the Venetians who studied the ruins. A Venetian polymath named Francesco Barozzi spent a year in 1577 touring the island's ruins and copying down ancient inscriptions. He recorded many structures, noted their locations, described their decorations, and noted that the city must surely have been 'very grand, and very famous'.[281] Around a decade later, Onorio Belli, another intellectual from Italy, toured the island with his employer, the Venetian governor of Crete. He was an artist with a gift for drawing plans, and set about drawing as many ruins as he could. In Ierapetra he reportedly found a lot to draw, though the sketches themselves are now lost. Ruins were also still clearly visible to the fabulously named Thomas Abel Brimage Spratt in 1865. During a sterling career in the Royal Navy, Vice-Admiral Spratt was tasked with surveying the Mediterranean, and he is most famous to archaeologists today as the author of 'Spratt's Map', where he mapped the Dardanelles. On this map, dated to 1840, he had carefully marked every ruin they'd surveyed, and he wrote 'Novum Ilium(?)', meaning 'New Troy', on the spot where he considered the likely location of the ancient city. When the German archaeologists Schliemann, Dorpfeld and Blegen used the map to rediscover the city in the 1860s, they found Troy exactly where Spratt had indicated.

In 1865, Spratt spent time exploring Crete and wrote a two-volume book about all aspects of the island, including its archaeology. He used his naval expertise to draw up detailed maps that located each of the ruins he encountered. Twenty years after Spratt's book, another book in English, Murray's Handbook for Travellers, mentions the visible ruins a tourist could encounter in Ierapetra. Crucially, all of these writers mention the same structures, and their descriptions of the ruins and their locations tally perfectly. Ancient Hierapytna boasted temples, colonnaded streets, two theatres, a bath complex and a very distinctively Roman amphitheatre. Belli's plans of the amphitheatre were so detailed that he was able to determine that the architects had built the seating on the slopes of two adjacent hills, and had constructed six buttresses at either end to complete the oval shape.

Unfortunately, no mythical wars were fought at Hierapytna and no antiquarians were rushing to excavate the maps that Spratt and others made of the area. By the time archaeologist Federico Halbherr arrived to excavate in 1893 much of the standing structures were being quarried by locals to build houses, and the structures that had been so clearly discernible were being dismantled piece by piece. Even so, ruins could still be seen in the early twentieth century. This soon changed, as yet another empire seeking control of the Mediterranean occupied the island and inflicted violence on anyone who resisted: this time, it was Nazi Germany. The Germans would retain control of the island for almost exactly four years, during which time they continued to punish resistance fighters by tearing down villages. As well as homes, the Nazi soldiers also demolished any buildings of historical significance that had withstood their bombs, and built gun emplacements and bunkers where they had once stood. Portable antiquities were looted by Nazi soldiers. Was this the fate of the Roman amphitheatre?

In Crete, as in so many places, it is hard to tell whether heritage sites have been damaged by imperial occupiers or local efforts to build lives for themselves: the amphitheatre may have already been built over in 1911 by a factory that made soap. The factory was demolished in the late 1970s and has yet to be redeveloped, as many of the sites destroyed by Nazis quickly were. As recently as 2009, archaeologists had begun to doubt whether the amphitheatre had existed at all. In 2012, a map made by Spratt once again provided an 'X' on the right spot, but this time archaeologists chose not to physically dig. Instead, a team used non-invasive archaeological techniques on the site of the old soap factory, which according to the map (and corroborated by the other antiquarian writers) was precisely where the amphitheatre should be. Ground Penetrating Radar (GPR) and Electrical Resistivity Tomography (ERT) both fall under the archaeological umbrella of geophysics; they allow archaeologists to get a sense of structures laying beneath the surface of the ground without the need of digging a trench. Both were used at the soap factory site, allowing the archaeological team to spot a large, oval building.[282] It is undoubtedly the amphitheatre. More information will be gathered if a full excavation ever does take place, but modern technology has so far vindicated the travellers of old.

For now, the ruins of the amphitheatre remain unexcavated and GPR and ERT can only tell archaeologists so much; whereas the finding of an inscription or coin that might help date the construction would answer a lot of questions about the development of amphitheatres in this region, small finds would tell us about how spectators experienced the games. For instance, intensive excavation at the amphitheatre of Chester not only revealed that spectators brought braziers with them to cook their own snacks, but rubbish deposits revealed that the snacks mainly consisted of chicken. Without such access to the remains of the amphitheatre at Hierapytna, we can make assumptions about such experiences, but can't say anything for certain.

Palmyra, Syria

Palmyra, also known as Tadmor, was an oasis caravan city in the middle of the Syrian desert, almost exactly equidistant from the great ancient cities of the eastern Mediterranean coast on one side and the Euphrates river on the other. Over its long history, because of its position at the nexus of many trade routes, it had been in contact with the many different cultures of ancient West Asia, whether we classify those traditions as Arabian, Hellenistic, Persian or Roman. The citizens of Palmyra developed a distinctive local visual culture that adapted elements of these various traditions and styles to their own tastes. From afar, the colonnaded streets look very much in the classical Roman style and they certainly date to the period Palmyra was part of the Roman empire, but closer inspection of the art and architecture reveals much more complexity and diversity. Though many have tried, Palmyra defies all attempts to categorise it into one neat 'box', because it is a blend of monuments built by a diverse array of peoples.

The city was, mercifully for historians, fond of inscriptions, which are frequently bilingual; Palmyrenes used both Greek and Aramaic for public inscriptions (although, intriguingly, the funerary inscriptions were primarily in Palmyrene Aramaic). Perfectly positioned as a trading post between empires, Palmyra grew in importance. The city was absorbed into Roman Syria when that province was expanded, probably under Tiberius in around 19 CE, and the Romans really turned the city's trade up a notch, with the city reaching its heyday in the second century CE. The wealthier its inhabitants got, the bigger the monuments they built. Colonnaded boulevards led to an elegant agora of civic buildings, and the city boasted temples to local gods and those from further afield alike. An enormous theatre was built in the second century CE, and its design shows that it was intended to be a multifunctional space: as well as the normal plays and pantomimes, a parapet safety wall around the *orchestra* allowed for gladiatorial displays without injury to the audience, which is a common feature in eastern theatres.[283]

But was this the only local venue where Palmyrenes could see gladiators? Until 2008, this was the consensus amongst archaeologists. That is, until an archaeologist named Manar Hammad spotted something while looking at some old aerial photographs from 1930. Aerial photography can be invaluable for spotting archaeological features in a landscape, particularly ones that lie just below the surface of the ground, but the conditions have to be just right. The colour and growth patterns of plants differ depending if the plants are rooted in deep soil or on top of the remains of stonework just below the topsoil. Archaeologists call these 'cropmarks'. In the verdant fields of the UK, droughts are the ideal time to spot subterranean structures with aerial photos because those differences become a lot starker; ancient ditches can appear a darker green than the rest of the field, while the plants on top of the remains of walls will dry out faster and turn yellow. Cropmarks in deserts are incredibly difficult to spot in comparison, though thankfully Palmyra's oasis allows for agricultural fields. The photos used by Hammad were taken in the spring of 1930 by French cartographers, and this was the season when the fields were ploughed.[284] This was awfully lucky for Hammad in 2008, because this agricultural process made buried structures that little bit easier to spot. While scouring photos of the entire site, two photos of a field near the museum showed two concentric oval walls, just beneath the surface.

Because the shape of an amphitheatre is unique in the ancient world, it is the only plausible candidate for what the buried building could be. Hammad measured the structure, and with a major axis of 100m it is a modest, if larger than an average legionary amphitheatre.[285] Hammad suggests that the upper walls are just below the surface, meaning that the arena itself is buried under metres of sand; full excavation would reveal many answers about its date and architectural style. Palmyra has been the subject of extensive excavation since 1902, and its buildings were a huge draw for tourism. It stands to reason that the amphitheatre, now located, would inevitably make its way onto the 'To Do' list of many archaeologists at some point and provide another monument for tourists to explore.

However, all archaeological work on the entire site ceased only a few years after Hammad's discovery. A series of anti-government protests and rebellions in several countries across North Africa and the Persian Gulf in 2011 became known as the Arab Spring. In Syria, massive protests were held against the Assads, a family who had ruled since 1971. Within months, Syria was plunged into civil war, and the Assad family responded with brutal violence. An unknowable number of Syrian protestors were brutalised, and many 'disappeared'. Several resistance groups sought to topple the Assad regime and assert their own dominance; the largest and most successful became known as ISIS, the Islamic State of Iraq and Syria. ISIS militants claimed the site of Palmyra in 2015, and for the following two years the ancient city changed hands between ISIS and the Syrian military forces, neither group caring if their military occupations damaged the fabric of the city. Whenever the site was in the control of ISIS, their militants set about destroying key ancient monuments with deliberately dramatic, controlled explosions, including the temples of Bel and Baalshamin, a castle and a monumental archway. Smaller artefacts such as statues were looted and sold on the black market to help fund the extremist movement. This was part of a wider programme of cultural destruction that affected other Syrian archaeological sites, religious buildings, and libraries; any remnants of a multi-cultural, multi-religion Syria were marked for destruction, as if they had never existed.

One of the many civilian casualties of the conflict around Palmyra was the archaeologist Khaled al-Asaad, who was not only local, but was the Head of Antiquities of the archaeological site for four decades. Nobody knew or loved Palmyra quite as much as al-Asaad, and he had been instrumental in smuggling out or hiding as many of his museum's artefacts as possible before ISIS could steal or destroy them. Al-Asaad was captured by ISIS terrorists, but, even under torture, he would not give up the location of the hidden antiquities. He was subsequently executed by decapitation in a public display of ISIS violence. He was eighty-three years old.

Much of the iconic architecture of Palmyra is now irrevocably lost, casualties of this hostile ideology. In the case of the amphitheatre, its burial and its obscurity seem to have saved it from the wrath of ISIS militants. Our inability to see and analyse this ancient site, where violence was performed as part of ongoing negotiation of local-imperial identity, is limited by more recent acts and performances of violence that have themselves emerged in local response to layers of imperial history. For now, it remains hidden; its existence is known only to a few, and its precise location by even fewer. When archaeologists are able to return to the site the arena will hardly be a priority, and rightly so; the horrified reaction to the destruction of Palmyra centred largely on the enduring antiquarian idea that Palmyra was 'Roman', and therefore the ideological, if not actual, property of the 'West'.[286] Its destruction was taken as an insult to Western powers (a deliberate motivation for ISIS demolition crews) and there was much public hand-wringing about the destruction of Roman (understood as Western) heritage, but not so much public sympathy for the many innocent Syrian civilians murdered by militants.

When the dust settles, archaeologists may be able to re-enter the site. It will be a monumental task to preserve and restore *all* of Palmyra's cultural monuments, not just those with perceived ties to European civilisations, and to remind the public that, as ISIS identified and resented, Palmyra was a vibrant city of intermingling cultures. But before archaeologists from foreign universities rush in to survey the destruction, the focus should be on foreign governments sending humanitarian aid to the millions of Syrians who desperately need housing and infrastructure. The amphitheatre, safely sleeping beneath the surface, can wait.

Salamis, Cyprus

The ancient town of Salamis on Cyprus has a history dating back to the Late Bronze Age, when its harbour made it an important part of growing trade networks. The town had important links to the Aegean in the west and the rich territory of Assyria in the east. Over the centuries, Cyprus was under the control of Assyrians, Egyptians, Persians and, in the wars that followed Alexander the Great's death, it was the Ptolemies who won dominion over the island. In 58 BCE, Salamis passed to Roman control when the entire island was annexed, and the town continued its centuries old tradition of trade. Of all her overlords, it was Rome that left the greatest impression on the archaeological record.

Salamis was first excavated by the British in the Victorian period; in 1887 the Cyprus Exploration Fund was created to conduct various excavations around the island and to bring back archaeological treasures that are still displayed in prominent English museums and public schools today. At the time, Cyprus was newly under British control,[287] and British archaeologists wanted to take advantage of their position (although they lost interest after a decade or so, and it wasn't until 1952 that excavations would resume). The archaeological work in the city continued for more than two decades, revealing enough artefacts to fill two museums (this time local). The site lies on low land right next to the beach, and sand blown over the site for centuries meant that buildings lay well-preserved. As well as a famed necropolis, a theatre and gymnasium were uncovered and received considerable global attention.

However, the excavations coincided with a turbulent period of Cypriot history. The majority of the population were Orthodox Christian Greek Cypriots, and the minority were Muslim Turkish Cypriots. Under centuries of foreign rule, first under the Ottomans and then the British, the two groups had often struggled to live in harmony, and tensions were rising once again. From 1955, a Greek Cypriot far-right group named EOKA started a guerilla campaign against British rule of Cyprus, with the aim of Cyprus becoming part of Greece; this 'big idea' is known as *enosis*.

Turkish Cypriots preferred British rule to *enosis*, and the British administration happily stoked this division between local communities for their own benefit; such feuding prevented the colonised from uniting against the coloniser. EOKA were attacking British soldiers whenever possible, and British authorities who could find no informants (because EOKA made sure to execute anyone who might try) resorted to torturing locals they suspected of having information. The British decided to hire Turkish Cypriots to police Greek Cypriots, which resulted in violence from both sides. Gradually, the consensus grew that neither side would be able to live in peace amongst the other. While far-right influenced Greek Cypriots pushed for absorption into Greece, Turkish Cypriots started to float their own solution; *taksim*, a two-state solution. Violence was encouraged and facilitated on both sides by external states with vested interests. In 1960, the British washed their hands of the situation, granting Cyprus independence (while retaining British military bases on the island, their main priority in claiming Cyprus in the first place). In 1967, the democratically elected government in Greece was supplanted by a far-right military junta who immediately lobbied for *enosis* over the fragile, multicultural new Republic of Cyprus. In 1974, the junta supported the Cypriot National

Guard staging a coup against the Cypriot government, and to many watching events unfold it seemed like a Greek merger was now inevitable. The Turkish government appealed to the British to intervene, but Britain refused to make any move, as did the United States. Politically isolated and citing concern for the safety of Turkish Cypriots, Türkiye sent military troops into Cyprus on 20 July 1974. Whether this should be classed as an intervention or an invasion is still hotly debated half a century later. Over the course of a month, Turkish troops secured about a third of the island, and, after a failed attempt at a ceasefire, this area has remained in Turkish hands ever since.

Greek Cypriots were expelled from this area in the north, and Turkish Cypriots were similarly forced to flee to Turkish territory. It was an echo of the Graeco-Turkish population exchange of 1923.[288] Atrocities were committed on both sides during this time, and civilians from both communities remain missing. Mass graves subsequently discovered do not account for the total number of the missing. The border between the two portions of the island, known as the Green Line, is a heavily monitored and patrolled buffer zone, and crossing was for a long time impossible. The team of archaeologists working on Salamis found themselves unable to visit the site, let alone work.

The Greek Cypriot archaeologist Vassos Karageorghis had, by 1974, been working at the site for more than two decades. In his 1969 book about the site, Karageorghis mentions that he has located the amphitheatre, wedged in between the excavated and partially restored theatre and gymnasium.[289] The sand had been removed to reveal the shape of the structure, but the removal of debris necessary for excavation to begin hadn't been conducted yet. As Karageorghis says, other projects needed to be completed first before the arena could have its moment in the sun. Because of the invasion, that moment has been delayed for half a century. Modern satellite imagery reveals that the dark oval of the arena is once again almost entirely covered by sand and plants.

For Greek Cypriots, the site is under the occupation of an invading force. For Turkish Cypriots, the site is part of their infant state, the Turkish Republic of Northern Cyprus having been formed in 1983. Only Türkiye, on whom the TRNC is highly dependent, officially recognises it as a state. Turkish universities have sent a few archaeological projects to Northern Cyprus since around the turn of the century, to the horror of Greek Cypriot archaeologists. UNESCO prohibits occupying forces from conducting archaeological excavations, but the Turkish universities argue that the TRNC is not occupied territory, it is a de facto state and as such the excavations are entirely legal. So far, Turkish archaeologists do not seem to have excavated the Salamis arena.

Modern Cyprus has bigger problems than archaeological excavation; its citizens are divided into groups who are still pro *enosis*, pro *taksim*, and those who remember the multicultural communities of the past. I am neither qualified nor inclined to distribute blame or offer solutions to the ongoing tensions in the area, but I hope to have demonstrated why geopolitics sometimes has a hand in which sites are revealed, and which sites must lay unstudied. The arena at Salamis still lies waiting for the archaeologists' trowel, though who will wield it and when is unknowable at this point.

There is one more reason why I have chosen to discuss the amphitheatre at Salamis specifically. Before the partition, archaeologists did find that most valuable form of evidence: an inscription that gives us an approximate date for the construction of the amphitheatre. The inscription reveals that a local dignitary named Servius Sulpicius Pancles Veranianus was responsible for rebuilding the gymnasium (complete with brand new Roman-style bathhouse) and theatre, and also built the amphitheatre all entirely at his own expense. The inscription itself mentions no date. Because other inscriptions mention his unusual name, his family tree can be partially reconstructed as well as his network of patrons and clientele, some of whom do have inscriptions that can be dated. Also, we know that Salamis was rocked by destructive earthquakes in 76/77 CE, but was in such great shape again by 123 CE that Hadrian granted it the prestigious status of metropolis.[290] Extensive building work had to have been completed in that window of time, and archaeologists have deduced that the construction of the arena, together with the rebuilding of the theatre and gymnasium complex, should be placed in the late 70s or 80s CE.[291] This means it was constructed fairly early in the progression of eastern amphitheatres, and was perhaps one of the first permanent imperial examples.[292]

Cyzicus, Pergamon and Anazarbos

There were three more amphitheatres built from the second century CE that reward further investigation: Cyzicus, Pergamon, and Anazarbos. All are situated in Anatolia, but are separated by quite some distance: Cyzicus sat in the ancient region of Mysia on the south coast of the Marmara Sea, Pergamon was in Aeolis near the Aegean coastline, and Anazarbos was a Cilician city, not far from the modern Syrian border. With three identified amphitheatres, we could theoretically have a goldmine of information about their construction and use, and yet details are hard to come by.

Here we return to our old problem of excavation. There are ongoing excavations at Cyzicus, but they are not currently focused on the amphitheatre there. Pergamon amphitheatre has recently been the focus of an interdisciplinary excavation, and information is slowly being released by the archaeologists. News reports suggest that Anazarbos amphitheatre might soon be paid archaeological attention, but academic publishing is a punishingly slow process and no information has yet been shared. We have three arenas, with three different levels of excavation, and three levels of available information. We might begin, at least, by trying to find out what, if anything, they have in common.

Some of our observations must therefore necessarily come merely from what can be observed with the naked eye. The first thing that we can definitely say is that these three arenas are built differently from the early, rock-cut amphitheatre at Corinth. Instead of digging down, these arenas were built *up*: using concrete and masonry, all three utilised sloping topography to build seating upon, with vaulting to complete the seating where necessary. In Pergamon, the slopes on either side of the valley that the amphitheatre straddles led to its unusual design – the amphitheatre is circular, not an oval. From construction style, it seems that the Cyzicus and Pergamon amphitheatres date from the early second century CE, and it's unlikely that the (as yet) undated Anazarbos arena was built earlier than them.

These amphitheatres were larger than the earlier amphitheatres of the wider region, even if they couldn't compete in size with the contemporary great western amphitheatres of Thysdrus (El Djem), Verona, Tarragona, or Nîmes. These were large enough to accommodate far more people than simply stationed soldiers, as at Dura Europos: they could seat large swathes of each city's civilian populace as well as visitors from nearby towns. Amphitheatres drew in spectators like moths to a flame.

Unfortunately, a second thing that these arenas have in common is that they were all almost completely dismantled so that their stone could be repurposed elsewhere. In Cyzicus, several large monuments were torn down to provide building materials for the emperor Justinian's rejuvenation of Constantinople. It is possible that some of the arena is now part of the fabric of the Hagia Sophia. In Cyzicus and Anazarbos, nearly all that is currently visible are the stubby remains of the substructures – the corridors beneath the seating – sticking out of the ground like decaying teeth in a rotting mouth. The Pergamon amphitheatre today looks a little like an iron age hill fort in Britain; a ring of heaped earth covered with vegetation. The only hint of its original form comes from a row of three tall, interconnected masonry arches. They were once part of a ring of vaulting that allowed the Romans to make the seating area so vast. What's left is nevertheless enough to surmise that they were far grander than the few arenas the Greeks had yet seen; larger and more architecturally advanced.

The Pergamon and Anazarbos amphitheatres seem to have both been part of designated entertainment districts, as both were closely situated next to a theatre and stadium. Situated away from the city centre, as was typical in western cities, these entertainment quarters would have been buzzing on festival and games days, with thousands of spectators milling around chatting, and dozens of food and souvenir stalls for them to purchase snacks and mementoes.

The Cyzicus and Pergamon arenas were built over streams, and it's been suggested that this allowed architects to flood the arenas for aquatic shows, which, as well as dancers and acrobats, may have featured *naumachiae*, mock sea battles with combatants in boats.[293] Pergamon's arena certainly does show evidence of a waterproof flooring, though this alone isn't definitive proof; until Cyzicus is thoroughly investigated, potential *naumachiae* there must also remain conjecture.

Even with so much of the structures missing, intensive excavation could provide vital clues as to how these buildings were used.

- Were there shrines used by the gladiators?
- Were there subterranean areas where wild animals were caged?
- Could we take precise measurements to estimate how many people the seating could accommodate?

One day, we may have comprehensive answers to these questions. Academic interest in the amphitheatres of this region is a very recent trend, and proper archaeological studies of monuments so large take several years, as well as being expensive to run. With a limited amount of money and archaeologists available, it is only in the last few years that Anatolian amphitheatres have been deemed worthy of study. Results here might spur interest in studying the buried amphitheatres of Crete and Cyprus. Of all the amphitheatres in the eastern regions of the Roman empire, only Eleutheropolis (in Palestine) has been fully revealed. Imagine how much information we would have about our Greek gladiators if this were to change.

We know that amphitheatres are few and far between in the Greek world, and we have learned that we don't know nearly as much as we could know about them. But, even if these arenas were complete and excavated, they wouldn't tell the full story of eastern gladiators. To truly get a grip on how widespread the phenomenon was, we need to turn to other evidence, and other cultural phenomena. First, we should apply our existing knowledge to another case study.

Relief showing a gladiator fight in chronological stages. Found in Hierapolis. The fighters are named Pinnas and Odysseus. Image courtesy of Carole Raddato.

Relief showing a gladiator fight in chronological stages. Provenance uncertain, possibly from Ephesus. The inscription names the fighters as Parthenopaios and Nympheros, both of the First Rank and hailing from Cappadocia. Image courtesy of Yale University Art Gallery.

Relief showing a gladiatorial fight in chronological stages. Found in Kibyra. Image courtesy of Carole Raddato.

Terracotta lamp depicting a gladiator fight. Made in Anatolia. Image courtesy of Getty's Open Content Program.

Funerary stele of Satornilos, a *thraex* from Ephesus who was buried in Smyrna. His tombstone was erected for him by his colleagues. Image courtesy of Rijksmuseum voor Oudheden, Leiden.

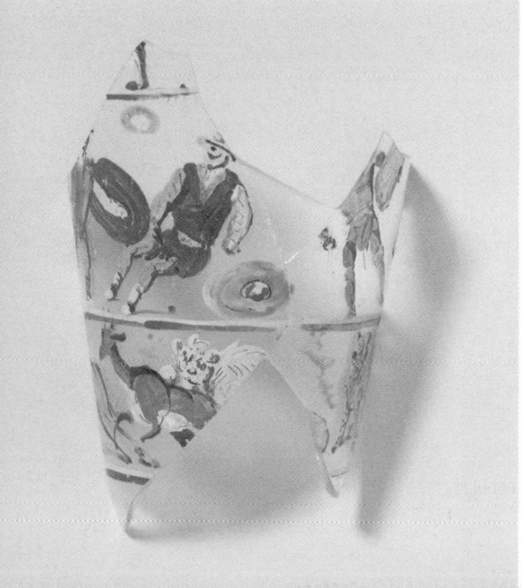

Fragments of a glass beaker painted with gladiatorial images. Found in Egypt. Image courtesy of The Metropolitan Museum of Art, New York.

Architectural remains of Cyzicus Amphitheatre. Image courtesy of Carole Raddato.

Pergamon Amphitheatre, viewed from the acropolis. Image courtesy of Carole Raddato.

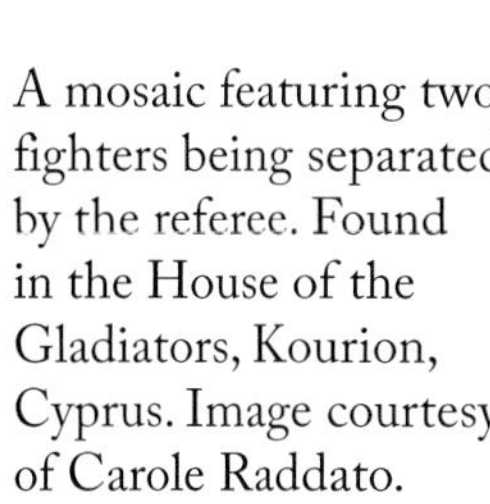

A mosaic featuring two fighters being separated by the referee. Found in the House of the Gladiators, Kourion, Cyprus. Image courtesy of Carole Raddato.

A mosaic featuring two gladiator fights. Found in the House of Silenos, Kos. Image courtesy of Robert Caudill, www.roamintheempire.com.

An unusual gladiator monument in the shape of a *scutum* and helmet. Found in the necropolis of Claudiopolis, now in the Bolu Museum. Erected by a priest named Secundus, the inscription names the gladiators of his *familia*: Campanus, *scutarius* with sixty-five victories; Myron, *essedarius* with forty-three victories; Apleros, *provocator* with fifty-two victories; Chrysampelos, thirty-five victories; Margareites, *essedarius* with seventy-five victories; Victor, fifty-eight victories; Poseidonius, twenty-four victories; Skirtos, *retiarius* with eighteen victories; Spekles, *eques* with thirty-five victories; Achilleus, forty victories; Euchorous, fifty victories; Panter, *retiarius* with fifteen victories.

Perge stadium, viewed from the *sphendone*. Note the addition of a wall bisecting the track, creating an arena.

Aphrodisias stadium, viewed from the *sphendone*. Note that the stadium has not been as extensively restored as Perge, yet the same additional arena wall is discernible.

Kibyra stadium excavations. The trench shows that the track level of stadiums is typically lower than the current surface, and the restoration work demonstrates how the high *podium* wall was constructed.

Xanthos theatre, with a high *podium* wall separating spectators from combatants.

The Theatre of Dionysus in Athens, with parapet wall *in situ.*

The rough-hewn parapet wall of Patara theatre.

The rough-hewn wall of Alabanda theatre, showing the blocked row of seating in the front.

Halicarnassus theatre, the likely location of Amazon and Achillea's bout. Post holes are discernible around the arena edge.

The theatre at Myra, with *podium* wall topped with a parapet wall of orthostates, of which only a few stand upright.

Gravestone of a *murmillo* from Tralleis.
Now in Aydin Archaeological Museum.

Gravestone of the *murmillo* Penelais,
probably from Sparta. Now in the National
Archaeological Museum in Athens. Note
the four victory wreaths and palm frond.

Stele of a *thraex* named Stephanos.
Ephesus Museum.

Stele of Anicetus, a *secutor* from
Aphrodisias.

Chapter 12

CSI Case Study: Armies and Amphitheatres

The unexcavated nature of the amphitheatres we *do* know about means it is difficult to construct a timeline of their development in the eastern provinces. Again, we have to look to the west for a potential parallel: despite the cultural differences, we have a far greater understanding of the development of gladiatorial architecture there, and so it remains a crucial source of information. We can take what we already know about the Greek world, carefully combine it with what we know about practice in Rome's western territories, and apply it in this case study.

We have already seen that, in Rome, early venues were temporary and usually made from wood, situated in the forum. We see this repeated elsewhere in the western provinces too. Vitruvius, the first century BCE architect, lays out his advice for constructing a forum specifically with the capability for hosting spectacles in mind.[294] One law, the *Lex Ursonensis*, suggests that a Caesarian colony in Spain had to make do with gladiatorial shows in its forum at the same time that Corinth got a permanent amphitheatre, but also indicates that local *aediles* and *duumvirs* sponsoring gladiatorial games as part of their magistracies was already an expectation.[295] Crucially, it seems that the permanent western amphitheatres that replaced ad hoc structures initially followed the legions: soldiers wanted to enjoy gladiatorial shows while on duty abroad and continue to enjoy them when they retired. This important detail helps us understand the patchier evidence we have for the Greek world.

Legions on campaign built forts, some temporary and some less so. Of all Roman groups, it was soldiers who had the greatest interest and familiarity with gladiatorial combat. As fellow combat experts, soldiers had a deep appreciation in gladiatorial manoeuvres and techniques which were very different to their own (despite sharing some weaponry). The two professions had much in common: discipline, intensive training, and high levels of violence. In fact, gladiators had played a key role in one of the most significant military periods of Roman history – a small but potentially significant part of the transition from civilians with armour in the backroom to a professionalised, standing army. They had also helped face down one of the biggest perceived threats to Rome's existence.

From 113 BCE, Germanic and Celtic tribes, including the ones we call the Teutones and the Cimbri, started to migrate south, close to the Italian peninsula and the newly minted Roman province of Gallia Narbonensis in southern France. They were confronted by a Roman army at the Battle of Noreia, where only a fifth of the Roman army survived. At this point, the army was a citizen militia; builders, farmers, shopkeepers, and so on, who were conscripted when required. Practically all able-bodied male citizens (or, at least, those that met the personal wealth requirements for conscription) had considerable combat experience. In this specific period, the male citizenry was particularly busy; Rome was fighting the Jugurthine War in Numidia as well as the Teutones and Cimbri. In Numidia, the famed general Gaius Marius was experimenting with the army reforms for which he remains famous. In Gaul, another general had his own novel methods.

In 105 BCE, the Romans had been dealt another harsh blow at the Battle of Arausio in southern France. The two generals, Quintus Servilius Caepio and Gnaeus Mallius Maximus, couldn't stop squabbling long enough to cooperate and organise a united front. Outnumbered nearly two-to-one, the battle was a disaster. All of the estimates of battlefield casualties given by Roman historians should be taken with a pinch of salt, but Livy states that 80,000 Romans and 40,000 of their auxiliaries were killed that day.[296] If that's true, it was a bigger catastrophe than the Battle of Cannae. As Rome reeled with shock, Publius Rutilius Rufus decided that his citizen militia had much to learn about combat from gladiators, but that perhaps watching gladiatorial combat was insufficient. He called in the gladiators of a gladiatorial school based in Capua, owned by Gaius Aurelius Scaurus, and employed them as battle consultants.[297] The gladiators taught the soldiers new techniques with their weaponry, and drilled them incessantly until they grew stronger and more nimble. When Marius swept in to take over command of the Cimbrian War, he found a far more disciplined and skilled force who were more than ready to meet their enemies; within four years, both the Teutones and Cimbri were all but annihilated.[298] The gladiator training had helped.

The relationship between gladiators and legions continued as the army morphed from a citizen militia into a professional standing force. Cicero, reminiscing about the military training of his youth, twice mentions that he had undertaken training in a gladiatorial *ludus*.[299] Clearly, both professions found that they could learn from each other, and their symbiotic relationship proved mutually beneficial. Eventually, a small amphitheatre was often considered an excellent addition to legionary forts, both for training and entertainment purposes.[300] This is why Britannia and the Danubian *Limes*,[301] both requiring heavy and constant military presence, boast so many amphitheatres on the very edges of the empire. In many cities, as towns grew up around some of these forts, the local population joined the soldiers as spectators, requiring the amphitheatres to be enlarged or improved, as at Chester.[302]

The transition to a professionalised army and the constant wars required to maintain Roman rule gave Rome a headache, the solution for which meant that gladiator games spread further. Constant wars also meant a surplus of veterans who all demanded good land to retire on as thanks for their loyal service, because now the Roman military was a professional force, rather than civilians who returned to their primary jobs once a campaign season was over. Retired soldiers now had no family business and home to fall back to. This caused several of their generals a significant political headache, because several thousand angry well-armed, well-trained, unemployed and homeless soldiers could wreak a lot of havoc. Veteran colonies were thus set up in newly conquered territories, often in the existing towns of allies and enemies alike; for example, Pompeii, home to the oldest permanent amphitheatre, was settled with Roman veterans after the town rebelled against Rome in the Social War. Following a successful siege by Sulla,[303] around 2,000 veterans of that war were settled in the town. The amphitheatre was built a mere two decades later, a very visible statement of 'Rome is in charge here now, get used to it'. Gradually, these alien settlers became embedded into wider local life, along with their culture and customs. Legionary amphitheatres were built as a symbol of imperial dominance, and while in the western provinces they came to be used by locals as well, evidence for a broader acceptance of a legionary amphitheatre on the easternmost edges of the empire is scant.

What seems clear, however, is that Roman amphitheatres often followed Roman armies. What does that mean for our investigation into Greek enthusiasm for gladiators in the Greek parts of the Roman empire?

Dura, Syria

In the eastern territories across West Asia and Egypt, military amphitheatres were not common, despite heavy military presence along the borders. This can perhaps be attributed to soldiers finding mature cities with existing buildings that could easily be borrowed and used for gladiatorial purposes, rather than using materials and manpower making arenas from scratch like they had to do in Britain or along the Germanic borders; this is perhaps the case, but we would need further evidence to prove the hypothesis. For now, all we can say is that fewer military amphitheatres were built in the eastern portion of the empire. An exception is found at the remote town of Dura Europos in Syria, which was a Hellenistic settlement on the Euphrates river, dating from around 300 BCE, shortly after Alexander the Great's campaigns and likely founded by his general Seleucus Nicator. It doesn't boast all of the Hellenistic features that we consider essential parts of a Greek settlement; there is no theatre in Dura for instance, nor a gymnasium, though it did have a 'Hippodamian' street plan and substantial city walls.

To begin with, it seems like the town was primarily a Seleukid military outpost. The Parthians took over the town when Seleukid powers were waning, in the late-second or early-first century BCE, and their influence can most clearly be seen in their temples. In the imperial period, Roman tussled over Dura with the Parthians for a while, with the town changing hands more than once. The town developed its own personalised identity, building on at least three peoples and cultures. At the start of the third century CE, Rome decided to beef up the military presence in the town, and a clutch of buildings for the soldiers were constructed in quick succession. One of these was an amphitheatre, and it is one of the few examples where we have a secure date; an inscription reveals that soldiers of Legio IV Scythica and Legio III Cyrenaica dedicated the new building in 216 CE.[304] It's the easternmost amphitheatre in the empire, and also one of the strangest.

It was constructed in an older bathhouse that seems to have been left derelict following a fire. The bathhouse had a *palaestra*, an open, squared space for practising Greek contact sports. The arena was built to fit into the *palaestra*, and the contact sports practised within the space became firmly Roman, with swords replacing fists. One half of the seating was built up over the ruins of the once-indoor area of the bathhouse, and the other expanded out over the existing street, which had to be closed to traffic. The arena walls were masonry topped with mudbrick, and the seating was entirely wooden. As Simon James notes, 'On one side perched on the ruins of the bath and on the other on a mass of timbering over 8th St, [the amphitheatre] must have looked like a building-site from the outside; yet the interior was a careful exercise in graceful curves and visual symmetry.'[305] Neither the arena nor the *cavea* were large, and it's estimated that the number of spectators might have only reached around 1,000.

What are we to make of this? The legionaries usually constructed purpose-built amphitheatres, from what we can tell, but here they adapted a local space. Perhaps the small capacity gives us a hint: it may be that this amphitheatre was purely for the enjoyment of the soldiers who constructed it, and that the civilian population were not inclined or perhaps not even invited to attend, which would be a parallel of the situation in Judaea. Perhaps it reflects a different mindset from the troops, who adapted their standard approach because of the specific requirements of the city. Perhaps they just never got around to constructing a purpose-built amphitheatre. The city changed hands again within a few decades of the inscription dating this converted amphitheatre.

The example of Dura Europos is a reminder that we can only ever get so far with our investigations of the past, for one thing. Perhaps it is also a reminder that, no matter how carefully we construct our categories, our evidence doesn't fit neatly the way we might like.

We may never answer these questions. However, this case study also offers two crucial pieces of information for our investigation that we can be confident about. Firstly, it is a reminder that military and martial prowess (real or imagined) was inextricably linked with the cultural phenomenon of gladiators. Sometimes those connections were real, sometimes they were perceived or performed, but we cannot understand gladiators without understanding the military context. Secondly, it tells us that gladiator combats could be performed in adapted venues. We must keep these two discoveries in mind as we turn to other evidence to truly get a grip on how widespread the phenomenon was in the Greek world.

Chapter 13

Homeric Cosplay

The Greeks loved stories. Listening to stories was an excellent way to pass the time, and became a popular form of community entertainment. As we will see, this tradition is essential to understanding gladiators in the Greek world: why they were popular, how they styled themselves, and where they fought.

Most people these days have heard of the Greek epic poems the *Iliad* and the *Odyssey*, even if only from Hollywood adaptations. Watching movies like *Troy*, *The Return*, and Christopher Nolan's *Odyssey* is remarkably similar to how most ancient Greeks engaged with the *Iliad* and *Odyssey*; few Greeks sat down with the texts in the form of a book. Initially, long before anyone thought to write the poems down, bards known as *aoidoi* recited them aloud. It would take too long to recite the entire poems at once,[306] so they may have spent a few days in a king's court or aristocrat's palace, reciting chunks of the poem in nightly instalments. Sometimes, the *aoidos* might have chosen to recite the most compelling scenes as excerpts, like a highlights reel.

When the poems first developed, there were no official versions, and nothing was written down. The bards knew the main beats of each story, and extemporised the actual lines using stock phrases that helped them to remember what to say. This is to say, the poet named Homer didn't really exist; he's the personification of a conglomerate of itinerant bards who were all telling slight variations of the same stories. At some point, single versions of each poem became fairly canonical, and eventually someone decided to write them down. The dating for each of these stages of development are frustratingly fuzzy, because no source from antiquity provides any firm dates. There is not a lot of evidence, and a lot of what we have is open to interpretation. Historians have been trying to nail down dates for centuries, and, even now, if I were to put twelve professors of Homeric literature into a room with the scant evidence that we have, like a jury in deliberation, a unanimous decision would never be reached.[307] I am not going to miraculously succeed where scores of scholars have failed before me, so suffice to say the poems were probably first developed by the 700s BCE, perhaps the 600s, and had solidified into their final, tidied-up forms by the time the Athenians began to really obsess over them in the 520s BCE. This is the point where we start seeing recognisable scenes from the poems painted onto vases, and passing references to the narratives in other literary sources. Up until this point, it's hard to determine who the audiences for the poems were, and whether the average Greek would have been privileged enough to listen to a bard. However, thanks to the Greek love of competition, opportunities for wider audiences started to open up when it was decided that bards should compete by each reciting a section of the poems, so that audience members could listen to large chunks of it in one sitting. This took place at the Panathenaic festival, probably in the Theatre of Dionysus, and contributed to the rising popularity of these two particular works. Even ancient writers can't agree on who instigated this competition and when, but it is at around the same time that vase paintings of particular scenes really took off.[308]

Both the *Iliad* and the *Odyssey* relate to the Trojan War, which lasted for a decade. The *Iliad*, however, only covers a couple of weeks in the war's latter stages which culminates in the death of the Trojan prince Hektor, and the *Odyssey* covers the decade-long voyage home of a Greek warrior king named Odysseus as he travelled back home to Ithaca after the war ended. The famous beats of the poem – the beautiful Greek queen Helen leaving Sparta to live with the Trojan prince Paris, the Greek warriors hiding in a huge wooden horse, and Achilles being killed when he is shot through his weak heel with an arrow – do not appear anywhere in the poems. That's because these two poems were joined by many more poems about this war. Known now as the Epic Cycle, a group of poems cover the prelude to the Trojan War, what happened before and after the events in the *Iliad*, and the immediate aftermath of the war. Unfortunately, none of these other poems survive. All we have is fragments, quotations in other literature, and a couple of descriptions. That the *Iliad* and *Odyssey* have survived, it has to be said, is a minor miracle; we are indescribably lucky to have two entire poems survive so long. This is, in part, because they were the most popular of the poems about the Trojan War, and there were simply more copies of them which increased their chances of survival. Beyond being able to determine that the other poems were probably less popular, it's difficult to say by how much, or why. We don't have enough fragments to be able to say that they were inferior in style or content, but we are able to tell that the poems weren't part of a planned collection that deliberately covered the entire war in chronological episodes, and that their (estimated) dates don't quite align with our (estimated) dates of composition for the *Iliad* and *Odyssey*. They weren't even all attributed to 'Homer'.

Just because we have less evidence of them doesn't mean we should write these poems off. After all, the Trojan Horse is still a really popular tale that most people are familiar with. We should assume that the same is true for the Greek world; even if the average Greek didn't own a copy of a poem on papyrus, or hadn't listened to the poems in their entirety, there was likely a modicum of familiarity with the overall tales. For instance, I can quote from television shows I've not seen every episode of, and I can just about explain the plot of movies I've never actually seen, as I'm sure you could too. Most anglophones can recall a line or two from a Shakespeare play that they studied in school, decades after they've forgotten the complicated storylines or historical contexts. Many works of fiction enter popular culture to the point where someone can be familiar with details about them without ever actually engaging with them in the intended manner, be it on stage, on screen or on a page. I propose that the same was true in the ancient Greek world; for many Greeks, a full recitation of every poem wouldn't have been necessary to become familiar with the core story beats. Snippets, adaptations and simplified versions (perhaps even as children's bedtime stories) would have been perfectly sufficient.

What are some of those other poems? The *Kypria* was a summary of the entire Trojan War, covering its cause and major plot points. Other poems follow the *Iliad's* lead in focussing on specific events. The *Aethiopis*, which we'll encounter in Chapter 17, picks up the story immediately following the finale of the *Iliad*, and includes the death scene of the *Iliad's* most prominent character, the Greek warrior Achilles. The *Little Iliad* covers the immediate aftermath of Achilles' death and the construction of the Trojan horse, while the *Sack of Troy* (*Iliou Persis*) describes how the horse was successfully used to finally bring about the fall of the city of Troy. Where the *Odyssey* describes Odysseus' voyage home, *Homecomings* (*Nostoi*) describes how the other Greeks including Agamemnon and Menelaus got home, and, finally, the *Telegoneia* acts as a sequel to the *Odyssey* and tells us Odysseus' fate at the hands of his son, Telegonus.

There were other epic poems that have been lost forever. Several were about the Greek city of Thebes, which apparently had more than its fair share of woes. The *Oedipodea* tells the story of Oedipus, the abandoned boy who grew up to murder his father, the King of Thebes, and marry his mother; then the *Thebaid* follows the next generation of the Theban royal family: Oedipus and his mother Jocasta had twin sons named Eteokles and Polyneikes who, after the death of their parents, waged a brutal war to determine which should inherit the throne. The *Epigoni* is about the third generation: the sons of Polyneikes' seven warriors, who, to honour and avenge their fathers, launched a second attack on the city of Thebes. Other epics feature stories of heroes like Theseus and Herakles. The word 'hero' or ἥρως (*hērōs*) in Greek, is a very different concept in ancient Greek thought than it is today. We think of heroes in a Superman sense: a morally good person who, when not fighting injustice, is probably saving a cat from being stuck in a tree. Homeric heroes weren't required to be kind, or to help damsels in distress or defenceless civilians. Their function was to be the ultimate warrior, and a moral compass was optional. They were usually very tall and handsome, and should utterly dominate a battlefield. Tactical thinking was highly valued, while ethics were less of a concern; for example, Diomedes is not concerned about whether it is morally wrong to kill thirteen Trojans as they sleep, unarmed, in their tents.[309] The heroes on both sides of the Trojan War and wars over Thebes are there to kill their enemies, and treat killing almost as an art form. In this sense, there are clear parallels to gladiators – emphasis on techniques, tactics, and physical strength was a common theme, as were the duels that the poets describe so vividly.

None of these stories have any basis in historical fact. While archaeologists have found the city of Troy, for instance, and found evidence of very ancient warfare around its walls, there is no evidence that characters like Priam, Helen, Achilles or Paris ever existed. There is similarly no evidence for an (accidentally) incestuous royal family in Thebes. These are wonderful stories, and entirely fictional. For Greeks, though, they were stories of their past, preserved for posterity. For an ancient Greek, the Trojan War was an incontrovertibly true historical event, and the details of this event were passed down through the medium of epic poetry.

Mythology

As well as tales of war, the Greeks (and later, the Romans) enjoyed stories of gods and heroes, who were as real to the ancient Greeks as Achilles and Odysseus. With a pantheon of dozens of gods, most of whom had at least a handful of children born of mortals, there were hundreds of stories to choose from. Gods battled against the other gods (because Mount Olympus was essentially one giant dysfunctional household), fell in love with nymphs and mortals, and turned humans into monsters if they felt slighted. Heroes were dispatched to defeat those terrifying monsters against all the odds, traversing the ancient world in search of glory and fame. Heracles completed the famous Twelve Labours, Jason assembled the ultimate crew to board his ship *Argo* and sail for adventure, Theseus entered the Labyrinth to face the mighty Minotaur, and Perseus chopped the head off Medusa. These are but a handful of popular myths. There are different versions of each story, sometimes with conflicting details, and regional variations as cities sought to exploit their mythical connections; the places where mythical events 'happened', or the birthplace and 'tombs' of favourite characters became landmarks. Poets and playwrights devised prequels, sequels, retellings from the perspectives of minor characters, and alternate endings for a public who thrilled at approaching these stories from every perspective.

Myths penetrated life on every level. Civic buildings were decorated with sculptures of famous scenes, painters and sculptors filled cities with images and statues of famous characters, and people decorated their homes with pictures and knickknacks depicting their favourite stories. Religious life was centred around the stories, which like the Trojan War were also taken to be historical fact, and deities were worshipped in temples and sanctuaries, with festivals held to honour them where the stories would be retold to rapt audiences. At many religious festivals, the recitation of mythical stories was a competition in itself, as *rhapsodes* performed poetry in the hopes of winning a prize. Famous athletes who won events at the Olympics and similar competitions commissioned special victory odes to celebrate their achievements, wherein the poets would recount a myth that was relevant to the event or particular athlete; for instance, Bacchylides' ode for Pytheas of Aegina retells the story of how Heracles killed the man-eating Nemean lion by bashing it with a club, because Pytheas was a *pankratiast* who won at Nemea where the lion had once prowled.[310] These would be sung by a chorus when the athlete returned to his proud hometown.

Myth really did saturate life in the Greek world; the stories explained the Greek concept of their collective history and sought to explain how the universe worked. It's hard to overstate how important myths were to the ancient Mediterranean. It's little wonder that the stories became a form of entertainment.

The Play's the Thing

It's difficult to say how many Greeks would ever have listened to the *Iliad* or *Odyssey* from beginning to end, but then, as now, truly great stories were adapted into other forms. Epic poetry, due to the sheer length of each poem, was difficult to perform and to consume. But these stories were never confined to epic poems; they were told in other ways. One particularly important example is through Greek plays.

The famous plays that still survive from the ancient Greek world were all written in Athens. The study of the ancient Greek world often ends up meaning the study of Athens. Ancient historians call this 'Athenocentrism', and those who study other *poleis* sometimes roll their eyes in frustration when Athens gets most of the attention. In large part, this is because we have a disproportionate amount of evidence from Athens compared to other cities; they loved to write things down both in stone inscriptions and on papyrus. In contrast, we don't have a single source written by a Spartan: we only have writers from other cities writing about how weird they thought Spartans were, and these accounts are too much of a caricature to be reliable. Everything we think we know about the tight-lipped Spartans comes from bemused neighbours (we call this the 'Spartan Mirage'), while the Athenians were more than happy to write down the minutiae of daily life in such a volume that lots has managed to survive the ravages of time. Just as with the heavy focus on Pompeii in Roman studies, Athens hogs the limelight because that's where the densest pile of evidence comes from. That said, the development of drama happened in Athens because, at that specific time, Athens was doing something truly weird compared to the rest of the Greek world: it was developing democracy. The rise of drama and democracy was a symbiotic relationship, even if drama caught on in other *poleis* where democracy certainly did not.

It was common in many cities for stories to be told through the medium of dance and song, performed by a chorus of performers. They were, in essence, narrators who described the plot. That is, until someone decided to break from the chorus and pretend to be one of the characters themselves. Acting was born: for the first time, the performer embodied the character by saying the character's lines and acting out their movements, rather than simply describing what was going on. According to Themistius, a scholar of Aristotle in the fourth century CE, Aristotle named this innovator as a playwright called Thespis.[311] Even if this is not the strongest evidence, we still call actors *thespians* today.

Choral performances thus morphed into plays, and were categorised into three genres: tragedy, comedy and satyr play, the latter of which were a bawdy combination of the first two. Several tragedies by Aeschylus, Sophocles and Euripides survive in full, as do comedies by Aristophanes and Menander. Today, we have complete scripts for only thirty-two plays, but we have fragments or sometimes even only titles of hundreds more, and the names of playwrights whose works are entirely lost. The fourth century BCE playwright Carcinus, for instance, apparently wrote 160 plays, and we don't have a copy of a single one. In other words, our knowledge of ancient drama is really patchy, and we can only estimate the characters and plots of the lost plays.

What we do know is that the chorus never became obsolete, even as their importance waned: every surviving play has a chorus who spoke and sang as one, commenting on the action and narrating events occurring 'off stage'. As far as we know, Aeschylus was the first to introduce a second actor who could converse with the first, rather than having a sole actor who could only talk to the audience or chorus. Sophocles then really pushed the boat out and wrote scripts requiring three, at which point three seems to have been capped as a maximum number for the cast.[312] There could be many more characters in each play, however, and so actors were required to play multiple roles in a single play. All actors wore masks, so it was easy enough to have a different mask for each character to help the audience tell them apart.

The stories told in the tragic plays were already familiar to the audience, because the plots were drawn from existing myths and epics; plots referring to contemporary events were taboo. In 493 BCE, a playwright named Phrynikos had written about a real and recent event in his play *The Sack of Miletus;* the Persians had destroyed this Athenian colony the previous year during the Ionian Revolt. Watching the disaster re-enacted on stage so soon was clearly triggering to the audience, who apparently wept during the performance. All further performances of the play were banned.[313] Undeterred, in 476 BCE, his play *The Phoenician Women* was also about a recent event, but this time the Battle of Salamis. The Greeks had won that battle, which had turned the tide of the Second Persian Invasion in their favour. Four years later Aeschylus (who had fought the Persians at the Battle of Marathon during the First Persian Invasion), followed his lead with another play celebrating the victory at Salamis, titled *The Persians*. The characters are the Persian queen Atossa, her defeated son Xerxes, and the ghost of her husband Darius, who makes a point of condemning the Persian hubris of invading Greece. While the play could be (and has been) read as verging on jingoistic xenophobia,[314] the war-weary Athenians loved it. Nevertheless, from then on, contemporary events were alluded to through mythical stories rather than directly related characters and events.

Here's where we see the characters of the epic poems return, as playwrights sought to put their own spin on familiar tales. This might involve centring characters previously on the periphery of stories, such as Sophocles making Antigone, sister of Eteokles and Polyneikes, the main character of a play about the aftermath of their deaths, or Euripides devoting an entire play to the women of the Trojan royal family as they contemplate the destruction of their city and imminent enslavement across the sea in Greece in his *Trojan Women*.

As we have already seen, and will see several more times, one of the dearest passions in Greek culture was competition, or *agon*. Any activity was made better if it became a contest with a prize, and theatre was no exception. The first aspect of *agon* in the theatre is that plays were not merely produced for entertainment, as we do today. Plays were performed at religious festivals, and two in Athens were particularly significant: the *City Dionysia* and the *Lenaia*, which were both sacred to Dionysus. Each festival featured many rites, and the contest between plays was the major part. The *City Dionysia* took place in spring, and was attended by Athenian and Greeks from other cities too. At each *City Dionysia*, three of the top playwrights in the city presented their work; three tragedies (that could form a trilogy featuring the same theme or characters[315]) followed by a satyr play. The four plays would be shown in sequence across an entire day, and then the following morning the next playwright would present his four plays. From 487 BCE two additional days were devoted to comedies during which five playwrights presented a single play each. Tragedians and comic playwrights considered themselves specialists, and did not attempt to compete in both genres.

The *Lenaia* was held in winter, when foreigners were unable to travel to attend. It was therefore a little more relaxed, and comedy took precedence. Both competitions took place in the Theatre of Dionysus on the slope of the Athenian acropolis. A panel of judges awarded prizes to the victorious playwrights, which was a wreath of ivy at the *City Dionysia*. Each playwright was sponsored by a *choregos*, a wealthy citizen who funded all aspects of the production. This was a compulsory act of civic duty for the citizen involved, and paying for actors, costumes, sets and rehearsals was no small venture. That said, it was considered an honour to be selected and many volunteered. The *choregos* also won a prize if their playwright was successful, and often celebrated by erecting commemorative monuments.[316] An award for best actor was also introduced at the *City Dionysia* in 449 BCE. Prizes had no monetary value, but a cash windfall wasn't the point; playwrights, actors, and sponsors were competing for prestige and fame attached to their name. There were no prizes for the runners-up, that concept would have baffled any ancient Greek.

The second element of theatrical *agon* was within the structure of the plays themselves. The point of tragedy was not merely to elicit an emotional response, but to prompt the audience into thinking carefully about the decisions characters made and the consequences of those decisions. There are no simplified 'Goodies' and 'Baddies', but complex characters who often disagree on an important issue. Which character has the strongest argument? Which character makes the wisest choices? The audience is asked to consider ethical and moral dilemmas, and to examine how they themselves would navigate the situation. This goes a long way to explain why tragedy avoided turning real Athenians into characters, and placed very real issues into the hands of mythological figures instead. Comedic playwrights had no such qualms, parodying figures like Socrates and Cleon in plays even as they sat in the audience.

These questions were of utmost importance to this newly democratic city; now that all (male) citizens (over the age of eighteen) were able to and encouraged to vote on political matters, it was crucial that individuals developed critical thinking skills, thought carefully about the cost and consequences of certain actions, and considered the wisest path for a society to take.

Athens produced around 1,200 plays in the fifth century BCE, and they quickly caught on elsewhere. In the 470s BCE Aeschylus was invited to stage his recent prize-winning hit *The Persians* in Syracuse, where the local tyrant Hieron was an early fan of tragedy. Hieron even managed to convince Aeschylus to pen him a play named *The Women of Etna* in honour of his conquering the city of Catania, expelling its inhabitants and repopulating it with Syracusan settlers.

Some decades later, an anecdote demonstrates that Attic tragedy was still a big deal in Syracuse, Sicily; thousands of Athenian soldiers were captured after the disastrous failure of their 'Sicilian Expedition' in 415–413 BCE. The Syracusans kept their prisoners of war in huge quarries on the outskirts of the city; they became convenient labour camps in times of war.[317] The conditions were harsh, with no shelter from the cold in the night nor the burning sun during the day, meagre rations, and disease. Few Athenians left alive, and, of those who did, many only left as enslaved men.

Plutarch tells an interesting tale about the soldiers held captive there. The Syracusans (who had built one of the first theatres outside of Attica) were especially fond of plays by Euripides, and would leap on any chance to listen to excerpts to later quote among themselves. Some of the captive Athenians had seen enough of the plays to have memorised snippets, and those who could entertain their captors by saying a few lines from a speech or singing parts of the choral odes were given preferential treatment, and sometimes their freedom. Apparently, many men managed to return home to Athens, hugging Euripides in the street and thanking him profusely for indirectly saving their lives.[318] Euripides himself retired to Macedonia on the invitation of its king Archelaus, who was assembling a court of poets, playwrights and musicians. This anecdote tells us more than the prestige of Attic tragedy further afield: it shows how central tragedy specifically and storytelling in general were spread across the Greek world.

By the fourth century BCE theatres were becoming an essential component of city life across the Greek world as their populations began to demand the sophisticated entertainment enjoyed in Athens. It was a century of a myriad of inter-*polis* wars, and cities fought for political dominance on the battlefields of mainland Greece. They also competed in a cultural arms race, each vying to become more sophisticated than their neighbours. Performances of plays, whether in whole or in part, were all the rage. Many cities had their own Dionysian festivals that featured performances of plays, poems and songs, as well as private performances for those who could afford such luxurious entertainment. As such, actors started to become even more lauded than the playwrights, much to the chagrin of Aristotle.[319] Actors were now masters of their craft, memorising enormous repertoires and perfecting their physical and vocal instruments. They now found themselves in demand year-round and across the eastern Mediterranean, as a circuit of theatres, festivals (with cash prize competitions) and recitals for exclusive parties kept them booked and busy, with the best being able to charge huge fees for appearances.

A new generation of tragedians continued to compose hundreds of plays for the Athenian festivals, as up-and-comers sought to place new twists and perspectives on the myths retold by their predecessors. In 386 BCE a new component was introduced in the *City Dionysia*; as well as new tragedies and satyr plays, an older play by the fifth century tragedians would be performed. The works of Aeschylus, Sophocles, and Euripides were now considered 'classics', and Lycurgus of Athens made a motion to keep official copies of their plays in the city archive and erect their statues by the Theatre of Dionysus.[320] Already, these plays were being promoted and preserved as products of Athenian greatness, evidence of their (fast fading) cultural dominance, and precious relics of their golden age. Athens was losing its influence and significance in all spheres except this one. We can imagine troupes of actors taking these older plays, still in demand, on 'tours' around the Greek *poleis*. For Athens, drama was their prime export – a gift to the rest of the Greek world.

That Greek world changed forever when Alexander the Great seized and expanded it with breathtaking rapidity. Born a Macedonian prince, Alexander had benefited from the finest education available and Aristotle was his private tutor. As such, he was well-versed in all forms of literature, able to perfectly recite tragedians by heart. Macedonia had continued to be the cultural hub that had once lured Euripides, and Alexander had mingled with some of the best writers and performers in the Greek world at the court of his father, Philip II, the most generous patron of the arts in his lifetime. When Alexander launched into his staggering invasion of Persia, he kept a copy of the *Iliad* with him on campaign, supposedly sleeping with it underneath his pillow.[321] While fighting in what is now eastern Türkiye, Alexander ran out of things to read and so he reportedly sent home for the complete works of Aeschylus, Sophocles and Euripides that he planned to read in his leisure time.[322]

This love affair with Greek literature was one that he encouraged in his inner circle, and promoted on his travels. Plutarch tells us that Alexander commemorated a successful campaign in Egypt by hosting a competition of tragedies and dithyrambic choruses, with Cypriot kings acting as the sponsors for each performance.[323] Alexander even poached the finest actors straight from Athens, even if it meant that they weren't able to fulfil their obligations at the festivals there. He paid their fines from his own pocket.[324] Alexander even had a habit of quoting literature as witty bon mots, with a clear preference for Euripides.[325] Quoting plays only makes sense when the speaker knows that his listeners will understand the reference and its relevance to the point he wants to make, so we can guess that Alexander's milieu were all expected to be familiar with the plays too.

Following his premature death in 323 BCE, Alexander's generals tussled over the fracturing empire and created their own empires from the splinters. For historians, this is when the Hellenistic period begins. Our evidence for theatre here is not as extensive, but we can detect the continuation of theatre if we know where to look. We know that passages of the great tragedians were used by schoolboys, because we have fragments of their exercise books. Similarly, famous excerpts have been found in rhetoric handbooks for aspiring orators. Greek culture had spread further than ever before, as Alexander and his successors had conquered enormous tracts of territory, and Greek colonists travelled in huge numbers to the territories further east. Some settled in Greek quarters in ancient cities, while dozens and dozens of new 'Greek' cities were founded, such as Alexandria in Egypt. The colonists brought their culture with them, and theatres were constructed in large numbers. Many cities, including Alexandria and Ephesus, possessed vast libraries, where epics and plays were stored for the perusal of scholars, and their summaries, quotations and thoughts on the works often provide valuable information about lost works. Hellenistic kings were keen to promote the performances of myths in various forms as part of the wider export of Greek culture into these new, vast empires.

It is clear from the continuation of the telling of stories, either by bards or actors, that myth retellings remained an enduring facet of Greek entertainment. As the Greek world was sucked into the Roman sphere, one of the best pieces of evidence we have that epic and drama were still immensely popular was that the Romans very quickly caught on to the idea of theatre. As we've seen, the Romans had been interacting with the Greeks of Magna Graecia for centuries through trade, and, by the third century BCE, through violence as Rome sought to consolidate its power throughout the entire Italian peninsula. When it finally conquered the powerful city of Tarentum (which, you may recall, had previously fought and won two wars against Rome to maintain their independence) in 275 BCE, the city was looted, and 30,000 of its culturally Greek inhabitants sold into slavery. According to tradition, one young Tarentine was brought to Rome and, owing to his own exemplary education in Greek literature, was employed as a tutor for an aristocratic Roman family who wanted their sons to have a sophisticated upbringing. This man was named Livius Andronicus, and he was to become famous for translating Greek literature into Latin, including the *Odyssey*.

In 240 BCE, less than two decades after the first gladiatorial fight, Livius Andronicus staged the first play performed in Rome, and, though only fragments of his tragedies remain, we know that they followed the tradition of adapting Greek myths, only this time they were performed in Latin. Titles of these lost plays include *Achilles, Andromeda* and *The Trojan Horse*. Roman tragedy (i.e. Latin adaptations of Greek stories) thus began to flourish, and for about a century, Roman tragedians like Ennius, Pacuvius and Naevius were all following Livius Andronicus' lead by making Latin adaptations of Greek myths.[326] The Roman population soon discovered a preference for comedy over tragedies, however, ironically using a Greek medium to ruthlessly mock the stereotyped 'Stupid Greeks' that populated Roman stages. Rome also developed their own forms of play, including farces and pantomimes (which were solo masked dances with no dialogue). Tragedy continued to be a literary pursuit among aristocratic Romans, however, who usually had Greek tutors at home, or travelled to Greek cities to further their education. Engaging in this (by now ancient) writing style allowed elite Romans to flaunt their sophistication. Over the centuries, the medium and style of storytelling had changed, but it was still the same stories getting retold again and again.

Theatres

Whether as part of a poetry competition, a recital or a play, there was one place designed specifically to hear these stories performed: the theatre.

Hundreds of Greek cities had an open-air theatre. Some were modest, and some truly monumental, with seating capacities of up to 25,000 people. Early designs aside, the archetype seems simple: utilising a handy slope of a hillside, valley or mountain, seating was constructed in a major arc (that is to say, slightly exceeding a semicircle) around a circular, flat space where the actors performed. In Greek, the seating area was known as the *theatron* ('viewing place') or *koilon* ('hollow cavity'), and the performance space was called the *orchestra*, which means the 'dancing place'. The *koilon* was divided into wedges, called *kerkides*, separated by staircases ascending the *koilon*, and some had a *diazoma*, 'the girdle', which was a horizontal walkway demarcating the lower rows of seats from the upper seating. The apparent simplicity of the design is deceptive, for the gradients of the theatres were engineered with mathematical precision to ensure perfect acoustics from any seat. It's still a favourite activity of tourists to test this out, and someone speaking at a normal volume can indeed be heard by those in the uppermost rows. The curved design ensured that everyone has a clear, unrestricted view of the *orchestra*, which many modern auditoriums still struggle with today.

The design of the ancient Greek theatre was constantly being tweaked. As plays were developing from the choral songs and dances about gods and heroes, the use of a tent or hut behind the *orchestra* and facing the *koilon* was deemed necessary. It was called the *skene*, and was initially merely a place to stash props and instruments. Aeschylus revolutionised early drama when he added a second actor with whom the first could converse, and Sophocles added a third. The rules of dramatic festivals quickly set three as a limit to how many actors could perform in plays, but playwrights simply made sure that each actor portrayed multiple characters. Actors would enter the tent as one character by 'entering the palace' or 'leaving the city', quickly swap their mask and a few costume details before re-emerging as a different character altogether. A tent or hut quickly became insufficient, and so wooden structures replaced them, the facades of which could be decorated with a backdrop resembling the play's setting. Some of these new wooden *skene* buildings were raised, with a platform between the backstage area and the *orchestra* which we would recognise as the stage and known as the *logeion* in Greek. Elaborate stone buildings decorated with columns and statues soon replaced them, allowing for complex machinery like cranes that allowed for the creation of special theatrical effects. By the

Hellenistic period, few theatres still had wooden seating and most boasted rows and rows of elegant stone. The supporting wall of the stage (*paraskenion*) was often decorated with carved reliefs, and more and more of the dramatic action moved from the *orchestra* to the *logeion* stage. As a result, the circular shape of the *orchestra* was more often than not changed into a horse-shoe shaped space that was becoming increasingly obsolete.

And so, by the time the Romans began to exert control over the Greek world and put their own stamp on various monuments, we should remember that Greek theatres were already going through several phases of change. Many Roman alterations to Greek theatres had little to do with gladiation. The Roman mastery of vaulting allowed for oblique seating to be built where no natural slopes could be utilised, and so the *koilon* of many theatres such as Miletus could be extended. In cities with very level topography, completely free-standing theatres could be built for the very first time, as in Side. The high, narrow *logeion* stage was replaced with lower, deeper stages known as the *pulpitum*. Where the Hellenistic stages had turned circular *orchestras* into U shaped spaces, the *pulpitum* restricted the *orchestra* further into a semicircle. The *skene* was replaced by the *scaenae frons*, which served the same function as a backdrop and backstage building, only now on a massive scale. Some were three stories high. Traditionally, theatres had open pathways leading into the *orchestra* on either side running along the supporting walls of the *koilon's* edges, as an entrance first for audience members and then for chorus members during performances. The Romans preferred these to be enclosed by a wall on the other side and vaulted over, making these passages roofed. The primary benefit was seating could be extended further, above the vaulting, often connecting to the ends of the *scaenae frons*.

Certain changes are evident whose purpose is more specific and more relevant to our investigation. Traditionally, the lowest row of seating was such that the feet of the audience members were on the edges of the *orchestra*. There was no need for further separation between audience, dancer and actor. When the performance space migrated from *orchestra* to stage, the *orchestra* became an empty, purposeless space. However, canny officials looking for a permanent home for gladiators without the fuss of amphitheatre construction soon found a new use for the *orchestra*. Rows of stone theatre seating meant that no more benches and balconies needed to be erected, and theatres were already calibrated to ensure that every seat had a clear view of the *orchestra*.

The only issue was one of spectator safety. Gladiatorial combat and the beast hunts that accompanied them involved a lot of blades, teeth and claws moving quickly and unpredictably, all within an uncomfortably short distance of the audience members in the lowest rows. To prevent accidental stabbing and maulings, three simple solutions were swiftly found to ensure every audience member left with their limbs firmly attached. The first was the quickest, cheapest and most unobtrusive. Post holes would be drilled at regular intervals around the perimeter of the *orchestra* just in front of or along the first row of seating. During *munera*, vertical posts were inserted that could support rope barriers, wooden railings or metal grilles. The animals and combatants were now fenced off from the audience, whose view remained unimpeded. For conservatives, this was the ideal solution as the barriers could be removed as soon as the spectacle was over, returning the theatre to normal with minimal fuss. However, spectator safety relied on the barriers being robust enough to withstand rogue wild animals, and it is perhaps for this reason that this is the solution we see the least. Most cities replaced the barriers, or added further safety measures, though cities such as Argos, Halicarnassus and Apamea deemed the fencing sufficient on its own.

The second was to replace the temporary fencing with a free-standing, permanent wall, called a parapet. The parapet could be made of elegant *orthostates*, neat masonry walls or even walls of rough, uneven recycled blocks if that was all that was available. At Patara, a rough masonry wall of uneven blocks was erected using the front row of seats as a base, and was probably covered in a thin layer of plaster that obscured how uneven the blocks of stone really are. Unfortunately, the height of this wall blocks the view of the *orchestra* for the first few rows, with the first row not even being able to see the actors performing plays on the raised stage. In creating a wall that was placed on top of one row of seats rather than in front of them, the theatre at Patara effectively lost multiple rows of seats to obstructed views. A similar issue is seen at the theatre of Alabanda, where the wall is thicker, and built upon the first entire first row with buttresses rendering the second row unusable too. At its surviving height, the wall doesn't cause as much obstruction as in Patara, but is equally roughly worked. One major difference is the type of row it was built on top of; at Patara the front row was a standard, backless row of seats, but at Alabanda the wall is built onto a special row of backed stone seating called the *prohedrai*; these were more comfortable, and usually had some form of sculptural decoration such as worked arm rests or lion's paw bases. These seats were reserved for priests of Dionysus, god of the theatre, and for important magistrates. To not only fail to remove these privileged seats but to use them as a foundation for a rough wall is a significant choice for the city to make; safety measures for gladiatorial shows, however lazily implemented, took precedence over centuries of traditionally reserved special seating for local VIPs. A parapet needn't be an eyesore, if the city officials put enough thought into the addition. The theatre at Perge has a decorated parapet wall, of which most does not unfortunately survive. From what is left, we can see that the parapet has been constructed like a fence; narrow stone uprights hold up fairly thin panels of stone that are all equally sized. Some of the panels have been pierced with carved holes in a trellis-like design. We can see, then, that different cities had differing opinions on how to build parapets, as well as differing approaches to how they appeared.

Aesthetics and budget aside, the primary concern was again spectator safety, and the parapets were incredibly sturdy. The secondary concern was that the spectators should have a clear view; though plays were now performed exclusively on the stage building, there was little point having gladiators fight in the *orchestra* if the parapet blocked people from seeing them. Sturdier than a fence of wood or rope, the parapet wall was a fairly simple method of permanently altering the theatre to make it suitable for gladiatorial combat and beast hunts, but, with most not exceeding one-and-a-half metres, it does raise questions as to which species of animal could be safely staged.

These concerns perhaps explain the third option of adaptation, which was to raise the spectators above the *orchestra*. This was the most drastic and by far the most popular form of architectural change. In western amphitheatres and circuses, the audience is raised above the arena or track, and the front row of spectators is looking down. The seating is placed upon vaulting, and the front row has a barrier wall in front of it. Unlike a parapet, if an audience member attempted to cross this wall, there was a significant drop to the arena. In Greek theatres, the feet of the first row of audience members rested on the edge of the *orchestra*. To replicate the disparity in level between performer and spectator, the *orchestra* could be excavated to a greater depth, but the better method was to remove the front rows of seats entirely. This created a supporting wall known as a *podium* (from the Greek word νōδιον, or pódion, meaning 'base' or 'foot'), giving much needed height to protect spectators, but it also widened the *orchestra* to form a larger arena. To return to the theatre of Patara, if the city had chosen to remove three or four rows of seating rather than building their wall, no views would be obstructed *and* the *orchestra* would have been enlarged to allow for larger performances.

The most modest adaptations removed two or three rows, and the most radical change was at the theatre of Corinth, which removed ten entire rows of seating. The height of seating rows in theatres varied slightly across the ancient world, depending on the slope that the theatre was built into. The average height of a seat in Greece and Asia Minor was 39 cm, but ranged from 34–46 cm, and theatres in the Levant had taller seats averaging 43 cm.[327] Few theatres had short podia of less than a metre in height, which again raises the question as to whether audiences in cities such as Aspendos and Dio Caesarea were able to enjoy a full spectrum of wild animals during *venationes* because the walls of those theatres were so much shorter than usual.

It's interesting to note that, in 1918, the American ancient historian Roy C. Flickinger noted this habit of creating *podium* walls but attributed the change to the Roman alterations to the stage; the deeper *pulpitum* extended further into the *orchestra* than the narrower *logeion*, and Flickinger theorised that the first rows of seating were removed to give the now higher front row, traditionally VIP seating, a better view.[328] Of course, Flickinger was writing before Louis Robert published his 1940 book *Les Gladiateurs dans l'Orient Grec*, which first revealed how widespread gladiatorial combat was. Flickinger knew about gladiators in theatres, but had no idea how prevalent the phenomenon was. If the alterations were purely for the purpose of giving audience members a better view of plays, I would question why this wasn't a change made earlier when the *logeion* was higher than the later Roman stages, and also why seat removal wasn't more prevalent. Today, it is accepted that the architectural changes were made for Roman spectacles, though some squeamish scholars often mention *venationes* alone, refusing to acknowledge the presence of gladiators.[329] In reality, beast-hunts and gladiatorial combats were a package deal by the time spectacles reached the provinces.

On occasion, one method of adaptation wasn't considered enough, and different cities used several methods in combination. A parapet wall could sit on top of a *podium* wall, replicating amphitheatres in the western territories. This was the ideal solution for cities that wanted to feature agile animal species in their hunts, particularly big cats. *Podiums* and parapets could also each have sockets drilled into their top in order to insert nets or grilles. By its peak, the theatre at Stobi had had seating rows removed to create its podium, which was topped off with a parapet that had sockets for grilles. In cities of the Greek world that had no theatre, the Romans often decided to build ones from scratch. Their expert knowledge of concrete and knack for barrelled vaulting allowed for huge theatres to be built where no slope was available, and *podiums* to keep the front row of seating higher than the *orchestra* were often included in the initial plans, meaning that Roman theatres in these Greek cities were multi-functional by design. This is in contrast to the theatres built by the Romans in the western provinces, which did not include adaptations for animal shows or combats.[330] In western provinces, the function of buildings was much simpler, and with a narrower scope: amphitheatres were for spectacle, and theatres were for plays. Where Roman theatres in the eastern Mediterranean had built-in *podium* walls, the front rows of western theatres were level with the *orchestra* in the Greek style, because western cities typically had an arena so didn't have to alter Greek theatre design.[331]

Logistical Concerns

The amphitheatre at Mastaura had been known to antiquarians for a century, until vegetation hid it from view once again. Recently rediscovered, the amphitheatre has now been cleared of much of this vegetation and surveyed, if not excavated. Mastaura sits in a valley on a major road and was well connected with neighbouring cities. Construction of the amphitheatre used local stone, utilising a valley slope on its northern and some of the eastern sides, with the southwestern portion of the building built upon vaults. Excavation of the structure is still in the initial stages, and yet archaeologists have already theorised that the amphitheatre was actually adapted from a Hellenistic theatre that previously occupied the slope, and that Romans extended the orchestra into an arena and added new seating to turn the semicircle into an oval. Dating estimates suggest that the amphitheatre conversion was a Severan construction. Currently, the most extreme confirmed theatre transformation is that of Cyrene, in which the stage building was demolished and around twelve rows of seating were removed to turn the *orchestra* into a massive *arena*. Nine rows of seats were then built to enclose the newly extended *orchestra/arena* and supported by large arches, transforming the theatre into a close facsimile of a canonical amphitheatre, a transformation also dated to the Severan period. The continued investigations at Mastaura may reveal an adaptation far more radical even still, with local topography less challenging than that at Cyrene aiding the transformation. It may also reveal if the full amphitheatre conversion replaced a previous, unobtrusive adaptation akin to the other theatres discussed. Thus far, the motives behind such a dramatic adaptation in Mastaura have yet to be revealed. Caria was a vibrant region for gladiation, with one of the densest distributions of venues and the highest concentration of gladiatorial epigraphy in the eastern Mediterranean, and so the need/desire for a canonical structure capable of hosting large-scale spectacles is a reasonable one, though the choice of Mastaura over other cities in the region with noted gladiatorial tastes is less obvious.

The largest theatre *orchestra* was equivalent in size to only the most modest of amphitheatrical arena floors; the diameter of the enlarged Corinth *orchestra* is 27x36m,[332] compared to the tiny arena of the recently discovered amphitheatre in Ategua, whose long internal axis measures only some 27m.[333] Even the most basic of legionary amphitheatres on the borders of the Roman world provided a larger performance space than a theatre. However, engaging and elaborate spectacles could still easily be displayed in a theatre *orchestra* without losing the essence of spectacular martial excellence that was at the heart of gladiation. The Croatian group *Spectacvla Antiqva* regularly stage recreations of gladiation in the ruins of Pula amphitheatre, but have also successfully presented a show for the public in the city's smaller Roman theatre.[334] They use replica arms and armour, and perform re-enactments of fights in shows for modern spectators. The *orchestra* of the unadapted theatre in Pula is twenty-eight metres in diameter, so smaller than the *orchestra* at Corinth.[335] Such recreations, albeit simulated, demonstrate that gladiatorial combat is easily transported from extensive arenas to smaller theatre *orchestras* with minimal need to alter performance techniques or style, as performers are not as restricted in their movements as one might assume. Only larger set battles between multiple pairs of fighters competing simultaneously would have been difficult to stage, but these were fairly rare even in the west.[336]

Odea (sing. *Odeon*) have often been discounted as viable venues for spectacle because they are an even smaller performance space than theatres, but I would hesitate to disregard them based on this. An *odeon* has a very similar plan to a theatre, but they were smaller in scale and were enclosed by walls and a roof. Their function wasn't to stage plays, but they were perfect for poetry and musical recitals. Many cities had both a theatre and an *odeon*, so that each kind of performance had its ideal structure. Because the *orchestras* in *odea* are much smaller than in theatres, some have assumed that they weren't used for gladiatorial combat, citing the need for ample space to attack with weapons. But the evidence suggests that *odea* weren't deemed unsuitable in the ancient world: *odea* that show features intended for spectacle include Corinth, Canatha, Ephesus and Aphrodisias, which all have the tall *podium* wall between seating and *orchestra* that we know indicated a space had been adapted for gladiator combats. *Odea* adapted or designed for multifunctionality are admittedly rarer than multifunctional theatres, but their presence suggests a different sort of gladiatorial performance, at least in terms of how the combat was experienced by audience members. While an *odeon* may be an impractical venue for large-scale *venationes*[337] the smaller performance space might have provided interesting novelty when hosting isolated gladiation. Spectators were fascinated by gladiatorial techniques and manoeuvres: combat in a more confined space would have provided an additional challenge to combatants because they would have had to adjust their tactics and methods accordingly. Hybrid *odea* have a minimum *orchestra* diameter of around 9 metres, with Corinth once again providing the largest example at 17 metres.

Once again, the experimental archaeology group *Spectacvla Antiqva* have shown this to be a feasible performance space: a modern UFC ring was erected in the centre of Pula arena for an event of modern contact sports, and re-enactors from the group performed a short display of combats.[338] The standard UFC octagonal ring has a diameter of 9 metres, smaller than the average converted *odeon* width of 12 metres. Among the 'combatants' were a *hoplomachus* and a *thraex*. Again, while simulated, such recreations demonstrate the performance potential for smaller arenas, including gladiators with spears and tridents. Such a space is more than large enough for a pair of *monomachoi*, but provided fewer opportunities for evasive manoeuvres or moments of respite. A combat within an *odeon* may therefore have been a more intense battle, at closer quarters, as the Croatian re-enactments suggest.

Having briefly speculated about how combatants might have performed differently in an *orchestra* of a theatre or an *odeon* compared to a canonical arena, we must also take into consideration the experience of spectators. After all, it was the experience of watching these combats that drove demand. In the Colosseum, the seven rows closest to the arena were reserved for senators, priests of major religious cults and foreign dignitaries.[339] The men possessing power and prestige were elevated high above the *infames* in the immense arena, their marked physical separation emphasising the chasm between their respective social statuses. In theatrical spaces of the eastern Mediterranean, this chasm is significantly lessened. The centre of an amphitheatre's arena is farther from the seating than the centre of an *orchestra*, and *podium* walls were noticeably taller than in adapted theatres. Performer and spectator were drawn closer together in a theatre. The spectators in a Greek theatre, particularly those in the front rows of the *koilon*, had a markedly different relationship with and experience of gladiators than the Romans in the Colosseum. Seeing spectacles in theatres allowed for spectators to be far more up close and personal and, as with modern performances of music, theatre and comedy, the intimacy of the venue can affect the vibe for everyone involved.

A recent study has examined close physical distance between audience members and performers, in this case modern dancers performing in a studio (roughly 7x13 metres), to investigate how proximity affects the experience of spectation down to a neuronal level.[340] It found that how close audience members are to performers can strongly affect how both experience the performance. Being close enough to hear the performer breathing, or to see the white of their eyes, can intensify our emotional responses to a performance. While some people relish that proximity, it can sometimes seem too intimate to feel comfortable. A comparable study with spectator proximity to bloodsports is thankfully unlikely to be considered ethical, but tentative, speculative comparisons can still be drawn here. The key response to physical closeness in the study was an appreciation of being able to discern the facial expressions of the performers, which aided audience members in forging an empathetic relationship with each dancer. The same effect would clearly not be present in a gladiatorial show, given that only one *armature* did not require a helmet with the entire face obscured. However, experienced theatre goers in the control group also reported a greater ability to view, recognise, and appreciate finer details of choreography, costume and technique in each dance.

Here we can easily imagine a direct comparison: connoisseurs of gladiatorial techniques would be able to appreciate the finer, subtler movements in a way not possible from canonical amphitheatre seating. If we consider gladiation in an *odeon*, we can particularly easily imagine aficionado spectators scrutinising every manoeuvre in forensic detail, especially when we remember that fans greatly enjoyed the technical aspects of gladiation. On the other hand, some in the control group felt that being closer than usual to dancers felt too emotionally intimate, which ruined their enjoyment of the performance. We can only wonder how much more tense a member of an ancient audience felt seeing fighting (and dying) that close. It was certainly an experience that a citizen of Rome would never have.

The primary function of venues dictated their design: amphitheatres, circuses and stadia all prioritised visual perception of performers, while theatres and *odea* centred on excellent acoustics.[341] We should remember that acoustics would also have altered the experience of gladiation held in these buildings, enhancing the experience for spectators. Clashes of weapons against armour would have been amplified, as would the exclamations or even, perhaps, laboured breathing of participants. *Odea* also provided the only indoor locale for gladiatorial combat; it is interesting to ponder if the increased ability to smell sweat and blood altered the sensory experience in ways that couldn't be replicated in open-air venues. Theatre and *odeon* adaptations are more numerous than sports venue adaptations in the Greek world, and it would be too hasty to assume that this is for reasons of financial and architectural ease. We should consider that gladiatorial *munera/philotimia* performed in theatrical spaces also fundamentally altered the experience for both performer and audience member, with spectators having a sensory and emotional experience that differed significantly from spectators in sports venues or canonical amphitheatres, and that this may have been taken into consideration when a *polis* deliberated over which building should be adapted to host shows.

There are just over 400 theatres in the Greek eastern Mediterranean, and at least 20 per cent of them have been adapted or built to host gladiators. Archaeologists love patterns, particularly if they demonstrate a delightfully clear process of development. I would really love to be able to say that post holes were all dated to the first century CE, and replaced in the second with parapets on the eastern side of the Aegean and *podiums* on the west, or that walls were of uniform height and that dozens of inscriptions had been found detailing exactly when changes were made and by whose authority and generosity. The truth is, however, that there is no discernible pattern to the changes we see made to theatres because we simply don't have enough information. Securely dating a wall is often difficult enough, but dating a drilled hole is nigh on impossible. Excavation reports often have to resort to dating adaptations to 'the Roman period', which is frustratingly vague. Dating an architectural adaptation to a specific century is as accurate as one can usually hope for. When each adaptation type is charted on a map, there are no neat regional delineations either. Posts, parapets, and *podiums* are distributed seemingly randomly.

What are we, as detectives on this case, to do? Let's explore another case study to think about the issues and the possibilities.

Chapter 14

CSI Case Study: Was Dodona a Stage for Augustus' Ambition?

For our case study, we will take a closer look at the theatre of Dodona. This performance space is usually described as having been adapted in the Augustan period, when some of the front rows of seats were removed to enlarge the *orchestra* and create a tall *podium* wall. However, as we have just established, dating is a tricky process, fraught with uncertainty. To get our heads around this, we'll weigh up the evidence both for and against the Augustan dating for the theatre at Dodona.

Dodona is in Epirus, a region that was on the fringe of the Greek world (for example, both Thucydides and Strabo considered the Epirotes to be little better than barbarians),[342] with a thick dialect and a disinterest in the type of grand cities found in other Greek regions. It wasn't a particularly rich area and held little interest for most visitors, but Dodona was the exception to that rule.

Dodona wasn't a city or a town; it was a religious sanctuary inhabited only by priests and caretakers (in the same way as Olympia, Delphi, and Eleusis). The sanctuary was dedicated to Zeus, and was home to one of the most famous oracles in the Greek world. There is archaeological evidence of cult activity dating as far back as the eighth century BCE, and the oracle there is namechecked in some of the most significant literature of the ancient world, suggesting that this small, seemingly unassuming sanctuary punched above its weight.

Achilles mentions Dodona in the *Iliad*, when he prays to Zeus 'the Lord of Dodona' to let Patroklos survive an upcoming battle.[343] In the *Odyssey*, the hero Odysseus is finally nearing his home of Ithaca after a decade of travelling. Before he returns, he sails further north than he has to, specifically to visit the oracle at Dodona to ask if he should enter his palace in disguise.[344] The sanctuary clearly had a deep cultural importance, even if, at that time in the Late Bronze Age, the sanctuary was little more than a grove containing the sacred oak tree of Zeus.[345] In Apollonius of Rhodes' *Argonautica*, a third-century BCE retelling of the story of Jason and the Argonauts, the prow of the ship Argo was made from oak brought from the sanctuary of Dodona, handily allowing the ship to spout prophecies on the move and guiding the heroic crew through many dangers.[346] This particular story was written in the same century that Dodona got a monumentalising makeover: King Pyrrhus enlarged the temple, and built a grand *stoa*, a *prytaneion* and a *bouleuterion*. He also provided the sanctuary with a grand theatre and stadium in which to host his Naia festival, consisting of athletic and dramatic competitions.

Dodona pops up in literature again in the Augustan period, this time in the *Roman Antiquities* by Dionysius of Halicarnassus. In this story (which Dionysius is adapting from a tale already centuries old), the Trojan prince Aeneas flees the defeated city as a refugee, and sails west to Latium, where his descendants are destined to found Rome. En route to Italy, Aeneas stops off at Dodona to consult the oracle of Zeus about the colony that is destined to be founded: Rome.[347] And so we have a sanctuary that has deep cultural resonance with Greeks and Romans alike. For Rome's first emperor, who wanted to both bring about a Pax Romana and also Make Greece Great Again, leaving a permanent mark on Dodona might be a savvy move. Likewise, local elites who wished to cosy up to the latest Roman big shot might wish to flatter him with some form of tangible honour, and we have archaeological evidence for this type of addition to the sanctuary at this time.

A statue was erected there of Livia, Augustus' wife (although only the inscribed base survives). Statues to Livia were erected in other Greek sanctuaries, such as Eleusis and Epidauros, so this statue fits in with a wider pattern. There are other matching bases in its vicinity, suggesting that this was in fact a collection of dynastic statues of Augustus' family members, which are also attested elsewhere.[348] These can be securely dated, thanks to the inscription, to Augustus' lifetime.

Does the secure dating of the statues extend to the adaptations of the theatre for gladiatorial shows at Dodona? Should these be seen as part of Augustus' mark on the sanctuary? The statue inscription mentions no new buildings at this point, which we would usually expect, and it also reveals that the statues were erected by local elites *for* Augustus and his family, not by Augustus himself. So we have no clear evidence matching the dating of the theatre adaptation to our securely dated statue. Absence of evidence is not necessarily evidence of absence but, in this case, it is a significant absence.

There are other problems with the Augustan dating. At the time the statue was dedicated, Augustus himself was busy just thirty-five miles away, on the southern promontory of the Ambracian Gulf at the site of a small town once known as Actium. The Battle of Actium, you might remember, was where Augustus famously ended the civil war between himself and Mark Antony. A couple of years after the battle, Augustus decided to found a city to celebrate the historic event, and he placed it exactly where his army had camped. He called it Nikopolis, which means 'Victory City' in Greek. In founding a city to commemorate a military victory, Augustus was taking his cue from Hellenistic kings, most famously Alexander the Great. From the outset, Nikopolis was designed to be a major centre and Augustus poured a lot of thought and cash into its construction. It was conceived of as the ideal combination of Roman city and Greek *polis*, with its population a mix of locals and Augustus' veterans. It was also to be home to Augustus' Actian Games, which featured the traditional athletic, dramatic, equine and musical contests. As such, the city was furnished immediately with a brand-new theatre, stadium, gymnasium and baths. There was a huge, monumental trophy commemorating the battle, decorated with the rams of Antony's destroyed fleet, and a sanctuary to Augustus' patron god Apollo.

We have seen that Augustus was keen to control gladiatorial shows in Rome, and, if he wanted to export them eastwards, Nikopolis would surely be the place to do it, where he melded Roman and Greek traditions together. The stadium at this point was not ideally suited to gladiatorial shows, but would be adapted about a century later.[349] The theatre similarly shows no intentional hybridity at this point, with no safety features built into the design. No amphitheatre has been detected in the city. If Augustus was intent on including gladiators in the culture of his new city, he forgot to build them somewhere to perform, and while thirty-five miles is not too far for a modern audience to travel, it makes no sense for an ancient ruler to build a quasi-Olympic village in Nikopolis but place gladiators at Dodona.

With this context, we can return to the question of whether local elites at Dodona might adapt their theatre to curry favour with Augustus. To be frank, there is nothing to suggest Augustus thought much about Dodona at all. Further to this, there is no evidence of Augustus pushing gladiation elsewhere in the eastern provinces of the Roman empire. If local elites wanted to flatter Augustus with the adaptation, why choose to adapt a monument for a performance Augustus showed little interest in?

Let's take another look at the Dodona theatre, then. The style of adaptation is an advanced one, and, though dating can be difficult, no other examples of this type are seen elsewhere for more than a century: even in the broad field of dating, this is a while. If the theatre was adapted like this in Augustus' lifetime, it becomes a further anomaly. We can't discount that the theatre might have previously had a minor adaptation with some kind of temporary barrier, but the *podium* wall signals that the permanent conversion is probably no earlier than the second century CE, when we see this sort of thing elsewhere. It's tempting to connect constructions like the theatre conversion to great men or to memorable events, particularly if there is something securely dateable sitting close to it, but an Augustan conversion makes little sense with what we know.

Another case study might help here, this time to show what we *do* know. On rare occasions, we do have a smoking 'date' gun, like an inscription that states 'this particular politician/priest/emperor built this', which we then can cross reference with other inscriptions and literature to determine when that person was alive and in office. This is the case with the Theatre of Dionysus in Athens.

There was a political mover-and-shaker in the city during the reigns of Claudius and Nero named Tiberius Claudius Novius. Between 41 and 61 CE, he held the prestigious civic post of 'Hoplite General' eight times, and was priest of Nero's imperial cult. This is the kind of man who leaves a mark, and there are multiple inscriptions about him that help us piece together his career. One of the most important texts about him, for our purposes, technically doesn't exist anymore. It was added to the architrave of the Parthenon in 62 CE, with bronze letters attached to the stone with sockets. There were enough traces of the letters on the stones of the Parthenon to allow archaeologists to determine that the letters spelled out a dedication to Nero, on the order of Tiberius Claudius Novius. The bronze letters were removed shortly after Nero died in 68 CE, as he had become dreadfully unpopular and the Roman Senate ordered that every image and public reference of him be destroyed – a form of condemnation we call *damnatio memoriae*.

The Athenians were no doubt happy to see the letters come down, as adding honorific inscriptions about men to temples was a Roman custom, and very thoroughly non-Greek. It just wasn't the done thing. Clearly, Tiberius Claudius Novius was the type of Athenian who was willing to suck up to the Romans and to conduct his affairs the Roman way, even if some of his fellow citizens found this sycophantic and unpatriotic.

A second relevant inscription from the career of Tiberius Claudius Novius comes from what remains of the Roman additions to the Theatre of Dionysus.[350] The inscription reveals that Tiberius Claudius Novius had paid for the theatre to be 'Romanised' sometime between 54 and 62 CE. The Roman additions were a low *pulpitum*, a relatively small *scaenae frons*, and a low parapet wall around the *orchestra* to protect spectators from animals and gladiators. For a theatre conversion, not only is it a relatively modest one compared to later ones, with their massive scene buildings and higher walls,[351] but it's astonishing that we can date it to an eight-year window. Usually, we must be content to date a theatre conversion to a century! We can narrow this date for two reasons: the inscription mentions that the conversion was carried out in honour of Nero, who became emperor in 54 CE. The change can't have started before this point. Secondly, because we know the dates of many of Tiberius Claudius Novius' magisterial appointments, and because he mentions that he arranged (or completed) the conversion in his seventh term as 'Hoplite General', we know that the conversion was finished by 62 CE. This makes the Theatre of Dionysus in Athens the first securely dated theatre conversion that made the *orchestra* safe to use as an arena.

Whether or not it truly was the first conversion, we cannot know with the limited evidence that we have. We do know that dozens of cities followed suit and held their gladiatorial games in the theatre, which became the most prevalent location for all Roman spectacle in the Greek world.

As well as physical changes, the *nature* of Greek theatres changed with the arrival of the Romans. No longer were they places to watch dramatizations or listen to recitations that talked of warriors. They became places to see those warriors in the flesh, and now the fighting was very much 'on stage'.

Chapter 15

The Stadia of Ares

The Greeks were famous for their love of sport, an obsession that dated back to the Bronze Age. Athletics were an essential component of life for men across the eastern Mediterranean, and part of a daily routine for the citizens who could afford to spend their time this way.[352] As well as the rich traditions of mythology, poetry and drama, it is just as important to look elsewhere in the Greek cultural landscape in order to get a fuller understanding of gladiators in the Greek world. One major clue can be found in another type of venue where gladiators fought: the stadiums originally built to host the premier athletes of the Greek sporting world. If gladiators were looking for inspirational men who thrived on competition and physical prowess, they need only attend a traditional athletic festival to find them.

For the Greeks, exercise wasn't fun unless someone could excel at it, and the clearest demonstration of excellence was being the best. Exercise became competitive, and men strived to become the fastest runner or strongest fighter. A beautifully honed body was a very good advertisement for one's own prowess at the *gymnasium*, and as the statues show, a tautly muscled body was the ideal male form for centuries.[353] Constant warfare also provided a strong incentive for the male population to be physically fit with a modicum of skill, agility and strength, though this was more of an added bonus – the main incentive for athletic prowess was winning competitions. Physical strength and capability were important components of Greek *arete*, which measured the excellence of an individual.

From an early stage, athletics was wrapped up in religion. Religion touched every element of communal life in Greece, and sport was no exception. Greeks couldn't remember the exact details of how this started, so they explained the process through the medium of myth: athletic festivals had been founded to commemorate a god or hero defeating someone or something in a vaguely athletic manner. As well as honouring these gods, there was always the possibility that watching mortals run around very fast entertained the gods as much as it did spectators. The first recorded Olympics were held in 776 BCE, and were held every four years for more than a millennium. For the first handful of those festivals, the only events were footraces, but, in 708 BCE, wrestling was introduced both as an individual event and as a component of the pentathlon. Five festivals later, boxing was added to the programme, and, in 648 BCE, the *pankration* was included, rounding out a trio of contact sports that would be emulated at festivals across the region.

There were hundreds of athletic festivals across the Greek world, and most self-respecting *poleis* had its own competition with its specific rituals and programme of events. Some were for local lads, and the bigger ones welcomed competitors from all over the Greek world. These bigger games tended to offer valuable prizes, either in the form of cash or expensive goods like olive oil. Each victor received a headband of ribbons, and we see these depicted in statues and on vases. Any athlete looking for glory could spend an entire career on the prize-games circuit, but only the exceptional made it to the Big Four festivals of Zeus at Olympia, Apollo at Delphi, Poseidon at Isthmia and Zeus (again) at Nemea. The prizes here were symbolic crowns of sacred plants rather than ribbon, with no other prize offered. It didn't matter; the fame and glory earned by a victory at these more prestigious games was worth more than any amount of cash. These special victory wreaths led to these four festivals being known as the *Stephanitic* Games, after the Greek word *stephanos*, meaning 'crown'. A win at one of the Games often meant a hometown showering a victor in honours and freebies, and immortality in the form of a statue in the sanctuary and perhaps one in one's hometown as well, more than making up for the lack of cash prizes.

The sanctuaries of the Big Four were Panhellenic hubs; as well as drawing pilgrims to the temples, the festivals themselves saw tens of thousands of visitors from all corners of the Greek world descend for a week of athletic events. As well as seeing athletes compete, celebrities were spotted, political gossip swapped, business deals brokered, and scandals made.

For our purposes, we'll leave the track and equine events to the side, and concentrate on Greek contact sports.[354] Combat athletes were instantly recognisable, not just because of their cauliflower ears and misshapen noses, but because their training gave them very different physiques to the track stars. They took training seriously, with diets of carbs and red meat, and exercises designed to bulk them out. Speed wasn't always the best tactic, not when a fighter could be simply too massive to knock down. Modern combat events have weight classes, but there was no such thing in ancient athletics. Nobody wanted to be the scrawny underdog, because a huge physique was necessary to win. So combat athletes usually boasted barrel chests and thick thighs. All combat events hinged on strength and endurance.

Combat events took place in the stadium, in an area called the *skamma*. It was created by breaking up an area of the running track with picks and softening the dirt there with water, which helped absorb the impact of throws and falls. There were referees to ensure that combatants stayed in the designated area during the events, and to closely monitor for illegal manoeuvres. Because there were private, preliminary knockout rounds before each festival began, spectators would be watching the crème de la crème of combat athletes competing, and could expect to enjoy what we might call the quarter-, semi-, and grand finals. Competitors were drawn by lot, until the last pair standing reached the final. That meant that the finalists had to fight several times, all in the space of a single afternoon. The finals were therefore not as explosive as the earlier rounds, and it was a wise athlete who didn't exhaust himself too soon. To prepare for a fight, the athletes oiled their skin, then covered themselves in dust (as being too slippery might give an unfair advantage). There were three main types of combat sports, and all of them help us to understand the phenomenon of gladiators in the ancient Greek world.

Wrestling (pálē, πάλη)

A wrestling match was won by the first competitor to score three points. Points could be gained in the following manner:

- causing an opponent to touch the dirt with his back, hip or shoulder
- causing an opponent to yield, or
- causing an opponent to leave the *skamma*

Wrestling was all about holds, grapples and throws, so no punches or kicks were allowed. Athletes couldn't bite either, or try to poke eyes out, or tug at exposed genitals; the referee was allowed to whip any offending athlete until he desisted. As such, it was all a very gentlemanly affair compared to other contact sports. For instance, a wrestler might try to choke his opponent by squeezing his neck, or he could snap a limb, or break his opponent's fingers. All of these were legitimate approaches. After each point, the wrestlers could have a quick breather before beginning again, which was a luxury boxers were not afforded.

Wrestling produced some legendary competitors, like Milo of Croton. Milo first won the wrestling at Olympia and Delphi in the youth category in the sixtieth Olympiad, winning again as an adult a further five times at Olympia and six at Delphi. He also won nine titles at Nemea and ten at Isthmia. That meant his professional career lasted for about thirty years from 540 BC, and twenty-four of those years were as the unbeatable champion at every one of the 'Big Four' Panhellenic Games. An athlete that won at all four Panhellenic Games was called a *periodonikes*; Milo achieved this an astonishing five times. He finally lost in 512 BCE to another wrestler from Croton called Timasitheus, who simply stayed at arm's length and waited until Milo eventually tired himself out.

Milo apparently built up his strength by carrying a calf on his shoulders every day for four years until it was a fully grown bull. He also had an awe-inspiring diet, reputedly eating twenty pounds of meat, twenty pounds of bread and drinking eighteen pints of wine a day. In 520 BCE, he strutted around a festival to Zeus dressed as Herakles, casually carrying a bull that he later ate in one sitting. Ten years later when the city of Croton attacked nearby Sybaris, Milo donned his Herakles costume again as well as his athletic crowns and led the charge onto the battlefield. Milo was fond of party tricks and enjoyed tying a cord around his forehead, holding his breath and snapping the cord with only his bulging veins. He would also love to challenge opponents to steal a pomegranate from his hand. Not only could no man loosen his grip, Milo would not even have bruised the fruit. In fact, a favourite game was for Milo to ask somebody to bend his outstretched finger. No-one ever did.

Boxing (pygmachia, πυγμαχία)

Another major combat sport was boxing. Unlike our modern iteration, ancient boxers didn't fight their bouts in rounds with a short break for a drink and a pep talk from their trainer. Fights were continuous and lasted as long as they needed to. There were no rounds, and no respite. The event could only be won if an athlete tapped out, was knocked unconscious, or died. Bearing in mind that the athletes wore nothing to protect their heads, the latter was a distinct possibility. Neither did they use large, padded gloves. Ancient boxers wound four metres of leather softened with oil called *himantes* around each hand and wrist, leaving the fingers free. This protected the hands of the wearer but certainly not the skin of the opponent. *Himantes* caused such stinging cuts that they were nicknamed 'ants'. Any type of blow from the hand was acceptable apart from gouging.

Certain boxers boasted that their faces were still unmarred because of their great skill. One, named Meloncomas of Caria, remained undefeated for his entire career without ever throwing or receiving a punch, relying on nimble footwork and the ability to keep his guard up for up to two days at a time. Otherwise, veteran boxers would have been instantly recognisable from their broken noses and numerous scars, perhaps with a few teeth knocked out for good measure. Eurydamas of Cyrene lost every single one of his teeth in a single fight. Apparently an aristocratic Roman entered the Olympic Games and when he got home was disowned by his family, losing his inheritance. He was so badly disfigured during his bout his family didn't recognise him. Fatalities were not only possible, but sometimes even preferable, if it meant winning. There was a memorial at Olympia from the first century CE to a boxer known as the Camel of Alexandria. It reads: 'He prayed to Zeus, "Give me victory or give me death!" And here in Olympia he died, boxing in the Stadium at the age of 35. Farewell!'

It appears from ancient depictions of boxing that the head was the primary, or even sole legitimate target, but blows to the body were not unheard of. Pausanias recounts the story of Damoxenos of Syracuse and Creugas of Epidamnus, who were competing in the boxing final at the Nemean Games. The bout seemed never ending, so the two made an agreement to end the match with a knockout. In turn, they would land an undefended blow until one of them could no longer stand. Creugas landed a blow to the head, Damoxenos didn't yield. Damoxenos, on his turn, didn't aim for the head. He outstretched his fingers, jabbed them into Creugas' side beneath the ribs, grabbed onto his internal organs and yanked as hard as he could, pulling them out of Creugas' torso. Creugas died instantly, but Damoxenos didn't win; his open hand move was judged a foul, and Pausanias suggests that each of his fingers was counted as a separate blow. The bargain had been to strike one blow each. The corpse of Creugas was declared the victor, and a wreath placed on its head.

Boxing also produced celebrities. In 480 BCE, the fighter Theagenes won the Olympic boxing title in a fight against Euthymos of Locri. Theagenes wanted to win the boxing and *pankration* in one day, but Euthymos had put up such a fight in the final that Theagenes was too exhausted to then compete in another event. His *pankration* opponent won by default, and Theagenes was fined for dropping out (as well as for entering the boxing for the sole reason of annoying Euthymos, as far as the judges could make out). At the next Olympics, Theagenes won the *pankration* and didn't enter the boxing, which Euthymos won. Euthymos seems to have travelled to Tamesa at some point after this, where he reportedly beat a murderous ghost in a wrestling match, saved the city, and married a beautiful maiden who was to be sacrificed to the ghost … (historians think there was likely some exaggeration going on here!) Meanwhile, Theagenes became the first Olympian to win both boxing and *pankration*, even if they weren't won on the same day as he'd planned.

He did later manage to win both in a single day (twice) at the Isthmian Games. Theagenes won several wreaths in boxing and *pankration*; he earned ten wreaths at Isthmia, nine at Nemea, and three at Delphi. He apparently also won 1,400 victories at various other, smaller Games during his stellar career. At Phthia he even ran and won the *dolichos* race, just to prove how versatile he could be.

After Theagenes died, his hometown of Thasos erected a large statue of him, which was common practice if a *polis* boasted a local Olympic superstar. A long-time rival who had never managed to best Theagenes took out his humiliation and frustration by sneaking up to the statue after dark each night and whipping it. The statue toppled one night and killed the hapless man. The statue was accused of murder and thrown into the sea, as the punishment in Thasos for murder was exile. A drought then hit the island, and the desperate citizens looked for the cause. The Oracle of Delphi eventually told the people to recall their exiles to end the famine, and it wasn't until the people of Thasos retrieved the statue of Theagenes from the sea floor did the drought stop. From that point on, sacrifices were left at the statue, which was reputed to have healing powers. Then, as now, legends sprang up around local celebrities who were the hot topic of conversation.

Pankration (παγκράτιον)

If boxing sounds violent, it was nothing in comparison to the third combat sport: *pankration*. The word comes from '*pan*' meaning 'all' (i.e. Panhellenic, all of the Greek world) and 'kratos' meaning 'power' (i.e. democracy: *demos* 'people' + *kratos* 'power': 'Power of the People'). So *pankration* literally means 'all forms of strength/power'. There were only two rules: no biting and no eye-gouging. Grapples, holds, throws, kicks, punches and everything in between were all considered fair game. To a modern eye, *pankration* is utterly savage. To the ancient audience it was a highlight of the games and a masterful display of skill, strength and determination. Like boxing, there were no rounds or points. Yielding, unconsciousness or death were the only way a match ended. With such freedom came a host of imaginative fighting styles within the event and the random lots must have made bouts between famous pankratiasts with differing techniques a must-see event. Determination and the endurance of pain were seen as honourable in the eyes of spectators and, as we often do now, crowds would sometimes cheer for underdogs if they showed fortitude. *Pankration* wasn't just a competition of who could inflict the most pain, but who could take the most pain. And pain they definitely inflicted and took: *pankration* caused broken bones, dislocated joints, and massive bruising, both internal and external. Despite only having two rules, *pankration* wasn't actually a free-for-all. There were different methods and tactics to choose from, and each athlete had their own style. No bout was the same. Even if, to us, *pankration* seems like an ultra-violent brawl, there was an immense amount of skill involved and talented pankratiasts were highly regarded.

As with boxing, fatalities were not uncommon. One famous example is the story of Arrichion of Phigaleia, who had reached the *pankration* final at Olympia at the fifty-fourth Games. He had been victorious at the previous two games, and was hopeful for a third win, until his opponent had him trapped in a brutal stranglehold which Arrichion could not loosen. Starved of oxygen, Arrichion was losing the match and his life, and could have tapped out to concede the match and live another day. However, conceding was not an option for an athlete like Arrichion. It was not enough to win twice at previous Olympics if he lost once – a single loss diluted his glorious career and reputation. We're told that his trainer yelled out to him from the crowd: 'What an epitaph it would read, if it said, "he was undefeated at Olympia!"'[355] This spurred Arrichion into action; accounts differ, but he either dislocated his opponent's toe or snapped his ankle in half. The hapless opponent tapped out in agony, and the effort of this (entirely legitimate) manoeuvre used up the last of Arrichion's strength and oxygen. He slipped out of consciousness and never woke up, but his corpse was crowned the victor. This was Arrichion's choice, and the story speaks to his ambition and priorities.

When we investigate the Greek propensity to adopt Roman gladiation, we need to keep their very ancient tradition of contact sports in mind. The popular image of the typical Greek as a bookish and bearded philosopher is an enduring stereotype (perpetuated by centuries of bookish and bearded scholars who value ancient philosophy over other aspects of Greek culture), but athletics and philosophy weren't ever mutually exclusive in the ancient world. Plato, for instance, was a talented wrestler, who wrote that athletic exercises were as crucial for the health of the soul as intellectual pursuits.[356] To be a great man, one needed to cultivate brains *and* brawn. As far as contact sports were concerned, the violence of the fights didn't mean mindless brutality: it was a vehicle for cultivating and demonstrating one's outstanding calibre. Excelling in these violent martial arts wasn't indicative of 'barbarian' negative traits, something to be stigmatised for. Combat athletes were well-respected in Greek communities, as demonstrated by the honours heaped upon them, the huge numbers of spectators who clamoured to attend their fights and the semi-mythologising of the celebrity athletes discussed above.

In other words, the Greeks had no reason to reject gladiation because it was an inherently violent sport; they had three incredibly brutal sports already. A martial art involving arms, armour and the occasional fatality was not an unimaginable leap to make.

Sports Buildings

As we've seen elsewhere, popular entertainment in the Greek world required appropriate facilities. In the case of athletics, these facilities were needed by those who wanted to get Olympics-ready and by other men who could afford to spend their day away from manual labour.

The earliest gymnasiums, which date to the Archaic period, were simply open spaces where young men could train, but soon developed into a specific civic building type that all self-respecting *polis* considered essential. They typically featured a running track, perhaps shaded with trees, and colonnades and porticoes along the sides (for use in inclement weather) that led to changing rooms and equipment storage. Some had dedicated bathing facilities, but the most basic would have a small room where athletes could anoint themselves in oil. *Gymnasium* translates to 'place to be naked', as all men trained in the nude.[357] What better way to broadcast one's training than to flaunt its results? A portion of the *gymnasium* was devoted to contact sports, and was usually an open-air square or rectangle surrounded by shady colonnades. This was called the *palaestra*, where wrestlers and boxers trained with their coaches. The *gymnasium* was also the favoured location for philosophers to train their pupils in geography, history and science, utilising the shaded porticoes; even the greatest philosophical schools such as Plato's Academy and Aristotle's Lyceum were centred around a *gymnasium*. As for local athletic festivals, a city might build itself a stadium.

Stadia

As well as theatres (as seen in Chapter 13), numerous sports venues in the Greek world were utilised for the performance of Roman-style spectacle, providing a safer venue for *venationes*, space for larger-scale gladiatorial performances with multiple pairs or groups performed at once, and potentially catering to larger audiences comparable to or exceeding the seating capacity of all but the largest western canonical amphitheatres. For instance, the stadium of Aphrodisias had an estimated seating capacity of 30,000, compared to the significant amphitheatre in Nîmes which could seat 30,500. Very few Greek theatres could rival the capacity of a western amphitheatre, but stadia definitely could.

Stadia were already numerous in the Greek world because, as we have seen, athletic competition was firmly embedded into the cultural landscape. The design popular in the Archaic and early Classical periods was a simple rectangular track enclosed by grassy banks for spectators to stand on.[358] The best surviving example is the stadium at Olympia, which barely changed from the early Classical period through to the banning of the Olympic Games in 393 CE. Elsewhere, in the Late Classical and Hellenistic periods, more attention was paid to developing seating, and stone benches were placed in prominent areas of the raised banks, likely reserved for VIPs. Permanent seating along the straight edge of the stadium could provide a scenic view beyond the track, as was also common in theatres; otherwise, theatre-like seating at one end of the rectangular track created a U-shape at one end to provide optimal viewing of combat sports.[359] Curved, enclosed ends like this were known as the *sphendone*. With the U-shape not needed for the foot races, it was ideal for a *skamma*. With rare exceptions, Greek stadia with entirely permanent stone seating only started to be built during the Roman period and were more common in Asia Minor, whose rich cities could afford such elaborate adaptations more easily than the *poleis* of the Greek mainland.[360] We should consider multifunctionality as a deliberate feature of the architectural adaptations to stadia at this time.

The Stadium of Domitian, built in Rome in 86 CE, likely built on the site of an earlier, temporary stadium, was constructed with a *sphendone* and a *podium* wall surrounding the track to a height of three metres.[361] Its shape is preserved in the later Piazza Navona, and its architecture is still visible (and visitable) in the subterranean museum beneath the Piazza. We know that, as in the Circus Maximus, the Stadium hosted gladiatorial fights. Following a fire in the Colosseum in 217 CE, Cassius Dio reports that gladiatorial spectacle moved to the Stadium of Domitian for 'several years'.[362] Spectator safety provided by the Spectator *podium* wall would have been extremely useful during this time, as would the *sphendone* at the southern end, which was likely roped off to make a temporary oval arena for the gladiators to fight in. We should consider that these features were included in the stadium's initial design specifically to make it suitable for gladiators as well as athletes,[363] and the fire of 217 CE was probably not the first time the stadium had hosted spectacle.

So we know that multifunctionality was built into a major stadium in Rome to allow it to host gladiatorial events as well as athletics. We have also seen previously that theatres and other performance venues in the eastern Mediterranean were often adapted to allow them to host different types of entertainment. It seems reasonable, therefore, to consider *podium* walls and *sphendonai* in Greek stadia as an indication of multifunctionality – a deliberate feature in the transformation of eastern stadia for new purposes.

In this case, the example from Rome is more than a comparison that helps us make sense of fragmentary evidence. We know that a *podium* wall and single *sphendone* were added to the existing stadia at Delphi and Athens when Herodes Atticus finally provided them with stone seating, as well as a parapet wall around the racetrack at Athens.[364] Herodes Atticus was Athenian, but spent a lot of time in Rome in his role as a Roman senator. He owned a large tract of land on the Via Appia, where he built himself an enormous villa (and where a modern street still bears his name, the Via Erode Attico). It is not an unreasonable stretch of the imagination that a senator of Greek descent may have attended Greek athletic games in the Stadium of Domitian, where he would, as a man with a known interest in architecture, have noted the Roman additions of a *podium* wall and *sphendone* to their version of a Greek structure, and that he had the Stadium of Domitian specifically in mind when he restored the stadia at Delphi and Athens.

As well as adapting existing stadia in the eastern Mediterranean, new structures were also built with hybridity in mind, such as the stadia of Aphrodisias and Patrai, replete with *podium* wall and two *sphendonai*.[365] This kind of stadium, which was totally enclosed by seating rather than having one or two open ends, is referred to as an *amphistadium*. 'Amphitheatre' and 'amphistadium' have the same etymological roots: 'amphi' means 'all around' or 'on both sides'. When added to 'theatre', it indicates that the seating area looks like two theatres that have been stuck together, so instead of a semi-circular seating, the seating is 'amphi': it continues all around into an oval. When a stadium is built with or has semicircular *sphendone* seating added to each minor side of the rectangle, the seating also becomes 'amphi': there is seating on all sides. The point is the same in amphitheatres and *amphistadia* alike: the curved wall means that every spectator could see as much of the show as possible, and gladiators weren't able to hide in a corner.

The *amphistadium* at Patrai, also built under Domitian, boasted a *podium* wall higher than other eastern stadia, but at three metres it is identical to that of its contemporary in Rome.[366] The Augustan stadium at Nikopolis was initially conceived with a single *sphendone*. It was again under Domitian that the stadium was altered to include a second *sphendone* and a *podium* wall of on average 2 metres in height, created by the removal of the lowest four rows of seating.[367] We can see, then, that alterations and adaptations were common even in later, purpose-built venues.

The *amphistadium* at Aphrodisias was built in the first century CE and was one of the largest in the Roman world. Clearly, one of its main functions was to host a traditional, Greek-style athletic festival, and archaeologists were even able to find a list of prizes for the victors; notably, the combat athletes won bigger piles of cash than the track stars.[368] But we know that *podium* walls were not deemed a necessity for hosting *pankratiasts*, and the whole length of the track was more than one and a half metres below the front rows of seats. When tourists visit the site today, they are unaware that the original track surface is still buried, as the wall isn't easily visible, but other than this minor quibble the stadium is one of the best preserved and most evocative in the entire ancient world. Because we know that altered/hybrid stadiums had a tall *podium* wall around the entire track, we know that the entire track must have been required for beast hunts, as well as the special classes of gladiator who required horses. The *eques* fought on horseback, and the *essedarius* fought from a moving chariot, just as Homeric heroes are described as doing in the *Iliad*. For cities that didn't want to build an amphitheatre, theatres were simply too small to accommodate mounted gladiators. A stadium, however, would be ideally sized for such a combat. *Venationes* and mounted gladiators may well be the reason that several cities chose to alter their theatre *and* their stadium. A full stadium track could also accommodate group gladiatorial fights featuring rookies and less notable combatants, which were a rare but not unheard-of event.

What about one-on-one fights between famous fighters? These kinds of combats were hot tickets, so where would they be performed to ensure everyone got a really good seat? If amphitheatres and theatres were ideal designs for spectators because their curved design allowed everyone a clear view, then it makes sense that the *sphendone* would make the ideal location for watching events too. Gladiatorial combat being performed in the *sphendone* was a natural progression from its initial purpose as a location for *pankration* and other combat sports, and, as interest in gladiatorial combat peaked, *sphendonai* could be temporarily or permanently enclosed to create an amphitheatrical performance space. For architects with a tight budget, the *sphendone* might have been turned into an oval arena by building a wooden bank of seating that jutted into the straight part of the track. We know that wooden amphitheatres were often constructed, so the architect simply had to construct half of a wooden amphitheatre into the existing stone stadium.

This all seems quite persuasive, although I should stress there is a problem: this is hypothetical, as this solution, if adopted, would leave almost imperceptible traces for archaeologists to try and find. However, we do know that some cities chose to do the same thing: create an oval arena that doubled the seating capacity of the *sphendone*, but they chose to do it permanently with curved, stone walls. Such walls can still be clearly seen at Messene, Aphrodisias and Perge, though others are attested but no longer easily visible, such as the stadium at Ephesus. The *sphendone* of the Panathenaic Stadium in Athens was clearly walled off in the plans and engravings of Ernst Ziller in 1870, but were likely removed in the restoration of the stadium in preparation for the second Zappas Olympics, after which the wall cannot be seen.[369] Using this wall as a base, wooden bleachers could be placed on top of it. This was a drastic change, as it irrevocably shortened the length of the running track, which suggests that as time went on in the imperial period, at least some Greek cities were prioritising Roman spectacles over the older, more traditional Greek foot races. We can't say for sure, then, but it does seem quite likely, considering the various different piles of evidence.

It seems that gladiators were quite proud of performing in Greek stadia. Several of them mention stadia in their epitaphs, and, just as athletics was considered a religious rite, the gladiators found a way to articulate their combats with reference to ancient Greek religious traditions. Across multiple cities, gladiators were giving themselves the same nickname: 'soldiers of Ares'.[370] Ares was one of the Greek gods of war; Athena was the goddess of strategic warfare, whereas Ares was the god of courage on the battlefield. He embodied the more visceral, destructive aspect of war, over Athena's measured cunning. Ares was the warrior deity of choice for gladiators. It's noteworthy that he is referred to as Ares; his Roman counterpart was known as Mars. I don't think this is for the benefit of locals, but rather that it's indicative that these fighters were Greek to their core, and not western gladiators shipped in to give the provincials a show. It's also worth mentioning that western gladiators never associate themselves with Mars, despite the symbiotic relationship between gladiators and legionaries. This was a nickname for Greek gladiators, and one that we see them give to themselves, not how they're advertised by the *munerarii*. It's a bold claim; that these men were representatives or even favoured by Ares, but one that made absolutely logical sense in the context of the sport, the society, and the god. If these gladiators were the soldiers of Ares, then the stadia in which they fought were connected to the god too, and in the epitaphs we do indeed see these venues similarly referred to as 'stadia of Ares'.[371] The stadium at Olympia was in a sanctuary of Zeus, Delphi was sacred to Apollo, and the stadium of Athens was used for games honouring Athena – but as far as the gladiators were concerned, every stadium became the domain of Ares as soon as a gladiator set foot on the track.

Hippodromes and Circuses

Many Greek sanctuaries that held athletic competitions also had a hippodrome to host equine sports like horseback racing and chariot racing, which were popular at all four of the Panhellenic festivals as well as prize games across the eastern Mediterranean. If Greeks had hippodromes, Romans had circuses. There are crucial differences between the two, which explains why Romans still felt the need to build the latter in their eastern territories. The first is that Greek hippodromes were very much *un*-monumental. Like stadia, the hippodrome was a flattened racetrack with banks of seating on one or both long sides, usually due to the fact that hippodromes were constructed in valleys or besides hills. Spectators would sit or stand on the slopes, with wooden or occasionally stone seating cut from the living rock for VIPs. Monumental racetracks for chariots weren't built in the Greek world until the Roman period, who not only made sure to include complete seating (utilising barrel vaulting as a support in the same manner as their theatres and amphitheatres), but also added a feature of the racetrack that the Greeks had never deemed necessary. The *spina* was a long masonry barrier that ran along almost the entire length of track, to ensure a one-way system. In Greek hippodromes that lacked this barrier, riders, and charioteers who had made the hairpin turn at the far end of the track ran the risk of a head-on collision with riders and chariots who had not yet turned and were coming straight towards them. This feature, combined with raised, permanent seating, are the two indications that a racetrack is a Roman circus and not a Greek hippodrome.

To better understand the Roman circus, we should look to the oldest, largest and most famous example: the Circus Maximus. As we've already seen, in Rome, chariot racing was easily the most popular entertainment event. Horse racing had taken place in the area since Rome's earliest years, and it was under the early kings that its form was laid out.[372] While it initially had many similarities with a Greek hippodrome, with seating on grassy banks in the valley between the Aventine and Palatine hills, the characteristically Roman *spina* was likely present even during Rome's earliest years. Its development seems to have been quite haphazard, requiring a complete overhaul by the Late Republic.[373] The transformation of the Circus from makeshift racetrack with a mishmash of permanent and temporary seating sections to formalised monument is largely the work of an innovator we have encountered already: Julius Caesar.[374] As we've seen time and again, his grand plans were continued by his successor Augustus. Under their supervision, the seating was rebuilt in a solid strip around three sides of the track, with stone seats at the front for prominent citizens and wooden seating higher up for the lower classes; it was not until the reign of Trajan that the seating was entirely formed of stone, at which point the Circus could accommodate 250,000 spectators (around a quarter of the city's population).

There was racing in the Circus Maximus at least once a week on average, with between ten and twenty-two races per day. Each lasted about ten or twelve minutes, easily providing a substantial programme of entertainment per race day. Roman chariots could reach speeds of 25 miles per hour, and crashes were both common and dangerous. Not only were charioteers frequently killed, but audience members could also be hurt by debris. The architecture was adapted to solve this problem; builders chose to raise the seating up and away from the racetrack, with a tall *podium* wall separating the two. The *podium* wall of the Circus Maximus may well have influenced Domitian's architects' decision to include one in his stadium. When charioteers misjudged a turn, or were edged off the track, the wall meant that horses and chariots crashed into solid stone, and didn't trample spectators. These chariot crashes were called *naufragia*, meaning 'shipwrecks', and, while they remained fatal for horses and charioteers, the people watching the races were now safe from harm. We've seen that this *podium* wall is really useful for making gladiatorial fights safe to stage in adapted theatres and stadia as well as amphitheatres, and the *podium* was convenient in the Circus Maximus for the same reason.

Again, Rome provides a significant precedent for our investigation; we know that iron fencing around the top of the *podium* wall was attested in the Late-Republican phase of the Circus Maximus to protect spectators from *venationes*.[375] Livy reports that such events could be extensive; an example from 169 BCE featured sixty-three big cats and forty bears and elephants.[376] Once gladiatorial combat in the city required larger venues than could be temporarily erected in various *fora*, a suitable location was sought. It appears that Julius Caesar, who was among the first to appreciate the political potential of most spectacles, may have been the first to use the Circus Maximus for gladiation too. Cassius Dio reports that it was here that, for the first time in the history of gladiatorial combat, Caesar presented gladiators fighting in groups instead of in pairs.[377] In keeping with the location, he also presented *essedarii* and even forty combatants mounted on elephants; he was a gladiatorial pioneer at home and abroad. The architectural nature of the Circus, with its *podium* wall and *sphendone*, allowed for imaginative and substantial programmes of spectacles aside from chariot racing, and it should be assumed that this dual functionality was employed elsewhere also, even if it was not a regular occurrence.

The circuses that Rome built in the eastern Mediterranean were based on the Circus Maximus, which had already proved to be suited to gladiation with absolutely no architectural adaptations necessary. Everything a gladiatorial show needed was already built into the design. If a Greek city wished to adopt Roman style spectacles, they didn't need to build both a circus and an amphitheatre (though some did); a single monument could provide a home to both chariot racing and bloodsports.

Despite a long history of Greek chariot racing, circuses of the Roman design were nevertheless comparatively rarer in Greece and Asia Minor compared to most other provinces, because Greek-style chariot racing in hippodromes remained preferable.[378] Chariot racing was still seen as part of an athletic programme for religious festivals in many Greek cities, rather than a spectacle in itself, so maintaining the hippodromes made more sense than building circuses in a lot of cases. It's interesting that some of the major circuses of Roman design in the eastern Mediterranean appear in cities with a lesser interest in Greek athletic festivals, like Tyre, Bostra and Berytos. Just over a dozen Roman-style circuses were built in the entirety of the eastern Mediterranean, and they were frequently slightly smaller in size compared to western circuses,[379] a change that is likely an indication of deliberate multifunctionality at the point of construction.[380] Racetracks for chariots could be smaller than the Circus Maximus and still provide an excellent show, but finding enough gladiators and wild animals to fill a track the size of the Circus Maximus was a big task in cities smaller than Rome; the solution was a smaller circus, ideal for both. For cities with limited resources or space, a hybrid racing-gladiation venue was an alternative to adapting their theatre for gladiatorial shows, particularly if *venationes* were popular. Even so, many of the eastern cities with a Roman-style circus also adapted theatres or built amphitheatres as well; Corinth and Bostra both boasted all three.

One eastern venue in particular must have been an early venue for gladiatorial combat. Josephus describes Herod Agrippa's euergetism regarding the provision of various civic buildings in Berytos (modern Beirut), including the additions of a theatre, baths, porticoes and an 'amphitheatre', where Herod Agrippa hosted gladiatorial games.[381] It is probable that this amphitheatre started as a temporary wooden structure.[382] Where was it? Certainly, no trace of a stone amphitheatre has been found. The presence of a canonical amphitheatre under Herod Agrippa's reign would also place it among the very first in the east; only Caesar's amphitheatres in Corinth and Antioch-on-the-Orontes would be dated earlier.[383] It would also be unusual for Herod Agrippa, who learned the use of monumentalisation from his grandfather Herod the Great, to deviate from the family tradition of building hybrid venues. Partial excavations of the Beirut Hippodrome reveal a stone circus complete with *spina*, in other words a canonical replication of the Circus Maximus, and its earliest walls (in the excavated areas) date to the latter half of the first century CE.[384] The stone circus cannot therefore be the venue for Herod Agrippa's games, in which he presented 1,400 gladiators, as he died in 44 CE.[385] However, the excavations also indicate that the area of the Hippodrome was being levelled as early as the late first century BCE, and that the first phase of the Hippodrome was likely of wooden construction.[386] It is therefore possible that the wooden amphitheatre and the wooden circus are one and the same building. Josephus had a habit of using the term 'amphitheatre' literally: a curved building where the seating completely surrounds the performance space. When he uses 'amphitheatre', he could mean a normal amphitheatre, a stadium with two *sphendonai*, or in this case, a small circus with two *sphendonai* that was used for both chariot racing and gladiation. This solution allows for both Josephus' use of terminology and the matching dating of Herod's attested 'amphitheatre' with the earliest phase of the Beirut Hippodrome.

While it is unclear what form the wooden construction took, a hybrid venue certainly follows the examples of Herod's earlier entertainment venues, and those of his grandfather Herod the Great. That the later, larger stone phases of the Beirut Hippodrome are in the form of a canonical circus does not detract from its hybridity, given that the main required safety feature of a *podium* wall for both chariot racing and gladiation was present, at a height of three metres.[387] It may just be that, in Berytos, chariot racing took precedence over gladiators, and that, when the venue was monumentalised in stone, it made sense to make it more like the Circus Maximus and less amphitheatrical. Titus celebrated Vespasian's birthday with Games there in 70 CE,[388] and we cannot know if the building was then made of wood or stone, though we know his Games at Caesarea Maritima were hosted in the permanent hybrid hippostadium earlier that year.[389] Clearly, as far as gladiation was concerned, multiple types of building were found more than appropriate.

Looking at the evidence for venues that hosted gladiators is an essential part of building our case; these are the buildings where our gladiators competed. But what of the men themselves? What evidence do we have of their own views of their profession and identity? It's time for another case study.

Chapter 16

CSI Case Study: An ID to Last for All Eternity

The case for the defence rests on two main arguments: that there is scant evidence for amphitheatres in the Greek world and that Greeks were too culturally sophisticated to appreciate the violence of gladiatorial combat, especially when it was so closely identified with the violent Roman conquerors. We have seen, however, that there is a great deal of evidence for gladiatorial venues, we just haven't been looking at it properly. The myriad of performance venue types that Greek cities already had – conceptually and literally – were routinely adapted into multi-purpose spaces for gladiator spectacles, just as they had previously been adapted for other needs and requirements. Not only do they make it clear that gladiator spectacles were frequently absorbed into the cultural and social fabric of the Greek world, but these adapted venues likely also enhanced various aspects of gladiatorial combats in ways that would have been meaningful to Greek audiences.

We also have enough context about the earlier Greek cultural phenomena that these venues were originally designed for (specifically, performances of Greek myths and athletic contests) to make an educated guess about how the spectacle of gladiators was absorbed, adapted and enthusiastically adopted by Greek audiences. But let's not simply make a guess, however educated, when we can start by tackling another case study together. This time our focus will be another major evidence group: gravestones.

Gravestones allow us to see how people *wanted* to be remembered. They offer an amazing insight into identity (if not always reality) and a perfect way to investigate the cultural function of gladiators. In fact, gravestones are such a good source of evidence for our investigation that we can't possibly explore every aspect in one case study. Here, we will focus more on individual elements: how gladiators presented themselves within long-standing Greek cultural traditions. Later, we will also look at gravestones to explore what they can tell us about the attitude towards gladiators in Greek society more generally.

We have seen that Greeks had long lived in militaristic societies, with warfare (largely among themselves) a constant feature of Greek life. Up until the end of the Classical period, cities had relied on citizen soldiers to go to war, using military conflict as the default solution for all kinds of political disagreements. Basically, warfare was a common aspect of Greek life for century after century. Warriors were idealised and idolised in equal measure, and every self-respecting Greek male wanted to be in peak physical condition so that he could serve his city with distinction and honour. In many cities, military training was a fundamental part of the education of the city's male youth. Greek warfare didn't produce many individual heroes, because the tactical, tight formations that the soldiers fought in encouraged soldiers to hold their lines and not break from formation to launch into any one-on-one combat. Nevertheless, soldiers were highly respected for their bravery and valued by their city. Such deeply embedded ideals didn't change even when the geopolitics changed: Alexander the Great and his successors preferred to use professional standing armies and mercenaries, as did the Romans. The Greek competitive spirit continued in other outlets, as we've seen, and the Greek enthusiasm for martial combat also found other outlets including, it would seem, gladiator combats.

Warriors of myth and legend

Of course, the most famous Greek warriors were found in myth, where warriors definitely did fight in one-on-one combats on the battlefield. We've already seen how children grew up hearing stories of legendary battles, and the epic exploits of their favourite heroes would have been as familiar as the backs of their hands. It's little wonder, then, that a quarter of the gladiators we know of in the eastern Mediterranean chose to use the name of a mythical hero as their stage name. By choosing the name of someone with a well-known story, the gladiator could favourably compare himself to them in terms of skill and charisma, and it created the same kind of audience expectations as the gladiators who chose names based on desirable attributes. A Heracles might be huge, or an Ajax might be particularly ferocious. By choosing names of mythical warriors, gladiators added a touch of narrative to their fights. It is easy to imagine that spectators each had emotional connections to the heroes they admired or identified with by hearing the stories, particularly from childhood.

This must have been particularly effective when gladiators performed in the theatre. Imagine an audience who were used to attending plays there, and seeing these stories performed by actors. As an example, let's take the mythological

Eteokles and Polyneikes. These two brothers, the princes of Thebes, feature in many of the stories that ancient Greeks told each other about themselves and each other. Their popularity is key to understanding another aspect of ancient Greek gladiator culture, so let's explore the key beats of the narrative. They were the sons of King Oedipus, who was thrown out of the city when it was discovered that years ago he had killed his estranged father and married his own mother, Jocasta. Eteokles (whose name meant 'truly glorious') and Polyneikes ('much strife') were supposed to share the throne of Thebes. There are many differing versions of the story, as we'd expect given what we know about stories and myths in the ancient Greek world, but both Apollodorus and Diodorus Siculus say that the plan was for the brothers to rule on alternate years. Eteokles took the throne for the first year, but, when Polyneikes was due to take the reins a year later, Eteokles refused to hand over his power. Furious, Polyneikes went down to the Peloponnese to recruit some champions who would lead an army against his stubborn brother, and these became known as the Seven Against Thebes.[390] After a long battle outside the city walls, Eteokles' defenders were victorious, but it didn't matter. The brothers had met on the battlefield to fight in a duel, and each lay dead by the other's hand. It was supposedly an epic fight.

In his play about the war, *Seven Against Thebes,* Aeschylus describes the brothers as *monomachoi,* meaning one-on-one fighters.[391] It's a word that is used in other plays for duelling heroes,[392] and was the preferred word that Greek elites used for the gladiators, even if the gladiators didn't use it themselves on their gravestones. Still, this word choice shows us one of the many ways that Greek culture absorbed gladiators into existing cultural traditions. The duel between the brothers was the emotional finale of Aeschylus' play, but, like all Greek drama, the actual fight occurred offstage. In tragedy, murders, kidnaps and battles were not depicted. The characters would leave the stage and a messenger character would shortly enter to tell the audience what had happened.[393] The reasons are debated, but Sommerstein makes a compelling suggestion that violence wasn't depicted because it would have distracted from the emotional thesis of the play.[394] The catalysts and aftermaths of violent acts were the focus, not the violent acts themselves—the violence wasn't really the point of the play. Even so, there would surely have been audience members who did want to see the fight enacted, and would have found it an emotional experience to do so. When the Romans came along with their gladiators, it finally provided an opportunity. In the same theatre as one could watch *Seven of Thebes,* a spectator might sit down a week later to watch two gladiators named

Eteokles and Polyneikes duke it out with a realism never before imagined. While this may have been a step too far for some theatre purists, it seems there were plenty of Greeks who were thrilled at the prospect. We have dozens of gladiators naming themselves after mythical warriors.

This raises an interesting question: were civilians choosing heroic names for their children? If we delve into a resource called the *Lexicon of Greek Personal Names* (*LGPN*), where 400,000 instances of preserved names are collated and organised by region and date, the name Eteokles appears a mere twenty-three times, but never in the Roman period.[395] By contrast, the name Dionysius occurs more than 5,000 times. The name Polyneikes appears fifteen times, and this time the name continues to be used into the third century CE. In other words, it was highly unusual for a regular Greek to be named after the brothers. But we do have three gladiators named Eteokles and four named Polyneikes. One stone in Smyrna reads: 'Eteokles erected this monument for his brother Polyneikes, the *essedarius*'.[396] Whether these two were biological brothers as well as gladiatorial comrades is unclear, but it does suggest that a savvy *lanista* saw the potential in having two gladiators named after two fraternal rivals on his roster. Other gladiators across the region also evoke the battle at Thebes, taking their names from Polyneikes Argive champions.[397]

The Trojan War was another predictably popular source for inspiration when it came to gladiator naming practices. Again, it's helpful to get an idea of the wider narrative beats of the story. As we've seen in Chapter 13, everyone in the ancient Greek world was familiar with the story from the *Iliad* and plays in the theatre but not everyone now is. The chief protagonist of the *Iliad* was Achilles, whose name naturally crops up among the gladiators most often. Achilles was the son of Peleus, King of Phthia, and the sea goddess Thetis. A prophecy had declared that any son born to Thetis would overshadow his father, and so her divine suitors (including Zeus and Poseidon) hastily married her off, against her will, to the mortal Peleus. Their wedding would unwittingly be the catalyst for the entire Trojan War; when the couple failed to invite Eris, the goddess of discord, Eris decided to gatecrash the wedding feast and cause a little chaos. It was here that Eris threw the golden apple inscribed 'to the fairest' between Hera, Aphrodite and Athena, launching a rivalry that ended in the deaths of thousands of Greeks and Trojans alike.[398] It's a bitter tragedy that a war set in motion before his own birth would cause his death, with a second prophecy that decreed he would die young on a battlefield but remain famous forever.

In the *Iliad*, Achilles leads a crack squad of soldiers known as the Myrmidons, and is the darling of the Achaean fighting force comprising soldiers from all over Greece. When King Agamemnon takes Achilles' battle prize for himself (a Trojan noblewoman named Briseis, who had survived the Greeks massacring her entire hometown of Lyrnessus earlier in the war only to be taken captive and treated as a prize), Achilles gets huffy and refuses to fight. It is only when his close companion Patroklos is killed that Achilles is stirred to rejoin the war, and we, the readers, get to witness his martial prowess and ungovernable rage.[399] Stubborn and irate as he was, Achilles was undeniably a legendary warrior. Little wonder that six gladiators named themselves for him, including one woman (we'll come back to her in Chapter 17).

The Romans, while admiring characters like Achilles, also couldn't help but disparage his many rather considerable character flaws. In fact, many of the legendary Greek warriors who fought at Troy that pop up in Roman literature are given rather a short shrift. Romans, on the whole, were fonder of the Trojans. In fact, they claimed to be descendants of those who fled Troy. Aeneas was a young Trojan prince during the war, and is mentioned in the *Iliad* as a minor character who was favoured by the gods. His mother was Aphrodite, making him a demigod. He was saved from the battlefield a couple of times by Aphrodite, Apollo and Poseidon, so he was clearly special, and yet Homer doesn't really mention what happened to him. The Romans picked up the story with Virgil's *Aeneid*, a sequel to the Trojan Cycle that follows what Aeneas did next.[400] Leading the Trojan refugees after the city falls, Aeneas leads them on a long journey via Carthage (where he meets Queen Dido), pops down to the Underworld to chat to some dead people, and, after a small war, settles down on the Italian peninsula where he marries the King of Latium's daughter.[401] Their descendants, Romulus and Remus, will later found Rome.

Just as Romans in the period of our investigation weren't particularly interested in the Greek characters of the Trojan War legends, so the Greek gladiators almost entirely ignored the Trojans of the story. Only one gladiator named after a Trojan is attested out of the nearly 300 names that we know of from the Greek world: a gladiator named Homeros names his final opponent as 'Hektor' on his tombstone in Nicomedia.[402] Hektor was described as the best of the Trojans, so it may seem odd that only one gladiator (that we know of) chose his name as an homage. As well as being generally more sympathetic than many of the Greek heroes, Hektor was pretty formidable. He had the highest kill rate of any Trojan by some margin, and compared to the Greeks, only Diomedes has more kills to his name (partially because Diomedes killed thirteen defenceless men in their sleep, and because Achilles spent a significant portion of the poem sat on the beach in a strop). Hektor is the only character to be mentioned by name in every single book of the poem. It's certainly easier for modern readers to root for Hektor over some of the more morally ambiguous Greeks; he's a devoted family man who knows the city can't hold out much longer, and who is honourable to a fault.[403]

Despite all of this, perhaps he was never the type of hero gladiators wished to model, despite the fact that in the first book of the poem Achilles speaks of Hektor as the type of warrior that only he himself could better, because while Hektor is admittedly great at killing unimportant Greeks, it's been noted that he frequently becomes quite cowardly when in a one-on-one fight against a Greek hero.[404] He's likeable, but Greeks and Trojans both overestimate his ability in duels against the kind of Greek closest to him in rank. There's also the niggling issue that Hektor's death is one of the most important parts of the poem: he is bested rather dramatically in front of two entire armies and then the victor, Achilles, proceeds to have great fun desecrating his corpse for an extended period. Hektor might be the most prominent example of why no other Greek gladiator chooses a Trojan name: the Trojans lost. They are, by definition, losers. Even in pure statistics, Trojans account for 78.8 per cent of soldiers killed throughout the poem, and their other heroes are on average far less deadly than the most mediocre of Greek counterparts. The Romans may have had a soft spot for the Trojans, but for a Greek gladiator competing in front of Greek spectators, anyone choosing a Trojan stage name might as well have entered the arena holding up a sign saying, 'Dead Man Walking'.

That isn't to say that gladiators weren't picky when choosing which Greek hero to name themselves after. There were two warriors named Ajax in the *Iliad*; Ajax the Greater was a prince from Salamis, also known as 'the Telemonian Ajax', and Ajax the Lesser was the prince of Lokris. Emily Wilson describes Ajax the Greater as 'the best Greek defensive fighter and the best at hand-to-hand-combat, dignified, brave', while Ajax the Lesser is 'the quickest sprinter on the Greek side after Achilles himself, who also excels with a light throwing spear'.[405] The name Ajax was not common in the ancient world. The *LGPN* contains only eight entries for it, and yet we find two gladiators who called themselves Ajax. One of these gladiators was laid to rest in Thasos. His epitaph opens like this: 'You see me, Ajax, not the Lokrian nor the Telamonian, but the one who aroused favour in the stadiums of Ares' battles'. This gladiator has shown deliberation in choosing his name, one that was not popular in the civilian population but would evoke an immediate response from any audience as they spectated his fights. He chose a name shared by two of the most prominent and memorable Greek warriors of the *Iliad*, which this Ajax could use to bolster his own image and reception. It may even have been a name chosen to emphasise one of his own qualities, perhaps enormous size like the Greater, or speed like the Lesser. By mentioning not one but both Ajaxes on his tomb, this gladiator wanted to leave viewers of his tombstone in no doubt as to the inspiration of his own name. In death, as in his career, he would be irrevocably connected and associated with two of the greatest warriors of legend. Not only was he connected, but he perhaps presented himself as their peer. His epitaph continues with a proud report of his career, in which he boasts of saving many men, and surviving many opponents to die a natural death.

So, two gladiators called themselves Ajax, and one deliberately evokes both namesakes featured in the *Iliad*. It is interesting that the sad fate of both Homeric Ajaxes after the part of the story when the *Iliad* cuts off didn't overshadow their earlier deeds for these two gladiators. After Achilles is finally killed, Ajax the Greater and Odysseus both want his armour, forged by Hephaestus himself. Ajax is the archetypal warrior, while Odysseus was always portrayed as a bit of a sly sneak, even before the war started. Both want the armour because it would set them apart as the greatest of the Greeks, now that Achilles is gone; they would be seen by all to be his successor as the best warrior in the Greek army. In the *Little Iliad*, the armour is awarded to Odysseus.[406] Ajax loses all control and tries to slaughter those around him, though the divine intervention of Athena ensures he only kills cattle. It might be assumed that an ignominious death in literature would have been a deterrent for choosing this stage name, but this does not seem to be the case for Ajax. At the end of the Sophoclean tragedy about his suicide, Ajax's final speech includes a plea for the Erinyes (more commonly known as the Furies) to destroy Agamemnon and Menelaus, who he holds responsible for his predicament.[407]

Agamemnon, of course, had an even more ignominious death, so vividly described in the *Oresteia*; when he arrived home to Argos after a decade of war, his wife Clytemnestra waited until he was dozing in his bath before fatally stabbing him. She was seeking retribution for him sacrificing their daughter Iphigenia ten years previously, when he thought such a gesture would cause the gods to send him favourable winds to sail his fleet to Troy. This somewhat pathetic death, as well as his truculent characterisation in the *Iliad*, perhaps explains why no extant gladiatorial memorial features a man with this nom de guerre, and that similarly, his name features a mere ten times in the *LGPN*.

Diomedes is another famous hero also conspicuous by his absence. We have to remember that we are working with the names that have survived on stone, which is not an accurate representation of the thousands of gladiators who fought in the Greek world. Even so, given the numbers of other names from the epic that are present in the collection of commemorations, it is surprising that Diomedes is missing. In the *Iliad*, Diomedes is the deadliest Achaean warrior, killing thirty-one enemies to Patroklos' twenty-seven. Even if we subtract the twelve Thracians Diomedes murdered in their sleep, he is still responsible for nineteen battlefield fatalities, as well as the wounding of Aphrodite and Ares in Book Five. As self-proclaimed soldiers of Ares, is it this sacrilegious attack on this god in particular (that was, in the story, sanctioned by other gods) that deterred gladiators from taking his name? Diomedes' actions do not seem to have bothered Greek civilians, with the *LGPN* containing 341 instances of the name, more than double the civilian instances of men named Achilles. Attempting to kill gods aside, Diomedes is characterised throughout the *Iliad* as an excellent warrior; Achilles' decision to sulk on a sand dune doesn't mean that the Greeks are suddenly on a losing wicket at all. Diomedes steps up to fill the Achilles-shaped void, and he does a tremendous job of killing Trojans. If anything, Diomedes' willingness to get stuck in, even if he personally does voice that he thinks the war is not a just one, emphasises how petulant Achilles was really being. Diomedes was one of the youngest Achaean heroes, but one of the most experienced in warfare; even before the Trojan War began, he was one of the seven Epigoni that marched on Thebes to avenge their fathers who had fallen in Eteokles' and Polyneikes' war. I can only speculate that loyalty to Ares led to Diomedes being ignored by gladiators, but right now this is merely a theory that would align with current available evidence.

The naming choices that we know of from extant gravestones reveal how gladiators expressed their heroic identities and, perhaps, connected with audiences within existing Greek cultural traditions.

Gravestone Poses

What else can we glean from the amazing group of evidence that is gladiatorial gravestones? For the gladiators, keen to promote their profession as one of quasi-heroes, funerary art was also a crucial tool to present themselves as pre-eminent warriors.

The proud and victorious pose adopted by many gladiators in their funerary reliefs is reminiscent of the gravestones of Greek soldiers of centuries past, which would still have been standing in the necropolis of many a city. There is another pose that would have been immediately recognisable to anyone familiar with Greek art, then or now. It is called the 'heroic diagonal', a term coined by the art historian Kenneth Clark to describe a formula used by Greek sculptors to represent heroes in martial motion.[408] While warriors are depicted standing perfectly static and vertical on tombstones, in reliefs on temples and other similar buildings, warriors are carved as if they are in the midst of battle. They might be lunging forward, or leaning defensively back, holding shields and weapons aloft. Their limbs and torsos thus create diagonal lines in the scene, which make the figures seem as if they have been frozen in the midst of furious fighting. When we look at friezes and metopes of famous mythical battles from monuments like the Parthenon or Pergamon Altar, we can begin to identify exactly where the sculptor has placed limbs in a diagonal line to emphasise the movement of each figure. And once we learn to spot it, we see it in the sculptures of buildings across the Greek world. After all, a culture so preoccupied with war liked to feature images of mythical wars on as many public buildings as possible, like the battle between gods and giants (known as the Gigantomachy),[409] the war between the Lapiths and Centaurs (the Centauromachy),[410] the wars against the Amazons (the Amazonomachy),[411] and the Trojan Wars.[412] This pose, then, became synonymous with heroic battles.

Most gladiators who featured art on their tombstone chose to present themselves in profile, in a combative stance. While the poses don't copy the heroic diagonal exactly, there is the definite suggestion that the relief artists were aiming for the suggestion of movement within the tighter confines of a tombstone.

The majority feature the gladiator facing the right, but the left is also present, most often in *familia* memorials and, geographically, in the polis of Mytilene. This is not a style popular among gladiators in the western Roman empire, where dynamic poses are reserved for other artworks such as mosaics and reliefs for *munerarius* commemorations. It's also not seen in Greek tombstones of soldiers, who all stand straight and gaze at the viewer head on. For the Greek gladiators, however, it's common. It is a dynamic pose, almost like the warriors on monuments, and promotes the martial skill of the gladiator. The gladiators are presented in an active stance, primed to strike. The viewer is invited to view the gladiator in action in intimate proximity: the art allows the viewer to consider the active gladiator closely and in detail, in a way that was difficult to achieve from the uppermost seats of a theatre or stadium while the gladiator fought. Because this pose was reminiscent of the great mythical battle sculptures, the gladiators could liken themselves to great mythical warriors, even if this meant deviating from standard soldier tombstones.

Gladiators seem to have come up against two issues in representing themselves as warriors through funerary art. Firstly, the heroic diagonal works best when it depicts opponents in the middle of combat, and these gladiators are depicted alone. Secondly, the reliefs are generally not of the highest quality and this is likely the result of the limited budget each fighter had to spare; none of these reliefs would be as finely wrought as those on civic monuments. As a facsimile, they were simply not quite as dynamic as the reliefs they sought to emulate. No matter: a fairly simplistic combative stance was a solid compromise for both artisan and customer, without losing the comparison to mythic warriors.

As for the inscriptions on the tombstones of Greek soldiers in the Hellenistic and Roman periods, we can turn to an expert for help with our investigation, Silvia Barbantani, and compare the epitaphs she studies with those of our Greek gladiators. Here, we see that gladiators followed the lead of the text on soldiers' tombstones more closely than they did the art. One notable aspect of soldiers' epitaphs is that they were often written in the style of a Homeric epic in miniature.[413] They're concise, but written with the same solemnity as Homer, and with the same kind of imagery and language. A scholar of Homer's epics, Oliver Taplin, notes that the goal of Homeric warriors was *kleos*, which was a Greek concept of fame and renown, particularly that which was earned on a battlefield. All warriors, real and fictional, had a desire for *kleos*. But Taplin also explains that this fame was won not by the warrior, but by the poet/*rhapsodes* who sing of them and the audiences who hear of them in the centuries that followed.[414] In other words, a warrior could achieve a wonderful feat, but if no writer immortalised that feat in poetry or song, the warrior would remain an anonymous nobody.

The epitaphs of soldiers, written by professional poets and often metrical, just like the epic poems, were therefore a way of broadcasting the glorious deeds of soldiers for decades or even centuries after their death, earning them that renown which they craved. We can definitely see parallels between Barbantani's soldiers and our gladiators, then, for many of their epitaphs are metrical and could be considered 'miniature epics.' Take this epitaph, written in hexameter, of a gladiator named Melanippos who died in Alexandria Troas:

> *Traveller, you see me, a corpse, brave in the stadia, the retiarius Melanippos from*
> *Tarsus, second rank. No more do I hear the voice of the bronze trumpet, nor do I*
> *rouse the sound of the unequal pipes in contests. They say that Heracles accomplished*
> *twelve labours. I accomplished the same number; in the thirteenth I met my end.*[415]

Melanippos must have been confident in his abilities and popularity to compare himself to the mighty Heracles, and his own twelve victories in the arena with Heracles' famed twelve labours. Comparing oneself or one's demise to a mythological character is therefore another method by which gladiators sought to align themselves with Greek soldiers, who were already incorporating mythical figures into their epitaphs to emphasise their own qualities and biographies. Barbantani notes that, during the Hellenistic period, Homeric allusions in military epitaphs increased significantly, with many soldiers likening themselves to Greek warriors, just as the gladiator Ajax had done.[416] Take, for instance, this epitaph about a soldier named Epigonus from Laodikeia-ad-Lykos:

> *This monument that you see, passerby, is of none other but of Epigonos, whose virtue Time will not corrupt; he left among the living the pre-eminence of temperance and divine beauty. Neither Achilles, the one who killed Hektor, son of Priam, nor Hippolytos who avoided his father's bed, were like Epigonos, son of Andreas, noble son of a father equal to a king. But Epigonos leaves a lasting memory among the living; not even Achilles, son of Thetis, escaped the destiny ...*[417]

This military epitaph evokes Homeric epic in a similar way to that of the gladiator Ajax who we met earlier in this chapter. Most gladiators preferred not to wait until their death to compare themselves to literary warriors by choosing *noms de guerre*, with the epitaphs of soldiers providing a precedent for the habit.

Western gladiator commemoration closely followed the formula of western military commemoration, in that they were both markedly less florid than elsewhere,[418] so we can see a second parallel. However, there are two remarkable differences between Greek military and gladiatorial commemorations. Barbantani notes that soldiers, particularly from Asia Minor, greatly admired Hektor as a 'symbol of selfless sacrifice for the homeland' and a 'model of valour for Asian military men', which she notes was particularly evident in the Roman period.[419] Hektor is mentioned in multiple epitaphs, with at least one putting him on a par with Achilles. As we have seen, gladiators did not share the sentiment, with a Hektor appearing only once, compared with numerous 'Achaean' gladiators. Soldiers and gladiators from the Greek world do seem to share an indifference to other Homeric Trojans, like Aeneas and Sarpedon, however.

Secondly, the epitaphs of soldiers tend to mention the *paideia* (formal education) the men received in the *gymnasion* as part of their military training; the Homeric allusions featured as another signifier of their stellar education.[420] The soldiers were flaunting their pedigree. Barbantani does note that the epitaphs are skewed to richer, elite soldiers, as those from a common background were buried in common graves.[421] If we assume that a majority of gladiators were buried in a similarly anonymising way, what does this tell us about the gladiators represented in the gravestones?

While in the western territories, social status was sometimes included in commemoration, Greek gladiators are uniformly silent on whether they were enslaved, freedmen, or freeborn *auctorati* (the term used for volunteers).[422] Rare lists of gladiators created by owners and *editores* suggest that percentages of freeborn and enslaved fighters varied across *ludi*, and slaves did not always outnumber *auctorati*. If gladiators were at liberty to choose their *noms de guerre*, perhaps Homeric allusions were included to demonstrate, if not a full, *gymnasion*-style *paideia*, then a level of cultural education that elevated these particular fighters above some of their less fortunate colleagues.

Fighters from a more sophisticated background than some of their colleagues could show off their refined tastes by flaunting a little knowledge of literature. I suspect, however, that mythical warrior names had less to do with superiority over colleagues – given that equal training would render a *ludus* egalitarian in the skills that truly mattered – but was more a case of presenting themselves in a manner that brought both Homeric warriors and contemporary soldiers to mind for the spectators. Though not sacrificing themselves defending a homeland like a soldier, the gladiators still refer to themselves as fighting in the 'Stadia of Ares' in the 'Battles of Ares', making sure to connect themselves with the god of war. This epitaph was made for a gladiator named Achilles who fought and died in Prusa (modern Bursa):

> *Very proud was I, Achilles, in the stadium of Ares, and many I subdued with my deadly hands. Now, I lie here, completing the bitter divine will of the Moirai. My wife Ammion erected the memorial for me, the deceased, and she set the tombstone, the comforting image of remembrance.*[423]

It is unclear if gladiators, retired or otherwise, had the same role in military training in the Greek world as we know they had in Roman history, where they were sometimes drafted in to teach legionaries tips and tricks.[424] After all, far fewer amphitheatres in the Greek world were associated with a garrison, as they were elsewhere, meaning that the relationship between soldier and gladiator may not have been as symbiotic in the Greek world. However, by claiming comparable martial prowess to soldiers and using mythical allusions to give the illusion of a similarly cultured education as soldiers, gladiators were making a clear statement about how they considered themselves as having the same abilities and values, communicated in the same Greek cultural terms.

The quality of epigrams on gladiatorial tombstones ranged from clumsy to rather sophisticated, which was no doubt a reflection on the budget of the deceased or those close to him and the availability of decent epigrammists and stonemasons.[425] Even so, many successfully functioned as miniaturised epics in the same way Barbantani identifies in the epigrams of fallen soldiers, spreading comparable *kleos* by preserving the memory of the gladiators in perpetuity. And this renown, while temporarily lost, has been revived by you reading about their arena exploits in this book!

The key audience of any tombstone, just like a poem or a song, was the wider public. Spectators who were used to listening to epics being recited, *epinikion* odes sung, and tragedies performed were invited to engage with these funerary texts praising the gladiators. Spectators who walked past images of real soldiers in the necropolis and mythical warriors on the monuments of their city every day would be able to spot the deliberate resemblances between warriors and gladiators when they passed by gladiator graves. The warrior, in Greek culture, was noble, strong and a vital member of society. Was it any wonder that gladiators wanted citizens to make favourable comparisons between them? In a way, weren't soldiers and gladiators alike both fighting for the benefit of their city?

Two of a Kind?

There is one more cultural strand – and accompanying venue type – that we have already encountered that is essential to understanding the active integration of gladiators within Greek cultural traditions: athletics.

We have seen that it was common to find Roman gladiation in circuses, originally designed for chariot racing, and we've also seen that the Greeks happily let gladiators perform in Greek athletic stadiums, even the ones in religious sanctuaries. Unlike the Theatre of Dionysus, we don't find any writers worrying about desecrating the stadia. It seems that athletes and gladiators were able to coexist in stadia, even if the two were never recorded as performing on the same day as each other. This is perhaps unsurprising. Much of what we know of ancient combat sports, particularly in the (sometimes semi-mythical) anecdotes about its greatest stars, is similar to what we know of gladiators.

Of course, Greek athletes tended to be rich citizens who could afford the extensive training and travel required for a successful career, while gladiators were either enslaved or financially stretched enough as a free man to consider such a drastic career-change. Socially, the two groups were poles apart.

However, the two groups did have much in common. Both trained incessantly to perfect their craft, taking the progression of their skills very seriously indeed. Both paid great attention to their diet and had specialised regimens and routines in order to get their bodies into peak shape for their respective fighting styles. Both groups needed mental strength as well as physical strength, a requirement for the stern self-discipline and courage needed for these most dangerous professions, and both were considered excellent examples of idealised masculinity. Death was a very real possibility for contact athletes and gladiators alike. It is the measured attitude to death which is strikingly similar; death was to be met without fear, and death needn't be a disgrace if met in the correct circumstances. We don't have any evidence for what the great wrestlers, boxers and *pankratiasts* of the Roman period thought of gladiators, but gravestones do provide some evidence of how gladiators definitely looked up to combat athletes and wanted to define themselves in similar ways.

In 1894 de Coubertin, known as the father of the Modern Olympic Games, compared the athletes of ancient Greece with the gladiators of ancient Rome, saying: 'Human imperfection tends always to transform the Olympian athlete into a circus gladiator. One must choose between two athletic methods which are not compatible'.[426] This was certainly not a view shared by the gladiators of this region of the empire, who seem to have very firmly placed themselves in the Greek athletic tradition. The proof for this comes from the tombstones of the gladiators themselves, and in multiple forms.

Across the empire, gladiators were rewarded upon victory with a palm branch which was itself a practice borrowed from many Greek athletic competitions and adopted by gladiators in Rome.[427] For athletes, it was supposedly, according to Pausanias, a tradition started by Theseus himself when he inaugurated the athletic festival of the holy island of Delos.[428] In the Greek world, then, the palm held significant symbolic value. Western gladiators don't mention these palm frond prizes on their tombstones, but the Greek gladiators certainly do. Partly, this is because a palm frond is an easy visual cue that they were a successful gladiator in life, and had won at least one victory, but it also placed them in the same social strata as athletes. The gladiators in the Greek world made sure to include images of their palm branches, either held aloft by the figure of the fighter or standing proudly beside him.

Another important – and helpful – visual cue from tombstones is the addition of *stephanitic* wreaths. As we know, athletes could earn victory ribbons, but the best athletes earned wreaths at Olympia, Delphi, Nemea and Isthmia – they were a well-known sign of excellence. Gladiators wanted to signal their own excellence in a way that locals would understand, and so wreaths became a popular addition on their tombstones. The statistics of a career also seem to be very important for gladiatorial individuals all the way across the empire. Just as modern athletes keep a running tally of goals scored, medals earned or records broken, so western gladiators mention their own fight record as a simple number in Roman numerals on their tombstones and Greek gladiators also often include a tally of victories in the text. However, in the Greek world, this is more often augmented or replaced by wreaths depicted on the tomb. We have no way of knowing if physical wreaths were given to gladiators when they won a match, but this was their favourite way to display their career statistics. Around 20 per cent of all Greek gladiator tombstones feature wreaths as a visual display of their careers, with some squeezing a dozen or more wreaths into the image on the stone. It wasn't just a handy pictorial shorthand for showcasing their success in their careers, because, by choosing this particular iconography, borrowed from athletes, gladiators in the Greek world were placing themselves alongside and among those same athletes. After all, they competed in the same venues, had a similar training regimen, and fought before tens of thousands of cheering spectators.

Language on tombstones also conveyed the ways gladiators wanted to be seen, both by their contemporaries and those that followed (including us). Words beginning with the stem 'Πυγ', or pyg/pug, appear eleven times in the gravestones. Words beginning with this stem include πυγμαχία (*pygmachia*), which was the name for boxing, and the term for boxers themselves, πυγμάχος (*pygmachos*). This was how a gladiator from Apollonia described himself, which initially led to scholars believing that the grave belonged to a boxer. It was only when Louis Robert noted that the gladiator (whose name has been lost due to damage to the stone) specified he'd fought in twelve combats that the truth came out: athletes did not state their career statistics this way, the deceased was clearly a gladiator.[429]

A gladiator named Gaius who died in Gortyn on Crete goes one step further. He elevates himself and his colleagues *above* combat athletes, saying that: 'We don't just fight for wreaths, we fight for our lives!'[430] The stakes are higher for gladiators, he is saying, so therefore they are more courageous. Two gladiators refer to their opponents as 'ἀντίπαλος', or *antipalos*, a technical term used in Greek wrestling.[431] Transliterated, the word can be broken down into 'anti', meaning 'against', and 'palos', meaning 'fight' or 'wrestle', so the word does refer to an adversary. Clearly, there were some gladiators who were very fond of using athletic lingo.

Another valuable source of information is the collection of stage names the gladiators took. For any ancient historian, the best resource for this is the *Lexicon of Greek Personal Names* (*LGPN*). It's a searchable database of nearly every name found in all kinds of literary and archaeological sources. A historian can search for a name and find out which century it was most popular in, whether it was regionally specific, and how many individuals had it. It's not a perfect resource, as the archaeological record is so patchy and it would take an army of scholars to keep it fully updated, but it can give a very solid indication of naming practices and trends.

Greeks took given names seriously, and used them to promote cultural ideals and values, a phenomenon that is clearly illustrated in the lists of Olympic victors.[432] For instance, a sprinter who was victorious in 676 BCE was named Kallisthenes, meaning 'Beauty and Strength'. The names of Olympic victors were obviously given at birth as something for the child to live up to, but beyond the idea of nominative determinism we can deduce that names that emphasise personal attributes reflect the values and attributes of Greek culture, of which athletic festivals were a demonstration. Therefore, parents who hoped their son would be an Olympic champion might give him a compound name like 'swift-footed' or 'beautiful body'.

For gladiators, *noms de guerre* were assumed in adulthood, but often reflected the same kind of attributes valued by athletes. However, we don't see gladiators taking the names of famous combat athletes as their stage names, even athletes who became legendary, such as Milo of Croton, Leonidas of Rhodes, Theagenes of Thasos or Diagoras of Rhodes. Greek gladiators clung on to their Greek combat names well into the imperial period, and only three that we know of used a Latin name. Conversely, victors in combat sports were using Roman tripartite names as early as 49 CE, when Tiberius Claudius Patrobius of Antiochus first won the wrestling competition at Olympia. After 69 CE, all but two champion *pankratiasts* at Olympia used Latin tripartite names, suggesting that combat athletes were among the first groups to adopt this foreign naming convention.[433] Roman-style fighters in the Greek world insisted on Greek names, while Greek-style fighters were keen to adopt Latin ones. Gladiators were not assuming the same names as historic athletic victors, but were using elements of compound names in their own combinations. For example, seven gladiators incorporate 'καλλιν' (beautiful) into their names; of particular athletic relevance are Kallidromos ('beautiful runner', or perhaps 'beautiful racetrack', because gladiators fought in stadia) and Kallimorphos (beautiful form). Kallidromos and Kallimorphos were not common names among civilians, so the gladiators were choosing these names with care. And if a gladiator didn't choose their name because of their beauty, they could always make an allusion to mythical beauty instead. The epitaph of a gladiator from Attaleia named Meiletos says:

You see the handsome warrior of the stadia, the beautiful Meiletos, who has won (in the arena) eight times, like Adonis, who was once beautiful on the hunt, the son of Kinyras, or the handsome boy Hyakinthos who was struck by the discus. But now, while fighting, the Moirai have taken me there by force and laid my body in the dear Pamphylian earth. The noble Odysseus placed this tomb here for my glory, because of commemoration and friendship.[434]

Adonis was the mortal boy so beautiful that Aphrodite fell in love with him, but there's an additional athletic connection to the beauty of Hyakinthos. The boy was handsome enough for Apollo to fall in love with him, but, when they were exercising with the discus, Apollo forgot his godlike strength, and he threw the discus so hard it shattered the poor boy's skull. The heartbroken Apollo then created flowers from the spilled blood, which we still call hyacinths today. Meiletos was comparing himself to two boys beloved by gods for their beauty.

Names containing the stem 'niko' are also well-represented, as a testament of ability to succeed; it derives from the name for the goddess of victory, Nike. Pasineikos (all/total victory) is particularly popular. Several gladiators are called Stephanos, perhaps to boast of their ability to win wreaths. The most popular prefix is 'Χρυσ-' (golden), and although this might emphasise the beauty of a combatant, it was also an incredibly popular prefix during the imperial period, with nearly 600 civilian families also choosing a name including 'golden' for their sons.

We can see, then, that Greek gladiators liked to portray themselves as a profession closely related to ancient Greek contact sports, and, in a lot of respects, they were entirely justified in doing so. They had much in common, with their specialised training, honed bodies and careers that required the participants to inflict serious and potentially fatal damage towards each other. In the west, gladiators were stigmatised because of the violence they dealt each other, even as the spectators demanded it.[435] But this was not true in the Greek world, where traditionally combat athletes were valorised. So is it any wonder that gladiators there took pains to use athletic terminology and imagery?

In a culture where both martial artists and the martial arts were valued, many gladiators were clearly keen to be seen as alternatives, if not equals to, the wrestlers, boxers and *pankratiasts* who graced the myriad of festivals across the region and starred in local legends. Gladiation was never absorbed into those festivals as a fourth contact event, but it was performed in the same spaces as contact sports, clearly with the blessing of local populations. Unlike athletes, a significant percentage of the gladiatorial profession had no choice in their career, but for the ones who were successful enough to be able to afford an inscribed stone for their grave, they wanted to emphasise that they could achieve greatness too, and were keen to remind anyone reading the headstones that it wasn't just rich boys who could excel in combat sports; an enslaved gladiator could fight just as well as a freeborn *pankratiast*.

We can see from the gravestones we have explored in this case study that gladiators were presenting themselves in deeply culturally relevant ways: within military traditions, within mythical traditions and within athletic traditions. Through names and visual imagery, they used cultural allusions and references to connect themselves to elements of society that were essential to collective Greekness. Having seen this, I think we can turn to another case study – this time, one that has perplexed experts for generations.

Chapter 17

CSI Case Study: Amazon and Achillea

The mystery we are applying ourselves to with this case study involves an utterly unique stone relief that is currently housed in the British Museum. It came from present-day Bodrum, a city on the southwest coast of Türkiye once known as Halicarnassus. This was one of the major cities of the ancient region of Caria, and is probably most famous for two things: the giant tomb of King Mausolus that was included in the list of the Seven Wonders of the World (from which we get the word 'mausoleum'), and being the birthplace of the ancient Greek historian Herodotus. Under Roman rule, it was a part of the province of Asia. It boasted a stadium as well as a theatre, where excavations have revealed the telltale signs of adaptation, with sockets drilled around the *orchestra* edge for temporary barriers to be erected. The stone we are interested in comes from a larger monument. Many pieces of marble belonging to commemorative gladiatorial monuments have been found across the eastern Mediterranean, but this one is perhaps the strangest. The marble was initially presented as a gift to the British ambassador to Constantinople, Viscount Stratford de Redcliffe, by the Ottoman Sultan Abdülmecid I in 1846. The Viscount brought it to London, where it has been in the British Museum ever since.

Like several other stone blocks from Asia Minor, it features two gladiators squaring off for a fight, carved in relief. They face each other, both adopting a classic combative stance with shield and sword in hand. An inscription reading ἀπελύθησαν (apelithēsan) records that the fight concluded in a draw; the word translates to 'they were released'. In Latin, the term was *stantes missi*, or 'sent away standing', but Greeks much preferred to translate gladiatorial lingo in Greek. Although a tie was a fairly common result of a combat,[436] it is incredibly rare to see it depicted in art, which typically features the moment of victory instead.[437] This peculiarity is not the only reason why the image is rare, however. This stone is unique because the gladiators are both women. The inscription names them as Amazon and Achillea, and they are the only female gladiators depicted in (surviving) art, and also the only ones we know by name.

The Stories in a Stone

Stratford de Redcliffe didn't think to ask exactly where the stone was found in the city, nor if it was found beside any others, or embedded into a wider monument. This is frustrating for archaeologists, because so much information lies in the findspot of an artefact; but we can make some educated guesses as to the purpose of the stone when comparing it to others in the Greek world. Stones showing two fighters are much rarer than stones showing a single gladiator; the latter are usually gravestones and if they do feature a second figure in the pictorial relief, it is usually a family member or even a beloved pet dog.

The reliefs depicting two combatants are thought to be memorials, but for a *munerarius* rather than a gladiator. Wealthy citizens and priests of the imperial cult sank considerable cash into providing electrifying spectacle for the citizens of their city, and this beneficence bought them respect and favourable opinion for a considerable time afterwards. Many sought to capitalise on this boost to their prestige by commemorating the fleeting event in a permanent manner. In other cities, such as Hierapolis, the *munerarius* that presented a programme of Roman spectacle would commission a monument with an inscription bearing his name, titles and a list of the performances the city had enjoyed at his behest, including which exotic species he had sourced for the hunts and the number of gladiators who fought. The monument would also usually feature pictorial representations of particularly memorable moments from the games. The larger of these monuments had several images; some fights were depicted in several stages, like a comic strip, but most had a series of blocks each depicting a pair of fighters in a combative stance. The names of the gladiators were usually inscribed above their heads or below their feet, and sometimes the result of the fights would be recorded as well. Unlike the art from gladiatorial gravestones, there were no wreaths or victory palms depicted and no heroic poses: these dynamic images were showing the gladiators in action to record the incredible experience the *munerarius* had provided, not convey the identity of the individual fighters.

So far, this general description matches the image of Amazon and Achillea. Both women hold their swords at hip-height, ready to lunge forwards. Their feet are firmly planted shoulder-width apart, knees slightly bent, perfectly balanced. Amazon has her weight on her forward leg, Achillea leans defensively away on her back leg. Their shields are held at the ideal height to protect their bare necks and torsos. Their movements are clear; the women are not posing. One detail is more reminiscent of gravestones, however, in that their helmets are removed and placed on the ground behind them. While other art does depict helmets being discarded or knocked off and gladiators continuing to fight bare headed, this positioning of the helmet by the feet is seen in gladiatorial gravestones across the Greek world where the individual wants to show their face as well as their professional garb. One explanation for the helmets both being removed and neatly placed is that the image needed to clearly signpost that these particular gladiators were women. The women appear to be fighting bare-breasted, in keeping with their *armaturae*. However, with the shields held in position, the side of a female breast may appear indistinguishable from a well-formed male pectoral. With the removal of helmets, the facial features can be appreciated, and Amazon in particular is shown with a very feminine hairstyle; her hair is simply braided around the crown of her head and gathered into a bun at the nape of her neck. The style is reminiscent of other women of the period as depicted in coins, frescoes and statues. Their femininity had to be accentuated in the relief not only to commemorate the fight itself, but also to differentiate Amazon and Achillea from their male counterparts. We have no way of knowing how skilfully they fought, but their presence alone is highly unusual. Their *munerarius*, whose name is forever lost, would have been keen to remind citizens that *he* had given them female fighters, a true novelty.

And a novelty they were! The presence of the *gladiatrix* in the Roman arena tends to be somewhat overstated in the public imagination, a distinct oddity in an already odd ancient phenomenon. Cinema certainly hasn't helped us appreciate how rare these warrior women actually were. In fact, the Romans didn't even use the term *gladiatrix* at all, despite having well-attested names for other odd gladiator classes. This artwork depicting female fighters is not just unique to the eastern Mediterranean, it is unique to the Roman world in its entirety. We've seen that gravestones, mosaics, terracotta lamps, frescoes and graffiti depicting male gladiators were abundant across the entire Mediterranean, yet only a single artwork featuring women survives.

Some ancient writers do allude to the presence of women in western amphitheatres, but they are frustratingly vague. Most of the time, these writers don't specify the role these women played. We should remember that a day at the Games featured performances by musicians and dancers, which would be seen as an appropriate profession for a woman in Roman society (albeit not for a well-born one). When ancient writers are specific, women are most frequently described as animal hunters. Even with training, beast-hunters were firmly differentiated from gladiators and the two professions were not interchangeable. The second most-noted reason for a woman to enter an arena was to be executed for various crimes. The martyrdom of several Christian women happened in amphitheatres and stadia during the *meridiani*, including Perpetua and Felicity in Carthage and Blandina in Lyons. Women executed for other criminal offences are also described, though their names are not of interest to Roman historians. The executions were carried out with the same enthusiasm and imagination as for men, although we cannot be sure if women were executed in similar numbers.

Looking to other literary sources for clues about female gladiators, we find only vague accounts. In Rome, the first recorded women to fight were presented by Nero, during Games to commemorate the mother he'd had murdered in 60 CE. Presumably, the fights took place in his own amphitheatre in the city. The women he presented cannot be considered true gladiators; Cassius Dio specifies that these were the upper-class wives of senators who had been forced into the arena to humiliate their husbands.[438] Their presence in the amphitheatre would have left a permanent stain on their social standing, but they received no training and any details suggesting appropriate equipment are not given. Suetonius helpfully states that women fought on the same roster as men in Domitian's games in Rome a couple of decades later, but doesn't go into detail about whether the women had been taught combat in a *ludus*.[439] When Statius mentions women fighting during Domitian's reign he does specify that, while they fought bravely, they were entirely ignorant of weaponry and technique.[440] So can we count these women as gladiators, or do they belong in a separate category of novelty act?

There is, to date, no extant evidence for any women being trained in a Roman *ludus*. To train a woman would be to run the risk that she could learn, or (even worse) excel at a masculine skill. Such a transgression would threaten the acceptance of rigid gender roles for all women present in the amphitheatre seats, and potentially emasculate male spectators. Presenting women who had never held a sword before, as Statius implies, emphasises just how unsuitable women were in a combat situation: the (likely frightened) women would not be able to improvise as well as a man with a modicum of military training or even brawling experience in taverns or streets. By ensuring that the women in Roman amphitheatres were both terrified and unprepared, their attempts to fight would be feeble at worst and clumsy at best, thereby reinforcing to the Roman audience that each gender had its culturally assigned behaviours and that breaching the divide was inadvisable.

Historians are naturally influenced by their own convictions, and feminism has increasingly influenced scholarship of the ancient world for decades: there is an innate desire to uncover evidence of women succeeding outside of the rigid constraints of ancient patriarchy.[441] However, I would caution against seeing proto-feminist icons in the women of ancient arenas; no evidence suggests that such women were much lauded. Tacitus snippily remarks that the women sent into the arena under Nero were disgracing themselves (though we should question how much say they had in their participation).[442] Statius is more sympathetic, but when we step back from his comments about female gladiators to place them into wider context, a sadder picture emerges. The poem in which Statius makes his remark is describing a Saturnalia feast thrown by Domitian. Among a long list of raucous entertainments, the women performed as gladiators alongside (but not against) men with dwarfism. The date is the most significant clue as to how Romans viewed such spectacle, as the Saturnalia was a holiday characterised by humourous role reversal across the social spectrum.[443] Enslaved people were relieved of duties for the duration of the festival, and not only dined with their masters, but were often served by them. Freeborn women and children were also allowed greater freedom. During Saturnalia, society turned upside down. Here, then, we see two groups of people fighting as gladiators for the very reason that their presence in a normal gladiatorial context was deemed absurd, the women for their gender, the men their stature. They were not presented to put on a competent show, their role in the festival was to provoke laughter. Domitian's gladiatorial Saturnalia show made a deliberate mockery of the gladiator as the epitome of the perfect, masculine warrior with the idealised strong body. I suspect that other attempts to present female gladiators in normal spectacles would have similarly attracted a significant amount of derision or even disgust from Roman spectators.

Traditional gender roles?

Yet this unique piece of evidence is hinting at a genuine combat between two apparently trained women found in Caria. How can that be? I believe we can find the clue in their stage names. As we've seen earlier, around a third of gladiators in the eastern Mediterranean had stage names chosen from mythology, and names from the Trojan Cycle were particularly popular. Of the many characters in the *Iliad* and its companion poems, Achilles is the name most frequently selected by gladiators in the epitaphs that have survived to us. That a woman should take a feminised version of this name should perhaps not be surprising, particularly given the name of her opponent. Romans were not fond of warrior queens: the misogynistic accounts of Boudicca's rebellion in Britannia during Nero's reign hints at the distaste towards women wielding weapons. However, the Greeks had a deep and enduring respect for the female fighters known as the Amazons and it is for this semi-mythical race of women that Achillea's opponent is named.

There were several stories involving Greeks encountering Amazons, and, as far as Greeks were concerned, these stories were entirely historical. Various versions of the myths existed, but they were generally believed to live on the coast of the Black Sea, and the stories probably arose from the early Greeks trying to make sense of the (very real) warrior women of Scythian tribes.[444] Far from a misandrist society, which is a modern misinterpretation of ancient evidence, Scythian women seem to have lived in relative equality alongside men.[445] They were experts on horseback, and peerless archers. No Scythian woman was dependent on her male relatives or husband for her survival: she was self-sufficient and able and willing to join skirmishes or defend her tribe. On the steppes, excavated burials of women interred with their horses, scores of weapons, and even golden crowns strongly suggest that these women were highly valued and respected. Many had sustained wounds from battle, some of which had healed, allowing the formidable women to fight another day.

In contrast, the lives of women in ancient Greece varied greatly depending on the city and century they lived in. Some men expected more genteel ladies to remain cloistered away, confined almost entirely to their homes, though this was harder to put into practice in families where women were required to contribute to trade or production. Some Greek cities allowed women a modicum of more freedom, but this was rare and garnered criticism; Aristotle made sure to blame Sparta's downfall on giving women too many rights and freedoms.[446] Even in the Roman period, when women were afforded more liberties, Greek women remained socially inferior to men as part of a rigidly patriarchal society. While the concept of women being restricted to an area of their father or husband's house is an ideal that likely rarely worked out in practice,[447] no Greek woman ever experienced society with the same equality that women in Scythian tribes appear to have enjoyed. The idea was certainly an anathema to Greek men, and their fascination with this foreign culture resulted in the mythologising of warrior women. Thus, mythical Amazons soon found themselves incorporated into Greek stories.[448] The stories bore the faintest of resemblances to real Scythian warrior women, of course, but they were just as central a part of Greek storytelling as the other myths we have encountered.

Heracles, the ideal Greek hero and paragon of masculine strength and courage, was the first to face the Amazons in mythology. Retrieving the war-belt of the Amazon queen Hippolyta was one of his famous Twelve Labours.[449] The belt had been a gift from her father – Ares, the god of war. As with all Greek myths, the story has variations, but most concur that Heracles and his retinue of warriors didn't want to approach the Amazons aggressively.[450] That would have been far too dangerous and potentially fatal. Instead, the Greeks were respectful. Hippolyta greeted Heracles warmly, and they clearly considered themselves equals. Both had divine fathers which gave them both demi-god status and they have equally excellent martial reputations. Hippolyta's gender is not a reason for Heracles to see her as inferior, for she can match him or even best him in combat. That is the quality that Heracles values the most, and so he gives Hippolyta her due deference. The myths suggest that the pair got along famously during that initial meeting, and that there was perhaps even romantic chemistry: two extraordinary people meeting their match and finding joy in it. Hippolyta offers up the belt as a gift.

Unfortunately, the stories generally had a tragic result. Heracles was being obsessively plagued by Hera, who hated her husband's bastard child with a passion. Furious to see the Labour being so easily completed, Hera disguised herself as an Amazon and started whispering to Hippolyta's retinue that Heracles had ulterior motives. The Amazons started to attack the Greeks to protect their queen and Heracles now assumed that Hippolyta was the one with the hidden agenda. Heracles attacked Hippolyta immediately. In some versions of the myth, Hippolyta was killed instantly, caught entirely unawares. In others, she refused to go down without a fight and very nearly killed Heracles. His men defeat the furious Amazons, but with great difficulty and at great cost. The implications are clear; even Heracles was reluctant to fight the Amazons, and was only drawn to do so by hostile divine intervention. That's how formidable the Amazons were.

Heracles' comrade Theseus was present at the battle and abducted another Amazon named Antiope as a war prize, taking her back to Athens where she bore him a son named Hippolytus.[451] The furious, vengeful Amazons launched an invasion to win her back and bring her home. By the Roman period and the time of the gladiatorial fight in Halicarnassus, there were a myriad of versions about how the war played out, but the gist is that the women breached the city walls, camped on the Areopagus and besieged the acropolis itself.[452] Theseus, genuinely frightened, consulted oracles, and sacrificed to Phobos, the god of panic – specifically, of panic in violent situations.[453] Theseus faced the Amazons with his army, who were nearly all massacred. Reinforcements managed to drive the women back up onto the rocks of the Areopagus, where many Amazons too fell. After months more of fighting, during which Antiope was also killed, a peace treaty was finally signed. The war, which the Athenians considered to be a very real, if ancient, event, was a defining moment for the nascent city. The Athenians boasted that they had withstood a siege from no less than a full Amazon army. Any Greek city could claim to have been attacked by armies of very ordinary men, but Athens had withstood very extraordinary women. This is important: despite the deep misogyny of Greek society, the fearsome reputation of the Amazons as warriors is central to the city's identity as exceptional. The idea of a war with these specific women was not a joke, and the Athenians admitted that the war was hard-won. Otherwise, it could not have been claimed as a sign of Athenian supremacy.

These first two traditions of Amazons provide important context but it is the third clash between Greeks and Amazons that is most relevant to our gladiators: the Trojan War, which we have already encountered a few times as central to Greek identity and the absorption of gladiators into Greek society. One of the poems in the Epic Cycle, the *Aethiopis* by Arctinos, picks up the story after the *Iliad* closed, with Priam begging Achilles for the body of his son, and Hektor's eventual funeral back behind the city walls. The war is rumbling on, and Achilles' thirst for glory was not yet quenched. A full text of the *Aethiopis* has not survived, but we can reconstruct the story from fragments and quotations or retellings in other texts. The Trojans are in mourning and dejected, until their allies arrive: the Amazons and the Aethiopians, a group that were probably understood to be from the area of modern Sudan. The Amazons arrive first, led by their queen Penthesilea, who is relishing the chance to face up to the famous Achilles. She is accompanied by twelve of her fiercest Amazons, who proceed to cut swathes through the Greek army. Penthesilea taunts the Greeks and challenges the Greeks' two mightiest warriors, Ajax and Achilles, to duels.

Fascinatingly, the poem then recounts a young Trojan woman, Hippodamia, who is so inspired by the Amazons that she briefly rallies the other women to take up arms and join them in protecting Troy. She points out that women are physically little different from men, and that the women have just as much at stake in the war's outcome as their husbands, sons and fathers currently fighting for their lives and families below them. The women are making their way to the armouries before an older woman points out that, unlike their menfolk and the Amazons, these women have never held a weapon in their lives and therefore cannot help. Penthesilea has been trained since she could toddle, and is a daughter of Ares himself. It's significant here that the modicum of gender equality in an extreme scenario isn't considered impossible in and of itself but for practical reasons; they're witnessing the results of women being given a very specific education and extraordinary independence. Herein lies the rub: the Amazons are the result of exceptional circumstances that would never be allowed to be replicated in Greek or Trojan communities. Moreover, we must remember that worthy adversaries existed in these stories to ultimately lose to Greeks, whose subsequent glory is multiplied because the foe was such a challenge.

This is as true of the *Aethiopis* as it was in Heracles' Labours and the Siege of Athens: Penthesilea and her comrades cut down opponent after opponent. Achilles and Penthesilea fought many, many times and Penthesilea bested Achilles on multiple occasions.[454] This Penthesilea gives Achilles a real run for his money. On one occasion, he is only saved because his shield was forged by Hephaestus himself, and is unbreakable. Even Achilles needs a little divine assistance when facing an Amazon. As for Penthesilea, her ultimate defeat and death is one which she, and indeed any other epic hero, aspired to: Achilles has to hit her with not one but two of his mighty spears. For Penthesilea, to die on the battlefield like this brought her a *kalos* and *euklees thanatos*: a beautiful and glorious death, just as Hektor had days before. Such a death ensured that their deeds would be forever remembered.[455] Old age withers the body, but death on the battlefield preserves the hero in their prime. A death that secures immortal fame was frequently seen as preferable to a long life of deterioration and obscurity, as Achilles himself had already come to terms with.

Such is the heroic nature of her death, in fact, that Achilles falls in love with her. Just like Heracles and Theseus before him, he cannot resist the eroticism of a warrior woman. In the *Iliad*, Achilles mistreated and abused the corpse of his enemy Hektor to the extent that the gods intervened and supernaturally kept Hektor's cadaver unmarked and free from decay. His treatment of Penthesilea in the *Aethiopis*, an enemy and a woman, is starkly different. Achilles is devastated, admitting that he had already accepted that he was never returning home, but in this brief moment he mourns for a future that they could have shared together, had they not been both fated to die on the plains of Troy. One poet says Achilles was as shattered by the death of this stranger as he was over the death of his beloved Patroklos. Her death is perhaps the ultimate moment of tragedy in his narrative, the point where we see what a heroic reputation truly costs. He sends her body to the city of Troy so that Penthesilea and her comrades can have funerals befitting their status, with full honours.

So, here we have seen Amazons interacting with several Greek heroes and being a credible threat to each of them. The Amazons were never allowed to win, for how would Greeks be able to revel in their own feelings of exceptionalism if they could be bested by barbarians? But we can detect a high-level of respect and even an erotic fascination with fighting women. The women warriors of all three of these myths were household names in the Greek world: even the secondary Amazons such as Aella, Phoebe and Molpadia were considered on a par with the stable of masculine Greek heroes.

As we would expect, given their literally legendary reputation, Amazons were also a mainstay of Greek art. Vases were painted with mythological scenes, and more than 1,300 surviving vases depicting Amazons are housed in museums today.[456] In the Archaic period, Amazons were the second most popular theme in Greek art,[457] and remained popular for centuries. They graced sarcophagi, cameos, and murals. The Parthenon, pointedly built after the Persians razed the Acropolis in 480/479 BCE, was decorated with several battles wherein Greeks triumphed over perceived eastern barbarians. The city was on a high, having defeated the Persians at the battles of Salamis and Plataea, and they commemorated their victory by deliberately choosing an artistic programme that suggested that the Persian invasion was but one in a long line of barbarians foolishly attempting to best the Greeks. The *metopes* feature the Fall of Troy, the Gigantomachy and the Centauromachy. Last, but by no means least, the Amazonomachy takes up the entire west side of the temple. Warrior women were ferocious enough to warrant being placed alongside mythical beings famed for their strength. The Amazonomachy can also be found in the frieze of the Temple of Apollo at Bassae (now housed in the British Museum), and the Temple of Artemis at Magnesia, whereas Heracles' Labours, featuring Hippolyta, graced the metopes of the Temple of Zeus at Olympia and the Temple of Hephaestus in Athens.

Perhaps most significantly for our purpose, the story of the Amazons at Troy was portrayed on the Mausoleum at Halicarnassus in relief. Local citizens would have recognised the characters as they walked past the monument every day and been reminded of the story. A block from the Mausoleum, which may depict Achilles and Penthesilea, is also now in the British Museum. It's unlikely that spectators would have condoned sending a woman, even one with a modicum of training, into the arena to face a male gladiator. Spectators craved well-matched fights. But by turning Achilles into Achillea, the *munerarius* provided novelty on a number of levels. Female fighters, presenting a recreation of one of the most memorable duels of the Trojan War, a story that everyone in the city was familiar with, and one that locals were reminded of regularly. This wasn't the usual bloodless poetry recital; this was a chance to see the fight from the *Aethiopis* recreated for their delectation. Happily, this time both combatants survived to tell the tale.

When we take everything into consideration – the style of the art, the likely purpose of the monument, the names of the fighters and the stories that those names are drawn from – we arrive at a fascinating scenario. Unlike the unfortunate women in the western territories, being thrown into arenas as laughing stocks, it's entirely possible that this relief is evidence for a fight between female gladiators that was taken seriously by spectators. Kitted out in an appropriate fashion, and depicted with decent combative stances, perhaps Amazon and Achillea even received some combat training before their bout. Of course, the use of these specific stage names and their commemoration in stone doesn't rule out the possibility that the women were presented as a joke novelty act, perhaps with sexual undertones for added titillation in a re-enactment of the romantic aspects of the poem. On the other hand, we've seen that the Greeks had long had a fascinated admiration for the very real barbarian warrior women who lived on the edges of their world. It does seem plausible that in Halicarnassus there was a serious combat between two women; a sight so incredible that the *munerarius* made sure no-one forgot it.

You will have to decide for yourself. However, whether or not this relief depicts trained women gladiators, it does demonstrate that gladiators were accepted as a legitimate form of performance (in serious combats and, perhaps, novelty acts) within the long-standing, deeply held cultural tradition of Greek mythology. This unique, fascinating example allows us to see the wider cultural phenomenon more clearly.

Chapter 18

Show Me the Money

As we approach the end of our investigation, a crucial question remains and no good detective can leave such a question unaddressed. How were gladiators seen by Greek society?

The spectacles, the combats, were clearly popular – I think it is fair to say this much is now clear. Rich and powerful men sponsored Games to curry favour with locals as well as imperial elites and they spent extra to leave a record of their generosity. Some philosophers may have disapproved of gladiators and used their platforms to express that disapproval loudly, but many people across the Greek world clearly enjoyed this form of entertainment. Local venues were adapted to host gladiatorial combats for local fans, rather than the Roman amphitheatres that the legionaries used, which suggests they also thought that gladiator shows were compatible with their existing, culturally 'Greek' traditions. That isn't the same as respecting gladiators themselves, however. As we have seen, gladiator combats were hugely popular in the western Roman territories but the gladiators themselves were considered *infames*: socially unacceptable. Was this the same in the Greek world? To answer this crucial question, we must return to that astonishing collection of evidence: gravestones.

As we've seen, a huge amount of biographical information about individual fighters can be found on their tombstones. This is deliberate, because a tombstone functioned to communicate exactly the biographical details that the deceased wanted to be remembered for. This information could be conveyed either through text, or through images carved into the stone in relief. One important element to bear in mind is that for those who could afford it, bigger was better. The aim was not quietly understated memorials; Greeks of means were not content with a dash in between two dates that represented a whole life lived. The ideal gravestone was large enough to display a large block of text and an eye-catching image full of easily identifiable iconography. Not all the gravestones we have are complete, so it's impossible to come up with an accurate number as to their sizes. Of all the full gravestones we have, around a third are less than half a metre high. We shouldn't imagine small or plain tombstones to be the bargain basement selection, however; a formal burial complete with rites and a modest stone grave marker were a significant investment for many citizens of the ancient world, and the poorest were often buried in unmarked mass graves. We should assume that many of our gladiators – the untalented and the unlucky alike – would have had their bodies disposed of in this way. In affluent cities, around 60 per cent of graves would have been unmarked. That we have so many gladiatorial gravestones, even modest ones, is therefore remarkable. We have a significant chunk of the gladiatorial milieu that had money to spend on memorials in a society where everyone would have understood how much said memorials would cost. Choosing to spend money on a memorial was a statement not only of personal pride, but of financial success.

We can explore much more about the social position of gladiators from their gravestones than just wealth, however. With a partial set of data, it's always going to be problematic to declare what constitutes average. We can assume that most gladiatorial gravestones are either destroyed, remain buried or have been reused to construct later buildings, and that the gravestones we have represent a mere selection. We also have gravestones with damage to the text or relief, or have parts of the stone missing. When it comes to the size of gladiator tombstones, we can only really use the relatively complete ones that we've excavated and studied, which don't necessarily represent the full range of the stones we have lost. As we've seen elsewhere, this is always a problem with studying the past but, with careful contextualisation and analysis, we can still use this limited evidence to investigate.

Using the material we have, what we can say is that around a third of gladiatorial gravestones were less than half a metre high, then around half are between half and a full metre in height. The rest are rather grand, and a couple are nearly two metres tall. Only a few of our gladiators opted for a full sarcophagus, which were much more expensive. The rest of the stones are typically *stelae*, rectangular slabs of stone that often had rounded or pointed tops, or a funerary altar. These were typically rectangular, with four equally sized sides. Less frequently, they were cylindrical, like the stump of a column. The funerary altars were sometimes hollowed to house the urn containing the ashes of the deceased, but, like the *stelae*, could also merely mark a place of burial or commemoration.

Even the smallest stones display a modest dedication, and they give us valuable information. Many announce that they were erected by family members or colleagues. The former category is mostly populated by women, the wives of the gladiators. Sometimes they also mention children. We learn from this that their wages could be enough to support a family, as well as invest in a tombstone. Talent and a solid fight record generally took precedence on gravestone records, particularly when limited space restricted how many details could be included but, out of the nearly 270 gladiatorial tombstones we have (bearing in mind that many are lost, and that many gladiators would never have been able to afford one), ninety mention a wife. We should assume that many more anonymous gladiators also had partners and families. As some of the epitaphs mention specifically that the gladiator in question died in the arena, we can also confirm that gladiators were not required to wait for retirement to wed.

This is a deceptively major nugget of information, in that it prompts a lot of further questions. Were these marriages formal or common law? Were all gladiators permitted to have romantic partners, or was this reserved for a specific rank or status? Did the gladiators live with their families outside of the *ludus*, or did their families share their room within the gladiatorial school? After all, a barracks is not the obvious home for a young family. There are enough wives and offspring mentioned in epitaphs that we can determine that at least some gladiators were able to have a romantic and family life alongside their career, rather than having to wait for a retirement that might not materialise, and that they took their family life very seriously, even if we cannot yet say where they called home.

These questions are frustratingly difficult to answer; though we know the eastern Mediterranean possessed *ludi*, including Pergamon and Cyzicus, they have yet to be identified and excavated, which would go a long way to reveal what day-to-day accommodation was like for the gladiators. We also don't know whether matrimony was a privilege afforded to the higher ranks of gladiators, or the volunteers who were not enslaved. This is because Greek gladiators seem to have been very keen to hide this facet of their identity from their epitaphs, particularly in comparison to the western Mediterranean.

Money, Money, Money

It's difficult to say anything more than that about how much a gladiator might earn, because we know frustratingly little about what any ancient Roman earned. Our best piece of evidence is the *Senatus Consultum de Pretiis Gladiatorum Minuendis*, a decree that dates to the late 170s CE. It was issued by the Senate during the reign of the emperor Marcus Aurelius, and was a decree that set out maximum prices for gladiatorial shows. This makes sense: gladiators were in demand and the *lanistae* knew it. When local magistrates in cities across the empire were required to provide spectacles as part of their duties, *lanistae* knew that they could charge whatever they liked and magistrates would have little choice but to pay. Prices grew to be astronomical, and intervention was deemed necessary. We know that Marcus Aurelius had instituted limits on the fees charged by gladiators (and actors) because a biography of emperors called the *Historia Augusta* mentions it twice.[458] Details weren't available, however, until copies of the decree itself were found; one fragment was found in Sardis (in Türkiye) and a larger fragment in Italica (in Spain). The findspots indicate that this decree applied to gladiatorial shows across the entire empire, not just in Rome. The fees fluctuate depending on the size of the show and the rank of the individual fighter. We know that ranks were very important to the gladiators, and unlike elsewhere, nearly forty of our Greek gladiators specify their rank in their epitaph as a source of pride.

For games costing between 30,000–60,000 sesterces in total:

- Primus Palus: ≤5,000 sesterces
- Secundus Palus: ≤4,000 sesterces
- Tertius Palus: ≤3,000 sesterces

For games costing between 60,000–100,000 sesterces in total:

- Primus Palus ≤8,000 sesterces
- Secundus Palus: ≤6,000 sesterces
- Tertius Palus: ≤5,000 sesterces

For games costing between 100,000–150,000 sesterces

- Primus Palus: ≤12,000 sesterces
- Secundus Palus: ≤10,000 sesterces
- Tertius Palus: ≤7,000 sesterces
- Quartus Palus: ≤6,000 sesterces
- Quintus Palus: ≤5,000 sesterces

For games costing between 150,000–200,000 sesterces:

- Primus Palus: ≤15,000 sesterces
- Secundus Palus: ≤12,000 sesterces
- Tertius Palus: ≤9,000 sesterces

- Quartus Palus: ≤7,000 sesterces
- Quintus Palus: ≤6,000 sesterces

These figures aren't the cash prizes for victory; they are performance fees. The *lanista* collected fees for every gladiator appearing, even if they didn't win. In essence, he was leasing the gladiators to the *editor*, the magistrate or the priest providing the games. We have no evidence for how *lanistae* chose to pay their fighters. Marcus Aurelius' decree says: 'The following rule regarding the proceeds: each gladiator should make an individual bargain for the money he gets for his fighting, and a free man should receive one quarter, a slave one fifth'. This means that 25 per cent for free gladiators and 20 per cent for the enslaved was only a suggestion, because Marcus Aurelius specifically says that gladiators were to be allowed to negotiate fees with their *lanista*. It does not say whether the money was paid to gladiators in a lump sum, or whether it was distributed in a regular allowance.

It is reasonable to think that the most of the appearance fees were used by *lanistae* for the day-to-day costs of keeping a troupe of gladiators happy and healthy; to keep a fighter in peak condition, he required a place to sleep and rest, training with an expert coach, a full belly provided by cooks, equipment supplied by blacksmiths, and healthcare provided by specialist physicians. As such, each appearance fee actually paid the services of a diverse group of workers attached to the *ludus*. For many rookies (known as *tirones*), a roof over their head and regular bowls of food would have been incentive enough to accept the career, but, for the seasoned veterans, the ability to negotiate their cut of the appearance fee as well as a percentage of any prizes won would have been a great motivator in wanting to ascend the *palus* ranking system.

Let's imagine two hypothetical gladiators. A freeborn gladiator who has risen up the ranks to *Tertius Palus* in 197 CE, and is fighting a modest Games held in Thessaloniki. He has managed to negotiate the full 25 per cent of his appearance fee, i.e. 1,250 sesterces. At the time, a basic foot soldier in the Roman legions could expect to earn 2,400 sesterces per year.[459] Our middle-of-the-road gladiator could exceed that salary by fighting twice a year, not including the bonuses he would receive for winning. Our next gladiator is enslaved, but he's a first-rate fighter at the *ludus* in Pergamon, where a fabulously wealthy priest of the imperial cult is putting on particularly elaborate games. Our second gladiator negotiates his 20 per cent of the 15,000 sesterces fee, raking in 3,000 sesterces in a single day.

It's more difficult to estimate gladiatorial wages in comparison to other professions, because few Romans outside of the legions had a steady wage as most skilled labourers had to seek out work in what was essentially a gig economy. Our best method for calculating annual earnings is to work out the daily wage for each profession and multiply it by 250, which takes festival days into account. The best evidence for daily wages is Diocletian's *Edictum de Pretiis Rerum Venalium,* which set the maximum to be charged both for a good day's worth of labour. It dates from 301 CE, more than a century after the *Senatus Consultum de Pretiis Gladiatorum Minuendis* was enacted, and we know that the economy massively altered in the intervening years. Under Maximinus Thrax, for example, the annual pay for basic legionaries had risen to 7,200 by 235 CE,[460] which suggests that all wages had similarly risen.

We don't know how long Marcus Aurelius' rates for appearances were in effect, and Diocletian's edict can't help us. We have a partial copy, and gladiators are either missing from the list or were not included. The chronological gap between our two documents makes it hard to hazard a like-for-like comparison between the earning potential of a gladiator and a carpenter, teacher or farmhand. Even so, if we assume that gladiator fees rose in a trajectory similar to that of a legionary's annual salary, talented gladiators would still be able to earn decent wages even if only fighting in a few contests per year. Even if most cities held gladiatorial games once or twice a year, because there were many, many more cities with venues than *ludi* in the Greek world, it stands to reason that an enterprising *lanista* might take his troupe on tour to boost the earning potential of all involved.

A couple of the larger epitaphs seem to corroborate this theory. Polos[461] was a gladiator who was buried in Gortyn, a major city on the island of Crete. The stone is damaged and some lines are missing, so we only have about half of what is clearly an exhaustive record of his career. A partial line at the top hints at some kind of connection to Antioch, perhaps his birthplace. Then eight lines worth of text are fully missing, and the following surviving lines are a list of combats that Polos participated in, naming both his opponents and the city in which the combat was fought. The first two cities are difficult to decipher, but the full lines state that he fought (and won) in Ephesus, Tralleis, Laodikeia and Aphrodisias, as well as Gortyn. Phoibos[462] was born in Cyzicus, but was buried in Larisa in Thessaly, because that's where he died. His career took him to so many places that he summarises them in a list of provinces rather than cities; he'd fought in Macedonia, Thrace and Asia. So, a gladiatorial career, for those talented enough, had significant earning potential and travel opportunities, on top of benefits such as in-house training and healthcare.

We can now understand why some gladiators could afford to take a wife and start a family, and why the most successful were able to pay for elaborate gravestones. Statistically, Greek gladiators were far more likely to invest in one than gladiators from elsewhere in the empire, but there is evidence to suggest that gladiators may have been more interested in gravestones than the civilians they entertained. In 2016, a scholar named Sven Ahrens published a study based on social status and tomb monuments in Asia Minor during the Roman period.[463] He studied the multiple volumes of *Inschriften Griechischer Städte aus Kleinasien* ('Inscriptions from the Greek Cities of Asia Minor'), searching for epitaphs that specifically name the profession of the deceased. The results were astonishing; for each trade like sailor, contractor, or architect there were only a handful of gravestones; less than ten each. Then, there was a huge jump to the three most numerous mentioned professions; soldiers counted for nearly 110 monuments, 'elites' had nearly eighty, and gladiators number more than fifty. Ahrens then checked another collection of stones, *Die Ostgriechischen Grabreliefs* ('Eastern Greek Grave Reliefs'), collated by Pfuhl and Möbius, wherein he looked for pictorial reliefs that featured any reference to the profession of the deceased. Here, the results were even more astonishing; nearly all professions were depicted in art only once or twice per trade. Craftsmen and sailors number about a dozen gravestones each, and farmers have around thirty or so gravestones with their equipment depicted. Gladiators, on the other hand, eclipse all other professions in the desire to display their careers in art; nearly seventy of the tombstones collected by Pfuhl and Möbius show gladiators in their full regalia.

It was also possible to have an epitaph written in the form of a poem, which in this context is known as an epigram. They show that the deceased possessed a level of sophistication, but at a price; a specialised poet was usually commissioned to write them (though the quality of some of these epigrams suggests there was a poet for every budget). For this, Ahrens used the volumes of *Steinepigramme aus dem Griechischen Osten* ('Stone Epigrams from the Greek East') compiled by Merkelbach and Stauber. In this category, gladiators have the largest number of poetic epitaphs, followed by doctors, elites and actors. So, we can confidently say that in the Greek part of the empire, gladiators prioritised having a gravestone that specified their profession either in text or iconography. No-one mentioned their profession more in art, and only two professions outstripped them by mentioning the profession in text. Moreover, the gladiators were more likely to add some flair, making their epitaphs metrical. Looking at the stones, we can tell that gladiators couldn't always afford the best stonemasons or epigrammists, but were still determined to have as elaborate a commemoration as possible. While the statistics aren't exactly the same in Asia

Minor as for other culturally Greek provinces in the empire, we can see this urge to emphasise their professional accomplishments across the whole region.

Remember Me Fondly

Considering that gladiation is often presented as a Roman import, the statistics we can draw from gravestones are incredibly interesting. Why were gladiators in the Greek world so keen to be remembered for their career, long after their lives and deaths?

I believe that social status plays a significant role. In Ahrens' study, skilled professions like physicians were not nearly as keen as gladiators to include their job in their epitaph, despite their careers arguably being more prestigious and requiring extensive (and expensive) training. These men were far more likely to have a higher socio-economic status and have had a more privileged upbringing than the enslaved and poor men who made up the majority of each gladiatorial troupe. To quote Margaret Atwood, 'old money whispers, new money shouts'. For Greeks in elite careers, mentioning their job on a tombstone was probably a little too gauche for most. Reliefs of funeral scenes including family members were deemed more appropriate for an epitaph.

For Greeks in unskilled roles, any stone at all would have been out of reach for most. Consider our gladiators: some were purchased in slave markets. Others were poor and willing to take a risk to earn some cash or to escape debt. There may have been a few well-heeled adrenaline junkies entering the arena for the fun of it, but they were the minority. We should remember that our gladiators usually started their careers with either no choice in the matter, or with limited options. As we've already noted, the *lanistae* were incentivised to keep the gladiators well-nourished and cared for, in order to have the best calibre of fighters with the highest earning potential. It was not in the interests of the *lanista* to treat their gladiators poorly. For many *tirones*, the high risk of entering the profession (willingly or not) brought high rewards and a rise in living standards and earnings. It is worth noting that conditions of enslavement were usually so awful that, for many enslaved people, even a profession centred on bloodsports had a higher quality of life and longer life expectancy than being sent to a quarry or mine. The arena was a perilous workplace, but at least positive outcomes were realistic. The reason for this boils down to money.

Remember that it is a misconception that gladiator fights always resulted in death. This was actually quite an unlikely outcome, and as the fight records on the tombstones attest, most fights ended with the loser walking out of the arena with his life. It's unlikely that all gladiators wished to kill; they typically speak of each other with professional respect in their epitaphs, and in towns with a single *familia* or reliant on travelling troupes, gladiators were paired with opponents that they trained and lived with. Unless a match was advertised as a 'no mercy' fight, gladiators had no incentive to kill their opponent. They certainly received no monetary bonus for doing so, and may even have been shunned by their comrades if they were seen to behave in an unnecessarily murderous manner.

Moreover, neither the *lanista* nor the *editor* were keen for gladiators to die. For the *lanista*, he would lose a fighter that he had taken a long time to carefully train (not to mention feed and house) and lose future earning potential. For the *editor*, fatalities changed the contract from leasing a performer to purchasing a performer – you break it, you buy it. *Editores* had to reimburse the *lanista* for the gladiator's full worth at time of death, and, when fully trained, gladiators were valuable commodities. Higher ranking gladiators were worth even more, so training hard to ensure that one ascended the *palus* ranks quickly may have resulted in a modicum of protection; the better a gladiator was, the more expensive his death became, and the less willing an *editor* would have been to pay for it.

We should also factor in name recognition and popularity among the spectators, who used chants to sway the *editor*'s decision about whether or not to grant mercy to the losers of each bout. For *editores* who owned their own troupe, such as imperial high priests, their term in office lasted a year. At the end of this year, they sold their *familia* to their successor.[464] They would not want to end the year on a loss by seeing their most talented and experienced gladiators die unnecessarily unless they were absolutely sure that the crowd's approval outweighed the financial loss. Money mattered. Better to let the gladiators survive, improve and be promoted so that the outgoing priest left his position with a profit, particularly after Marcus Aurelius' new regulations meant that gladiators were to be sold individually, and not as a familial group.

In other words, gladiators were incentivised to work hard, perform well, and to impress and charm the local population. Skill and celebrity increased the odds of an extended career and even the possibility of manumission and retirement. In a world where those born into poverty or slavery were usually fated for uncomfortable and short lives due to back-breaking labour, malnutrition, and lesser access to rudimentary medicine, even a brutal career in the arena was a chance to lift oneself out of that existence, into a life of having one's needs met, and to be admired and respected by citizens who would never look twice at them in any other scenario. The gamble was whether a gladiator would ultimately die at the hands of his opponent as thousands spectated, but, as this was not an inevitable outcome, it was worth the risk for many. For losing gladiators who were condemned to death, either because they were deemed expendable or had failed to perform in a satisfactory manner, their opponent was trained to dispatch them quickly with their sword, with dignity and respect. This manner of death might also have been deemed preferable to starvation, prolonged illness, or being worked to death, which were all distinct possibilities outside of the arena. In an ideal society, no man would have to make this gamble, but the ancient world was far from being an ideal society. Perhaps, then, we can attribute gladiators being so keen to invest in commemorating their careers in stone, to the fact that it was their career that allowed them upward mobility, and that they never would have been able to afford ostentatious memorials if they hadn't worked so hard and risked so much.

Context is King

As we've seen in Chapter 8, western gladiators were branded with the social stigma of *infamia*. The shame of selling one's body for entertainment was designed to be dehumanising; this dehumanisation manufactured the consent for spectators to watch men harm and kill each other. It's okay to watch somebody fight for their life if you don't consider them to be a full person. This indifference to human lives too frequently remains, as we still see in the news every day. We can see this shame reflected in the gravestones. The gravestones of western gladiators are few in number, and hardly any are decorated. They are terse in their epitaphs, and give no clues to the lives of individual men, the opposite in every way to the funerary commemorations of gladiators in the Greek world.

It seems likely this was because gladiators did not face *infamia* from Greek spectators. When we look at the evidence we have, Greek gladiators saw no shame in being exactly what they were. They used the names of mythical heroes, they positioned themselves as an extension of ancient contact athletics, they carried themselves like warriors, and they were bold in their unignorable commemorations of their lives. It's hard to believe that local populations would tolerate such proud monuments, so unabashedly Greek in style and inspiration and so many in number, if gladiators were treated with disdain outside of the arena, as they were in Rome. The dates of the gravestones range over two centuries, and none show any signs of ancient deliberate defacement, which we might expect if locals resented socially unacceptable people having prominent commemorations.

This comparison with the western practices leads us to another interesting element of our investigation. It is generally accepted that western gladiators were buried in segregated cemeteries, away from respectable civilians. Their headstones were less prominent, and perhaps less likely to be read with any interest, which may explain why they're so concise. Many gladiator gravestones from the Greek world aren't found *in situ*, they were removed from necropoleis to be reused as building blocks for newer construction. In 2007 in Ephesus, however, archaeologists found the first identifiable gladiator graveyard, complete with human remains and gravestones *in situ*. The striking thing about this particular discovery is its location; the graveyard wasn't hidden away in an unfrequented and remote plot far from the bustle of the city, it was on the prominent road that led to the famous Temple of Artemis. These gladiators were given an eminent position in Ephesian civic life, even after they had died. The gladiators were buried some 300m from the stadium in which they had competed. This area, on the Anodos section of the Via Sacra Ephesiaca, was in a prominent position with significant footfall between the Koressian Gate and the Artemision sanctuary, particularly during the annual procession of statues celebrating the goddess Artemis' birth, where the entire city would pass the cemetery and be able to read the inscriptions. The Ephesian gladiators were not hidden away in death, but were buried in a visible and distinguished location.

This, then, was another thing we can see that Greek gladiators and contact athletes had in common: they were well-respected in their communities, which is reflected in their final resting places.

This has a lot to do with the gravestones themselves, because the gladiators consciously used them to promote their own Greekness, to remind everyone who read the epitaphs that, while they had had a quintessentially Roman profession, that they were still Greek to their core, and that they were proud to be so. Moreover, gladiators were actively rebranding their profession in Greek terms; they transliterated the long list of gladiatorial jargon into Greek, chose Greek stage names, and the tombs depict these men in the same poses as Greek soldiers and wrestlers. The fighters touch upon Greek religious beliefs, and reference Greek myths. Gladiators were taking great care and expense to communicate their Greekness in death, which must have been a continuation of how the gladiators presented themselves in life. They were marketing gladiation as the perfect combination of all the cultural touchstones that Greeks loved so much:

- ἀγών ('agon': 'contest')
- καλός ('kalos': in this context, physical beauty of the body)
- ἀριστεία ('aristeia': the moment when a Greek warrior in epic poetry shines on the battlefield) and
- ἀρετή ('*arete*': a catch-all term for excellence and virtue, similar to Roman *virtus*, in this case referring to mastery of martial skills, discipline and courage)

Greek gladiators promoted themselves as the ultimate amalgamation of Olympic contact athletes, the heroes of Greek literature, and the warriors Greece was so proud of, and they performed in culturally Greek spaces: the agora, the theatre and the stadium. Not only were amphitheatres a huge drain of resources, manpower and funds, they were an incontrovertibly Roman addition to a Greek urban landscape. In the cities with a larger Roman population, this was clearly not an issue, but the Greeks were proud of their heritage and proud of their cities; not all Roman civic additions were as welcome as others. It made financial and cultural sense to stage Greek gladiators as the ultimate Greek mash-up entertainers in existing entertainment venues. Gladiators named Achilles or Ajax fought in the theatres where Greeks had heard the *Iliad* recited and the titular tragedies performed for centuries, and gladiators fought in stadia where boxers and *pankratiasts* had competed for generations. The gladiatorial combat itself was recognisably Roman across the empire, in that the categories of arms and armour universally stayed roughly the same, but the Greek spectacle took the bare bones of equipment and rules, and embedded allusions to existing Greek cultural practices wherever possible. This appears to be undertaken consciously by *munerarii*, spectators, and, particularly, participants – both in their lives and after their deaths. Gladiation became not just acceptable but respectable, and unmistakably Greek.

We should ask who chose the compositions of each gravestone? Were they truly autobiographical? It has been suggested that gladiatorial epitaphs cannot be used as evidence of individuals projecting their self-identity for three reasons: purchasing one's epitaph in advance may have been seen as inauspicious; death could occur in a *polis* far from a gladiator's base if 'on tour'; and the likelihood of not surviving a fight could be difficult to predict in advance.[465] It is true that many monuments were erected by family or colleagues, because the person responsible for producing the actual stone usually tells us so. But I do not think there is reason to believe that this merely results in wives and comrades deciding what goes on the stone that they are purchasing on behalf of the deceased. I have two suggestions here.

The first is that, while purchasing and preparing a stone for oneself while still alive might well have been a bad omen, discussing the nature of commemoration would not be. It is the very risk of fatality that would prompt a man in a dangerous profession to consider and prepare for not only his demise, but for what comes after. Plutarch seems to confirm this was true for Greek gladiators, saying:

> *Why, even among the gladiators I observe that those who are not utterly bestial, but Greeks, when about to enter the arena, though many costly viands are set before them, find greater pleasure at that moment in recommending their women to the care of their friends and setting free their slaves than in gratifying their belly.*[466]

Here, Plutarch is referencing the grand feast that all gladiators were invited to enjoy on the night before a Games, featuring the kind of elevated cuisine that they would not have been able to indulge in on any other day of the year. From Plutarch's tone, we get the impression that gladiators elsewhere took this as an opportunity to eat, drink and be merry, if not raucous. If this was their last night on Earth, these gladiators were determined to have as much fun as possible. But Plutarch is specific in saying that Greek gladiators spent this time preparing for how the people around them would cope after their death. Consider modern soldiers preparing for a tour of duty; a will is not seen as inauspicious, but an essential and practical way to ensure that if death does occur, matters are dealt with and wishes can be honoured. In such a comparable case, not preparing for one's death would be seen as irresponsible, and modern soldiers are strongly encouraged to do so. Will-making is made as easy as possible for all personnel. This tradition can actually be traced back to the Roman army, where will-making prior to potential dangerous battles was deemed so important that soldiers were allowed to create legally binding wills while on campaign without the usual rigmarole of hiring lawyers with their complex paperwork back home; a soldier of Rome was permitted to make his will in any way he was able.[467] If legionaries were encouraged to plan for what happened after death, it is plausible that gladiators were also – or at least felt that they could: after all, there were many other professional connections between soldiers and gladiators, as we have seen.

With gravestones being such a significant investment by the deceased (or someone close to him), I do not accept that proud fighters would leave family or colleagues to guess how to suitably represent their loved ones. I suspect that colleagues who shared such a risky profession may well have also shared a preoccupation with ideas of an ideal death and desired commemoration, and it is likely to have been a topic of conversation with both families and comrades. In which case, out of either love or respect, the surviving spouse or colleague would have striven to ensure that the individual's identity would have been presented as the deceased had already requested, rather than resort to a banal stereotype. While Greekness is homogenous across the gravestones, we've seen that there were many different parts of Greek culture that a gladiator might choose to emphasise on his gravestone, and different ways to do so, either through the iconography or content of the text. The Greekness is homogenous, the myriad combinations of Greek cultural touchstones incorporated into memorials are not.

It is also important to remember that individual identity and professional identity need not be mutually exclusive, and a monument can display both. This is particularly true when these fighters were not only proud of themselves, but of their profession and how they wove it into their existing Greek culture. The respect that gladiators held for both colleagues and opponents, who were so often both at once,[468] is demonstrated by the care with which they took to inflict minimal harm on each other in the arena itself (a feat which several gladiators make sure to point out[469]), but also by the care that was taken clearly in memorialising each other as individuals. These men mattered to their families and to each other as unique people, and not mere statistics, and the care taken over a tombstone reflected that. It was a respect not always borne from sentimentality, but always from professional esteem. In and out of the arena, gladiators were looking out for each other far more than they were harming each other.

Chapter 19

Final Words: The Fates,
The Underworld, and Death

There is one final stopping point in our investigation together and, appropriately enough, it is to explore the final stopping point of Greek gladiators: not the cemeteries where they were buried, but the Underworld. We have seen over and over that death is essential to understanding gladiators in the Greek world: the likelihood of it and whether that would make it a deterrent as a career; the financial cost to the rich and powerful men hosting such spectacles; the possible connection with the gods of the Underworld; the bravery of facing your potential death nobly and the ways that might connect you to the great heroes of the past to earn the favour of a crowd; and the role of gravestones in understanding both gladiators as individuals and their role in society. A career as a gladiator was inseparable from death and so it is perhaps not surprising to learn that gladiators were preoccupied with mortality. Nowhere do we have better evidence of this than the Greek world and the gravestones they left to record their place in life for posterity. It is time to take one last look at this incredible evidence group.

Firstly, however, we have to reflect on the long-held Greek ideal of the 'perfect death', encapsulated in the *Iliad*: a glorious death in battle. Achilles, the raging protagonist of the story of the Trojan War, chose a short, violent life that ended in fame and glory over a quiet life dying in bed, even though we see Achilles reflect on the consequences of that choice when he loses Patroklos and slays Penthesilea; the tragedy of loss also heightens the glory of success. Usually, glory in death was reserved for those defending their home city, but facing death on a constructed battlefield in an arena still required elevated levels of courage, which was highly prized and admired in Greek society. Even if the odds of surviving were generally high, death was still an ever-present concern; however, if a glorious death was preferable to Achilles, then why not to a gladiator?

That's not to say, however, that gladiators sought death in quite the same manner that Achilles did. As well as pondering their own deaths, Greek gladiators were also keen not to inflict death on their opponents; for example, a gladiator named Mestrianos (who fought under the name Meilesis) mentions in his epitaph that he fought five times without causing anybody grief.[470] After all, an opponent wasn't a real enemy, but a fellow professional who just happened to be an adversary for as long as the match lasted. Perhaps this is why when opponents are specifically named in the epitaphs it is usually in a neutral manner. When opponents are mentioned disparagingly, it is always because the opponent has fought in a dishonourable fashion, going against the unspoken code of mutual respect that these gladiators seem to have constructed. Professional pride is clearly signalled both in the language and artistic programmes of the majority of these epitaphs.

How then, do these men present their deaths, an event which in itself usually betrays that at least once, they were found wanting? An epitaph from Tralleis (modern Aydin in Türkiye) gives us a possible theory:

> *I, Victor, died while I was fighting in the stadium, defying the Moirai. I had defeated them all, when the strong Moirai seized me and led me to Hades, and now I lie here in the grave. The end of my life I received from the murderous hands of Amarantos.*[471]

Amarantos is definitely named and shamed in this epitaph, but only after Victor (whose name, perhaps chosen by himself, means 'winner') describes being pulled down into the Underworld by the 'strong *Moirai*'. Who were they? In English, we know them as the Fates: three sisters and the daughters of Nyx, the goddess of Night. Their eternal role was to determine the destinies of every living mortal, and each had a specific task. Klotho worked with her spindle, spinning a thread for each mortal on Earth. Her sister Lakhesis, known as the Allotter, measured each thread to decide how long and happy a life each mortal would receive. Atropos, known as the Inflexible, cut each thread when she decided that the life was to end and the mortal was to die. In other words, the *Moirai* predetermined birth, death and everything in between for each individual person. Myths tell us that even the Olympian gods did not dare challenge the decisions made by the sisters.

The Fates are mentioned on gladiatorial funerary stones at least thirty-one times, which is roughly ten per cent of all the epitaphs we currently possess. It has been suggested that this number of references to the Fates may have been a deliberate feature of gladiatorial training.[472] This theory suggests that fatalism in the form of belief in the *Moirai* was a form of indoctrination, used in order for gladiators to accept their deaths with the impassive forbearance that society demanded. In other words, a gladiator would be more likely to die without pleading or screaming if he was led to believe that the manner and date of his death had been fixed for him by goddesses on the day he was born. No gladiator wanted to die without dignity, and no spectator would feel comfortable watching a professional (as averse to a condemned criminal, for whom a humiliating death was *de rigeur*), struggling to escape or sobbing as the sword was plunged into his neck. However, there are no votives or dedicatory inscriptions from gladiators addressed to the *Moirai*. Neither do we have any evidence showing mentions of the sisters from spectators or organisers either. There are no shrines to the *Moirai* built into spectacle venues. If there was a standard programme that insisted on acknowledgement of the Fates as part of training, it seems likely that the *Moirai* would be mentioned in more evidence for Greek gladiators than only the epitaphs.

Rather, it seems that the Greek gladiators were thinking about the Fates by their own volition. It's unlikely that Greek gladiators specifically required supernatural rationalisation to satisfactorily fulfil the obligations of their role when other gladiators did not, and we only have one reference to the *Fatae/ Parcae* (the Roman term for the *Moirai*) in a gladiatorial epitaph written in Latin, in the region of Epetium (Stobreč in Croatia, quite close to the Greek world). Intriguingly, the primary religious association for gladiators in the western Roman territories is another Greek goddess and another sister of the Fates: Nemesis, goddess of Retribution. She had traditional sanctuaries in Rhamnous in Attika, Patrai, Smyrna, and Cyzicus, but, thanks to her association with western gladiators, she also had shrines in or close to major amphitheatres across the empire.[473] Small rooms off the arena floor are often found that contain altars and votives to Nemesis, as well as sculptural representations of the goddess.

In the Greek world, however, the evidence suggests that the majority of inscriptions and dedications to Nemesis in spaces relevant to gladiators were made by spectators.[474] For instance, in Prousa, in the province of Bithynia, a fragment of an architrave is inscribed with the name of Nemesis, dedicated by a local magistrate who provided games for the local people.[475] In Aphrodisias in Caria, the son of the local High Priest included a relief of Nemesis on his memorial to the gladiatorial troupe he owned, which was probably erected near the theatre.[476] A seat was reserved permanently for the incumbent priest of Nemesis in the Theatre of Dionysus in Athens, which was used for spectacles. In Rome, Nemesis was believed to influence state order, and we've already seen that the amphitheatre could be considered a microcosm of the Roman state and its control and dominion over life and death. Perhaps in this context, Nemesis was seen as an appropriate goddess to allot the deaths of those already considered *infamia*. If so, it might help explain why most of the evidence we find of her in connection with gladiators in the Greek world is coming from outside, rather than the gladiators themselves, who noticeably seem to prefer the *Moirai*.

As an alternative theory, I suggest that the many ways the *Moirai* are evoked is evidence of professional pride. The lengthiest recorded career in the epitaphs is Eurotas, who fought an astonishing fifty times,[477] but, of the epitaphs that specify how many combats a gladiator participated in, the average number is twelve. Of the gladiators who mention both their fight statistics and the *Moirai* in their epitaph, the majority were killed before they reached that average. There is less humiliation in defeat and death if that defeat was predetermined by Underworld deities. The gladiator becomes blameless, for nothing he could have done in the arena could have changed the outcome. It was simply that his time was up. For a group that took their profession so seriously, it's not a surprise that so many mention these divine mitigating circumstances when they talk about their death on the gravestones. A gravestone for a gladiator is already a pretty solid indication that someone had a dreadful day at work, and that one moment is not what the gladiators wanted to be remembered for – not when they had had a successful career up until that point.

Another gladiator named Victor, who this time fought and died in Xanthos on the Lycian coast, says in his epitaph:

I am Victor, of the Primus Palus (first rank). Look at me, passers by. I am Victor the mighty secutor, and all opponents feared me in the stadiums. My fatherland was Libya. Now the earth of Xanthos on the Auxanian Plain shelters me, according to the decree of the Moirai. Play and laugh, wanderer, knowing that you too must die.[478]

The composition here is important. Victor is quick to point out that he was in the top rank of gladiators, which only the best of the best could aspire to achieve. He tells us plainly that he was the kind of gladiator that opponents dreaded. He was formidable, and he is keen to remind us of it. So none of these quaking opponents could have possibly killed a man like him without a liberal amount of help from the Fates themselves, as far as Victor is concerned. He came from a group of men who boasted of being warriors of Ares and fighting like heroes; their 'thread' being cut while they were fighting not only attenuated their defeat, but it meant they weren't marked as inferior to their opponent in any way. The gladiators were too mighty for their death to be attributed to a mere mortal, despite the well-known fact that their opponents had exactly the same training and skill set as them, and were deliberately selected so that matches were fought between gladiators of the same skill level. That little detail gets in the way of personal ego, however, and so we find repeated mentions of the *Moirai*.

To really hammer home the point, a gladiator named Gaius who fought in Gortyn on Crete states on his gravestone that the *Moirai* killed him and presented his corpse to his opponent, rather than give his opponent any credit![479] Whether we see this as braggadocio or fear of a negative evaluation is a matter of opinion, but, given the risks these men ran every time they stepped into an arena (sometimes not by their own choice), it seems churlish to judge them for wanting to preserve their reputations post mortem. Besides, referencing the *Moirai* in epitaphs was a long-established tradition in Greek funerary commemorations, particularly if a death was premature or unnatural.[480] In other words, Greek gladiators were conforming with local funerary norms.

There are references to the journey to the Underworld mentioned in the epitaphs as well, and they align perfectly with the already ancient concept of the afterlife recorded in art and literature. For Greeks, the Underworld was a cold, dark, silent place. The souls of the departed lived in a largely featureless plain called the Asphodel Meadows, unable to interact with one another. According to Homer, when Odysseus is told he must visit the dead to obtain vital information about his voyage home after the Trojan War, the dead can only speak with him after they have drunk blood from a sacrificed sheep, otherwise they were barely recognisable as human.[481] Homer also describes some of the ghosts as being able to vocalise only in bat-like shrieks.[482] The Underworld is dank, miserable and not somewhere anybody wishes to go; the concept of an idyllic Heaven wasn't really a belief for many, apart from a few cults like the Eleusinian and Orphic mystery cults. The lack of light, warmth and comfort was a dim prospect, and is sometimes described as such in the epitaphs along with the Underworld deities. The standard formula allowed for poetic licence, resulting in some hauntingly beautiful phrasing:

- Achilleus, who died in Xanthos: 'The Moira's thread led me down into the abyss'[483]
- Diodorus, who died in Amisos: '*The pernicious Moirai and the sly* summa rudis *killed me; I left the daylight and came to Hades*'.[484]
- Unknown, who died in Philadelphia: '*The* Moirai *dragged me here by force and buried my body*'.[485]

- Stephanos, who died in Pergamon: '*I who was cheered in the stadium have obtained oblivion*'.[486]
- Eutychos, who died in Pessinus: '*I [...] have left the daylight and entered the unchanged realm of Hades [...] which is not desired by normal men, and is the most detested. I was struck with a murderous sword, I have left the beautiful daylight and now I face the end: death*'.[487]

In death, as in life, the ways that gladiators articulated their place in the world was firmly in the Greek tradition.

Your Honour, the Defence Rests

We have seen that so many theatres and stadia were converted to host Roman spectacle that a significant number of Greek cities had at least one venue in which gladiators fought, and that even if a city didn't possess a converted venue, a Greek would not have to travel very far from their hometown to find one. Looking at amphitheatres alone was not enough, and when we plot these theatres and stadia alongside them, a clearer picture emerges; Asia Minor shoots up the leaderboard to become the region of the Roman empire with the third densest distribution of spectacle venues, beaten only by the region we now know as Tunisia in second place, and the Italian peninsula itself in first. Gladiatorial art can be found all over the eastern Mediterranean in all genres, made by skilled craftsmen and idle doodlers alike. We also now know that more gravestones of gladiators have been found in the culturally Greek provinces than any other – not just because Greeks were more likely to use them, but also because Greek gladiators felt comfortable flaunting their profession for all to see. Every city doesn't necessarily have all three types of evidence that survive for us to investigate, and some only have one, but because we've looked at all of these forms of evidence in tandem, we can now see that gladiators were a feature of everyday life in hundreds of Greek cities.

In Chapter 6, we saw in the literary evidence that elite, educated Greeks were sometimes vocal in their disdain for gladiation, just as elites were elsewhere in the empire. What is different here is that, for the rest of the Greeks who did enjoy a day at the Games, gladiation was not seen as an import from Rome that unavoidably came complete with all the negative connotations of imperialism, xenophobia and degradation. When Plutarch discusses Greek gladiators, he argues that they are *not* 'utterly bestial' in comparison with their contemptible Roman counterparts, specifically because of their Greekness. While a man like Plutarch (a wealthy academic and priest at Delphi) was unlikely to be the target demographic for gladiation, this nonchalant comment is likely indicative of wider sensibilities; it was the cultural Greekness of the participants that elevated gladiation in the Greek world. In the western territories, gladiators were dehumanised and shunned to make them vaguely tolerable to society, but, in the Greek world, it seems that gladiators were an acknowledged part of the community simply because they could fit in. No wonder the gladiators sought to emphasise their cultural credentials at every given opportunity—it elevated them as individuals as well as their profession as a whole. The accentuation of Greekness by both combatant and spectator was a collective effort to ennoble both gladiation and gladiator.

Not all memories warrant preservation in stone. That so many Greek gladiators were memorialised according to their profession speaks not only to their own pride but to the admiration of their spectators: society deems what is worth memorialising, and the open pride with which these gladiators present themselves is indicative of wide social acceptance and endorsement. These gladiators commemorated themselves because the society that they lived in agreed that they were worthy of commemoration and desired to remember them as much as they longed to be remembered. Silvia Barbantani, who helped us study the epitaphs of Greek warriors through the Hellenistic and Roman periods, writes that the use of epigrams with call-backs to epic poetry preserved the memory of heroic deeds of individual soldiers and aimed to pass it on throughout centuries to future generations.[488] In which case, every military gravestone's text is like a mini-scene from the *Iliad*, immortalising the soldiers forever, which in turn granted them fame and honour. It's obvious that gladiators took note of this and wanted to emulate it for themselves; they too fought with immense bravery, and were their own remarkable deeds not worthy of everlasting fame? The metre of their own epigrams may have been occasionally clumsy, and the art sometimes rudimentary, but, when approached without modern sensibilities, the collective effect of this extraordinary collection of stones does fulfil that brief. Greek gladiators were able to use their limited resources, in combinations of various methods, to earn the lasting *kleos* ('glory') that eluded their counterparts elsewhere.

When we take all of the gravestones, inscriptions, artworks, and adapted venues and study them in tandem, it becomes clear gladiation was not only enthusiastically adopted by the Greeks on a scale thus far underappreciated, but that it was embedded and absorbed deeply into the existing Greek cultural landscape – and that gladiators played an active vital role in doing so. The Roman imperialism inherent in the ideology of the Colosseum[489] was not translated in the Greek world along with gladiator terminology, and Roman ideals of masculine *virtus* as a central function of gladiation were reformed and reframed into Greek masculine ideals of competition, military excellence, athleticism, and physical beauty, embellished with a dramatic, epic flair. Greek gladiators didn't minimise themselves in commemoration as their counterparts elsewhere did, and were not weighed down with the same levels of social stigma. Rome may have developed *armaturae* to represent conquered foes, but, as we have seen with stage names, Greek gladiators placed themselves among the victors of legend, rather than taking their place among the vanquished.

It is clear now that Greek gladiators can and should be considered, as they were in the ancient world, as a vibrant part of the Greek cultural landscape.

Epilogue: We Are Most Definitely Entertained

The city is buzzing with energy as the crowds swarm the streets around the stadium. Hawkers have set up stalls around the great marble monument, selling cushions, lamps and statuettes. A small child tugs on his father's tunic, pointing to a table of little gladiator dollies he wants to play with. A woman yells the prices she's charging for chicken thighs in a spiced sauce and honey-glazed cakes, she's already sold out of cheese and nut pastries. Thousands of people line up at the stadium entrance arches, clutching their precious entrance tokens. One man takes his seat early, and takes out a knife to stave off boredom – he scratches a caricature of a murmillo to while away the time. When everyone is seated, the trumpets sound; the procession of performers is about to enter. Infatuated young ladies crane their necks to catch a glimpse of the gladiators they crush on as the troupe's most handsome fighters enter; the retiarius with the golden hair is their favourite. The crowd cheers as the High Priest stands to greet them and officially announce that the Games have begun. They have been waiting for this day all year. The High Priest beams, soaking in the gratitude and adulation of 15,000 people. Today will be expensive, but the roar of the crowd is worth it.

On the stadium floor, Achilleus squints in the morning sun, the cacophony of the crowd filling his ears; he feels that familiar knot of anticipation in his belly. Today, he fights Hermes, a fighter from a rival ludus. Hermes is supposed to be a good fighter, but no matter. Achilleus is better. He glances around the stands of the stadium, at the thousands of people who have come to watch him perform. At the beginning of his career, he had viewed these people with suspicion, not sure what to make of them at all. They hadn't paid him much attention back then, and he'd resented having to fight for the entertainment of people who showed him such ambivalence, but they'd soon taken notice of him when he'd won his first match against a cocky murmillo. Now, four years later, everyone in the city knows Achilleus the Thraex. He'd worked hard during those four years, improving his manoeuvres, perfecting his techniques, studying the tactics of his opponents. Achilleus had become known as the master of the feint, confusing his opponents before moving with lightning speed to take them unawares. The crowd loved this move, and now they looked forward to it every fight. Whirling round his *lumbering foe, he tired them out until they had no choice but to concede. Achilleus has a spotless fight record, and he isn't about to let that change today. If he wins this afternoon, he is up for promotion, with all the benefits that a higher rank would bring: a better room, better food and extra massages at the end of a training session. The bonus he'll get for a victory will be nice, too, and he's already mentally spending it. All he has to do is win. He's less suspicious of the crowd now; he's fought for their respect, and their respect gives him a home and a purpose. It brings risk, of course, but Achilleus is a confident man, and isn't worried. He'd earned a gnarly scar on his thigh a couple of years ago, but the ladies seem to find it strangely alluring, so it feels churlish to complain.*

The names of the participants are being announced one by one, and when Achilleus's name is called the crowd erupt. It feels good to be a favourite, and he hoped that these fans would call for him as loudly if he ever relied on their affection for his survival. As he did every morning of the games, he resolved to give them such a show that they'd never leave him high and dry. As the parade wrapped up, he gives a collegial nod to the bestiarii *who are scheduled to hunt a lion that morning and leaves the sun-soaked stadium for a few hours of preparation away from the throng. He needs enough time for some stretches after he triple checks his armour, he doesn't want any straps coming loose …*

There's a persistent misconception, and perhaps even a desire from certain quarters, to see the ancient Greek world as a utopian idyll exclusively populated with honest, hardworking farmers and bearded old philosophers talking about the universe every night in the shade of an elegant *stoa*. It's a pretty picture, but it's not an accurate one. We've been taught for centuries that Greeks should be emulated; they invented democracy and theatre, and made huge advances in mathematics and science. We still use their political ideas, literature, architecture and theorems to this day. For this reason, there have been some scholars and archaeologists who have dismissed the idea that these erudite Greeks could possibly have welcomed the savagery they see in Roman arenas.

However, if we take off our rose-tinted spectacles, we can see that for the Greeks, gladiation was the perfect amalgamation of their favourite things; the thrill of competition, the drama of a mythical clash of heroes, the exhilaration of *pankration*, and the sheer beauty of a strong body, honed to perfection and pushed to its limits. The Romans had *virtus*, and the Greeks had *arete*: both concepts had much in common. Both required a man to strive for excellence, to show courage, fortitude, and mental and physical strength. They required a man to endeavour to push past fear to fulfil his potential, achieve the extraordinary and become truly supreme. Who better to demonstrate and embody these concepts than an expert warrior fighting for not only glory, but survival? The Romans and Greeks weren't so different after all, in many respects, and there is no reason to dispute that Greeks were capable of seeing *arete* in their adapted arenas.

Gladiators and spectators alike were keen to emphasise the Greekness of this most Roman of sports. They largely rejected the Roman amphitheatre in favour of the Greek theatres and *stadia*, they spoke of gladiators as athletes and warriors, and they ditched *infamia* because, to them, a gladiator wasn't somebody who should be shunned for their profession; their profession was a source of pride. We see this pride emanating from even the most modest of epitaphs. Greek gladiators could be proud of themselves for the very reason that they were Greek, born and bred, living in a culture that took pride in its heritage. We will never have a full account of the gladiators of the Greek World – our evidence is patchy and partial. But from what we do have, there is the distinct suggestion that these men did not see themselves as victims. Instead, it seems that they relished the chance to live fast and perhaps die young in a world where their lives could otherwise have been distinctly less comfortable, and their lives not much longer outside of the arena; we shouldn't underestimate how hard life was for thousands of people barely scraping by, or condemned to a life of back-breaking enslavement. The arena presented risk, but it also provided opportunity. For hundreds of men living in the eastern Mediterranean, becoming a gladiator was a gamble worth making.

The Roman Empire had grown too large to function, and upon the death of Theodosius I in 395 CE, the empire was divided into two, Western and Eastern. In the Western Roman empire, gladiator fights were finally abolished in 404 CE by the emperor Honorius. In the Eastern Roman empire (aka the Byzantine empire), we have no such clear-cut date for the end of gladiation. However, our evidence does trail off gradually in the fifth century CE, though animal hunts remained popular for a while longer. The day of the gladiator was over.

There is an astonishing volume of archaeological evidence for gladiators in the Greek world, despite us only possessing a fraction of what once existed, but there is the exciting prospect of new discoveries. Amphitheatres that were once overlooked are receiving fresh attention from archaeologists in Türkiye, and there is renewed interest in the amphitheatres of Crete and Cyprus. New gravestones and inscriptions are being uncovered during many excavations. Even large monuments are providing us with new evidence, as the stunning recent before-and-after-excavation photos of the theatre of Laodikeia on the Lykos and the stadium of Magnesia on the Maeander demonstrate; there are still treasures waiting to be found. The reality is that the process will continue to be slow;

excavation is expensive, time consuming and requires high levels of expertise, and there are simply too many ancient sites for archaeologists to choose from. We shall have to be patient. But, with gladiators getting a renaissance in modern pop culture,[490] perhaps they will continue to rise up the list of excavation priorities. In many ways, I look forward to my research, and this book, becoming out of date, because that will mean we have answered so many questions that I still have. In the meantime, we can determine that Greek gladiators had *kleos* on their minds – the idea that they could perform heroic deeds that would keep their names alive for generations, ensuring them a kind of immortality. For now, this book serves to grant them the *kleos* they fought so hard to earn.

Achilleus is hot, sweaty and panting furiously. His muscles are screaming with exhaustion, and he's pulled his shoulder. He's been fighting for a whole half an hour, and his opponent Hermes has put up a ferocious resistance. It's just as well Achilleus likes a challenge, and he's vaguely aware that the crowd are waiting with bated breath to see who in this battle of titans will emerge victorious. Hermes, who is finally showing some signs of tiring, is clearly summoning the energy for one last lunge. Achilleus can hear his own pulse thudding in his ears, and feel the heat of his own breath swirl around his helmet. One, two, three … Achilleus steps to the left and Hermes follows him, leaping towards him with his gladius extending towards Achilleus' chest, but Achilleus has already dodged to the right, his signature move, and spins round behind Hermes. The crowd erupts into a thunderous roar as Achilleus brings up his curved sica *blade to Hermes' throat. It has always gratified Achilleus when an opponent concedes defeat, and he feels that euphoria he loves so much surge through him as Hermes raises his index finger in capitulation.*

Achilleus, Hermes and the referee all look to the High Priest in anticipation, as the crowd calls for mercy. It was a tense fight, but a thrilling one, one that had challenged every ounce of skill and strength the fighters had. The crowd appreciated the efforts Hermes had gone through, and even Achilleus had to give him credit, nobody had made him fight that hard in a long time. The High Priest listens carefully to what the citizens were yelling, does a brief bit of mental arithmetic, and gives the signal: mercy.

Achilleus, still wrapped around Hermes, feels his opponent slowly exhale and his muscles relax. Achilleus lowers his sica *down and cordially slaps Hermes on the shoulder, who chuckles and mutters a playful bit of banter that Achilleus can't quite hear over the din. As the official hands Achilleus his victory wreath, he can finally take off his helmet and enjoy the exhilaration of 15,000 people chanting his name.*

Further Reading

Nearly every ancient source used in this book is available freely online, translated into English. Useful websites include *www.perseus.tufts. edu/hopper/* and *www.penelope.uchicago.edu/Thayer/ERoman/home. html*. Otherwise, Penguin Classics and Oxford World's Classics each have a large list of expertly translated texts with a short introduction by an academic. For the *Iliad* and *Odyssey*, my personal translator of choice is Emily Wilson. For resources and advice on reading primary sources, see *www.workingclassicists. com*.

If you would like to delve further into any of the topics mentioned in the book, here is a list of books, podcasts and documentaries that are a great place to start. I've endeavoured to include an easily accessible scholarship, though this isn't always possible on certain subjects. Happy reading!

An ideal introduction to the Seleukid dynasty is *Land of the Elephant Kings* by Paul Kosmin. For Antiochus III, an excellent biography is *Antiochus the Great* by Michael Taylor. For an excellent deep dive into Antiochus IV's late career, including the Daphne Festival, I recommend the episode '109: Sinful Root' from The Hellenistic Age Podcast.

The story of gladiatorial development in Rome is a fascinating one, and if you want to learn more I can recommend *Emperors and Gladiators* by Thomas Wiedemann and *Spectacles of Death in Ancient Rome* by Donald G. Kyle.

As this book suggests, the Greek world is a complex topic of study. Thankfully, there are many excellent sources available. The documentary series 'Ancient Worlds', written and presented by Richard Miles, is a wonderful overview of Greek history from the Bronze Age to the Roman period and is available on BBC iPlayer. John Ma's magnum opus is his book *Polis*; perhaps the least casual read on this list, it is nevertheless a masterclass in understanding exactly what Greek cities had in common, as well as how each one retained a unique identity of its own. Regarding the Greek fondness for warfare, Roel Konijnendijk gives an excellent interview with the History Hit podcast entitled 'Warfare in Ancient Greece.' For the stratospheric rise of Philip V of Macedon and his son Alexander the Great, Adrian Goldsworthy provides a thoughtful history in his biography *Philip and Alexander: Kings and Conquerors*. For the complicated Wars of the Diadochi that followed Alexander's death, try Robin Waterfield's book *Dividing the Spoils: The War for Alexander the Great's Empire*.

For further reading on the Hellenistic periods, you can't go far wrong with *A History of the Hellenistic World* by Malcolm Errington, Peter Green's *Alexander to Actium: The Historical Evolution of the Hellenistic Age* or Peter Thonemann's *The Hellenistic Age: A Very Short Introduction*.

Taken at the Flood is an eminently readable account of the Roman conquest of Greece, again by Robin Waterfield. For a more in-depth study, Arthur M. Eckstein's *Rome Enters the Greek East: From Anarchy to Hierarchy in the Hellenistic Mediterranean, 230-170 BC* is worth the effort. Erich Gruen looks at Rome's spread eastward from a Greek perspective in *The Hellenistic World and the Coming of Rome*, which is usually available in two volumes. For an overview of the Hellenistic World, the Hellenistic Age Podcast should be top of the listening list.

There are two excellent biographies of Lucullus: *Lucullus: The Life and Campaigns of a Roman Conqueror* by Lee Fratanuono and *Lucullus: A Life* by Arthur Keaveney. There is not a bookshop in the world that is short of Julius Caesar biographies; Adrian Goldsworthy provides a very readable one with his *Caesar, Life of a Colossus*. *Julius Caesar and the Roman People* by Robert Morstein-Marx and *Caesar* by Christian Meier are also worth a read. As for Mark Antony, I really recommend *A Noble Ruin: Mark Antony, Civil War, and the Collapse of the Roman Republic* by W. Jeffrey Tatum.

Key to understanding the appeal of gladiatorial spectacle is *The Lure of the Arena: Social Psychology and the Crowd at the Roman Games* by Garrett G Fagan. For more information about the Games themselves, Roger Dunkle's *Gladiators: Violence and Spectacle in Ancient Rome* is a good starting point.

Whilst an academic book, the first port of call for learning about amphitheatres is *The Roman Amphitheatre: From Its Origins to the Colosseum* by Katherine

Welch. D. L. Bomgardner's *The Story of the Roman Amphitheatre* is also highly recommended.

If you're interested in Dura Europos, try *Dura-Europos* by the peerless J. A. Baird.

For all things Homer, head to Joel Christensen's exhaustive website www.sententiaeantiquae.com, where you will find analysis, explanation and recommendations for what to read next. As for Greek mythology, Liv Albert is a walking encyclopaedia; you can find her work in her book *Greek Mythology: The Gods, Goddesses, and Heroes Handbook* and her podcast 'Let's Talk About Myths, Baby!' For Greek plays, The Center for Hellenic Studies has provided an invaluable free resource on YouTube, called the 'Reading Greek Tragedy Online' series. Each episode features a reading of an ancient play (translated into English) performed by actors, accompanied by academics providing some crucial analysis and context. Plays were meant to be heard, and so I encourage you to hear the plays before you read them.

For a survey of athletics in the ancient world, I recommend *Sport and Spectacle in the Ancient World* by Donald G. Kyle, *Sport in the Greek and Roman Worlds: Greek Athletic Identities and Roman Sports and Spectacle* by Thomas Scanlon, *Arete: Greek Sports from Ancient Sources* by Stephen Miller, and *Combat Sports in the Ancient World* by Michael B. Poliakoff. *Sport: Antiquity and Its Legacy* by Peter Miller explains how much modern athletes, like gladiators, owe to their ancient peers.

Much of the scholarship used in this book is not freely available to the public. However, many scholars listed in this bibliography have uploaded their research, without paywalls, on websites such as academia.edu, Researchgate. net and hcommons.org.

Where to See Greek Gladiators

This book has a companion Instagram account, @GladiatorsoftheGreekWorld, where you can find an archive of images relating to venues, gravestones, art and objects excavated across the ancient world.

To see these objects in person is sometimes more difficult than one may imagine; objects stored in museums may not necessarily be on display, as curatorial staff choose what objects and aspects of the ancient world to prioritise. The vast majority of the evidence studied for this book is not on public display. However, the relief of Amazon and Achillea can be seen in the British Museum, and the gravestone from the book's back cover is in the Rijksmuseum van Oudheden. The Kibyra relief on the front cover can be viewed at the Burdur Museum.

When travelling in Greece, Cyprus and Türkiye, I can only give a warning about unexpected museum and archaeological site closures. At the time of writing, gladiatorial objects in the museums of Aphrodisias, Antalya, Fethiye and Muğla are all inaccessible due to indefinite closures for renovations. Once reopened, their collections are well worth travelling for. Objects available to view currently include the gravestone of a Spartan gladiator at the National Archaeological Museum in Athens. The Archaeological Museum of Patras has an excellent display of both gravestones, graffiti and a mosaic. The Aydin Archaeological Museum also has an exceptional gladiator mosaic found at Orthosia. The Archaeological Museum of Thessaloniki has a particularly rare find on display; a gravestone of a *secutor* complete with surviving paint. The Burdur Archaeological Museum houses a rare frieze of gladiatorial combats from Kibyra, and the Archaeological Museum of Manisa, and the History and the Archaeology and Ethnography Museum in Izmir both have displays of gladiatorial tombstones.

No amphitheatre in the eastern Mediterranean is currently open to the public. I suspect that this may change in the near future, given the recent excavations at Mastaura, Pergamon and Cyzicus.

Because of the habit of placing *stadia* at the very edges of a city, many are excluded from the visitor routes of many archaeological parks, or are fenced off, as at Ephesus. Others, like Delphi, are only visible externally. Exceptions that are well worth visiting are at Aphrodisias, Athens, Kibyra, Messene, Perge, Nysa on the Maeander and Magnesia on the Maeander, which has gladiator reliefs carved into its *podium* wall.

Theatres and *odea* are usually easier to visit, given that they are more numerous and less likely to be situated away from the ancient heart of a city. A word of caution: several excellent examples of adapted theatres in Türkiye are closed at the time of writing, including Side, Tlos, Ephesus, Perge and Stratonikeia. These indefinite closures are apparently for restoration, though whether this work is necessary and not merely for aesthetics is not for me to say. The choice to work on theatres that have already been extensively excavated and previously open to the public suggests that the venues are being primed for their extra earning potential as venues for modern concerts and shows, as is the case already at Aspendos, and not because of continued academic interest. There is also clear evidence of an ongoing programme of anastylosis across Türkiye – rebuilding of ruined or partially ruined monuments – that is targeting large monuments. Many ancient buildings across Europe have been partially rebuilt in this way, including temples across Italy, the acropolis buildings in Athens, the Tetrapylon of Aphrodisias and the Library of Celsus in Ephesus. The practice is not without controversy, particularly since debates continue as to whether rebuilding has academic value or has purely 'aesthetic' motivation (read: financial incentive; in an effort to draw in tourists as image sharing on social media continues to influence tourism hotspots, certain buildings with potential aesthetic appeal may be targeted for a makeover at the expense of, say, further excavations in less 'glamorous' areas, such as houses). Anastylosis, its critics argue, can never be truly accurate or authentic. Anastylosis can also be destructive; in an effort to present a building as it was in a certain period, additions from later periods can be dismantled at the discretion of the director of each project, and not always documented as they should be; the parapet wall of Aspendos theatre, drawn by Austrian archaeologist Franz Graf Lanckoroński in 1890, has been removed, but details of when this occurred are elusive. The less-than-elegant parapet walls of Patara and Alabanda may too one day be quietly dismantled. Time will tell.

Thankfully, other theatres with clearly visible adaptations are currently open elsewhere. These include Athens, Argos, Corinth, Thassos, Stobi, Plovdiv, Bodrum, Mytilene, Miletus, Myra, Nysa on the Maeander, Aphrodisias, Hierapolis, Xanthos, Sagalassos and Paphos. For an exhaustive list, see my article 'Venues for Spectacle in the Greek East: Architectural Adaptation and Cultural Adoption', available for download from ResearchGate.

Select Bibliography

Ahrens, S. (2017) 'Social Status and Tomb Monuments in Hierapolis and Roman Asia Minor', in Rasmus Brand, J., Hagelberg, E., Bjørnstad, G., and Ahrens, S. (eds), *Life and Death in Asia Minor in Hellenistic, Roman and Byzantine Times: Studies in Archaeology and Bioarchaeology* (Oxford: Oxbow Publishing) 131-148

Akkurnaz, S. (2022) 'Mastaura Antik Kenti'nde Yapılan Arkeolojik Çalışmalar', *Lycus Dergisi* 6, 99-125

Alanyali, H. S. and Çoksolmaz E. (2021) Tiyatro–Stadyum ve Amphitiyatro Çalışmaları, Anazarbos & Anavarza, Cilt 1, in Gülşen, F. (ed), *Ankara: Akademisyen Kitapevi*, 333-354

Alcock, S. E. (1997) 'The Problem of Romanization: The Power of Athens', in Hoff, M. C., Rotroff, S. I., Habicht, C., and Alcock, S. E. (eds*), The Romanization of Athens: Proceedings of an International Conference Held at Lincoln, Nebraska (April 1996)* (Oxford: Oxbow Monograph 94) 1-7

Antoniou, G. P. (2015) 'The Theatre of Dodona: New Observations on the Architecture of the Cavea', in Frederiksen, R., Gebhard, E. R., and Sokolicek, A. (eds), *The Architecture of the Ancient Greek Theatre* (Aarhus: Aarhus University Press) 177-192

Arslan, N. (2022) 'Asia Minor'da İyi Korunmuş Erken Hellenistik Çağ Tiyatro Örneği: Assos', *Höyük: Türk Tarih Kurumu* 10, 37-59

Aydas, M. (2006) 'Gladiatorial Inscriptions from Stratonikeia in Caria', *Epigraphica Anatolica* 39, 105-110

Bagnall, R. S., Casagrande-Kim, R., Ersoy, A., and Tanriver, C. (2016*), Graffiti from the Basilica in the Agora of Smyrna* (New York: Institute for the Study of the Ancient World and New York University Press)

Baird, J. A. (2018) *Dura-Europos* (London: Bloomsbury Academic)

Baird, J. A., and Kamash, Z. (2019) 'Remembering Roman Syria: Valuing Tadmor-Palmyra, from "Discovery" to Destruction', Bulletin of the Institute of Classical Studies 62.1, 1-29

Barbantani, S. (2016) 'Simplify Me When I Am Dead: War Heroes and Long-Lasting *Topoi* in Hellenistic Epitaphs', *Aevum Antiquum* 16, 183-239

Barbantani, S. (2018) '"Fui buon poeta e buon soldato": κλέος militare e paideia poetica negli epigrammi ellenistici', *Eikasmos* 39, 283-312

Barker, C., and Stennett, G. (2004) 'The Architecture of the Ancient Theatre at Nea Paphos Revisited', *Mediterranean Archaeology* 17, 253-274

Bennett, J. (2009) 'Gladiators in Ancyra', *Anatolica* 35, 1-13

Berns, C., and Ali Ekinci, H. (2015) 'Gladiatorial Games in the Greek East: A Complex of Reliefs from Cibyra', *Anatolian Studies* 65, 143-179

Berti, F., and Masturzo, N. (2015) 'New Studies of the Theatre at Iasos: 50 Years Since the First Excavation', in Frederiksen R., Gebhard E.R., and Sokolicek, A. (eds), *The Architecture of the Ancient Greek Theatre* (Aarhus: Aarhus University Press) 131-148

Bertolín Cebrián, R. (2020) *The Athlete in the Ancient Greek World* (Norman: University of Oklahoma Press)

Bingöl, O. (2005) *Menderes Magnesiasi Theatron Magnesia on the Maeander* (Istanbul: Homer Kitabevi ve Yayincilik Ltd)

Bingöl, O. (2008) 'Das Stadion von Magnesia am Maeander', in Borm, H., Ehrhardt, N., and Wiesehoefer, J. (eds*), Monumentum et Instrumentum Inscriptum, for P Weiss on his 65th Birthday* (Stuttgart: Steiner) 21-30

Bishop, M. C. (2016) *The Gladius: The Roman Short Sword* (London: Osprey Publishing)

Blum, I. (2009) 'Milet in der Römischen Kaiserzeit', in Dally, O., Maischberger, M., Schneider, P. I. and Scholl, A. (eds), *Zeiträume : Milet in Kaiserzeit und Spätantike* (Regensburg: Verlag Schnell & Schneider GmbH) 43-60

Bomgardner, D. L. (2000) *The Story of the Roman Amphitheatre* (London: Routledge)

Bouley, E. (1994) 'La gladiature et la venatio en Mésie Inférieure et en Dacie à partir du règne de Trajan', *Dialogues d'histoire ancienne* 21.1, 29-53

Bowes, K., Hoti A., Bowden W., Francis K., and Mitchell J. (2003) 'An Amphitheatre and Its Afterlives: Survey and Excavation in the Durres Amphitheatre', *Journal of Roman Archaeology* 16, 380–94

Broneer, O. (1928) 'Excavations in the *Odeum* at Corinth, 1928', *American Journal of Archaeology* 32.4, 447-473

Brown, S. (2021) 'Combat Sports and Gladiatorial Combat in Greek and Roman Private Art', in Scanlon T.F., and Futrell A. (eds), *The Oxford Handbook Sport and Spectacle in the Ancient World* (Oxford: Oxford University Press) 439-454

Buonocore, M. (1992) *Epigrafia anfiteatrale dell'Occidente Romano III. Regiones Italiae II-V, Sicilia, Sardinia et Corsica* (Rome: Edizione Quasar)

Carlsen, J. (2014) 'Gladiators in Ancient Halikarnassos', in Karlsson, L., Carlsson, S. and Blid Kullberg, J. (eds), *Labrys: Studies presented to Pontus Hellström* (Uppsala: Acta Universitatis Upsaliensis) 441-450

Carter, M. (1999) 'A Doctor *Secutorum* and the *Retiarius* Draukos from Corinth', *Zeitschrift fur Papyrologie und Epigraphik* 126, 262-268

Carter, M. (1999) '*The Presentation of Gladiatorial Spectacles in the Greek East: Roman Culture and Greek Identity*', Doctoral Dissertation: McMaster University

Carter, M. (2001) 'Artemidorus and the Arbelas Gladiator', *Zeitschrift für Papyrologie und Epigraphik* 134, 109-115

Carter, M. (2001) 'The Roman Spectacles of Antiochus IV Epiphanes at Daphne, 166 BC', *Nikephorus* 14, 45-62

Carter, M. (2003) 'Gladiatorial Ranking and the "SC de Pretiis Gladiatorum Minuendis" (CIL II 6278 = ILS 5163)', *Phoenix* 57.1, 83-144

Carter, M. (2004) 'Archiereis and Asiarchs: A Gladiatorial *Perspective*', *Greek, Roman, and Byzantine Studies* 44, 41-68

Carter, M. (2006) 'Gladiatorial Combat with "Sharp" Weapons' *Zeitschrift für Papyrologie und Epigraphik* 155, 161-175

Carter, M. (2012) 'Gladiators and Monomachoi: Greek Attitudes to a Roman Cultural Performance', in Papakonstantinou, Z. (ed), *Sport in the Cultures of the Ancient World: New Perspectives* (Abingdon: Routledge) 150-174

Carter, M. (2014) 'Romanization Through Roman Spectacle in the Greek East', in Christesen P., and Kyle D. G. (eds), *Sport and Spectacle in Greek and Roman Antiquity* (Malden MA: Blackwell Publishing) 619-632

Carter, M. (2015) 'Bloodbath: Artemidorus, Apotomos Combat and Ps. Quintilian's "The Gladiator"', Zeitschrift für Papyrologie und Epigraphik 193, 39-52

Carter, M., and Edmonson J. (2014) 'Spectacles in Rome, Italy and the Provinces' in Bruun C., and Edmonson J. (eds), *Oxford Handbook of Roman Epigraphy* (Oxford: Oxford University Press) 537-558

Cecconi, N. (2020) 'Lo Stadio Panatenaico', *ASAtene* 98, 417-455

Chamberland, G., (2021) 'Imperial Spectacle in the Roman Provinces: Combat Sports and Gladiatorial Combat in Greek and Roman Private Art', in Scanlon, T. F., and Futrell, A. (eds), *The Oxford Handbook Sport and Spectacle in the Ancient World* (Oxford: Oxford University Press) 379-390

Chaniotis, A. (2004) 'New Inscriptions from Aphrodisias', *American Journal of Archaeology* 108, 377-416

Chaniotis, A. (2005) *War in the Hellenistic World: A Social and Cultural History* (Malden MA: Blackwell Publishing)

Chaniotis, A., and De Staeble, P. D. (2008) 'Gladiators and Animals: New Pictorial Graffiti from Aphrodisias and their Contexts', *Philia* 4, 31-54

Clark, K. (1956) *The Nude: A Study in Ideal Form* (Princeton NJ: Princeton University Press)

Clinton, K. (1997) 'Eleusis and the Romans: Late Republic to Marcus Aurelius', in Hoff, M. C., Rotroff, S. I., Habicht, C., and Alcock, S. E. (eds), *The Romanization of Athens: Proceedings of an International Conference held at Lincoln, Nebraska (April 1996)* (Oxford: Oxbow Monograph 94) 161-182

Çoksolmaz, E. (2024) 'Destroyed Amphitheaters of Asia Minor', *Library Progress International* 44.6, 198-206

Coleman, K. (2000) 'Entertaining Rome', in Coulston, J., and Dodge, H. (eds), *Ancient Rome: The Archaeology of the Eternal City* (Oxford: Oxford School for Archaeology) 205-52

Coleman, K. (2000) 'Missio at Halicarnassus', *Harvard Studies in Classical Philology* 100, 487-500

Coleman, K. (2005) 'Bonds of Danger: Communal Life in the Gladiatorial Barracks of Ancient Rome', *Todd Memorial Lectures* (Sydney: University of Sydney) 1-25

Coleman, K. (2008) 'Exchanging Gladiators for an Aqueduct at Aphrodisias (SEG 50.1096)', *Acta Classica* 51, 31-46

Coleman, K. (2019) 'Defeat in the Arena', *Greece & Rome* 66.1, 1-36

Coloru, O. (2010) 'A Marble Relief Representing the Gladiator Dareios', *Zeitschrift für Papyrologie und Epigraphik 175*, 161-163

Commito, A. R., and Rojas, F. (2012) 'The Aqueducts of Aphrodisias', in Ratté, C., and De Staebler, P. D. (eds), *The Aphrodisias Survey Volume V*, 239-307

Corzo Sánchez, R. (1994) 'Notas sobre el anfiteatro de Carmona y otros anfiteatros de la Betica', in Álvarez Martínez, J. M., and Enríquez Navascués, J. J. (eds), *Bimilenario*

Del Anfiteatro Romano De Mérida: Coloquio Internacional El Anfiteatro En La Hispania Romana, Mérida, 26-28 De Noviembre 1992 (Merida: Junta de Extremadura. Consejería de Cultura y Patrimonio) 239-246

Cowan, E., and Parkin, T. (2024) 'Domestic Violence and Vulnerability in the Roman World: Setting the Scene', *Bulletin of the Institute of Classical Studies* 66.2, 1-15

Curvers, H. H., Gans, U-W., Held, W., Kotitsa, Z., Nurpetlian, J., and Wangen, J. (2017) 'The Hippodrome of Berytos Preliminary Report', *Bulletin d'Archéologie et d'Architecture Libanaises* 17, 7-78

de Chaisemartin, N. (2015) 'The Carian Theatre at Aphrodisias', in Frederiksen, R., Gebhard, E. R., and Sokolicek, A. (eds), *The Architecture of the Ancient Greek Theatre* (Aarhus: Aarhus University Press) 391-402

Di Napoli, V. (2010) 'Entertainment Buildings of the Roman Peloponnese: Theatres, *Odea* and Amphitheatres and their Topographical Distribution', *Melethmata* 63, 253-266

Di Napoli, V. (2015) 'Architecture and Romanization: The Transition to Roman Forms in Greek Theatres of the Augustan Age', in Frederiksen, R., Gebhard, E. R., and Sokolicek, A. (eds), *The Architecture of the Ancient Greek Theatre* (Aarhus: Aarhus University Press) 365-380

Di Vita, A. (1991) 'l'Anfiteatro ed il Grande Teatro Romano di Gortina', in Rizzo, M. (ed), *Annuario della Scuola Archeologica di Atene, LXIV-LXV*, 327-352

Dodge, H. (1999) 'Amusing the Masses: Buildings for Entertainment and Leisure in the Roman World', in Potter, D. S., and Mattingly, D. J. (eds), *Life, Death and Entertainment in the Roman Empire* (Ann Arbor: University of Michigan Press) 205-55

Dodge, H. (2008) 'Circuses in the Roman East: A Reappraisal', in Nelis-Clément, J. and Roddaz, J-M. (eds), *Le Cirque Romain et Son Image* (Bordeaux: Ausonius) 133-146

Dodge, H. (2014a) 'Building for an Audience: The Architecture of Roman Spectacle', in Ulrich, R. B. and Quenemoen, C. K. (eds), *A Companion to Roman Architecture* (New Malden: Wiley Blackwell) 281-298

Dodge, H. (2014b) 'Amphitheatres in the Roman World', in Christesen, P., and Kyle, D. G. (eds), *A Companion to Sport and Spectacle in Greek and Roman Antiquity* (Chichester: Wiley Blackwell) 545-560

Dodge, H. (2014c) 'Venues for Spectacle and Sport (Other Than Amphitheatres) in the Roman World', in Christesen, P. and Kyle, D. G. (eds), *A Companion to Sport and Spectacle in Greek and Roman Antiquity* (Chichester: Wiley Blackwell) 561-577

Dodge, H. (2016) 'Amphitheatres in the Roman East', in Wilmott, T. (ed), *Roman Amphitheatres and Spectacula: a 21st-Century perspective–Papers from an International Conference Held at Chester, 16th-18th February, 2007* (Oxford: BAR Publishing) 29-46

Dökü, F. E., and Kaya, M. C. (2013) 'The Architecture and Function of the Stadium of Kibyra', *Adalya XVI*, 177-201

Dolansky, F. (2011) 'Celebrating the Saturnalia: Religious Ritual and Roman Domestic Life', in Rawson B. (ed), *A Companion to Families in the Greek and Roman Worlds* (Chichester: Wiley Blackwell) 488-503

Duman, B. (2019) *Tripolis Araştırmaları* (Istanbul: Zero Prodüksiyon)

Dunbabin, K. (1979) *Mosaics of the Greek and Roman World* (Cambridge: Cambridge University Press)

Edmondson, J. C. (1999) 'The Cultural Politics of Public Spectacle in Rome and the Greek East, 167-166 BCE', *Studies in the History of Art 56, Symposium Papers XXXIV: The Art of Ancient Spectacle*, 76-95

Engelmann, H. (2004) 'Zum Stadium von Ephesos', *ZPE* 149, 71-72

Ertuğ Ergürer, H., and Keleş, V. (2018) 'The Gladiator Graffitis Found at the Theater of Parion', *Türkiye Bilimler Akademisi Kültür Envanteri Dergisi* 18.1, 22-32

Evangelisti, S. (2011) *Epigrafia anfiteatrale dell'Occidente Romano VIII. Regio Italiae I, 1: Campania praeter Pompeios* (Rome: Edizione Quasar)

Fagan, G. G. (2011) *The Lure of the Arena: Social Psychology and the Crowd at the Roman Games* (Cambridge: Cambridge University Press)

Fagan, G. G. (2014) 'Gladiatorial Combat as Alluring Spectacle', in Christesen, P., and Kyle, D. G. (eds), *Sport and Spectacle in Greek and Roman Antiquity* (Malden MA: Blackwell Publishing) 465-477

Farron, S. (1978) 'The Character of Hector in the Iliad', *Acta Classica* 21, 39-57

Finlayson, C. (2012) 'New Excavations and a Reexamination of the Great Roman Theater at Apamea, Syria, Seasons 1–3 (2008–2010)', *American Journal of Archaeology* 116.2, 277-319

Flickinger, R. C. (1918) *The Greek Theater and its Drama* (Chicago: University of Chicago Press)

Fora, M. (1996) *Epigrafia anfiteatrale dell'Occidente Romano IV. Regio Italiae I, Latium* (Rome: Edizione Quasar)

Franz. F., and Hinz V. (2015) 'The Architecture of the Greek Theatre of Apollonia in Illyria (Albania) and its Transformation in Roman Times', in Frederiksen, R., Gebhard, E. R., and Sokolicek, A. (eds), *The Architecture of the Ancient Greek Theatre* (Aarhus: Aarhus University Press) 335-350

Futrell, A. (1997) *Blood in the Arena: The Spectacle of Roman Power* (Austin: University of Texas Press)

Futrell, A. (2006) *The Roman Games: Historical Sources in Translation* (Malden MA: Blackwell Publishing)

Futrell, A. (2021) 'Games in the Republic', in Scanlon, T. F., and Futrell, A. (eds), *The Oxford Handbook Sport and Spectacle in the Ancient World* (Oxford: Oxford University Press) 135-154

Gallimore, S. (2015) '"The Saddest of Ruins": Travelers' Accounts as Evidence for Formation Processes at Hierapytna, Crete', *Journal of Eastern Mediterranean Archaeology and Heritage Studies* 3.2, 105-126

Garraffoni, R. S. (2012) 'Reading Gladiators' Epitaphs and Rethinking Violence and Masculinity in the Roman Empire', in Voss, B. (ed), *The Archaeology of Colonialism: Intimate Encounters and Sexual Effects* (New York: Cambridge University Press) 214-231

Gasparri, C. (1974) 'Lo Stadio Panatenaico', *ASAtene* 52-53, 313-392

Gebhard, E. (2014) 'The Theater at Stobi, A Summary', in Mano-Zisi, D. and Wiseman, J. (ed), *Studies in the Antiquities of Stobi Volume 3* (Princeton: Princeton University Press) 13-28

Golden, M. (2008) *Greek Sport and Social Status* (Austin: University of Texas Press)

Goldhill, S. (2001) *Being Greek under Rome: Cultural Identity, the Second Sophistic and the Development of Empire* (Cambridge: Cambridge University Press)

Golvin, J-C. (1988) *L'amphithéâtre romain: essai sur la théorisation de sa forme et de ses fonctions* (Paris: Diffusion de Boccard)

Gómez-Pantoja, J. L. (2009) *Epigrafia anfiteatrale dell'Occidente Romano VII. Baetica, Tarraconensis, Lusitania* (Rome: Edizione Quasar)

Green, J. R., Barker, C., and Stennett, G. (2015) 'The Hellenistic Phases of the Theatre at Nea Paphos in Cyprus: The Evidence from the Australian Excavations', in Frederiksen, R., Gebhard, E. R., and Sokolicek, A. (eds), *The Architecture of the Ancient Greek Theatre* (Aarhus: Aarhus University Press) 319-334

Greenhalgh, M. (2017) *Syria's Monuments: Their Survival and Destruction* (Leiden: Brill)

Gregori, G. (1989) *Epigrafia anfiteatrale dell'Occidente Romano II. Regiones Italiae VI-XI* (Rome: Edizione Quasar)

Gunderson, E. (1996) 'The Ideology of the Arena', *Classical Antiquity* 15.1, 113-151

Gutierrez, D., Frischer, B., Cerezo, E., Gomez, A., and Seron, F. (2007) 'AI and Virtual Crowds: Populating the Colosseum', *Journal of Cultural Heritage* 8, 176-185

Hägg, T. (2012) *The Art of Biography in Antiquity* (Cambridge: Cambridge University Press)

Hammad, M. (2008) 'Un amphithéâtre à Tadmor-Palmyre?', *Syria* 85, 341-346

Hayward, C., and Lolos, Y. 'Building the Early Hellenistic Theatre at Sikyon', in Frederiksen, R., Gebhard, E. R., and Sokolicek, A. (eds), *The Architecture of the Ancient Greek Theatre* (Aarhus: Aarhus University Press) 161-176

Heath, S. (2023) 'Nearness and Experience in a Network of Roman Amphitheaters', in Blakely, S. and Daniels, M. (eds), *Data Science, Human Science, and Ancient Gods Conversations in Theory and Method* (Columbus, GA: Lockwood Press) 135-174

Hofbauer, M. (2015) 'New Investigations in the Ephesian Theatre: the Hellenistic Skene', in Frederiksen, R., Gebhard, E. R., and Sokolicek, A. (eds), *The Architecture of the Ancient Greek Theatre* (Aarhus: Aarhus University Press) 149-160

Holliday, P. J. (2021) 'Circuses and Hippodromes', in Scanlon, T. F., and Futrell, A. (eds), *The Oxford Handbook Sport and Spectacle in the Ancient World* (Oxford: Oxford University Press) 426-437

Hope, V. (2000) 'Fighting for Identity: The Funerary Commemoration of Italian Gladiators', *Bulletin of the Institute of Classical Studies Supplement* 73, 92-113

Hope, V. (2021) 'Gladiators as a Class', in Scanlon, T. F., and Futrell, A. (eds), *The Oxford Handbook Sport and Spectacle in the Ancient World* (Oxford: Oxford University Press) 557-566

Hornum, M. B. (1993) *Nemesis, The Roman State, and the Games* (Leiden: Brill Publishing)

Humphrey, J. H. (1986) *Roman Circuses: Arenas for Chariot Racing* (Oakland: University of California Press)

Ilhan, N. (2002) 'Stadia of Anatolia', *ICOMOS* 38, 15-20

Isler, H. P. (2015) 'Traditional Hellenistic Elements in the Architecture of Ancient Theatres in Roman Asia Minor', in Frederiksen, R., Gebhard, E. R., and Sokolicek, A. (eds), *The Architecture of the Ancient Greek Theatre* (Aarhus: Aarhus University Press) 433-447

James, S. (2019) *The Roman Military Base at Dura-Europos, Syria* (Oxford: Oxford University Press)

Jola, C., and Reason, M. (2016) 'Audiences' Experience of Proximity and Co-Presence in Live Dance Performance', in Falletti, C., Sofia, G. and Jacono, V. (eds), *Theatre and Cognitive Neuroscience* (London: Bloomsbury Methuen Drama) 75-92

Jones, C. P. (2007) 'Gladiator Epigrams from Beroea and Stratonikeia (Caria)', *Zeitschrift für Papyrologie und Epigraphik* 163, 45-48

Junkelmann, M. (2000) *Das Spiel Mit Dem Tod: So Kämpften Die Gladiatoren* (Mainz: Philipp von Zabern)

Junkelmann, M. (2022) *Gladiatoren: Die Wirklichkeit hinter der Legende* (Oppenheim am Rhein: Nünnerich-Asmus)

Kantiréa, M. (2019) 'Servius Sulpicius Pancles Veranianus: le grand bâtisseur de Salamine', in Rogge, S., Ioannou, C., and Mavrojannis, T. (eds), *Salamis of Cyprus: History and Archaeology from the Earliest Times to Late Antiquity* (Göttingen: Waxman) 571-580

Kanz, F., and Grossschmidt, K. (2002) *Gladiatoren in Ephesos: Tod am Nachmittag* (Vienna: Österreichisches Archäologisches Institut)

Kanz, F., and Grossschmidt, K. (2009) 'Dying in the Arena: The Osseous Evidence from Ephesian Gladiators', in Wilmott, T. (ed), *Roman Amphitheatres and Spectacula: a 21st Century Perspective* (Oxford: BAR Publishing) 211-222

Karadima, C., Zambas, C., Chatzidakis, N., Thomas, G. and Doudoumi, E. (2015) 'The Ancient Theatre at Maroneia', in Frederiksen, R., Gebhard, E. R., and Sokolicek, A. (eds), *The Architecture of the Ancient Greek Theatre* (Aarhus: Aarhus University Press) 253-266

Karageorghis, V. (1969) *Salamis in Cyprus: Homeric, Hellenistic and Roman* (London: Thames and Hudson)

Karambinis, M. (2020) 'Gladiatorial and Beast-Fight Monuments in Mytilene', *American Journal of Archaeology* 124.1, 73-103

Karambinis, M. (2023) 'Gladiatorial Spectacles in Crete', *Tekmeria* 17, 45-100

Karambinis, M. (2025) 'The Gladiatorial Spectacles in Cyprus and the Enigma of the Amphitheater at Salamis', *American Journal of Archaeology* 129.2, 181-202

Kasapoğlu, H. (2018) 'Parion Theater Terracotta Figurines', in Başaran, C. and Ertuğ Ergürer, H. (eds), *Roman Theater of Parion* (Çanakkale: İÇDAŞ A.Ş. Publications) 237-276

Kayser, F. (2000) 'La Gladiature en Egypte', *Revue des Études Anciennes* 102.3-4, 459-478

Keaveney, A. (1992) *Lucullus: A Life* (London: Routledge)

Kelly, A. (2011) '"Occide, verbera, ure!" (Kill Him, Flog Him, Burn Him Alive! – Seneca Epistles 7); The Popularity, Extent and Duration of Roman Spectacula on Crete', *The 10th International Congress of Cretan Studies*, 77-94

Kloner, A., and Hubsch, A. (1996) 'The Roman Amphitheater of Bet Guvrin: A Preliminary Report on the 1992, 1993 and 1994 Seasons', *Atiqot* 30, 85-106

Kolendo, J. (1981) 'La répartition des places aux spectacles et la stratification sociale dans l'Empire Romain. A propos des inscriptions sur les gradins des amphithéâtres et théâtres', *Ktèma* 6, 301-315

Kontokosta, A. H. (2008) 'Gladiatorial Reliefs and Elite Funerary Monuments', in Ratté, C., and Smith, R. R. R. (eds), *Aphrodisias Papers 4: New Research on the City and its Monuments* (Portsmouth, RI: *Journal of Roman Archaeology Supplement* 70) 190-229

Kontokosta, A. H. (2021) 'Contests in Context: Gladiatorial Inscriptions and Graffiti', in Scanlon, T. F., and Futrell, A. (eds), *The Oxford Handbook Sport and Spectacle in the Ancient World* (Oxford: Oxford University Press) 330-341

Kourtzellis, Y. (2018) ʻαρχιτεκτονική του αρχαίου Θεάτρου Μυτιλήνης. Παρουσίαση των πρώτων αποτελεσμάτων της μελέτης*ʼ, in di Napoli, V., Camia, F., Evangelidis, V., Grigoropoulos, D., Rogers, D. K., and Vlizos, S. (eds), *What's New in Roman Greece? Recent Work on the Greek Mainland and the Islands in the Roman Period: Proceedings of a Conference Held in Athens, 8-10 October 2015*, 263-279

Kyle, D. G. (1998) *Spectacles of Death in Ancient Rome* (London: Routledge)

Kyle, D. G. (2015) *Sport and Spectacle in the Ancient World* (Malden MA: Blackwell Publishing)

Lafli, E., and Christof, E. (2020) ʻA New Stele of a Retiarius from Marmaris in Cariaʼ, *Dacia: Revue d'Archéologie et d'Histoire Ancienne* 64, 277-292

Larmour, D. H. J. (1999) *Stage and Stadium: Drama and Athletics in Ancient Greece* (Hildesheim: Weidmann)

Larsen, M. D. C., and Letteney, M. (2025) *Ancient Mediterranean Incarceration* (California: University of California Press)

Lattimore, R. (1962) *Themes in Greek and Latin Epitaphs* (Urbana: University of Illinois Press)

Lee, H. M. (2014) ʻGreek Sports in Romeʼ, in Christesen, P., and Kyle, D. G. (eds), *Sport and Spectacle in Greek and Roman Antiquity* (Malden MA: Blackwell Publishing) 533-542

Lösch, S., Moghaddam, N., Grossschmidt. K., Risser, D. U., and Kanz, F. (2014) ʻStable Isotope and Trace Element Studies on Gladiators and Contemporary Romans from Ephesus (Turkey, 2nd and 3rd Ct. AD) – Implications for Differences in Dietʼ, *PLoS ONE* 9.10, 1-17

Mandel, U. (1988) *Kleinasiatische Reliefkeramik der mittleren Kaiserzeit. Die ʻOinophorengruppeʼ und Verwandtes* (Berlin: de Gruyter)

Mann, C. (2009) ʻGladiators in the Greek East: A Case Study in Romanizationʼ, *The International Journal of Sport* 26.2, 272-297

Mann, C. (2011) *ʻUm keinen Kranz, um das Leben kämpfen wir!ʼ Gladiatoren im Osten des Römischen Reiches und die Frage der Romanisierung* (Berlin: Verlag Antike)

Martín González, E., and Paschidis P. (2020) *A Supplement to ΈΠΙΓΡΑΦΈΣ ΚΑΤΩ ΜΑΚΕΔΟΝΙΑΣ Α΄:ΕΠΙΓΡΑΦΈΣ ΒΕΡΟΙΑΣ* (Athens: Institute of Historical Research)

Mayor, A. (2014) *The Amazons – Lives and Legends of Warrior Women Across the Ancient World* (Princeton: Princeton University Press)

McLean, B. H. (2002) *An Introduction to Greek Epigraphy of the Hellenistic and Roman Periods: From Alexander the Great to the Reign of Constantine (323 BC-AD 337)* (Ann Arbor: University of Michigan Press)

Miller, S. G. (2014) ʻThe Greek Stadium as a Reflection of a Changing Societyʼ, in Christesen, P. and Kyle, D. G. (eds), *A Companion to Sport and Spectacle in Greek and Roman Antiquity* (Chichester: Wiley Blackwell) 287-294

Moretti, J-C. (1992) ʻL'Adaptation des theatres de Grece aux Spectacles Imperiauxʼ, in Landes, C. and Kramerovskis, V. (eds), *Spectacula: Theatres Antique et ses Spectacles* (Lattes: Musée archéologique Henri Prades) 179-185

Moretti, J-C. (2001) *Théâtre Et Société Dans La Grèce Antique* (Paris: Le Livre de Poche)

Moretti, J-C., and Mauduit, C. (2015) 'The Greek Vocabulary of Theatrical Architecture', in Frederiksen, R., Gebhard, E. R., and Sokolicek, A. (eds), *The Architecture of the Ancient Greek Theatre* (Aarhus: Aarhus University Press) 119-130

Murray, S. C. (2022) *Male Nudity in the Greek Iron Age: Representation and Ritual Context in Aegean Societies* (Cambridge: Cambridge University Press

Newton, C. T. (1862) *A History of Discoveries at Halicarnassus, Cnidus and Branchidae* (Cambridge: Cambridge University Press)

Nigdelis, P., and Tzelepidou, A. (2016) 'Two New Gladiatorial Monuments from Amphipolis', *Tekmeria* 13, 71-78

Orlandi, S. (2004) *Epigrafia Anfiteatrale dell'Occidente Romano, VI. Roma. Anfiteatri e strutture annesse, con una nuova edizione e commento delle iscrizioni del Colosseo* (Rome: Edizioni Quasar)

Papadopoulos, N. G., Sarris, A., Salvi, M. C., Dederix, S., Soupios, P., and Dikmen, U. (2012) 'Rediscovering the Small Theatre and Amphitheatre of Ancient Ierapytna (SE Crete) by Integrated Geophysical Methods', *Journal of Archaeological Science* 39, 1960-1973

Papanikolau, D. (2018) 'Notes of a Gladiatorial Inscription from Plotinopolis', *Tekmeria* 14, 203-213

Papapostolou, Y. (1989) 'Monuments de gladiateurs à Patras', *Bulletin de correspondance hellénique* 113.1, 351-401

Pastor, S. (2017) *Epigrafia anfiteatrale dell'Occidente Romano IX. Retia, Noricum, Duae Pannoniae, Dalmatia, Dacia, Moesia Inferior* (Rome: Edizioni Quasar)

Pedersen, P., and Isager, S. (2015) 'The Theatre at Halikarnassos: and some Thoughts on the Origin of the Semicircular Greek Theatre', in Frederiksen, R., Gebhard, E. R., and Sokolicek, A. (eds), *The Architecture of the Ancient Greek Theatre* (Aarhus: Aarhus University Press) 293-318

Petropoulos, M., and Pansini, A. (2020) 'The Roman Stadium of Patras: Excavations, Analysis and Reconstruction', *ASAtene* 98, 382-517

Pfuhl, E., and Möbius, H. (1977-79) *Die Ostgriechischen Grabreliefs* (Mainz am Rhein: Von Zabern)

Piccinini, J. (2013) 'Dodona at the Time of Augustus', in Galli, M. (ed), *Roman Power and Greek Sanctuaries: Forms of Interaction and Communication* (Athens: Scuola Archaeologica Italiana di Atene)

Piesker, K. (2015) '"Traditional" Elements in the Roman Redesign of the Hellenistic Theatre in Patara, Turkey', in Frederiksen, R., Gebhard, E. R., and Sokolicek, A. (eds), *The Architecture of the Ancient Greek Theatre* (Aarhus: Aarhus University Press) 403-418

Pirson, F. (2022) 'Pergamon–Die Arbeiten in Der Kampagne 2021', *Archäologischer Anzeiger* 2, 1–197

Poliakoff, M. B. (2021) 'Greek Combat Sport and the Borders of Athletics, Violence and Civilization', in Scanlon, T. F., and Futrell, A. (eds), *The Oxford Handbook Sport and Spectacle in the Ancient World* (Oxford: Oxford University Press) 221-231

Popova, V. (2017) 'On the Date and the Interpretation of the Complex at the Southwestern Gate of Augusta Traiana/Beroe', *Studia Academica Šumenensia* 4, 57-96

Posamentir, R., and Sayar, M. H. (2006) 'Anazarbos–ein Zwischenbericht aus der Metropole des Ebenen Kilikien', *Istanbuler Mitteilungen* 56, 317-355

Potter, D. S. (1999) 'Entertainers in the Roman Empire', in Potter, D. S., and Mattingly, D. J. (eds), *Life, Death and Entertainment in the Roman Empire* (Ann Arbor: University of Michigan Press) 256-326

Price, S. R. F. (1984) *Rituals and Power: The Roman Imperial Cult in Asia Minor* (Cambridge: Cambridge University Press)

Rauh, N. K. (1992) 'Was the Agora of the Italians an Établissement du Sport?', *Bulletin de correspondance hellénique* 116.1, 293-333

Redfield, J. M. (1975) *Nature and Culture in the Iliad: The Tragedy of Hektor* (Chicago: University of Chicago Press)

Reid, H. (2011) *Athletics and Philosophy in the Ancient World: Contests of Virtue* (Abingdon: Routledge)

Reynolds, J. (2000) 'New Letters from Hadrian to Aphrodisias: Trials, Taxes, Gladiators and an Aqueduct', *Journal of Roman Archaeology* 13, 5-20

Richardson, L. (1992) *A New Topographical Dictionary of Ancient Rome* (Baltimore: Johns Hopkins University Press)

Ritti, T., and Yilmaz, S. (1998) *Gladiatori e Venationes a Hierapolis di Frigia* (Rome: Accademia Nazionale dei Lincei)

Rizakis, A. (2019) 'New Identities in the Greco-Roman East: Cultural and Legal Implications of the Use of Roman Names', in Parker, R. (ed), *Changing Names: Tradition and Innovation in Ancient Greek Onomastics* (London: British Academy Scholarship Online) 237-257

Rizakis, Y. (1984) 'Munera gladiatoria à Patras', *Bulletin de correspondance hellénique* 108.1, 533-542

Robert, L. (1940) *Les Gladiateurs dans l'Orient Grec* (Paris: Champion)

Robert, L. (1946) *Hellenica III* (Limoges: Bontemps)

Robert L. (1948) *Hellenica V* (Limoges: Bontemps)

Robert, L. (1950) *Hellenica VIII* (Limoges: Bontemps)

Rohn, C. (2007) '*Der Theater–Stadion–Komplex von Aizanoi*', Doctoral Dissertation: Brandenburg University of Technology Cottbus

Romano, D. G. (1985) 'The Panathenaic Stadium and Theater of Lykourgos: A Re-examination of the Facilities on the Pnyx Hill', *American Journal of Archaeology* 89.3, 441-454

Romano, D. G. (2000) 'A Tale of Two Cities: Roman Colonies at Corinth', in Fentress, E., and Alcock, S. E. (eds), *Romanization and the City: Creation, Transformations and Failures* (Portsmouth Rhode Island: *Journal of Roman Archaeology*) 83-104

Romano, D. G. (2005) 'A Roman Circus in Corinth', *Hesperia* 74, 585-611

Romano, D. G. (2021) 'Greek Sanctuaries and Stadia', in Futrell, A. and Scanlon, T. F. (eds), *The Oxford Handbook of Sport and Spectacle in the Ancient World* (Oxford: Oxford University Press) 391-401

Roos, P. (2022) 'The Stadia in Caria', *The Journal of Anatolian Archaeological Studies* 5, 24-36

Rose, P. (2005) 'Spectators and Spectator Comfort in Roman Entertainment Buildings: A Study in Functional Design', *Papers of the British School at Rome* 73, 99-130

Roueche, C. M., and de Chaisemartin, N. (1993) *Performers and Partisans at Aphrodisias in the Roman and Late Roman Periods: A Study Based on Inscriptions from the Current Excavations at Aphrodisias in Caria (Journal of Roman Studies* Monographs; Vol. 6)

Sabbatini Tumolesi, P. (1998) *Epigrafia anfiteatrale dell'Occidente Romano I. Roma* (Rome: Edizioni Quasar)

Saltuk, S. (1995) *Antik Stadyumlar* (Istanbul: İnkılap Kitabevi)

Saraçoğlu, A., and Çekilmez, M. (2010) 'A Gladiator Stele from Tralleis', *Epigraphica Anatolica* 43, 57-58

Sayar, M. H. (2018) 'Death in the Theater: Gladiator Fights in the Theater of Parion', in Başaran, C., and Ertuğ Ergürer, H. (eds), *Roman Theater of Parion* (Çanakkale: İÇDAŞ A.Ş. Publications) 181-183

Scahill, D. (2015) 'The Hellenistic Theatre at Corinth: New Observations on the Architecture of the Cavea', in Frederiksen, R., Gebhard, E. R., and Sokolicek, A. (eds), *The Architecture of the Ancient Greek Theatre* (Aarhus: Aarhus University Press) 193-202

Scarborough, J. (2013) 'Galen and the Gladiators (Revised)', *Episteme: revista critica di storia delle scienze mediche e biologiche* 5.2, 98-111

Scharff, S. (2024) *Hellenistic Athletes: Agonistic Cultures and Self-Presentation* (Cambridge: Cambridge University Press)

Scullard, H. H. (1956) *From the Gracchi to Nero* (London: Routledge)

Sear, F. (2006) *Roman Theatres: An Architectural Study* (New York: Oxford University Press)

Sear, F. (2018) 'From Theatre to Amphitheatre: The Evidence of Taormina and Cyrene', in Vella, N. C., Frendo, A. J. and Vella, H. C. R (eds), *The Lure of the Antique: Essays on Malta and Mediterranean Archaeology in Honour of Anthony Bonanno* (Leuven: Peeters) 331-348

Shear, J. L. (2021) *Serving Athena: The Festival of the Panathenaia and the Construction of Athenian Identities* (Cambridge: Cambridge University Press)

Sills, A. (2023) *'Were Greek Boxers Ripped?'*, www.BadAncient.com

Sills, A. (2025) 'Venues for Spectacle in the Greek East: Architectural Adaptation and Cultural Adoption', *Melita Classica* 11

Şimşek, C. (2007) *Laodikeia* (Istanbul: Ege Yayınları)

Şimşek, C. (2023) 'Laodikeia Batı Tiyatrosu Çalışmaları', in Özme, A. (ed), *42. Uluslararası Kazı, Araştırma Ve Arkeometri Sempozyumu 42. Kazi Sonuçlari Toplantisi Cilt 1* (Ankara) 493-512

Skaltsa, S. (2019) 'A Place for Honours? Honorific Practices and Culture in the Bath-*Gymnasium* Complex in Roman Salamis', in Rogge, S., Ioannou, C., and Mavrojannis, T. (eds), *Salamis of Cyprus: History and Archaeology from the Earliest Times to Late Antiquity* (Göttingen: Waxman) 659-677

Smith, R. R. R. (2014) *Ancient Theatres of Anatolia* (Istanbul: Ege Yayinlari)

Sommerstein, A. H. (2010) *The Tangled Ways of Zeus and Other Studies in and around Greek Tragedy* (Oxford: Oxford University Press)

Spawforth, A. J. S. (2012) *Greece and the Augustan Cultural Revolution* (Cambridge: Cambridge University Press)

Speidel, M. A. (1992) 'Roman Army Pay Scales', *The Journal of Roman Studies* 82, 87-106

Starkey, J. (2018) 'The Origin and Purpose of the Three-Actor Rule', *TAPA* 148.2, 269-297

Stewart, D. (2013) '"Most Worth Remembering": Pausanias, Analogy, and Classical Archaeology', *Hesperia* 82.2, 231-261

Stewart, D. (2014) 'Rural Sites in Roman Greece', *Archaeological Reports* 60, 117-132

Stillwell, R. (1961) 'Kourion: The Theater', *Proceedings of the American Philosophical Society* 105.1, 37-78

Streinu, M. C. (2021) 'Buildings for Gladiatorial Fights in the Roman Black Sea Provinces', in Tsetskhladze, G. G., Avram, A. and Hargrave, J. (eds), *The Greeks and Romans in the Black Sea and the Importance of the Pontic Region for the Graeco Roman World (7th century BC–5th century AD): 20 Years On (1997-2017) Proceedings of the Sixth International Congress on Black Sea Antiquities (Constanta–18-22 September 2017)* (Oxford: Archaeopress Publishing) 337-341

Streinu, M. C. (2023) 'Gladiators in Caria: An Overview', *Bollettino dell'Associazione Iasos di Caria* 29, 11-25

Strootman, R. (2023) 'Chapter 11 "The Glory of Alexander and Philip Made Spoil by Roman Arms": the Triumph of Aemilius Paullus in 167 BCE', in de Jong, I. J. F., and Versluys, M. J. (eds), *Reading Greek and Hellenistic-Roman Spolia: Objects, Appropriation and Cultural Change* (Leiden: Brill) 189-214

Styhler-Aydin, G. (2015) 'The Hellenistic Theatre of Ephesus: Results of a Recent Architectural Invesitigation of the Koilon', in Frederiksen, R., Gebhard, E. R., and Sokolicek, A. (eds), *The Architecture of the Ancient Greek Theatre* (Aarhus: Aarhus University Press) 419-432

Taeuber, H. (2014) 'Einblicke in die Privatsphäre. Die Evidenz der Graffiti aus dem Hanghaus 2 in Ephesos', in Eck, W., and Funke, P. (eds), *Vol 4 Öffentlichkeit–Monument–Text: XIV Congressus Internationalis Epigraphiae Graecae et Latinae. 27.-31. Augusti MMXII. Akten* (Berlin: De Gruyter) 487-489

Taplin, O. (1992) *Homeric Soundings: The Shaping of the Iliad* (Oxford: Clarendon Press)

Tatum, W. J. (2024) *A Noble Ruin: Mark Antony, Civil War, and the Collapse of the Roman Republic* (Oxford: Oxford University Press)

Thompson, T. J. U., Errickson, D., McDonnell, C., Holst, M., Caffell, A., Pearce, J., and Gowland, R. L. (2025) 'Unique Osteological Evidence for Humananimal Gladiatorial Combat in Roman Britain', *PlOS ONE* 20.4 1-19

Thonemann, P. (2015) 'Heroic Onomastics in Roman Anatolia', *Historia: Zeitschrift für Alte Geschichte* 64.3, 357-385

Toner, J. (2014) 'Trends in the Study of Roman Spectacle and Sport', in Christesen, P., and Kyle, D. G. (eds), *Sport and Spectacle in Greek and Roman Antiquity* (Malden MA: Blackwell Publishing) 451-462

Tsontchev, D. (1947) *Contributions à l'histoire du stade antique de Philippopolis. Materiaux pour l'histoire de Plovdiv, vol 2.* (Sofia: Edition de la Municipalitate de Plovdiv)

Vagalinksi, L. F. (2009) *Blood and Entertainments: Sports and Gladiatorial Games in Hellenistic and Roman Thrace* (Sofia: NOUS Publishers)

Van Wees, H. (1994) 'The Homeric Way of War: The *Iliad* and the Hoplite Phalanx', *Greece & Rome* 41.2, 131-155

Velichkov, Z. (2016) The Amphitheatre of Serdica, Sofia, Bulgaria', in Wilmott, T. (ed), *Roman Amphitheatres and Spectacula: a 21st-Century perspective – Papers from an International Conference held at Chester, 16th-18th February, 2007* (Oxford: BAR Publishing) 119-126

Vickers, M. (1971) 'The Stadium at Thessaloniki', *Byzantion* 41, 339-348

Vickers, M. (1972) 'The Hippodrome at Thessaloniki', *The Journal of Roman Studies* 62, 25-32

Vismara, C., and Caldelli, M. L. (2001) *Epigrafia anfiteatrale dell'Occidente Romano V. Alpes Maritimae, Gallia Narbonensis, Tres Galliae, Germaniae, Britannia* (Rome: Edizione Quasar)

Waelkens, M., Poblome, J., and De Rynck P. (2011) *Sagalassos: City of Dreams* (Ghent: Openbaar Kunstbezit Vlaanderen)

Wallace-Hadrill, A. (1982) 'Civilis Princeps: Between Citizen and King', *Journal of Roman Studies* 72, 32-48

Wallace-Hadrill, A. (1990) 'Roman Arches and Greek Honours: The Language of Power at Rome', *Proceedings of the Cambridge Philological Society* 36, 143-181

Welch, K. (1994) 'The Roman Arena in Late Republican Italy: A New Interpretation', *Journal of Roman Archaeology* 7, 59-80

Welch, K. (1998a) 'Greek Stadia and Roman Spectacles: Asia, Athens and the Tomb of Herodes Atticus', *Journal of Roman Archaeology* 11, 117-145

Welch, K. (1998b) 'The Stadium at Aphrodisias', *American Journal of Archaeology* 102.3, 547-569

Welch, K. (2001) 'Recent Work on Amphitheatre Architecture and Arena Spectacles', *Journal of Roman Archaeology* 14, 492-8

Welch, K. (2007) *The Roman Amphitheatre from its Origins to the Colosseum* (Cambridge: Cambridge University Press)

Wiedemann, T. (1992) *Emperors and Gladiators* (London: Routledge)

Wilmott, T., and Garner, D. (2018) *The Roman Amphitheatre at Chester: The Prehistoric and Roman Archaeology* (Oxford: Oxbow Books)

Woolf, G. (1994) 'Becoming Roman, Staying Greek: Culture, Identity and the Civilising Process in the Roman East', *Proceedings of the Cambridge Philological Society* 40, 116-143

Worthington, I. (2021) *Athens After Empire: A History from Alexander the Great to the Emperor Hadrian* (Oxford: Oxford University Press)

Yiannakis, T. B., and Yiannakis, S. T (2007) 'The Meaning of Names in Greek Antiquity, with Special Reference to Olympic Athletes', *The International Journal of the History of Sport* 15.3, 103-114

Yurtsever, A. (2018) 'Gladiator-Themed Artefacts in the Side Museum', in Aurenhammer, M. (ed), *Sculpture in Roman Asia Minor Proceedings of the International Conference at Selçuk* (Vienna: Holzhausen)67-78

Zachos, N. (2016) 'The Stadium of Actian Nicopolis: Observations on Dating and Architectural Evolution', in Lamprinoudakis, V., Ohnesorg, A., Semantone-Bournia, E. and Zambas, C. (eds), *Architekton: Timetikos Tomos Gia Ton Kathegete Manole Korre* (Athens: Melissa) 541-522

Zekioglu, A., and Kalkan, N. (2019) 'Anatolian Cultural Heritage: Ancient Stadiums Related to Sport or Physical Culture?', *Universal Journal of Educational Research* 7.1, 106-110

Notes

1. Our key source for the festival is Polybius, a Greek from Arcadia who was himself held hostage in Rome for seventeen years following the Battle of Pydna in 168 BCE. There, he tutored the sons of the general who had successfully led the Roman army at that battle, Aemilus Paullus. One of the general's sons was Scipio Aemilianus, who had fought ferociously at Pydna aged just seventeen. This is the Scipio who would later win the Third Punic War and raze the great city of Carthage to the ground in 146 BCE. Polybius remained close to Scipio and accompanied him to Carthage, witnessing the slaughter first hand. These experiences prompted Polybius to write his *Histories*, an account of exactly how Rome managed to conquer the Mediterranean in such an astonishingly short amount of time.

2. The key aim of this particular clause was surely the capture of Hannibal Barca, great enemy of Rome and a friend and advisor to Antiochus III after he had been expelled from Carthage. Hannibal was able to escape to Crete before Antiochus could surrender him to Rome.

3. Allies of Rome who called in military favours soon found there was a price to pay afterwards. 'Liberation' from the hegemony of one empire simply led to Rome calling in reciprocating 'favours', which similarly limited their freedom.

4. Appian states that the Romans had cause for alarm, worried that the recently defeated Macedonians and Carthaginians may join the Seleukids as a form of revenge, dragging Rome into an extended war it was unlikely to win: *The Syrian Wars* IX.15.

5. Appian, *The Syrian Wars* XI.3.

6. Antiochus was well aware of the Roman policy to quell disruptions in the eastern Mediterranean and then withdraw, leaving a network of grateful clients behind.

7. Livy, 45.34.

8. See Taylor, (2020) and Devereaux, (2022).

9. An anabasis was a military expedition heading inland from the coast. The most famous example is Xenophon's account of Cyrus the Younger's Army of 10,000 and their campaign route from Asia Minor into Mesopotamia in 401 BCE.

10. The bronze shield bearers, the *chalkaspides*, are numbered in Polybius' account of the parade. The text has not been transmitted in its entirety, and so the number of silver shield bearers, the *argyraspides*, is lost. Elsewhere (5.79.4), Polybius suggests that the majority of a 10,000 strong unit at the Battle of Raphia were *argyraspides*, and so a number of at least 5,000 to equal the *chalkaspides* is plausible.

11. Horace, *Epistles* 2.1.

12. Latium is the region of the Italian peninsula in which Rome was founded, hence their language being called Latin.

13. See Chapters 13 and 15.

14. Chrubasik and King, (2017) 3.

15. Banducci, (2014).

16. Livy, 9.40.17; Strabo, 5.4.13; Silvius Italicus, *Punica* 11/51–4.

17. Livy, *Periochae* 16.

18. There is a modicum of confusion in the identity of the deceased; see Futrell, (1997) 20–22 for further discussion.

19. Valerius Maximus, *Facta et Dicta Memorabilia* 2.4.7.

20. Ausonius, *Griphus* 36–7.

21. Servius, *Ad Aeneid* 3.67.10–14.

22. Dunkle, (2008) 10–11.

23. Polybius, *Histories* 3.107.

24. Livy, *Ab Urbe Condita* 22.49.

25. Livy, 22.56.

26. Goldsworthy, (2001) 159.

27. Livy, 22.57.

28. Livy, 22.57.

29. Livy, 31.50.

30. Livy, 39.46.

31. His descendant, Marcus Licinius Crassus, of the Triumvirate with Caesar and Pompey, would also be famed for his wealth.

32. Livy, 41.28.

33. Polybius, 31.28.

34. Diodorus, 31.25.

35. A talent weighed approximately 32kg of pure silver each. The planned show would cost the equivalent of nearly ten tonnes of pure silver.

36. Terence, *Hecyra* Second Prologue.

37. Pliny the Elder, *Natural History* 35.33.

38. Plutarch, *Life of Gaius Gracchus* 12.

39. Valleius Paterculus, *The Roman History* 2.43.

40. Crassus, whose brother and father had been killed in Marius' own proscriptions of 87 BCE, gleefully aided his mentor Sulla in handling the

confiscation of the properties of the murdered Marian allies. The wealth he accrued from this kickstarted Crassus' path to becoming the richest man in Rome. Despite coming up on opposing sides of this conflict, Crassus was savvy enough to bankroll Caesar's early career for their mutual benefit.

41. Suetonius, *Life of Julius Caesar* 1.
42. Suetonius, *Life of Julius Caesar* 10. This was to be the beginning of a bitter rivalry between the two, who would share magistracies on multiple occasions. Later, when the pair shared the consulship, Bibulus tried to block one of Caesar's proposed laws. In response, one of Caesar's armed gang of thugs assaulted Bibulus in the Forum and he was pelted with faeces. Bibulus begged onlookers to kill him to spare him his embarrassment, and he spent the remaining eight months of their consulship agoraphobic, refusing to leave his house (Plutarch, *Life of Cato the Younger* 32.1-2; *Life of Pompey Magnus* 48.2-3).
43. Suetonius, *Life of Julius Caesar* 10.
44. Plutarch, *Life of Julius Caesar* 5.
45. Cicero, *Pro Sestio* 133–135; *In Vatinium* 37. An exception was allowed if the will of the deceased had specified a date for funerary games.
46. Known as the 'Vettius Affair', both Cicero and some modern scholars agree that the plot was a fabrication designed to scare an assortment of politicians.
47. Cassius Dio, 39.7.
48. Ironically, immediately before and after his assassination in 44 BCE, his assassins protected themselves with a troupe of their own gladiators.
49. Goldsworthy, (2006) 345.
50. Östenberg, (2022) 47–48.
51. Cassius Dio, 44.7.
52. Cassius Dio, 54.2.
53. His *Histories* essentially founded both the discipline of historical study and historical writing as a genre; previously events had been baldly noted in the lists of chronicles and records. Herodotus was the first to add context, attempting to answer *why* events unfolded as they did, and why people acted as they had done. In fact, *Historiai* is better translated as '*Inquiries*'.
54. Eratosthenes was astoundingly accurate, with a margin of error of less than 1 per cent.
55. Pausanias, 10.4.1.
56. Not that Greek cities were shy in rebelling when their autonomy was threatened, e.g. the Ionian Revolt, the Mytilenean Revolt, the War of the Allies and the Asiatic Vespers.

57. Respecting the individual autonomy of weaker cities in a league was not always put into practice, though a city may consider a degree of loss of control preferable to being without allies.

58. Once Athens' importance had waned in the fourth century, it ceased wishing to connect to the mythical past and turned its attention to trading on its fifth century BCE reputation for the remainder of antiquity.

59. Plutarch, *Life of Cimon* 8.

60. Herodotus, 1.67.

61. The Greek soldiers from Mantinea, Tegea, Orchomenus, Corinth, Phlius, Mycenae, Thespiae, Malis, Thebes, Phokis and Lokris are usually not mentioned, but also fought hard at Thermopylae. The idea that 300 Spartans fought alone is a myth.

62. Annual tributes were significant sums that, whilst carefully calculated to not bankrupt an ally entirely, were only feasibly affordable to local kings and oligarchies. Radical democracy, then, was only introduced when the wealthy oligarchs threatened not to pay up and revolt.

63. The speeches collectively became known as the *Philippics*, and Cicero later used the name for his own speeches denouncing Mark Antony.

64. No historian, ancient nor modern, can be certain as to the motive behind Philip's murder.

65. It should be noted that despite framing himself as 'liberator of the Greek cities', several cities in Asia Minor attempted to resist Alexander's invasion, preferring to stay in the frying pan lest they fall into the fire. In the end, resistance was futile.

66. When Marcus Licinius Crassus died at the Battle of Carrhae, his Parthian invasion failed miserably. Crassus' severed head was brought to the Parthian king Orodes II. The head was presented to him at a wedding and thrown into the centre of the banqueting room. A famous actor named Jason of Tralleis just happened to be reciting a scene from Euripides' *Bacchae*, in which a crazed Theban princess named Agave tears the head from her son Pentheus and parades it around. Jason, thinking quickly, grabbed the head of Crassus and used it as a prop as he recited the line: 'We bring down from the mountain this branch to the palace: a wonderful prey!' Plutarch, *Life of Crassus* 33. This story is perhaps exaggerated, and, in my opinion, Jason of Tralleis need not have been performing the *Bacchae* for the joke to work: merely quoting this line, which was famous in antiquity, would have had the desired effect. Either way, Plutarch expects the Parthian king and his court to appreciate the joke because they were clearly familiar with its context.

67. 'Punic' from *Poenus*, a Latin word derived from the Greek *phoinix* meaning 'Phoenician'. Carthage was believed to have been founded as a colony of the Phoenician city of Tyre.
68. Polybius, 25.3.
69. Polybius, 22.18.
70. Appian, *Syrian Wars* 10.
71. Pausanias, 7.14.
72. Polybius, 38.9.
73. Polybius, 38.15-16.
74. Polybius, who claims to have been present at the massacre and razing of the city, is too preoccupied with the ignorant destruction of Greek art to focus on the human suffering caused by Rome: Polybius, 39.13.
75. Cicero, *Letters to Atticus* I.19.10.
76. This method of death is apocryphally given to Crassus after the Battle of Carrhae, though it should be noted that in Crassus' instance the sources are less robust.
77. Lucullus' time in Asia spared him witnessing his mentor's viciousness during the protracted civil war firsthand.
78. Plutarch, *Life of Lucullus* 4.1.
79. During this period, his colleague in Asia, Murena, was not so careful and foolishly started a second war with Mithridates in which Lucullus was not involved.
80. This was the third time that a kingdom had been bequeathed to Rome. First Pergamon in 133 BCE, which allowed the Romans to form Asia as a province. Then Cyrenaica in 96BCE by Ptolemy Apion, but Rome showed little interest in it until 74 BCE, when it was officially granted provincial status.
81. Plutarch, *Life of Lucullus* 7.
82. More moderate estimates suggest five to one.
83. Plutarch, *Life of Lucullus* 18; Appian, *The Mithridatic Wars* 12.18.
84. Plutarch, *Life of Lucullus* 35.
85. Philip V received a harsh assessment from Polybius (an Achaean) which should not be taken entirely at face value; see Nicholson (2023). He seems to have been certainly no worse than his royal Hellenistic peers, or indeed, the Romans he fought.
86. Plutarch, *Life of Aemilius Paullus* 28.
87. Appian, *The Mithridatic Wars* 62–63.
88. It must be noted that while Lucullus may have been kind to culturally Greek cities in Asia Minor, he had no such empathy with non-Greek cities during his campaigns.
89. Keaveney, (1992) 97.

90. Plutarch, *Life of Lucullus* 23.
91. The term 'Lucullan' is still used today to describe particularly extravagant dining.
92. Plutarch, *Life of Lucullus* 23.
93. Livy, 28.21.
94. Futrell, (1997) 47.
95. Appian, *The Iberian Wars* 33; Livy, 28.22.
96. Livy, 41.20.13: '*gladiatorum munus, Romanae consuetudinis, primo maiore cum terrore hominum, insuetorum ad tale spectaculum, quam voluptate dedit; deinde saepius dando et modo volneribus tenus, modo sine missione, etiam familiare oculis gratumque id spectaculum fecit, et armorum studium plerisque iuvenum accendit. Itaque qui primo ab Roma magnis pretiis paratos gladiatores accersere solitus erat, iam suo ....*' – 'a gladiatorial exhibition, after the Roman fashion, he presented which was at first received with greater terror than pleasure on the part of men who were unused to such sights; then by frequent repetitions, by sometimes allowing the fighters to go only as far as wounding one another, sometimes permitting them to fight without giving quarter, he made the sight familiar and even pleasing, and he roused in many of the young men a joy in arms. And so, while at first he had been accustomed to summoning gladiators from Rome, procuring them by large fees, finally he could find a sufficient supply at home ....' (trans. Sage and Schlesinger, 1938, Loeb Classical Library).
97. Plutarch. *Life of Lucullus* 33.
98. Cicero, *Letters to Atticus* 6.1.
99. Sills, (20 25).
100. Suetonius, *Life of Julius Caesar* 4; Plutarch, *Life of Julius Caesar* 1–2.
101. Suetonius, *Life of Julius Caesar* 4.
102. Caesar, *The Civil Wars* 3.102.
103. Interestingly, at this point Lucan inserts a fictitious day trip for Caesar to 'the ruins of Troy' (much of the city was still inhabited at the time and its older buildings were a popular tourist attraction) in his epic civil war poem *Pharsalia*. This is important, as the vignette demonstrates the continuing popularity and cultural significance of Homeric 'history' and ancient warrior heroes. Also of note, Alexander the Great was known to have visited the site. Lucan had reasons for drawing comparisons between the two men, but for our purposes we should note the enduring legacy of the *Iliad* amongst educated Romans.
104. Plutarch, *Life of Caesar* 47.
105. Plutarch, *Life of Caesar* 48.
106. Caesar had already extended a hand of friendship to many senators who had fought against him at Pharsalus, including one Marcus Junius Brutus.

107. Some notably more literally than others ….

108. Alexandria was founded by Macedonians, and remained a staunchly Hellenistic city with a primarily Greek population.

109. Cicero, *De Rege* Alexandrino: see Scullard (first published 1959), Chapter 6.1 for more context.

110. Son of Mithridates VI, and clearly more amenable to Rome than his father.

111. The same route used by Antiochus IV on his own route to Alexandria as mentioned in Chapter 1.

112. The choice not to annex Egypt at this point was likely because Cleopatra relied so heavily on Caesar for her rank, which made her a far safer ally to him personally than a rival Roman installed as governor.

113. The flotilla of 400 ships mentioned by Appian in *The Civil Wars* 2.90 suggests that the voyage was far more business than pleasure; the rest of Egypt was being firmly shown who was now in control.

114. See Worthington, (2021) Chapters 10–11.

115. Appian, *The Civil Wars* 2.88.

116. For example, the stoas of Eumenes II of Pergamum and Attalus II of Pergamum in Athens, and Antiochus IV's cash injection to continue the massive Temple of Olympian Zeus there.

117. By this point, the Romans had had significant interactions with Greeks, particularly in Magna Graecia, and were beginning to absorb some aspects of Greek political thought and custom, while discarding other aspects with performative disdain. See Wallace-Hadrill, (1990).

118. See Wallace-Hadrill, (1982).

119. *CIL* 1² 1529.

120. Worthington, (2021) 225.

121. Cicero, *Letters to Atticus* 6.1.25.

122. Appius Claudius Pulcher had served under his brother-in-law Lucullus in the Third Mithridatic War, and his brusque manner with foreign kings was a significant cause of Tigranes of Armenia declaring war on Rome. His proconsulship was served in Cilicia, where he was particularly corrupt. Appius was there when his younger brother Clodius was murdered on the Appian Way.

123. Clinton, (1997) 164–5.

124. Cicero, *Letters to Atticus* 6.1.26.

125. Caesar, *The Alexandrian War* 70. This accusation doesn't appear in other sources, and should perhaps be considered a xenophobic example of a Caesarian smear campaign against a foreign enemy.

126. Appian, *The Civil Wars* 3.77.

127. Caesar did indeed continue his Parthian plans, mobilising around sixteen legions in 44 BCE in anticipation for a three-year campaign. He was assassinated three days before he was due to depart for the east.

128. The vast influx of Greek art and enslaved people had a profound impact on the city of Rome: it became the very height of fashion to own Greek antiquities, and Roman artisans started mass producing copies of the Greek masterpieces brought into the city.

129. It would be separated from Macedonia in 27 BCE, becoming the new Roman province known as Achaea.

130. Archaeological evidence attests that the site was never completely abandoned. See Romano, (2000).

131. Romano, (2005).

132. His grandfather (also Marcus Antonius) had waged such a successful campaign against pirates as governor of Cilicia that he'd been awarded a naval triumph. His father (another Marcus Antonius) had continued this campaign, though he had died in Crete having achieved little more than ransacking the island.

133. Cassius Dio, 49.41.

134. Suetonius, *Life of Augustus* 68.

135. Plutarch, *Life of Antony* 56.

136. All significant wills of Roman citizens were deposited at the Temple of Vesta for safekeeping.

137. Plutarch, *Life of Antony* 58; Suetonius, *Life of Augustus* 17.

138. Cassius Dio, 50.4.

139. Plutarch, *Life of Antony* 59; Cassius Dio, 50.4.

140. Plutarch, *Life of Antony* 69.

141. Plutarch, *Life of Antony* 68.

142. Cassius Dio, 51.7.

143. Plutarch, *Life of Antony* 72.

144. cf. Cassius Dio, 10–11; Plutarch, *Life of Antony* 76–77; Strabo, *Geography* 17.10.

145. A title that Augustus refused to use himself, preferring *Princeps*: 'First Amongst Citizens'.

146. Anyone wishing to stage their own gladiatorial games must now jump through several hoops to do so, including gaining permission from the Senate. Each of these Games was restricted to a mere 120 gladiators, quite modest by this point: Cassius Dio, *History of Rome* 54.2.4.

147. Augustus, *Res Gestae Divi Augusti* 1.1.

148. Whether or not Antony ever wanted to be more than a prominent Roman with significant powers in eastern provinces is debated. See Tatum, (2024) 325–6.

149. *Venationes* had not yet been coupled up with gladiators.
150. Augustus, *Res Gestae Divi Augusti* 23.1; Suetonius, *Augustus* 43; Cassius Dio, *History of Rome* 55.10.7–8.
151. Augustus, *Res Gestae Divi Augusti* 22.1.
152. See Spawforth, (2012) 31–32; and Woolf (1994).
153. The flow of people was by no means a one-way system of west to east, as even more Greeks came to the west to take up roles as educators, artists etc.
154. Meaning 'First Citizen', Augustus staunchly refused to call himself an emperor.
155. See Ritti and Yilmaz, (1998) 469–479.
156. Stones are often found recycled as building blocks in more recent buildings.
157. Carter, (1999), 167.
158. Carter, (1999) 145.
159. An excellent example of this is a large inscription from Ancyra (modern Ankara) on the Temple of Augustus and Roma (*IGR* IV 157) which records a list of *philotimiai* given by successive priests. Some chose gladiatorial games, (the earliest in around 30 CE, in the reign of Tiberius), but some chose public banquets or similar alternatives.
160. While much of ancient society is not to be emulated, perhaps the idea that the ultrawealthy in a society should share their wealth with the populace rather than hoard it is one that we should take another crack at in the twenty-first century.
161. Cicero, *Pro Murena* 40.
162. Seneca, *Epistles* 7.3–5, trans. Gummere.
163. Seneca, *Epistles* 76.2, trans. Gummere.
164. Robert, (1940) 263.
165. Dio Chrysostom, *The Rhodian Oration* 121–122, trans. Cohoon & Crosby.
166. See Chapter 11.
167. See Chapter 13.
168. There is no fixed date for this speech, and while Rhodes was a free city exempt from Roman interference most of the time, it did lose this status several times in Dio Chrysostom's lifetime. It is not clear if the city was free at the time of the speech, or even if this speech was delivered in one part on one occasion.
169. Philostratus, *Life of Apollonius Tyana* 4.22, trans. Jones.
170. See Chapter 13.
171. Hägg, (2012) 299.
172. Lucian, *Demonax* 57, trans. Harmon.
173. Pausanias 1.17.1.

174. Putting on a full-scale day of spectacle more than once a year (i.e. per term) would have bankrupted the average official, but having a single show per year likely added to the excitement on the day of the actual games.
175. This is not to say that the Roman establishment didn't benefit; making euergetism a function of the imperial cult ensured that the emperor was constantly associated with benevolence, albeit by proxy.
176. *SEG* 50.1096.
177. Reynolds, (2000).
178. Coleman, (2008).
179. There is indeed a 25km aqueduct that was subsequently built in Aphrodisias, known as the Timeles Aqueduct, whose ruins are still visible today. See Comitto and Rojas, (2012).
180. Gospel of Matthew 2.16–18.
181. Josephus, *Antiquities* 16.5.3.
182. See Chapter 15.
183. Josephus, *Antiquities* 15.268–77, 16.137–41.
184. Sills, (2025).
185. Tacitus, *Annals* 14.17.
186. For instance, a record of the year 354 CE called the Chronography of Philocalus specifies that 176 days in the calendar were devoted to various entertainments. That year, chariots raced on 64 days, plays were staged on 102, but gladiatorial displays were only staged over ten days in the entire year. These statistics are perhaps explained by the comparable cost of each form of entertainment.
187. Suetonius, *Life of Augustus* 44.
188. The carved barriers from the amphitheatre of Capua, on display in a museum on site, are a particularly beautiful example.
189. Bomgardner, (2000) 13.
190. For a more detailed discussion, see Kolendo, (1981).
191. The Colosseum had eighty entrances: four for VIPS and seventy-six for everyone else.
192. Gutierrez, Frischer, Cirizo, Gomez and Seron, (2007) 184.
193. Pliny the Elder, *Natural History* 8.2.
194. Thompson et al, (2025).
195. Larsen and Letteney, (2025).
196. Suetonius, *Life of Claudius* 34.
197. Martial, *Liber Spectaculorum* 31.
198. Cassius Dio, 73.19.
199. Some theories suffer from the sensibilities of the authors being allowed to cloud their scholarship, and so are of little value. See Chapter 6.

200. For further discussion, see Chapter 6.
201. See Cowan and Parkin (eds), (2023).
202. It should be noted that the ancient and modern uses of the word 'virtue' are indeed related but not the same.
203. Note that this applies to men only – *vir* means 'man'.
204. Mark Antony, for instance, was unashamed of his love affair with the actress Cytheris.
205. Gunderson, (1996).
206. Not without reason: Rome was sacked by the Gauls in 390 CE, the Visigoths in 410 CE, the Vandals in 455 CE, and the Ostrogoths in 546 and 549 CE.
207. Global Estimates on Modern Slavery suggest that 50 million people were enslaved in 2021, and that this number is rising.
208. The availability of execution videos on the 'dark web' means that executions are still very much a public affair.
209. Gladiators in Rome were trained in the *Ludus Aemilius* in the triumviral period owned by the *triumvir Lepidus*, and later in the *Ludus Magnus, Ludus Dacicus* and *Ludus Gallicus* built by Domitian.
210. We have enough evidence for the (common law) wives and children of gladiators to suggest that some were allowed to live independently as they progressed the career ladder.
211. Livy, 9.40.
212. Junkelmann, (2022) 68.
213. Carter, (2006).
214. Marcus Aurelius, the big softie, is recorded as making sure that the weapons were blunted in every fight under his rule (161–180 CE) according to Cassius Dio 72.29.
215. IK, *Ephesos* 1177, Kontokosta (2008, 17) and Carlsen (2014, 448) respectively.
216. Van Wees, (1994) 144.
217. Kanz et al, (2009) 216.
218. Gladiators trained with wooden facsimile weapons, and may have used leather or no armour in the *ludus*.
219. The potential is there: even extensively studied sites like Aphrodisias and Ephesus have acres and acres of unexcavated land. Uncovering an entire city, even one not impeded by modern construction, takes many, many decades.
220. Bishop, (2016) 54.
221. Potter, (1999) 314.
222. Vegetius, *De Re Militari* 1.12.
223. Junkelmann, (2000).

224. Scarborough, (2013) 102.
225. I'm looking at you, Kit Harington in *Pompeii* (2014).
226. Lösch et al, (2014) 13.
227. Pliny, *Natural History* 36.69.
228. It is worth mentioning that not every *ludus* followed the practice. Gladiators from the only other confirmed gladiator cemetery (in York, UK) had normal strontium levels, suggesting no prolonged use of such a drink.
229. Pliny, *Natural History* 18.14, trans. Rackham.
230. Galen, *On the Nature of Foodstuffs* 1.19.
231. Sills, (2023).
232. Kanz and Grossschmidt, (2002).
233. His involvement explains why the British Museum has more of the Mausoleum than Bodrum does, with more artefacts than they can display at any one time.
234. Pausanias, 2.22.3.
235. Newton, (1863) 369.
236. Mandel, (1988) 193.
237. Mandel, (1988) 172.
238. Kielau, (2018).
239. Kasapoğlu, (2018).
240. An image that will be familiar to all parents, even if the context gives pause; however, modern toy shops stock action figures of superheroes, soldiers and characters from well-known sci-fi epics, which are arguably just as violent as an ancient child playing with a gladiator doll.
241. A similar volcanic eruption preserved Thera on the Greek island of Santorini, but long before the period we are discussing.
242. See Chapters 13 and 15.
243. The second is in York, UK.
244. See Chapter 5.
245. Taeuber, (2014) 488.
246. In late antiquity, Christians repurposed basilicas as large churches, and built new churches using the same architectural form and keeping the name. In the period we are discussing, basilicas had no sacred purpose.
247. Bagnall et al., (2016) 25.
248. Ibid. 36.
249. To use Pompeii as a comparison once again, adverts for upcoming games were painted onto external walls on the streets, not inside public buildings. They also featured text written by professional sign writers, but no images.
250. Sayar, (2018) 182.

251. An excellent example of the 'unswept floor' genre is on display in the Vatican Museums.

252. Robert, (1940) 36–37.

253. Livy, 7.2.

254. See Sear, (2006) 54-57 for further discussion.

255. Dionysius of Halicarnassus, *Roman Antiquities* 7.72.1–3, 7.73.1–3; Livy, *History of Rome* 39.22.1–2; Polybius 30.22.2.

256. Welch, (2007) 32-35.

257. Welch, (2007) 49-51, figs. 21 and 22.

258. Welch, (2007) 56-7.

259. Suetonius, *Life of Julius Caesar* 39.

260. Cassius Dio, 43.23.

261. Cassius Dio, 51.23. *Praetors* were magistrates of considerable power and prestige and were typically elected by the Comitia Centuriata. Allowing Taurus to choose a *praetor* every year in perpetuity was a considerable demonstration of respect.

262. Welch, (2007) 109–110, 116.

263. Augustus, *Res Gestae* 22; Suetonius, *Life of Tiberius* 7.1.

264. Suetonius, *Life of Nero* 31. Future emperors were savvy enough to construct their own estates far from the city, such as Hadrian's vast complex at Tivoli and Diocletian's at Split.

265. Welch, (2007) 156-7

266. This villa was subsequently filled with rubble by Trajan, to form a platform on which to build his bathing complex. Ironically, in burying the last vestiges of Nero's *Domus Aurea*, Trajan inadvertently preserved them for posterity. Sections of the subterranean remains are now open to visitors and offer a tantalising glimpse of the true majesty of the Golden House.

267. The Circus Maximus could seat a quarter of the population in comparison, with 250,000 seats.

268. Referring to Nero as a king was a great insult. Romans had held monarchy with great disdain since the expulsion of their last king in 509 BCE, and ever since men in power had taken extreme care to avoid appearing regal. Julius Caesar, as rumours of his ambitions to rule alone swirled, arranged for some play acting during the Lupercalia festival. Mark Antony was to publicly offer him a crown with laurel branches woven around it. What followed was interesting; Plutarch (*Life of Julius Caesar* 61.1-10) reports that the crowd's response was lukewarm, but that cheers erupted when Caesar refused to accept the crown. Antony once again tried to offer the crown to a smattering of applause, only for the crowd to go wild when Caesar once again refused it. Some have interpreted this as a contrived attempt by Caesar to downplay his ambitions to the populace, but

Plutarch also notes that statues of Caesar had also been decorated with crowns that day, and that two tribunes who had torn the crowns down had been hailed as Brutuses, after the man who had expelled Tarquin the Proud. This addition suddenly suggests that Caesar and Antony had rather been hoping that the crowd would approve of him *accepting* a crown. Either way, the damage was done. A mere month later, Caesar was stabbed twenty-three times by a group of tyrannophobic senators, including one Marcus Junius Brutus. Rome may have morphed into an empire, but emperors remained careful not to refer to themselves as kings, or even emperors. Their preferred term *imperator* was a pre-existing term that merely became exclusive after Augustus and meant 'commander'.

269. Historia Augusta, *Life of Hadrian* 19.
270. Richardson, (1992) 94.
271. Vagalinski (2009), 111–12.
272. Popova (2017), 58.
273. Popova (2017), 75.
274. Most of these are found in Campania, which makes a lot of sense: Campanians had never felt quite as strongly as the Etruscans that gladiators should be reserved for funerals, and their enthusiasm for combat as entertainment predated that of the Romans. Campania, a region rich in volcanic tufa stone and pozzolana, a volcanic ash that makes superlative cement, were not carved out of rock. Katherine Welch has noted that their modest average size is a parallel of the wooden *spectacula* arenas built with wood in the Forum Romanum (2007, 192). With their pretty facing on external walls, it is likely that the Campanian amphitheatres looked a little fancier than Corinth's, though without excavation at Corinth we cannot know.
275. See Romano, (2005).
276. See Chapter 13.
277. Malalas, *Chronographia* 13.39.
278. Malalas, *Chronographia* 9.5.
279. See Stewart, (2014).
280. See Stewart, (2013).
281. Gallimore, (2015) 114.
282. Papadopoulos et al., (2012).
283. For more on this phenomenon, see Chapter 13.
284. Hammad, (2008) 342.
285. For a tangible comparison, the Palmyra amphitheatre is just a couple of metres larger than the one at Chester.
286. Baird and Kamash, (2019).

287. Disraeli needed a British naval base close enough to defend the Suez Canal, and so negotiated for control of the entire island to be passed to Britain from the Ottoman Empire.

288. During partitioning of the Ottoman empire following its defeat in the First World War, both Greece and Turkish nationalists fought a war over control of Asia Minor. During this time, the Turkish carried out genocides of Greek and Armenian residents of Anatolia, while Greek forces also carried out massacres of civilians. At the war's conclusion, the Republic of Turkey was founded and the two nations agreed to a massive population exchange, each ethnically cleansing the minorities from their territories. Nearly two million people were forcibly removed from their homes, and sent to live in places they had never even visited before.

289. Karageorghis, (1969) 196.

290. Kantiréa, (2019) 579.

291. Skaltsa, (2019) 670.

292. Archaeologist Michalis Karambinis (2025) refutes this date, suggesting that Salamis' amphitheatre is actually a later adaptation that enclosed a *sphendone* of the existing stadium as is seen elsewhere in the east (see Chapter 15). While I remain unconvinced, the only way to solve the issue would be a full excavation.

293. Çoksolmaz, (2024).

294. Vitruvius, *de Architectura* 5.1.

295. *Lex Ursonensis* 70-71.

296. Livy, *Periochae* 67.

297. Valerius Maximus, *Facta et Dicta Memorabilia* 2.3.2.

298. Following the bloodbath at the Battle of Aquae Sextiae (Aix-en-Provence), Plutarch reports that the citizens of Massalia (Marseille) made fences out of the hundreds of bones from fallen warriors from the Teutones and Ambrones tribes, and that the rotting corpses of the barbarians enriched the soil so much that the region enjoyed bumper harvests for several years: *Life of Marius* 21.

299. Cicero, *Pro Caelio* 5.2, *De Oratore* 2.20.84.

300. Excellent examples can still be seen at Caerleon, Budapest, Windisch and Xanten.

301. The military frontier that roughly followed the course of the Danube river, separating the Roman empire from the Germanic barbarian tribes beyond.

302. Wilmott and Garner, (2009).

303. Projectiles from Roman *ballistae* have been found in large numbers outside the city walls, and the scars can still be seen on the walls, particularly between the Herculaneum and Vesuvius Gates.

304. Baird, (2018) 31.

305. James, (2019) 58.

306. The average audiobook recording of translations is 24 hours long, for instance.

307. For a masterful discussion of the difficulty historians have faced in dating the poems, see Dr Gainsford's blog post: 'The Dates of Homer'; https://kiwihellenist.blogspot.com/2021/11/dates-homer.html

308. Shear, (2021) 175-6.

309. Homer, *Iliad* Book 10.

310. Bacchylides, 5.

311. Themistius, 26.316d.

312. For discussion of the 'Three Actor Rule' see Starkey, (2018).

313. Herodotus, 6.21.

314. This is perhaps a simplistic view, as many scholars have argued that the play invites the Athenian audience to sympathise with the defeated Persian characters. Art truly is subjective.

315. One notable example of a trilogy is Aeschylus' *Oresteia*. The first play, *Agamemnon*, features Clytemnestra murdering her husband Agamemnon upon his return from the Trojan War, then *The Libation Bearers* skips forward a few years and focuses on Agamemnon's son Orestes murdering Clytemnestra in revenge. The final play, *Eumenides*, follows Orestes to Athens, chased by the Furies for his matricide.

316. The Choragic Monument of Lysicrates is an excellent example which can still be admired in situ, erected by Lysicrates who sponsored the winning dithyramb performance at the 335/4 BCE City Dionysia.

317. Some of the Syracusan quarries are visitable today, such as the Latomie del Paradiso which is now a peaceful public garden.

318. Plutarch, *Life of Nicias* 29.

319. Aristotle, *Rhetoric* 1403b.

320. Plutarch, *Life of the Ten Orators* 841f. Note that, already, the fifth-century peers of Aeschylus, Sophocles and Euripides (including Phynicus, Aristarchus, Agathon et al) were not granted the same honours.

321. Plutarch, *Life of Alexander* 8,2.

322. Plutarch, *Life of Alexander* 8.3.

323. Plutarch, *Life of Alexander* 29.1.

324. Plutarch, *Life of Alexander* 29.3.

325. Plutarch, *Life of Alexander* 10.6, 53.3.

326. Only fragments remain of these plays, but through literary references we know that titles include *Aegisthus*, *Andromache* and *Hector Profiscens* by Naevius, *Thyestes*, *Medea*, *Achilles* and *Ajax* by Ennius, and *Antiope*, *Atalanta*, *Chryses*, *Pentheus* and *Teaucer* by Pacuvius.

327. Sear, (2006) 31.

328. Flickinger, (1918) 112–113.

329. I suspect that there is a degree of squeamishness involved, as the killing of animals is considered easier to accept than the killing of fellow men.

330. Theatres in Sicily are the rare exceptions, though the region had deep Greek roots.

331. Interestingly, the theatre at Tauromenium (modern-day Taormina, in Sicily) has an adapted theatre that matches the changes made in West Asia, despite being hundreds of miles away. There are two important factors that explain this. First, Tauromenium was a city in Magna Graecia – the area of southern Italy and Sicily that had multiple Greek colonies and a strong Greek culture – and so culturally Tauromenium had a lot in common with the Greek mainland and West Asia. Secondly, Tauromenium was built perched high on the side of Mount Taurus, where an arena was unable to be constructed.

332. Sear, (2006) 394.

333. Velasco, (2023).

334. Photographs of the event can be found here: https://www.facebook.com/spectacvla.antiqva/posts/pfbid0o6fe JBLitxAjH63r43AfZMPffS7rV27m4RkxcmX38MaK3y9LWjNjh 94gMR5dRpoql?__cft__[0]=AZWYPJUUwBhK-IP_efggflRm LyH02CscY6B0cDDeasp8t52nxTlIFUssCnyqwJ7sLzNWGXO dWorg9ZQjcodpskA_eRX1oqOafU_ZnajiHZbRDjDs7_9EeLs BTwFkkAznfs-1-Vu_LvZumd29MvK_1q_eeNeOAubqm KBW2Yy879AWuZZi8MsX5ssyf4XwL9TxohE&__tn__=%2 CO%2CP-R

335. Sear, (2006) 179.

336. Despite what Hollywood would have you think!

337. Some *odea* have been described as adapted specifically for *venationes*, though with *podium* walls generally lower than theatre *podiums* and *podium*/parapet or *podium*/barrier adaptations, the species of beast suitable would be limited. Gladiation is therefore a more likely catalyst for such change. Similarly, there is no reason to believe that *odea* described as being adapted to form a *kolymbethra* should not have also been altered with gladiation as an additional function in mind.

338. A video of which can be found here: https://www.facebook.com/ 100009457376118/videos/921683609990755/?__tn__=%2CO-R

339. Bomgardner, (2000) 12.

340. Jola and Reason, (2016).

341. Futrell, (1997) 36-37.

342. Thucydides, *History of the Peloponnesian War* 1.8; Strabo *Geography* 7.7.1.

343. Homer, *Iliad* 16.233–248.
344. Homer, *Odyssey* 14.327–330, 19.296–299.
345. The oracle spoke via the wind whistling through the leaves of the sacred tree.
346. This time, Zeus spoke in a conveniently human voice.
347. Dionysius of Halicarnassus, *Roman Antiquities* 1.51.
348. Piccinini, (2013) 186.
349. See Chapter 15.
350. IG II2 3182.
351. Tiberius Claudius Novius may well have desired to alter the theatre to please Romans while making his changes small enough not to annoy his Athenian peers too much.
352. In other words, those who could afford to enslave people to do menial tasks and provide their owner with leisure time.
353. Whether or not this ideal was achievable by the majority of the population is debatable, just as Hollywood superhero physiques are not feasible for many modern men in the normal population.
354. These were the three main genres of competition at Olympia, though other festivals also had competitions for music, poetry recitals, acting and painting. The Panathenaic Games in Athens even had boat races.
355. Philostratus of Athens, *Gymnasticus* 21.
356. Plato, *Timaeus* 88.
357. The beginnings of the Greek obsession with nudity are difficult to ascertain; see Murray, (2022) for a compelling argument.
358. Miller, (2014) 287; Romano, (2021) 391–2.
359. Welch, (1998a) 118.
360. Dodge, (2014c) 567; Welch (1998a) 131.
361. According to Gismondi, cited in Bernard & Ciancio Rosetto, (2014) 86.
362. Cassius Dio, 79.25.
363. Bernard & Cancio Rosetto, (2014) 86.
364. Welch, (1998a).
365. Welch, (1998b).
366. Petropoulos & Pansini, (2020) 406.
367. Zachos, (2016) 547.
368. Tok and Fowler, (2005) 212.
369. For Ziller's plans, see Gasparri (1974) fig.12
370. Such as Nikanor's epitaph in near Cyzicus IK *Kyzikos* 379
371. Such as Achilleus' epitaph in Prusa (modern Bursa) IK *Prusa* 60
372. Livy suggests that the fifth king of Rome, Tarquinius Priscus, was responsible: 1.35.
373. Humphrey, (1986) 72.

374. Pliny, *Natural History* 36.24; Suetonius, *Life of Julius Caesar* 39.

375. Humphrey, (1986) 71.

376. Livy, 44.18.8.

377. Cassius Dio, 43.23.3.

378. Dodge, (2014c) 565.

379. Dodge, (2008) 135.

380. Dodge, (2014c) 565–6.

381. Josephus, *Jewish Antiquities* 19.335.

382. Dodge, (2016) 35.

383. Welch, (2007) 182, and Malalas, *Chronographia* 216-217, respectively.

384. Curvers et al., (2017) 71.

385. Josephus, *Jewish Antiquities* 19.336–7. To circumvent local laws, the 'gladiators' were condemned criminals. It is unlikely that they received gladiatorial training, as this spectacle was intended as a mass execution.

386. Curvers et al., (2017) 70–71.

387. Curvers et al., (2017) 59.

388. Josephus, *The Jewish War* 7.39–40.

389. Josephus, *The Jewish War* 7.37–38. Caesarea's canonical circus was later built under Hadrian, and a canonical amphitheatre constructed in the second or third centuries CE. See Porath, (2018) 221, and Dodge, (2016).

390. Various versions of the myth feature different rosters of champions, and not always seven in number.

391. Aeschylus, *Seven Against Thebes* 798.

392. Euripides in *Phoenician Women* (lines 1300, 1325 and 1363) and *Children of Hercules* (line 819).

393. Similarly, in comedies, sex was never simulated on stage.

394. Sommerstein. (2010) 43.

395. The gladiators named Eteokles have yet to be published in the Lexicon.

396. Robert, (1940) 245.

397. For Tydeus, see Robert, (1940) 253 (also in Smyrna). For gladiators named Melanippos see Kontokosta (2008) 12, Robert (1940) 19 and 298. For Parthenopais, see Robert, (1940) 65.

398. To determine which of the goddesses would get to keep the apple, Zeus told them to ask a mortal, the Trojan prince Paris (though Paris was unaware of his royal status at the time). Athena offered him wisdom, Hera offered him control over all Asia and Europe, and Aphrodite offered him the hand of the most beautiful woman in the world. Paris didn't vote with his head. Aphrodite failed to mention that the most beautiful woman, Helen, was already married to King Menelaus of Sparta. When Helen leaves Sparta with Paris, Menelaus prepares for war.

399. Homer never explicitly suggests a homosexual relationship, though subsequent Greek writers such as Aeschylus and Plato did. As fictional characters, I believe their relationship is open to personal interpretation.

400. The Romans were apparently familiar with the story of Aeneas prior to Virgil composing the poem in the late first century BCE, though earlier versions, such as Cato the Elder's *Origines*, are now lost.

401. The *Aeneid* finishes abruptly on the battlefield; Livy's *History of Rome* and Ovid's *Metamorphoses* continue the narrative.

402. Mann, (2011) 164.

403. See Redfield, (1975) Chapters 3–5.

404. Farron, (1978) 40–41.

405. Wilson, (2023) 722–23.

406. Details from this poem are scant, as only thirty or so lines survive and the overall synopsis has only survived when referred to in other texts. The exact method of deciding who should have the armour is lost.

407. Sophocles, *Aias* 835–844. trans. Storr.

408. Clark, (1956) 187.

409. For example, the Siphnian Treasury (northern frieze) at Delphi, the Pergamon Altar frieze, the Argive Heraion, the coffers of the Temple of Athena Polis at Priene, and the eastern metopes of the Temple of Athena at Troy.

410. For example, the southern metopes of the Parthenon, the western pediment of the Temple of Zeus at Olympia, the frieze of the Temple of Hephaestus at Athens, the metopes of the Temple of Athena at Troy, the frieze of the Temple of Zeus at Mylasa, and the metopes of the Ptolemaion at Limyra.

411. For example, the frieze of the Temple of Apollo Epikourios at Bassae, the frieze of the Temple of Artemis Magnesia-ad-Maeandrum, the frieze of the Temple of Apollo at Alabanda, and reliefs from the Mausoleum of Halicarnassus.

412. For example, the northern metopes of the Parthenon and the eastern frieze of the Siphnian Treasury at Delphi.

413. Barbantani, (2018) 284.

414. Taplin, (1992) 5.

415. *CIG* II 3765, trans. Coleman.

416. Barbantani, (2016) 190.

417. GVI 1804, trans. Barbantani.

418. Hope, (2000) 111.

419. Barbantani, (2016) 198.

420. Barbantani, (2018) 291.

421. Barbantani, (2016) 229.

422. Mann, (2011) 92–94.
423. IK *Prusa* 60.
424. Welch, (1994) 63; Cicero, *Pro Caelio* 11.
425. McClean, (2002) 10–17.
426. Cited in Golden, (2008) 70.
427. Kyle, (2015) 246. It was similarly adopted by Roman charioteers.
428. Pausanias, 8.48.3.
429. Mann, (2011) 17.
430. *IC* IV 374.
431. Mann, (2011) 170 and 177.
432. Yianakkis and Yianakki (2007) 105
433. Rizakis (2009)
434. *SEG* XVII, 599.
435. The near dehumanisation of western gladiators may have helped spectators justify watching such violent acts.
436. Gladiators were an expensive commodity for their owners, requiring bed, board, training, and equipment. For this reason, fees charged to rent them for *munera* were high, and if a gladiator died the *editor* had to remunerate the *lanista* for the gladiator's full worth. Both the *editor* and *lanista* had incentive to make sure fights ended without fatalities in all but a few matches. Where no clear victor appeared from a lengthy fight, draws were a respectable way to reward both fighters as fatigue slowed them down. Of the eleven recorded fights that survive from the fragments of a gravestone belonging to Polos, a gladiator in Gortyn, he boasts of ten wins and one draw (IC IV 375).
437. Coleman, (2000) 490.
438. Cassius Dio, 61.17.
439. Suetonius, *Life of Domitian* 4.
440. Statius, *Silvae* 1.6.
441. There is similar tension among scholars as to whether the Aristophanes play *Lysistrata* is proto-feminist or (as is more likely) a scathing comedy revelling in the ridiculous notion of Greek women participating in political civic life.
442. Tacitus, *Annals* 15.32.
443. See Dolansky, (2011).
444. See Mayor, (2014).
445. See Mayor, (2014) 25–6.
446. Aristotle, *Politics* 1269b–1270a.
447. Economic concerns meant that few families could afford to keep women hidden away, and most would be compelled to work or find ways to contribute that involved leaving the house. Even *poleis* that aspired to

the ideal of cloistered women, such as Athens, provide ample evidence of women in religious roles at temples, women working in commerce, or appearing in law courts.

448. It should be emphasised that the concept of Amazons as 'man-hating virgins' is a modern one, and that ancient stories are full of Amazons happily bedding men, just not letting men suppress them. See Mayor, (2014) 25-6.

449. Misogyny still surrounds the Amazons, with 'war-belt' being frequently translated as 'girdle'. The two are not interchangeable.

450. Orosius, a Roman Christian writing his own version of the myth (at least a century after the gladiatorial fight in Halicarnassus) cannot fathom approaching any woman as an equal; his version has Heracles launch a surprise attack on the Amazons when they are off guard. The women, while given less deference by Orosius' Heracles, are still considered too dangerous to confront in the traditional manner. See Orosius, *Histories Against the Pagans* 1.15.

451. Plutarch suggests that Theseus travelled east on a separate mission specifically to find a wife; the abduction and subsequent rape remain the same. *Life of Theseus* 26.

452. Plutarch, *Life of Theseus* 27.

453. It is from his name we get the term *phobia*, to mean irrational fear. The Romans named him Terror.

454. Tzetzes, *Ad Lycophronem* 999.

455. 'And now my doom has come at last. But never let me die without a struggle and without acclaim. Let me achieve some greatness and be known to people in the days to come': Homer, *Iliad* 22.303–305, translated by Emily Wilson (2023) (lines 22.407–411 in Wilson's edition).

456. Mayor, (2014) 238.

457. Mayor, (2014) 255.

458. Historia Augusta Life of Marcus Aurelius 11, 27

459. Speidel, (1992) 350.

460. ibid.

461. IC IV 373

462. SEG XXXII 605.

463. Ahrens, (2017).

464. *SC de pretiis gladiatorum minuendis* 59–61, Galen 13.599–600

465. Mann, (2011) 137.

466. Plutarch, *Moralia* 1099b.

467. Known as a *testamentum militis*.

468. Coleman, (2005) 2–3.

469. 'Traveller! You see me, bold Olympus. Often I fought in the stadiums, and I saved many in the stadiums. When the Fates wished it, I paid my debt to them here, and died fighting for the ninth time': see Robert, (1940) 56.
470. Mann, (2011) 46.
471. CIG 2942c.
472. Carter, (1999) 128.
473. Including but not limited to: Chester (UK), Pula (Pola, Croatia), Aquincum (Budapest, Hungary), Carnuntum (Vienna, Austria), Tarraco (Tarragona, Spain) and Leptis Magna (Libya).
474. Hornum, (1993) 89.
475. Robert, (1940) 82.
476. Roueché, (1993) 15.
477. Mann, (2011) 55b.
478. Mann, (2011) 189.
479. Robert, (1940) 66.
480. See Lattimore (1962) 150
481. Homer *The Odyssey* Book 11
482. Homer *The Odyssey* Book 24
483. Robert, (1940) 107.
484. Robert, (1940) 79.
485. Robert, (1940) 140.
486. Robert, (1940) 262.
487. Mann, (2011) 176.
488. Barbantani, (2018) 284.
489. See Gunderson, (1996).
490. My begrudging thanks to Ridley Scott, though I wish he'd skipped the sharks …

Index